This is the first social and cultural study of the principal 'free' professions in Italy between Unification and the First World War. It is a major contribution both to the history of the bourgeoisie in Italy and to the developing role of professions in modern European society.

The first section discusses the formation of modern Italian engineering, notarial occupations, law and medicine, and the close involvement of members of the professions with the state and the university. The second section makes an important contribution to the study of Italian society of the period. It analyses the inter-relation between the professions, the nobility and parliament, and examines the social status of members of the professions – how they saw themselves, and how they were viewed by others. Together the collection offers a fresh review of the modern Italian bourgeoisie.

CAMBRIDGE STUDIES IN ITALIAN HISTORY AND CULTURE

SOCIETY AND THE PROFESSIONS IN ITALY, 1860–1914

CAMBRIDGE STUDIES IN ITALIAN HISTORY AND CULTURE

Edited by GIORGIO CHITTOLINI, Università degli Studi, Milan

CESARE MOZZARELLI, Università Cattolica del Sacro Cuore, Milan

ROBERT ORESKO, Institute of Historical Research, University of London

and GEOFFREY SYMCOX, University of California, Los Angeles

This series comprises monographs and a variety of collaborative volumes, including translated works, which will concentrate on the period of Italian history from late medieval times up to the Risorgimento. The editors aim to stimulate scholarly debate over a range of issues which have not hitherto received, in English, the attention they deserve. As it develops, the series will emphasize the interest and vigor of current international debates on this central period of Italian history and the persistent influence of Italian culture on the rest of Europe.

Titles in the series

Family and public life in Brescia, 1580–1650
The foundations of power in the Venetian state
JOANNE M. FERRARO

Church and politics in Renaissance Italy
The life and career of Cardinal Francesco Soderini, 1453–1524
K. J. P. LOWE

Crime, disorder, and the Risorgimento
The politics of policing in Bologna
STEVEN C. HUGHES

Liturgy, sanctity and history in Tridentine Italy
Pietro Maria Campi and the preservation of the particular
SIMON DITCHFIELD

Lay confraternities and civic religion in Renaissance Bologna
NICHOLAS TERPSTRA

Society and the professions in Italy, 1860–1914
Edited by MARIA MALATESTA
Translated by Adrian Belton

Other titles are in preparation

SOCIETY AND THE PROFESSIONS IN ITALY, 1860–1914

EDITED BY MARIA MALATESTA

University of Bologna

TRANSLATED BY ADRIAN BELTON

CAMBRIDGE
UNIVERSITY PRESS

Published by the Press Syndicate of the University of Cambridge
The Pitt Building, Trumpington Street, Cambridge CB2 1RP
40 West 20th Street, New York, NY 10011–4211, USA
10 Stamford Road, Oakleigh, Melbourne 3166, Australia

First published 1995

Printed in Great Britain at the University Press, Cambridge

A catalogue record for this book is available from the British Library

Library of Congress cataloguing in publication data

Society and the professions in Italy, 1860–1914 / edited by Maria Malatesta;
translated by Adrian Belton.
p.   cm. – (Cambridge studies in Italian history and culture)
ISBN 0 521 46536 2
1. Professions–Italy–History.   2. Elite (Social sciences)–Italy–History.
3. Italy–Social conditions.   I. Malatesta, Maria.   II. Series.
HD8038.I8S65 1995
305.5'53'0945–dc20   94-47222   CIP

ISBN 0 521 46536 2 hardback

CONTENTS

THE ITALIAN PROFESSIONS FROM A COMPARATIVE PERSPECTIVE

MARIA MALATESTA

I. THE PROFESSIONS AND ITALIAN HISTORY

Since the 1970s, the study of the professions has been animated by conflicts, incursions and new alliances. The rise of the power paradigm, and the analysis of mechanisms of collective action by professional groups and of the role of the state conducted by neo-Weberian and neo-Marxist sociologists in Britain and the United States, brought a first profound revision to the hitherto dominant functionalist approach by introducing the temporal dimension into the sociology of the professions.[1] The assault was continued by French sociology, which contraposed the idea of rationality inherent in the structural-functionalist concept of professionalization with analysis of the mechanisms of social selection that determine the growth of the professions and their reproduction.[2] Thanks to the sociology of Pierre Bourdieu, the professions and the processes of knowledge formation were incorporated into the study of elites, thereby encouraging fruitful contacts between sociologists and historians.[3]

Functionalism underwent further revision when historians joined the debate on the professions. The broadening of research into the

---

[1] R. Torstendahl, 'Essential Properties, Strategic Aims and Historical Development: Three Approaches to Theories of Professionalism', in M. Burrage, R. Torstendahl (eds), *Professions in Theory and History. Rethinking the Study of the Professions*, London, 1990; R. Collins, 'Changing Conceptions in the Sociology of the Professions', in R. Torstendahl, M. Burrage (eds), *The Formation of Professions. Knowledge, State and Strategy*, London, 1990. See also R. H. Hall, 'Theoretical Trends in the Sociology of Occupations', *Sociological Quarterly*, 24, 1983; K. MacDonald, G. Ritzer, 'The Sociology of the Professions. Dead or Alive?', *Work and Occupation*, 15, 1988.

[2] P. Bourdieu, J.C. Passeron, *Reproduction, in Education, Society and Culture*, Beverly Hills, 1970/1977; H. Jamous, B. Pelloile, 'Professions or Self-Perpetuating System?', in J.A. Jackson (ed.), *Professions and Professionalization*, Cambridge, 1970.

[3] See for example C. Charle, *Les élites de la République 1880–1900*, Paris, 1987.

history of the European professions revealed the shortcomings of a reconstruction of professionalization processes based solely on the
example of the Anglo-Saxon countries, and it dismantled evolutionary
schemes which sought to divide the history of the professions into evolutionary stages. It was the achievement of German historians to demonstrate the distinctive differences between the continental and
Anglo-Saxon patterns of professionalization, stressing the role of the
state in the control of knowledge on the one hand, and analysing the
place occupied by the professions in the nineteenth-century European
bourgeoisie on the other.[4] Historical and sociological revision thus met
and merged, giving rise to a further alliance, the most recent enterprise
of which has been to develop a theory of the professions which
extends its roots into social history.[5]

Italy remained substantially extraneous to these interdisciplinary re-
alignments in the rest of Europe. Although there was no lack of Italian
historical research into the professions, it was influenced by two
schools of thought, diverse in their methodology but convergent in
their conclusions. First, as Paolo Frascani has observed, the history of
the professions was long influenced by the theories of Antonio
Gramsci. Attention thus focused on figures such as schoolteachers,
general practitioners and country priests, who were marginal to the
grand systems of contemporary sociology but central to the Gramscian
interpretation of Italian history.[6] The influence of Gramsci's Marxist
philosophy restricted study of the political and cultural conditions of
Italian professionals to analysis of political parties and movements,
while studies conducted in the more specific sector of medicine were
also influenced by the *Annales* and hence concentrated on aspects of
disease and health care.[7] As a result of these two tendencies, specific
aspects of the history of the professions and their processes of profession-

---

[4]   W. Conze, J. Kocka (eds), *Bildungsbürgertum im 19. Jahrhundert.* vol 1. *Bildungssystem
und Professionalizierung in internationalen Vergleichen,* Stuttgart, 1985; J. Kocka (ed.),
Bürgertum in 19. Jahrhundert. Deutschland im europäischen Vergleich, vols I–III,
Munich, 1988; H. Siegrist (ed.), *Bürgerliche Berufe. Beiträge zur Sozialgeschichte der
Professionen, freien Berufe und Akademiker im internationalen Vergleich,* Göttingen,
1988; K.H. Jarausch, *The Unfree Professions. German Lawyers, Teachers, and Engineers,
1900–1950,* New York, 1990; G. Cocks, K.H. Jarausch (eds), *German Professions
1800–1950,* New York, 1990.

[5]   M. Burrage, K. Jarausch, H. Siegrist, 'An Actor-based Framework for the Study of
the Professions', in M. Burrage, R. Torstendahl (eds), *Professions in Theory and
History.*

[6]   P. Frascani, 'Premessa', in P. Frascani (ed.), *Professioni liberali. Campania XIX–XX
secolo,* Naples, 1993. A clear example of Gramsci's influence is provided by
C. Vivanti (ed.), *Intellettuali e potere,* in *Storia d'Italia. Annali 4,* Turin, 1981.

[7]   See F. Della Peruta (ed.), *Malattia e medicina,* in *Storia d'Italia. Annali 7,* Turin, 1984.

alization were neglected. The engineering profession was more fortunate, but nevertheless inquiry into the formation of the modern professions and the development of knowledge which extended beyond narrow sectoral analysis was generally lacking in Italy. A further factor responsible for this laggardliness was the rift between Italian history and sociology. Within the latter discipline, interest in the professions was long confined to a small group of researchers who were never concerned to establish any significant contacts with historians.[8]

It was a major shift of emphasis in Italian social history during the 1980s, largely brought about by the growth of studies on the bourgeoisie, that provided the recent interest in the professions with its first stimulus.[9] German *Neue Sozialgeschichte* combined with French economic and social history to exert a profound influence on Italian historiography, and its advent in Italy was also encouraged by the participation of Italian academics in groups of German social historians,[10] and by research on the history of the Italian professions carried out by German-speaking scholars.[11] However, fascination with the history of the bourgeoisie has led to the predominance of studies on the reproduction strategies of the professional classes,[12] with the consequent relative neglect – as Paolo Frascani has stressed[13] – of the formation, control and organization of knowledge. The beginning of research on the universities of united Italy,[14] newly established rela-

---

[8] W. Tousijn (ed.), *Sociologia delle professioni*, Bologna, 1979; *idem*, *Le libere professioni in Italia*, Bologna, 1987.

[9] P. Macry, 'I professionisti. Note su tipologie e funzioni', *Quaderni Storici*, 48, 1981; *idem*, 'Notables, professions libérales, employés: la difficile identité des bourgeoisies italiennes dans la deuxième moitié du XIXe siècle', in *Mélanges de l'Ecole française de Rome*, 97, 1, 1985.

[10] M. Meriggi, 'Italienisches und deutsches Bürgertum im Vergleich', in J. Kocka (ed.), *Bürgertum im 19. Jahrhundert*, vol. I.

[11] H. Siegrist, 'Gli avvocati e la borghesia. Germania, Svizzera e Italia nel XIX secolo', in J. Kocka (ed.), *Borghesie europee dell'Ottocento*, Venice, 1989; *idem*, 'Gli avvocati nell'Italia del XIX secolo. Provenienza e matrimoni, titolo e prestigio', *Meridiana*, 14, 1992.

[12] P. Macry, *Ottocento. Famiglia, élites e patrimoni a Napoli*, Turin, 1988.

[13] P. Frascani, 'Les professions bourgeoises en Italie à l'époque libérale (1860–1920)', in *Mélanges de l'Ecole française de Rome*, 97, 1, 1985.

[14] G.P. Brizzi, A. Varni (eds), *L'università in Italia fra età moderna e contemporanea. Aspetti e momenti*, Bologna, 1993; S. Polenghi, *La politica universitaria italiana nell'età della Destra storica 1848–1876*, Brescia, 1993; A. La Penna, 'Modello tedesco e modello francese nel dibattito sull'università italiana', in S. Soldani, G. Turi (eds), *Fare gli italiani. Scuola e cultura nell'Italia contemporanea*, vol. I, Bologna, 1993; M. Moretti, I. Porciani, 'Il sistema universitario tra nazione e città: un campo di tensione', in M. Meriggi, P. Schiera (eds), *Dalla città alla nazione. Borghesie ottocentesche in Italia e in Germania*, Trento, 1993; A. Mazzacane, C. Vano (eds), *Università e professioni giuridiche in Europa nell'età liberale*, Naples, 1994.

tionships with historians of science and with sociologists, and the first comparative studies,[15] have today brought further dynamism to historical analysis of the Italian professions.

The purpose of this book is to bring these various components of Italian historiography together, and at the same time to remedy its most evident flaws and omissions. The essays collected in the book have been written by historians from various backgrounds, statisticians and sociologists, within a methodological framework that combines social history with the history of the professions. The essays in Part I illustrate the processes whereby the four free professions inherited from the *ancien régime* and requiring university training were transformed into their modern counterparts. The essays in Part II take as their subject-matter the 'embeddedment' of the professions in Italian society as, between 1860 and 1914, it underwent two processes which brought major upheavals: the formation of the national state and industrialization. They analyse the relationship between the market and professional identity, the gradual uncoupling of the professions from the aristocracy, and the role of mediation and interest-representation which professionals performed in society and in the political system.

The chronology of the book, which is followed by the majority of the essays, stresses the role played by the unitary state in the history of modern Italian professionism. The essays on the engineers and lawyers also extend their range to the pre-Unification period in order to demonstrate the importance of the Napoleonic and Restoration periods both in the formation of the Italian professions and in their regional differences. The eve of the First World War, the *terminus ad quem* of the book, marks the conclusion of the first phase in the professionalization of the old liberal professions. The only exception are the engineers, whose professional order was created in 1923. The second phase, which coincided with the fascist regime and saw the emergence of the 'new' free professions (chemists, journalists, business consultants, etc.), has been studied in a recent book on the relationship between the professions and the fascist state.[16] But relations between the professions, society and the labour market under the fascist regime have yet to be explored. The present work therefore restricts itself to examination of

[15] G. Calcagno, 'Les ingénieurs et la gestion des processus de modernization en Italie à la fin du XIXe siècle et au début du XXe siècle', in J.P. Bouilloud, B.P. Lecuyer (eds), *L'invention de la gestion. Histoire et pratique*, Paris 1994; M. Santoro, 'Professione e professionalizzazione: approcci teorici e processi storici', *Polis*, 8, 1994; A.M. Banti, 'Borghesie delle "professioni". Avvocati e medici nell'Europa dell'Ottocento', *Meridiana*, 18, 1993.
[16] G. Turi (ed.), *Libere professioni e fascismo*, Milan, 1994.

the so-called liberal period, while waiting for Italian social history to extend its compass to the fascist years.

In order to afford better understanding of the 'Italian model' compared with those of the other European countries, this introduction discusses three issues: the etymological problem of the term *professione*, the place of the Italian professions within the continental model of the professions, and the influence of Italy's economic backwardness on the relationship between professions and society in the nineteenth century.

2. PROFESSION: THE WORD AND ITS MEANING

The campaign to revise the functionalist approach to the study of the professions has also been waged using the weapons of philology. Indeed, among the evidence adduced for the contention that modern professionism began with industrialization is the change that took place in the word 'profession' between the eighteenth and nineteenth centuries, when its generic meaning (job) was replaced by a more specific and abstract sense denoting the organized control of knowledge.[17] This etymological conclusion, which attributes the paternity of professionism to the Anglo-Saxon countries, has been challenged by German historians, who cite linguistic differences in order to demonstrate that the Anglo-Saxon model is inapplicable to the German professions. The terms *Akademische Berufstand* and *Freie Beruf*, an extension of the word *Beruf* (calling), do not carry (unlike the more modern *professionalizierung*) any connotation of the self-organized closure of the profession, but instead refer to a class-based distinction between intellectual and manual work.[18]

Nor has England been exempt from the revisionist offensive. Wilfrid Prest has refuted the identification between professionism and industrialization by showing that the class identity of the professions in the early modern period was based on possession of a specific corpus of knowledge. He demonstrates that the term 'profession' had three distinct meanings in pre-Victorian English: 'job', 'high-status job', and a specific sense relating to 'the ministry, physic and law'. According to Prest, 'profession' came to assume the third of these meanings not

---

[17] W.J. Reader, *Professional Men: The Rise of Professional Classes in Nineteenth Century England*, London, 1966, pp. 9–10; H. Perkin, 'Le professioni e il gioco della vita: l'Inghilterra dall'Ottocento ad oggi', *Quaderni storici*, 48, 1981, pp. 945–6.

[18] K.H. Jarausch, 'The German Professions in History and Theory', in G. Cocks, K.H. Jarausch (eds), *German Professions 1800–1950*, pp. 10–12; J. Kocka, 'Bürgertum and Professions in the Nineteenth Century: Two Alternative Approaches', in M. Burrage, R. Torstendahl (eds), *Professions in Theory and History*, pp. 62–3.

because of industrialization but because of its traditional association with the three faculties of the medieval university.[19]

This brief etymological analysis demonstrates the linguistic analogies between English, French and Italian. Sharing the same Latin root (*profiteor*) in all three languages, 'profession' was a polysemic term which comprised both the meaning of 'noble' and intellectual work and that of manual labour, thus reflecting the ancient distinction between the liberal arts and the 'mechanical trades'. But let us examine the evolution of the Italian word *professione* more closely in order to establish whether it has undergone changes in meaning comparable with those in English. After the Middle Ages, *professione* denoted two distinctive semantic fields: a wider area comprising various forms of public confession or avowal (in the sense of professing an idea, a religious faith, a doctrine); and a more restricted field in which it referred to any occupation, whether intellectual or manual. The learned literature of the sixteenth and seventeenth centuries offers numerous examples of the latter 'high' meaning of the word, where it was used specifically to connote the exercise of the law and medicine.[20]

In its 'high' sense, *professione* was closely associated, both historically and philologically, with the universities. From the Renaissance onwards, the verb *profiteor* was used in university Latin with the meaning of 'to teach' or 'to expound *ex cathedra*'. It was the technical term which denoted the role of a university instructor (*docente*) in a particular discipline.[21] The connection between university and professions was thus manifest in the word *professore*, which was in fact synonymous with *docente* but was also employed in the sense of 'professional' and indicated membership of the corporation of the liberal arts.[22] *Professare/professione* were terms which connoted the highest manifestation of culture, characterized by the distinction between theoretical knowledge, practical expertise and the governmental functions assigned to the Italian universities during the early modern period; a period when

[19] W. Prest, 'Why the History of the Professions is not written', in G.R. Rubin, D. Sugarman (eds), *Law, Economy and Society, 1750–1914: Essays in the History of English Law*, Abingdon, Oxon., 1984.

[20] G. De Luca, *Il cavaliere e la dama, ovvero discorsi familiari nell'ozio tuscolano*, Pavia, 1700, pp.170–3; A. De Simoni, *Memorie intorno la propria vita e scritti*, edited by C. Mozzarelli, Mantua, 1991, tome I (ca. 1780), p. 41.

[21] L. Avellini, 'Le lodi delle discipline come fonti per la "disputa delle arti"', *Schede umanistiche*, 2, 1988.

[22] E. Brambilla, 'Il "sistema letterario" di Milano: professioni nobili e professioni borghesi dall'età spagnola alle riforme teresiane', in A. De Maddalena, E. Rotelli, G. Barbarisi (eds), *Economia, istituzioni, cultura in Lombardia nell'età di Maria Teresa*, vol. III. *Istituzioni e società*, Bologna, 1982, p. 92.

university teaching, the practice of a profession, and governmental function were roles, especially for lawyers, which often (but not always) coincided.[23]

The system that arose in the ancient Italian states as the fruit of this union between high knowledge, professions and governing elite has been an enduring feature of the Italian professions; one that has accompanied their development in the contemporary age. Far from being obliterated with the demise of the *ancien régime* it returned, in new guise, during the Napoleonic period and in the political literature of the Restoration.[24] As envisaged by the jurist Gian Domenico Romagnosi,[25] the parliament of the new constitutional state was to consist of professionals. Lawyers, doctors and engineers were ascribed a function of government not because of their specific competence but because of their ability to build consensus on trust in their judgement and on their 'multiple clientele'.

Alongside the specific sense of *professione*, also to be found in the learned literature was a mixed linguistic usage whereby *mestiere* (calling) referred to the law,[26] while *professione* might designate even a manual trade or an *arte minore*.[27] At the end of the eighteenth century, the Italian dictionaries had institutionalized the generic meaning of the term into the sense of 'business' or 'calling'.[28] The distinction between intellectual activity and practical/manual work was drawn with greater clarity in the second half of the nineteenth century (learned profession as opposed to work or trade). However, the legacy of the past is still evident when one examines the specific meaning of *professione*. In the dictionary of the language of unified Italy, the *Dizionario della lingua italiana* by Tommaseo and Bellini, *libera professione* is still synonymous

[23] C. Vasoli, 'Le discipline e il sistema del sapere', in *Sapere e potere. Discipline, dispute e professioni nell'università medioevale e moderna. Il caso bolognese a confronto*, vol. II. A. Cristiani (ed.), *Verso un nuovo sistema del sapere*, Bologna, 1990; R. Savelli, 'Diritto e politica: "doctores" e patriziato a Genova', in *Sapere e potere*, vol III. A. De Benedictis (ed.), *Dalle discipline ai ruoli sociali*, Bologna, 1990.

[24] The Constitution of the Italian Republic enacted three constituencies, one of which was the *collegio dei dotti*, a body including professionals, clergymen, men of science, culture and law: C. Zaghi, *L'Italia di Napoleone dalla Cisalpina al Regno*, Turin, 1986, pp. 294–302; F. Sofia, 'Ancora "dal modello francese al caso italiano": gli appunti di P. L. Roederer per la costituzione cisalpina (1801)', *Clio*, 3, 1986.

[25] G. Romagnosi, *La scienza delle costituzioni*, Florence, 1850, p. 624.

[26] G. De Luca, *Il dottor volgare, ovvero il compendio di tutta la legge civile, canonica, feudale e municipale nelle cose più ricevute in pratica*, Cologne, 1755, pp. 147–62.

[27] T. Garzoni, *La sinagoga de gl'ignoranti*, Pavia, 1589 (2nd edition), p. 16; F. Griselini, *Dizionario delle arti e mestieri*, Venice, 1768–78, vol. III, p. 205.

[28] *Vocabolario degli Accademici della Crusca*, tome V, Verona, 1806, p. 223; G. Gherardini, *Supplemento ai vocabolari italiani*, Milan, 1855, vol. III, p. 868.

with *professione liberale* in the classical sense and does not convey the idea of autonomous work.[29] Consequently, together with doctors and lawyers, the dictionary also cites judges as exemplifying 'free professionals' – that is, as practising the liberal arts – although they were officers of the state.

During the fascist period, on completion of the second phase of the professionalization process, codified Italian still lagged behind the changes that had taken place within the professions. In some cases *liberale* designated the *libera professione*, autonomous and distinct from salaried employment; in others, it denoted only the intellectual content of a profession.[30] The same indecision is apparent in the definition of *professionista*. As a new term, one not to be found in the nineteenth-century dictionaries, *professionista* was used in the legal language of the early years of this century to refer to a person who carried out an occupation. It entered the dictionaries of the fascist period, however, as indicating the practitioner of a free or liberal profession.[31] This discrepancy between reality and codified language was probably also due to a conceptual difficulty. The inclusion of the free professions in the fascist corporatist system created problems of identity which were also reflected in the dictionary definition of the term. Curiously, in the *Enciclopedia Treccani*, the monument to fascist culture, the entry '*professione*' makes no mention of the various meanings attaching to the word *occupazione* (calling), which are merely listed under the entry '*statistica delle professione*' (statistics on the professions).[32]

During the last years of fascism, the first definition to reflect the changes that had occurred in the organization of the professions was formulated in the legal field. In the preparatory draft of the new civil code (which is still in force today), *professionista* was defined as 'one who, in possession of a university degree or higher diploma and subsequent professional certification, engages independently and continuously in intellectual activity for which enrolment on a professional register is required'.[33] Three elements in this definition should be stressed: the elliptical use of *professionista* for *libero professionista*; the emphasis on abstract knowledge acquired through higher education (the secondary-school diploma) but not necessarily at university; the

[29] N. Tommaseo, B. Bellini, *Dizionario della lingua italiana*, Turin, 1865–9, vol. IV, entry '*professione*'; vol. III, entry '*libero*'.

[30] P. Petrocchi, *Nuovo dizionario della lingua italiana*, Milan, 1931, vol. II, p. 54.

[31] *Monitore dei tribunali*, 1911. F. Palazzi, *Novissimo dizionario della lingua italiana*, Milan, 1939, p. 875.

[32] *Enciclopedia italiana Treccani*, vol. XXVII, Rome, 1935, pp. 300–2.

[33] *Atti del Comitato delle confederazioni sindacali dei lavoratori per il Libro del lavoro del Codice civile*, Rome, 1941, p. 210.

concept of self-regulation and closure of the market (the professional register). The latter two components – as distinguishing features of the modern professions throughout the Western world – had thus become part of the heritage of Italian language and culture.

Today, *professione*, which we may take as an abbreviation for *libera professione*, is distinguished from *occupazione* by the notions of abstract knowledge and of professional monopoly intrinsic to it.[34] Current colloquial Italian adopts the legal definition of *professione* as intellectual, autonomous, non-wage-earning and organized.[35] Thus the self-representation that the professions have developed and disseminated through the law is ultimately based on the ancient, high concept of *professione*, to which the further senses deriving from the process of professionalization have accreted. The polysemous nature of the term, however, is still evident in Italian national statistics, which classify all full-time and permanent occupations under the heading '*professione*'.[36]

Etymological analysis confirms that the process of professionalization culminated in Italy during fascism. The linguistic delay with respect to the first phase of the process during the liberal period can be read – apart from the physiological delay between current usage and codification of the language – as indicative of the difficulties faced by the free professionals in asserting their status as experts. Finally, we cannot rule out the possibility that linguistic delay has conditioned the perception and assertion of professionism as a specific problem, historically and sociologically important.

3. THE PROFESSIONS AND THE STATE

The process of professionalization which began in nineteenth-century Italy has adhered to the continental pattern, and is thus distinguished by the conspicuous and constant action of the state and by the less independent action of professional groups.[37] There is no doubt that in Italy the early process of state-building interwove with professionalization, and there is equally no doubt that the unified state played a crucial role in the constitution of the professions. However, when analysed as a whole, the first phase of the professionalization process

---

[34] 'Professioni', in *Enciclopedia giuridica Treccani*, vol. XXIV, Rome, 1991, pp. 5–6.

[35] S. Battaglia, *Grande dizionario della lingua italiana*, vol. XIV, Turin, 1988, entry '*professione*'.

[36] L. Speranza, 'Le professioni: un approccio sociologico', in P. Frascani (ed.), *Professioni liberali. Campania XIX–XX secolo*, p. 33.

[37] M. Burrage, K. Jarausch, H. Siegrist, 'An Actor-based Framework for the Study of the Professions', pp. 218–21.

reveals itself to have been a mixture of state initiative and corporatist pressures applied by professional groups. Hannes Siegrist has argued that the Italian case can be located midway between that of France, characterized by greater professionalization from below, and that of Prussia, which best fits the concept of professionalization from above. This intermediate position resulted from the traditional strength and independence of Italian professional groups and from the features of Italian society, as a mix between state-society and stateless society which impeded the process of regulation initiated by the unitary state.[38] The persistence of pronounced regional and provincial features on the one hand, and economic backwardness on the other, hampered the growth of the centralized state and encouraged independent action by social groups and classes, in the professions as well.

In the second half of the nineteenth century, the European processes of professionalization – the case of Germany is emblematic here[39] – were distinguished by the growth of corporate self-assertion for the protection of the professional market. Italian professionalization began in this period and was conditioned by European trends as well as by events specific to the country. It was a process in which pressures from above and from below converged, and public and private components combined, in a creative dialectic between the state and the professions. The indubitable influence exercised by the state was flanked by the action of the professional bodies as they negotiated with the state to enhance their prestige. In post-Unification Italy, the process of professionalization was initiated by the state in the legal sector, which, as in the other European countries, provided the model for the other free professions. The modern system of the professions was created in 1874 by the law on attorneys and prosecutors, which is still in force, and it rested on the twin institutions of the professional register (albo) and the professional order (ordine). The professional registers, which listed all those certified to practise a profession, were a corporatist legacy from the Old Regime. The professional order was instead an innovation. The combination of albo and ordine constituted the legal basis for re-cognition of a free profession, defence of its market, and enforcement of its code of ethics.

The Italian professional order bore many resemblances to the ordre of the French avocats, which was reconstituted by Napoleon and won further self-governing powers during the Restoration. The Italian

---

[38] H. Siegrist, 'State and Legal Professions. France, Germany, Italy and Switzerland 18th to Early 20th Centuries', Università degli studi di Macerata. Annali della Facoltà di Giurisprudenza, 1989/II, pp. 876–80.
[39] K.H. Jarausch, The Unfree Professions, pp. 22–4.

ordine differed from its French counterpart, however, in that it was applied to all the other professions: in France, as a result of the Le Chapelier Law, all the non-legal professions used the syndicate form in order to organize themselves collectively. The *ordres* were later extended by the Vichy government to all the professions and were reinstated during the Fourth Republic. Today France is the country whose professional system most closely resembles Italy's,[40] but in the nineteenth century greater affinities can be discerned between the Italian system and the Spanish one. The *colegiaciòn* introduced in 1837 at first only applied to lawyers, but was then extended in the second half of the nineteenth century to notaries and to the health professions, which, in Spain as in Italy, had organized themselves into private associations until the creation of their *colegio* in 1898.[41] One also finds analogies with the German *Kammern*, which was introduced in 1878 for lawyers and was later extended to doctors. However, the *Kammern* had limited jurisdiction in disciplinary matters – which it shared with the professional associations – and equally restricted self-governing powers.[42] By contrast the Italian orders were, and still are, genuine bodies of professional self-government: disciplinary power and the enforcement of professional ethics were their exclusive province. These competences mixed, in equal measure, private and public elements which reflected the features themselves of the Italian process of professionalization.[43]

The creation of the order of lawyers and prosecutors equipped a free profession with the instruments to turn itself into a national institution, whose rules of admission, exclusion and compatibility were standardized throughout the country and backed by a state law. The legal professions thus managed to enhance their prestige, which had waned during the Restoration,[44] relative to the state and the other professions. However, although they were the most powerful group, the lawyers

---

[40] P. Piscione, *Ordini e collegi professionali*, Rome, 1959, pp. 173–84.

[41] F. Villacorta Baños, *Profesionales y burocrátas. Estado y poder corporativo en la España del siglo XX (1890–1923)*, Madrid, 1989, pp. 3–19.

[42] C.E. McClelland, *The German Experience of Professionalization. Modern Learned Professions and their Organizations from the Early Nineteenth Century to the Hitler Era*, Cambridge, 1991, pp. 83–7.

[43] W. Tousijn, 'Tra stato e mercato: le libere professioni in Italia in una prospettiva storico-evolutiva', in W. Tousijn (ed.), *Le libere professioni*, pp. 33–34; V. Olgiati, 'Avvocati e notai tra professionalismo e mutamento sociale', in Tousijn, *Le libere professioni*, pp. 97–102.

[44] See the essay by A. Mazzacane in this volume and, on the bar in Milan, A. Liva, 'Le professioni liberali e i loro collegi: gli avvocati', in C. Mozzarelli, R. Pavoni (eds), *Milano fin de siècle e il caso Bagatti Valsecchi. Memoria e progetto per la metropoli italiana*, Milan, 1991, pp. 319–20.

did not develop a professional strategy. Instead, and also in order to achieve the juridical unification of the country that was by now urgently necessary, the initiative was taken by the state – in the institutions of which, however, lawyers were strongly represented.

The other professions took more direct and forceful action in applying pressure on the state to grant them monopoly of the market and thus to improve their status. Demands by the doctors for their own professional order, and by the notaries for the credentials required for admittance to their profession to include a university degree, stemmed from the desire by both groups to acquire a social and intellectual legitimacy equivalent to that enjoyed by the lawyers.[45] However, these were pressures from below exerted within an already established institutional framework (the Health Law of 1888 for doctors, the Professional Law of 1875 for the notaries). Thus the state furnished the normative resources which the professional bodies then developed or adapted to their own purposes.

The more than thirty-year delay between the regulation of first the legal profession and later the medical profession created a dual system in which the latter, without its own professional order but endowed with a professional register, endeavoured to catch up with the former. The doctors, pharmacists, engineers, accountants and surveyors equipped themselves with forms of self-government with which to address the state and the local administrations. Not all groups, however, pursued an explicit professional project based on an organizational effort to enhance their status.[46] One may speak of a professional strategy in the cases of the doctors, of the notaries (with regard to the Law of 1913), and of the accountants, but the strategic action undertaken by the engineers was much weaker, and it was conditioned by marked differences among local markets. For decades, the engineers working in the most industrialized region of Italy opposed the creation of a professional order. The Lombard engineers were an elite whose social status derived from its links with

[45] M. Santoro and P. Frascani, *infra*. For comparison with the French doctors' efforts to obtain collective social capital such as that possessed by the lawyers, see J. Léonard, *Les médicins de l'Ouest au XIXe siècle*, 3 vols, Paris, 1978; C. Charle, 'Histoire professionnelle, histoire sociale? Les médicins de l'Ouest au XIXe siècle', *Annales E.S.C.*, 4, 1979; idem, 'Pour une histoire sociale des professions juridiques à l'époque contemporaine', *Actes de la recherche en sciences sociales*, 76/77, 1989.

[46] M. Larson, *The Rise of Professionalism. A Sociological Analysis*, Berkeley, 1977, p. 67; W. Tousijn, 'Tra stato e mercato: le libere professioni in Italia in una prospettiva storico-evolutiva', pp. 42–6. L. Speranza, W. Tousijn, 'Le libere professioni', in M. Paci, *Dimensioni della diseguaglianza. Primo rapporto della Fondazione CESPE sulla diseguaglianza sociale in Italia*, Bologna, 1993.

the landed aristocracy and industry[47] – and like the American engineers of the East Coast or the great Berlin doctors,[48] they obstructed every form of professional regulation and trade unionism, preferring to rely instead on the mechanisms of a market in which they occupied a privileged position.

But the most serious obstacles against the rise of modern professionism in Italy were the force of tradition and the power of local interest-groups. Added to these were the typical disdain shown by the Italian bourgeoisie for social aggregation and the persistence of professional abuses symptomatic of the unitary state's inability to enforce the new laws. In the majority of cases, these were forms of resistance designed to entrench the identity of local professional groups according to a geographical pattern which duplicated that of the ancient Italian states. The influence of the pre-Unification legacy is apparent in the text of the law regulating the legal profession. Common to other professional groups, as well as to the Lombard engineers, was the fear that the creation of orders would cancel not only local traditions but local privileges as well, and there was also widespread concern that the orders would lead to the restoration of the old corporatist regime.[49]

The resistance of certain segments of the professions was flanked by action taken by others to improve their professional organization. As well as the notaries, who pressed for reform of the first law to regulate their profession, the general practitioners lobbied for an extension of the functions of the medical orders, which the Law of 1910 had restricted to regulation of the relationship between the doctor and private clients. Thus, as an effect of further pressures from below, by the First World War some of the medical orders had acquired broader powers and had even become forums for debate on national health policies. Apart from the engineers, the demands by professional groups for the passing, or the reform, of a law regulating their profession were only satisfied in the early years of this century. The reform policies introduced by the prime minister Giovanni Giolitti gave a voice to pressures from below. But the recognition and strengthening of such

[47] M. Malatesta, 'Gli 'ingegneri milanesi e il loro collegio professionale', in C. Mozzarelli, R. Pavoni (eds), *Milano fin de siècle e il caso Bagatti Valsecchi*.

[48] E.T. Layton, *The Revolt of the Engineers. Social Responsibility and American Engineering Profession*, Cleveland and London, 1971, pp. 109ff; P. Meiksins, 'Professionalism and Conflict: The Case of the American Association of Engineers', *Journal of Social History*, Spring 1986; C. E. McClelland, *The German Experience of Professionalization*, p. 79.

[49] M. Malatesta, 'Gli ordini professionali e la nazionalizzazione in Italia', in M. Meriggi, P. Schiera (eds), *Dalla città alla nazione. Borghesie ottocentesche in Italia e in Germania*.

scattered interests only came about through their incorporation into the state.[50] The free professions too became components of Giolitti's political strategy, in an equitable trade-off which satisfied the demands of the professional groups on the one hand, and the state's need to impose norm-based regulation on the other.

However, the relationship between the state and the professions went considerably further than legal recognition. Through its bodies and institutions, the state exercised other forms of control, legitimation and defence with respect to professionals; and it utilized their expertise in the public administration.[51] For their part, the professionals exploited their positions within the state to enhance their prestige and to expand their markets. The new state assumed responsibility for professional training and assigned it to the universities, thereby forcing the many private professional schools and institutes inherited from the pre-Unification states to close. In keeping with the continental model, technical training was also brought under state control. Although the creation of many of the country's higher technical institutes and polytechnics during this period was due to the initiative of industrialists and professionals, these schools too were soon granted recognition by the state.[52] Higher education thus represented the first stage in the state's gradual extension of its control over the professions. The judicial powers proved to be a staunch ally of the professions, and the judiciary was the principal instrument with which they combatted unlawful practice, by easing the passage of professionals to the inner circles of the state and by acting as the guarantor of professional monopoly.[53] The issue of the entitlement of women to exercise the professions exemplifies the behaviour of the Italian judiciary.

In the 1870s the Italian universities opened their doors to female students and, as in the rest of Europe, medicine was the first free profession that women were permitted to practise. The first women graduated from the medical faculties in 1877 and admission to the exercise of the profession, although it was long restricted to gynaecology and obstetrics, came shortly afterwards. Unlike the countries of northern Europe and France, Italy continued to exclude women from

---

[50] P. Farneti, Sistema politico e società civile. Saggi di teoria e ricerca politica, Turin, 1971; A. Aquarone, Tre capitoli sull'Italia giolittiana, Bologna, 1987.

[51] R. Torstendahl, 'Introduction: Promotion and Strategies of Knowledge-based Groups', in R. Torstendahl, M. Burrage (eds), The Formation of Professions, pp. 6–7.

[52] M. Minesso, infra; P. Audenino, 'The "Alpin Paradox". Exporting Builders to the World', in G.E. Pozzetta, B. Ramirez (eds), The Italian Diaspora. Migration Across the World, Ontario, 1992, pp. 10–11.

[53] A. Lonni, I professionisti della salute. Monopolio professionale e nascita dell'ordine dei medici, XIX e XX secolo, Milan, 1994.

legal practice for many years; indeed, it was only at the end of the First World War that their debarment was finally lifted (contemporaneously, in fact, with similar developments in England and Prussia).[54] The exclusion of women from practice of the legal professions was the work of the judiciary and, as in England and the United States, special legislation was required to remove the barriers against their entry.[55] The embargo imposed by the Italian judiciary embodied the professional closure sought by the majority of lawyers, and it provided male professional monopoly with a formidable weapon of defence. However, it was vigorously combatted by the other, more advanced segment of the legal profession which wished to assert its independence from the state, and did so by allowing women to enrol on the professional registers.[56] Judicial power, therefore, was principally to blame for the perpetuation in the legal sector of the 'sexual variable' and for the persistence of the positivist dogma that women did not possess sufficient abilities to practise the law. Not coincidentally, although women were admitted to the bar in 1919, and to notarial practice in 1928, it was only in the 1960s that the judiciary finally opened its ranks to women.

The advancement of the professions in the early nineteenth century, however, was offset by the growing subordination of the state-employed professionals to the decisions of politicians and bureaucrats. The bureaucratization of professional knowledge became more pronounced in a period in which, as a result of modernization, the civil service's demand for expertise grew apace. This process created a hierarchical division between the free and the state-employed professionals which – as the essays in this book by Michela Minesso and Paolo Frascani show – had significant consequences. The exodus of poorly-paid state engineers to the private sector in the Giolitti period;[57] the conflict that arose between the engineers and the military administration during the Great War; the dissent by the general practitioners which grew into

---

[54] S. Soldani (ed.), *L'educazione delle donne*, Milan, 1989; *idem*, 'Lo stato e il lavoro delle donne nell'Italia liberale', *Passato e Presente*, 24, 1990; M. De Giorgio, *Le italiane dall'Unità ad oggi. Modelli culturali e comportamenti sociali*, Rome–Bari, 1992, pp. 461–84.

[55] C. Menkel-Meadow, 'Feminization of the Legal Professions. The Comparative Sociology of Women Lawyers', in R.L. Abel, P.S. Lewis (eds), *Lawyers in Society. Vol. III, Comparative Theories*, Berkeley–Los Angeles–London, 1989, pp. 200–2.

[56] A. Liva, 'Le professioni liberali e i loro collegi: gli avvocati', pp. 330–4.

[57] On this subject see also E. Ferrari, 'Governo e organizzazione amministrativa in una città padana: Reggio Emilia nel primo Novecento', and A. Attanasio, 'Burocrazia e strutture amministrative del comune di Roma (1900–1915)', in C. Mozzarelli (ed.), *Il governo dalla città in età giolittiana*, Trento, 1992, pp. 265, 387.

militant socialism: these are examples of the reaction of professional groups to the unsatisfactory treatment meted out to them by the public administration.

The evidence provided by the essays in this book confirms the general judgement passed by historians on the Italian public administration: namely that it was run for eminently political purposes which, during the Giolitti period, turned the state bureaucracy into a governing party.[58] In the absence of specific research on the relationship between the professions and the public administration, one may hypothesize that Giolitti's strategy for curbing social change affected the professions in two principal ways. On the one hand, recognition was granted to the prestige that the free professions had acquired in society; on the other, this prestige was prevented from entering the public administration, where it might have created hierarchies based on professional competence.

The broad margins of action enjoyed by the free professions were most evident in their peripheral management of local interests, which they orchestrated by manipulating the resources supplied to them by the central state. The clientary networks woven together by the professionals represent the other side of the social coin. I refer to that stateless society which flanked state society in a combination that has been the distinctive feature of the history of unified Italy. The political use of nineteenth- and twentieth-century clientelism was probably a legacy from the ancient alliance between the professions and the governing classes. But a specifically professional use was made of it as well. As Luigi Musella explains in his essay, clientelism was one of the factors which cemented the system of state, professions and market together. Clients determined the wealth hierarchy of the professionals and gave them access to the centres of political power. The close-knit webs of social relations created by professionals, and the social standing they acquired as political operators, increased confidence in their professional expertise and thereby expanded their markets.[59]

A similar mechanism governed the relationship between profes-

---

[58] I. Zanni Rosiello (ed.), *Gli apparati statali dall'Unità al fascismo*, Bologna, 1976; C. Mozzarelli, S. Nespor, 'Il personale e le strutture amministrative', in S. Cassese (ed.), *L'amministrazione centrale*, Turin, 1984; S. Cassese, *Il sistema amministrativo italiano*, Bologna, 1985; G. Melis, *Due modelli di amministrazione tra liberalismo e fascismo. Burocrazie tradizionali e nuovi apparati*, Rome, 1988; F. Sofia, 'Alla ricerca di un'alternativa al partito: riflessioni su governo e amministrazione nell'Italia liberale', in G. Quagliariello (ed.), *Il partito politico nella Belle Epoque. Il dibattito sulla forma-partito in Italia tra '800 e '900*, Milan, 1990.

[59] P. Bourdieu, 'La réprésentation politique. Eléments pour une théorie du champ politique', *Actes de la recherche en sciences sociales*, 36–37, 1981, p. 18.

sionals and the universities. The ancient tradition of the lawyer-academic-statesman which had flourished in the Kingdom of Naples – as Aldo Mazzacane stresses in his essay – was inherited by the new state, and it is still today a distinctive feature of the Italian university system.[60] The professional elite consisted of university professors who combined teaching with the exercise of a profession while often pursuing a political career at the same time. The credentials acquired from their university role were spent in the professional and political markets. In this case, therefore, it was the university professor who was the key actor in the state/professions/market system. It is difficult to establish which of the two identities predominated in the case of the academic-professional.[61] Sociological analysis has stressed the existence of structural conflicts between theoreticians and practitioners.[62] One may assume that this 'symbolic division of labour' in the academic-professional sphere was resolved at the apex of the profession.[63] More than a conflict, therefore, the phenomenon seems to have been a sum of identities which were functionally resolved in the market.

4. AN ITALIAN PATTERN OF BACKWARDNESS?

Italy was one of various countries in the European periphery which started along the road to industrialization at the end of the nineteenth century.[64] The rise of modern professionism therefore began in a society that was still predominantly rural. Recent studies have questioned the validity of any attempt to establish a direct correlation between education, the professions and economic development; instead, they have identified a more immediate influence exercised by political and cultural factors on processes of professionalization.[65] There is no doubt, however, that a country's level of economic development closely conditions the growth of the professional market. Ac-

---

[60] P.P. Giglioli, *Baroni e burocrati. Il ceto accademico italiano*, Bologna, 1979, pp. 52–7; B. Clark, *Academic Power in Italy. Bureaucracy and Oligarchy in a National University System*, Chicago, 1977, pp. 77–8.

[61] M. Santoro, 'Per una storia sociale della giuspubblicistica italiana. Appunti sugli insegnamenti di diritto amministrativo e scienza dell'amministrazione nell'Italia liberale', *Cheiron*, 16, 1991, pp. 128–9.

[62] B. Barber, 'Some Problems in the Sociology of Professions', *Daedalus*, 92, 1963, pp. 669–88.

[63] P. Bourdieu, 'La force du droit. Eléments pour une sociologie du champ juridique', *Actes de la recherche en sciences sociales*, 64, 1986, p. 6.

[64] V. Zamagni, *The Economic History of Italy. 1860–1990*, Oxford, 1993.

[65] H. Siegrist, 'Professionalization as a Process: Patterns, Progression and Discontinuity', in M. Burrage, R. Torstendhal (eds), *Professions in Theory and History*, pp. 185–9.

cordingly, economic backwardness is an important parameter with
which to assess and understand numerous aspects of the history of the
Italian professions. The influence of the market was greater on those
professions which were directly tied to it than on the legal professions,
which depended more closely on the behaviour of the state. The
delayed self-assertion of the Italian industrial engineer, and the qualitative and quantitative inadequacy of the national health service,[66] were
direct consequences of the narrowness of the market. At the same
time, however, the difficulties provoked by the shortage of demand
stimulated the growth of professionalization. It is no coincidence that
the first demands for organization and regulation of the profession
were advanced by the engineers and by southern notaries.[67] The regional differences that so conspicuously mark the history of Italian professional groups did not stem solely from politico-cultural factors; they
should also be interpreted in the light of the economic disparity
between the North and South of the country; a disparity which was
exacerbated by economic take-off.

The relationship between economic backwardness and higher education has been examined in one of the most innovative studies produced by Italian sociology. Twenty years ago, Marzio Barbagli
demonstrated there was a direct correlation between the narrowness of
the market and a level of unemployment among Italian professionals
which was very much higher than in any other European country.[68]
The combination of a semi-universal educational system, created by
the unitary state in order to increase the socialization of the middle
classes, and the absence of channels of social mobility, created a vicious
circle. The results were, according to Barbagli, the bloating of the
public administration as the only source of employment for professionals, and large-scale intellectual emigration. Although Barbagli's
study fell into neglect a number of years ago, the essay by Andrea
Cammelli in this book revives its central thesis and partly revises it to
reflect recent statistics on higher learning published in various countries. Cammelli's essay disputes Barbagli's findings by showing that the
Italian university population expanded more slowly than in the other
industrialized European countries, that the growth in the number of
professionals was constant, and that the market of the public adminis-

---

[66] I. Waddington, 'Medicine, the Market and Professional Autonomy: Some Aspects
of the Professionalization of Medicine', in W. Conze, J. Kocka (eds), *Bildungsbürgertum im 19. Jahrhundert*, p. 406ff.
[67] See the essays by M. Minesso and M. Santoro in this volume.
[68] M. Barbagli, *Educating for Unemployment. Politics, Labour, Markets and the School
System – Italy, 1859–1973*, New York, 1982 (first published in Italy in 1974).

tration did not grow significantly in the period 1860–1914 with respect to population increase. Economic backwardness, therefore, produced, not an excessive imbalance between demand and supply in the professional market but the stagnation of both. The disequilibrium was manifest instead in the skewed geographical distribution of the free professions – with lawyers concentrated in the South and engineers in the North – caused by the disparity between the country's regional economies.

These new data, combined with the information now available on the social composition of Italian professionals, also suggest revising the thesis that Italian higher education provided significant opportunities for upward social mobility. Between the nineteenth and twentieth centuries, major changes occurred within the professional bourgeoisie of the industrialized European countries. With the advent of the Second Reich, the educated bourgeoisie ceased to be the main social origin of Prussian students, and there was a similar decline in recruitment from the landowning class. Contrasting with these downward trends was the growth in the numbers of Prussian students from the industrial and commercial propertied bourgeoisie and from the lower middle class. The ratio between the representation of the cultivated bourgeoisie and that of the lower middle class in the German student body had, by the First World War, reversed in favour of the latter.[69] A similar pattern of advancement by the lower middle class is exhibited by the French professions during the Third Republic. Student enrolments at the Ecole Polytechnique registered a numerical collapse in the sons of the landowning and *rentier* class, and a diminution among the sons of free professionals and high-ranking officials. This downturn in recruitment from the high bourgeoisie was off-set by the corresponding growth of students from the industrial and commercial middle class and from the *petite bourgeoisie*.[70] These latter were also well represented among the French doctors, in which profession they were almost as numerous as the sons of free professional families. In France too, professional self-recruitment and landowning origin tended to diminish in the second half of the nineteenth century with a concomitant expansion within the lower strata of the bourgeoisie.[71]

In Italy until the First World War, the world of the professions was dominated by a high rate of self-recruitment and by social origin tied

[69] K.H. Jarausch, *Students, Society, and Politics in Imperial Germany. The Rise of Academic Illiberalism*, Princeton, 1982, pp. 78–130.
[70] T. Shinn, *L'Ecole Polytechnique 1794–1914*, Paris, 1980, pp. 141–58, 184–8.
[71] G.G. Weisz, *The Emergence of the Modern University in France 1863–1914*, Princeton, 1983, p. 24.

to landownership. In 1911 the educated bourgeoisie accounted for 25 per cent of the families of university students, the propertied bourgeoisie for 49 per cent, and the lower middle class for 15 per cent. These shares were reversed in the course of the 1920s, when the constant percentage of the offspring of the educated bourgeoisie (26 per cent) in the student population was matched by a marked decline among the landowning bourgeoisie (30 per cent) and by the vigorous advance of the lower middle class (20 per cent) and the less prestigious professions (surveyors, accountants).[72] Still low was the percentage of sons of industrialists, who in 1913 represented around 10 per cent of engineering students, although those from property-owning families had dropped to 8 per cent from the 24 per cent recorded in 1911. However, the greater openness of the Italian university system compared with those of the other European countries was not sufficient to attenuate social inequality during the liberal period. Indeed, discrimination was exacerbated in the early years of this century when an increase in university fees restricted the social base from which the student body was recruited.[73] Although certain professions, most notably those in the health sector, became somewhat more open to members of the lower middle class, only after the First World War did they finally detach themselves from the landowning milieu.

The self-recruitment of the educated bourgeoisie was one of the most salient features of the Italian professions. The analysis set out in Alberto Banti's essay suggests that this phenomenon did not signal the existence of an educated middle class with a distinct social identity, but rather the persistence of corporatist traditions in a system with few paths of social mobility. The lack of social cohesion and a shared identity among the Italian professions may thus be viewed as the reverse side of economic backwardness. Using comparison with Germany as his benchmark, Banti argues that the Italian professionals were far from constituting a social formation comparable to the *Bildungsbürgertum*, and that they reproduced those phenomena of social disaggregation which typified the Italian nineteenth-century bourgeoisie. As a segment of a weak bourgeoisie traversed by deep social, economic, regional and political cleavages, the Italian professions patterned themselves into a variegated constellation devoid of a class identity. This conclusion is borne out by Fulvio Cammarano's essay, which shows that the behaviour of professionals with seats in the Chamber of Deputies displayed a marked lack of group self-representation.

[72] My reaggregation of statistical data quoted by M. Barbagli, *Educating for Unemployment*, pp. 127, 136–7.
[73] A. Cammelli, *infra*.

Another indicator of the influence of economic backwardness on the Italian professions is the persistence of the link between professions, the land and the nobility. To be stressed here is the case of the engineers, large numbers of whom belonged to the landowning milieu and to the ranks of the nobility; a pattern which was also reflected in the composition of Parliament, where titled engineers were the second largest group of aristocratic deputies after the lawyers.[74] The entry of Italian nobles into the engineering profession was not provoked, as it was in late-nineteenth-century England, by the agrarian crisis.[75] In the first half of the nineteenth century, sons of Italian aristocratic families would attend university courses in mathematics and then specialize in engineering. The link between nobility and engineering was particularly close in Lombardy. And, as Giovanni Montroni shows in his essay, it was also pronounced among the southern aristocracy, although the noble engineers of the *Mezzogiorno*, unlike their counterparts in the North, chose to work in the public administration rather than apply their technical expertise to the management of their estates. This three-way connection between engineers, land and nobility resulted from the persistence of rural society, and it was dissolved by the rise of the industrial engineer.[76] It was also a legacy from the *ancien régime*, under which – this being the case of Lombardy under the Austrians – the colleges of engineers were given noble entitlement.[77]

As in the rest of Europe, the free profession most frequently chosen by the Italian nobility was the law, even if the number of aristocrats in this sector declined noticeably between the mid-nineteenth century and the First World War.[78] Negligible though – as it was in the other European countries, for that matter – was the aristocratic component among doctors and notaries, both of which professions recruited from

[74] See the essay by Fulvio Cammarano in this volume.

[75] D. Cannadine, *The Decline and Fall of the British Aristocracy*, New Haven and London, 1990, pp. 396–7; R.A. Buchanan, 'Gentlemen Engineers: the Making of a Profession', *Victorian Studies*, 26, 1983, pp. 420ff.

[76] For a comparison with Spanish engineers see R. Garrabou, *Enginyers, industrials, modernizació econòmica i burgesia a Catalunya (1850–inicis del segle XX)*, Barcelona, 1982, especially pp. 75–8.

[77] C. Mozzarelli, 'Strutture sociali e formazioni statuali a Napoli fra '500 e '700', *Società e Storia*, 3, 1978, pp. 441ff.

[78] G. Montroni, *infra*; H. Siegrist, 'Gli avvocati nell'Italia del XIX secolo. Provenienza e matrimoni, titoli e prestigio'; R. Abel, *The Legal Professions in England and Wales*, Oxford, 1988, pp. 349–50; D. Higgs, *Nobles in Nineteenth-century France. The Practice of Inegalitarism*, Baltimore and London, 1987, pp. 122–8; C. Charle, 'Noblesse et élites en France au début du XXe siècle', in *Le noblesses européennes au XIXe siècle*. Collection de l'Ecole française de Rome, 107, Rome, 1988, pp. 408–22.

the middle and lower middle classes. Overall, in the second half of the nineteenth century, the professions split away from the nobility and became more pronouncedly bourgeois in character. Although the land continued to exercise its attraction as a form of investment for Italian professionals, this was not an economic strategy confined to a predominantly agricultural country like Italy. In France, the bourgeoisie continued to invest in the land throughout the nineteenth century, even if the share of landed property in urban wealth generally diminished, while in late-nineteenth-century England the successful professional often crowned his career by purchasing a rural estate.[79]

Lastly, one also discerns certain components of the 'backwardness pattern' in the relations between the Italian professionals and politics. This observation applies principally to the militant activism of the doctors in the ranks of the socialist party. As in Spain, Portugal and Russia – rural societies which started along the road to modernization at the end of the nineteenth century – so in Italy the medical profession was distinguished by its vigorous political and social commitment.[80] The political representation of doctors in these countries was greater than that of their counterparts in Germany, England, Austria and Hungary, but much lower than that of the French physicians. Indeed, there were twice as many doctors in the French parliament during the Third Republic than in the Italian Chamber of Deputies (10/12% as compared to 4/6.5%). The French doctors had the strongest medico-political tradition in Europe and their activism in the political arena stemmed more from their *esprit de corps* than from social commitment.[81]

Nineteenth- and early twentieth-century Italy was a country of lawyers; and as in France of the Third Republic, the political representation of this group far exceeded that of all the other professions. In Italy, too, this high political profile was the expression of a composite middle class rather than of a homogeneous professional group. The massive influx to the university law faculties, although a phenomenon in constant and conspicuous growth throughout Europe, acquired special significance in a country such as Italy which came late to national unification. As in Hungary during the same period, the creation

---

[79] A. Banti, *infra*; A. Daumard, *Les fortunes françaises au XIXe siècle*, Paris–La Haye, 1973; Y. Lequin, 'Les patriciats urbaines', in G. Duby, A. Wallon (eds), *Histoire de la France urbaine*, vol. IV, Paris, 1975, pp. 480–90; F.M.L. Thompson, *English Landed Society in the Nineteenth Century*, London, 1980, p. 297.

[80] W.A. Glaser, 'Doctors and Politics', *American Journal of Sociology*, 66, 1960.

[81] J.D. Ellis, *The Physicians-Legislators of France. Medicine and Politics in the Early Third Republic, 1870–1914*, Cambridge, 1990, p. 6.

of the national state oriented the old aristocratic elites and the bourgeois class towards legal studies, on the basis of which they could stake their claim to a share in the new state's resources.[82] Under this interpretation, the boom in legal studies represented both the continuation of a long-established tradition in Italian culture and society, and the creation of an alliance between new and old social strata intent on gaining control over the new state.

In liberal Italy, the professionals did not accomplish the rapid ascent to power and prestige that their counterparts in England or France were able to achieve. Although its links with politics and the universities enabled the elite of the Italian free professions to shape itself into a new patriciate, the fragmentariness typical of the professional rank and file duplicated the traditional failings of the Italian bourgeoisie. This judgement, however, should not obscure the fact that – as elsewhere in Europe – the Italian professionals contributed to the modernization of their country. They represented one of the crucial factors in the secularization of Italian society,[83] they replaced the landowning notability in the running of local government,[84] they were the first to assimilate changes within the family and to establish greater equality between the sexes.[85] They embodied a model of professionalization founded on the politics of ambiguity which would later provide the basis for the ascent of professionism in Italy after the Second World War.

[82] V. Karady, 'Une "nation de juristes"', Actes de la recherche en sciences sociales, 86/87, 1991, pp. 110–11.

[83] On the affiliation of Italian professionals with Freemasonry see J.P. Viallet, 'Anatomie d'une obédience maçonique: le Grand-Orient d'Italie (1870–1890 circa)', in Mélanges de l'Ecole française de Rome, 90, 1, 1978, p. 212.

[84] See for example the municipal council of Parma in 1889–1914, in which about 50 per cent of all the councillors were professionals: C. Sorba, L'eredità delle mura. Un caso di municipalismo democratico (Parma 1889–1914), Venice, 1993, pp. 21–46.

[85] M. Barbagli, Sotto lo stesso tetto. Mutamenti della famiglia in Italia dal XV al XX secolo, Bologna, 1984, pp. 485ff.

PART I

THE FORMATION OF THE PROFESSIONS

CHAPTER I

UNIVERSITIES AND PROFESSIONS*

ANDREA CAMMELLI

I. INTRODUCTION

The aim of this study is to analyse the dynamics of university training and of the practice of certain professions in nineteenth- and early twentieth-century Italy. After a brief survey of certain essential features of Italian society during the period of national unification, the first part of the essay seeks to quantify the numbers of Italians who practised professions which required a university education. This will entail analysis and critical appraisal of a source – namely, population censuses – of especial historical and documentary interest. The study will then examine, in quantitative terms, the evolution of university attendance in Italy between 1861 and 1911. The results presented derive from the first phase of research which will be completed in the near future with detailed analysis of the relationship between university and the professions at the University of Bologna's schools of Pharmacy, Veterinary Science, Notarial Studies and Obstetrics.

I.I. Quantifying the practitioners of a profession is a notoriously difficult and complex undertaking, especially when the aim is to ensure comparability over a long period and/or among different national contexts. Definition of the competences, functions and roles of each individual profession requires examination of variables which constantly vary in time and space with the evolution of society, of technical progress, of institutional reform, of government policies, and of the power relationships among different social groups and interests; an evolution which also alters the relationships among the

* I am particularly indebted to Francesco Casadei (with whom I am about to complete a comprehensive study of the university and university schools of Bologna in the period 1861–1911), Fabrizio Bernardi, Angelo Di Francia and Angelo Guerriero, for their assistance in writing this essay.

professions and the manner in which each of them is perceived by society at large.

Matters are further complicated by the arbitrary correspondence between professions as formally defined and as they are actually practised – between, that is, legal situations and *de facto* ones. As Ben-David has convincingly argued, there is no unequivocal – in time and space – definition of the professions. An added difficulty is that only few countries possess historical statistics on the professions which are of sufficient detail and reliability.[1] Bairoch, amongst others, has shown that international comparisons of the occupational structure – for reasons to do with differences in survey method, the definition and classification of individual professions, as well as the concept itself of working population – should be conducted with extreme caution.[2] Hence, the use of census data for the study of the diffusion and evolution of the professions has often proved difficult in practice and is, accordingly, rarely attempted. Researchers have instead insisted on the unreliability of census data; unreliability which is the greater, the earlier the date of the census and the more closely the figures reflect the rudimentary beginnings of official statistical surveys.

Because of these doubts and difficulties, study of the size and development of the professions has seemed more reliable, and also easier, if conducted using a different approach; one which concentrates on the supply of qualified personnel and therefore analyses figures on the intake (enrolments) by institutes of higher education and universities and, especially, figures on their output (diploma-holders and graduates). The focus of interest in this case is on the number of new entrants to the professional labour market in search of employment and in possession of the necessary formal qualifications. Ben-David, in the work cited above, argues against the measurement of the professions *per se* and advocates instead the use of university statistics, since these constitute a vital source of information on professionalism.[3]

According to educational statistics and a number of widely cited studies (carried out both in Italy and abroad), post-Unification Italy found itself in the curious position of having both an illiteracy rate and a rate of university attendance among the highest in Europe. The excessive production of graduates in the country – excessive with respect to its conditions, needs and prospects – created a marked disequilibrium between the demand for and supply of qualified personnel.

[1] J. Ben-David, 'The Growth of the Professions and the Class System', in R. Bendix, S. Lipset (eds), *Class, Status and Power*, New York, 1966.
[2] See *La population active et sa structure*, Institut de Sociologie, Brussels, 1968.
[3] Ben-David, 'The Growth of the Professions'.

This surplus of graduates on the labour market instigated a variety of phenomena: pressure on the civil service, with the resultant bloating of its staffing levels; large-scale intellectual emigration; and the (sometimes vehement) denunciations of the mismatch between demand and supply of qualified personnel which were a constant theme of Italian political and parliamentary debate for at least sixty years.[4] However, at least for the period covered by the present study (1861–1911), some specifications are in order.

1.2. As regards quantitative documentation, the contention that educational statistics (university statistics in particular) are more reliable than census data needs to be demonstrated. The first two decades after Italian unification were years of adjustment at all levels and in all areas – and this regarded the university just as much as censuses. Historians and specialists agree, however, on the substantial reliability of census data during the following period.[5] Indeed there are good grounds for doubting the statistics furnished by the universities, given their tendency to inflate their enrolments (and perhaps even the number of their graduates) in order to obtain greater public financing and to counter the insistent criticism by politicians and parliamentarians – and also by distinguished intellectuals – that they were inefficient, excessive in numbers and too costly (especially those universities with small student bodies). What is certain, though, is that the figures on student enrolments, and even more so those on graduates, are difficult to reconstruct, erratic, and in some cases altogether contradictory.[6]

It should also be pointed out that the studies claiming to show that the civil service was grossly inflated in order to accommodate the large numbers of graduates in search of employment[7] fail to cite their

---

[4] See M. Barbagli, *Educating for Unemployment. Politics, Labour Markets, and the School System. Italy, 1859–1973*, New York, 1982, especially pp. 13–70.

[5] See the important study by Ornello Vitali, *Aspetti dello sviluppo economico italiano alla luce della ricostruzione della popolazione attiva*, Facoltà di Scienze Statistiche, Demographiche ed Attuariali, Rome, 1970. See also S. Bruni, 'La realtà produttiva nei primi censimenti', in *Storia d'Italia*. Vol. VI. *Atlante*, Turin, 1976.

[6] See, for example, the historical series of graduates produced by Bodio and used by Nitti, which begins with 1881–82 and reports 2,699 graduates, and the figures for the previous year, from a different source, which cite 3,119: that is, 16.8% more. See F.S. Nitti, *La ricchezza dell'Italia*, Bari, 1966, p. 103, and Ministero di Agricoltura, Industria e Commercio, *Statistiche dell'istruzione per l'anno scolastico 1880–81*, Rome, 1883.

[7] See the book by the parliamentarian Giovanni Abignente, *La riforma dell'amministrazione pubblica in Italia*, Laterza, Bari, 1916, cited in M. Barbagli, *Educating for Unemployment*, pp. 37–8.

sources, and they reach conclusions very different from those to be drawn from demonstrably reliable census data.

Moreover, the figures used to quantify the phenomenon of emigration from Italy, and intellectual emigration in particular, are anything but convincing. In the attempt to demonstrate that the surplus of graduates (once it had enormously swollen the civil service) had no other option than to leave the country, insufficient attention has been paid to a number of important aspects. First of all, statistics on emigration for the entire period 1876–1903 concern, not the number of effective 'expatriates' but the number of *nulla osta* or 'permits for the issue of passports' granted by the authorities (and from 1904 to 1920 the 'passports' issued). Indeed the *Commissariato Generale dell'Emigrazione* itself warned, in a study conducted by its own staff, that inquiry

> based on *nulla osta* gave rise to an excessive estimate, in that the number of passports was always smaller than that of the *nulla osta*, both because many applicants, once they had obtained permission to be issued a passport, did not bother to collect them having decided not to emigrate, and because the political authorities sometimes refused to issue the passport for reasons of public order, even though the *nulla osta* had been granted.[8]

One should also verify the number of *nulla osta* (or passports) issued in the same year to the same person (for different destinations, or for repeated journeys to the same destination in cases of temporary emigration to European countries). This may be a matter of considerable importance, given that emigration within Europe (principally to France, Switzerland and Germany) accounted for 82 per cent of overall Italian migratory movement in the decade 1861–70, and that it was invariably higher than 40 per cent until the end of the first decade of this century.[9] In any case, detailed analysis should also take account of 're-patriations', since these, during the period for which figures are available (1872–76), were very numerous, accounting for between 57 and 80 per cent of expatriations in each of the years considered.[10]

A further unresolved issue in this area – perhaps one even more controversial than the question of census data – is the correspondence between the profession effectively practised by an applicant and the profession that s/he declared when applying for the *nulla osta* to emigrate. There seem to be good grounds for suspecting that in the hope

---

[8] Commissariato Generale dell'Emigrazione, *Annuario statistico dell'emigrazione italiana, 1875–1926*, Rome, 1926, p. XVIII.

[9] See Istituto Centrale di Statistica, *Sommario di Statistiche storiche dell'Italia 1861–1965*, Rome, 1968, p. 28.

[10] Istituto Centrale di Statistica, *Sommario di Statistiche storiche italiane 1861–1955*, Rome, 1958, p. 65.

of finding better employment in the destination country, those intent on emigrating would declare their employment potential or their future aspirations, rather than the profession that they were unable to practise at home. To what extent this reduces the scale (nevertheless huge) of Italian emigration – especially intellectual emigration – is difficult to say, and it is in any case not the subject of this study. It is important nonetheless to stress that the phenomenon has certainly been overestimated.

If these premises are valid, they suggest a different line of analysis: one which assesses the size and development of the professions by returning to the source; by re-examining, that is, census data, with all the caution necessary and in full awareness of their shortcomings. This approach enables direct interpretation of the phenomenon examined in the light of the findings of official surveys. It reveals how the profession exercised was perceived by the individual citizen (and likewise by the community in which he worked) in the version given of it when the census form was compiled (although it was not possible to check the declaration of educational qualifications because census surveys did not record this information until 1951). From this point of view, censuses restore the image not only of how the world of the professions appeared in the eyes of the census-takers but also of how this world was perceived in society by political and social forces, as well as by public opinion in this particular period.

The result will be a reading of the phenomenon 'professions' which can be usefully compared with the findings of other and different interpretations. Obviously, the validity and interpretative capacity of this approach depend closely on the existence of a unitary institutional, economic and social context. In short, ours is an approach which can be used to investigate developments in a single country; it is much less suitable (or indeed entirely inappropriate) for cross-country comparisons.

1.3. Turning to empirical matters, new documentation and a different, more careful use of the data already available enable the researcher to specify a number of important features of the period examined by this study (1861–1911). The rate of university attendance in Italy (measured by the ratio between enrolments and the population aged 20 to 24) was certainly high, but not nearly as high as has long been contended (see section 4.2). The international comparisons that are possible today scale down the phenomenon. They show that, in education, Italy lagged behind almost all the major European countries, and in the first decade of this century consider-

ably so. As we shall see, the fact that there was a boom in enrolments (first at secondary schools, then at universities) during this
period does not alter the issue; if anything it confirms it.

Compared with the increase in the population, there was no significant numerical growth in the practitioners of the principal professions.
Despite the predictable requirements of the public sector in a newly
created state confronted by enormous problems (suffice it to mention
the government's task of educating the majority of the population),
not only was the increase in the personnel employed by this sector
(comparing homogeneous categories) much less substantial than many
have contended, even in absolute values (the increase amounted to 38
per cent in fifty years, and to 33 per cent in the last thirty years, compared with the 68 per cent that some have claimed[11]), it was even
modest when set against the population as a whole (+9.4 per cent
between 1881 and 1911).

1.4. We have not yet addressed the problem of the disequilibrium
between the supply of, and demand for, qualified labour in the major
professions. We have suggested, however, that this disequilibrium may
have been directly inherited from before Unification – and that the
situation did not worsen during the fifty years following national
unity, but indeed remained substantially stable.

Whatever the case may be, this disequilibrium apparently did not
have the alleged effect of bloating staffing levels in the civil service.
The 'emigration' solution – which was undoubtedly a constant and extremely important feature of Italy's post-Unification history – was certainly resorted to by large numbers of secondary-school leavers and
university graduates. Yet it should come as no surprise if new studies
and further analysis reach the conclusion that the real size of this phenomenon (especially as regards its most highly qualified component)
was much smaller than has long been believed.

However, still unexplained is another enduring feature; a topic constantly returned to – almost obsessively so – by Italian political, parliamentary and cultural debate throughout most of the post-Unification
period. The concern and censure provoked by the excessive numbers
of university students and graduates have already been amply
documented.[12] And equally well documented is the fact that the cru-
sading spirit which emerged during this fierce battle was not a characteristic exclusive to obscurantists and conservatives.

---

[11] See Abignente, La riforma della pubblica amministrazione, p. 3.
[12] See Barbagli, Educating for Unemployment, pp. 41–8, and A. Banti in this volume.

If the above results concerning the real proportions of university enrolments, of the professions, of the civil service and of intellectual emigration are robust, then one must explain why the situation of Italy
between national Unification and the first decade of this century was
perceived in such dramatic terms. And one must also verify the extent
to which it was the reaction by the ruling class of the time, by the political class and by the professions, and by the intellectual milieu (traditionally the proponent of a Malthusian educational policy), to a semi-
universal educational system inherited, without any great enthusiasm,
from pre-Unification Piedmont. For various reasons, this school
system met with immediate scepticism, and it alarmed the ruling class
because it subtracted resources from primary education – and perhaps
also, and even more so, because it undermined existing power relationships and equilibria and was a potential source of political radicalization. So strong was the ruling class's anxiety that it set out to create a
different educational system – one, that is, with restricted entrance; an
endeavour in which it eventually succeeded, albeit only on paper, with
the Gentile reforms of 1923, sixty years after Unification. This was an
objective pursued with a determination perhaps greater than that necessary to invest the abundant availability of human capital in the
country's more equitable and rapid development.[13]

The five censuses carried out during the period with which we are
concerned here (i.e. the censuses of 1861, 1871, 1881, 1901 and 1911)
recorded the 'profession' (or the 'condition') declared by each citizen
(the last two surveys distinguished between the respondent's 'principal' profession and his 'secondary' one), without comparisons being
possible with the respondent's level of educational attainment. These,
in fact, were still the years in which assessment of educational level
went no further than the 'ability to read and write'. The key issue
here is the existence, and the most likely location, of areas of overesti-
mation and underestimation of the professions declared and of those
requiring a university-level qualification. We shall divide the professions into two categories: those involving dependent employment (in
the private and public sectors), and those involving self-employment,
i.e. the free professions.

It seems plausible that, at the moment of the census, in the former
case the dependent employee would opt for the declaration which
maximized his professional success and emphasized the social and economic prestige that he had achieved. That is, he would declare his

---

[13] See the hypothesis by V. Zamagni, *L'offerta di istruzione in Italia 1861–1987: un fattore
guida dello sviluppo o un ostacolo?*, Università di Cassino, Dipartimento di Economia
e Territorio, Cassino, 1993.

level or grade in the public or private sector if this was high (executive, director, etc.), but would declare his qualification required for the exercise of a profession if it was low. For example, in the case of two law graduates, one a senior executive (public or private) and the other a routine office-worker in some ministry, it is highly likely that they would give different descriptions of their professional statuses to the census officer: the former describing himself as an executive, the latter as a lawyer. The same would apply to doctors, veterinary surgeons and pharmacists. Thus, under this hypothesis, the census figures on the overall membership of the professions (especially those requiring a university qualification) underestimate a proportion of the professional activities performed by dependent workers (in both the public and private sectors) but overestimate another proportion of them (probably much larger).

In the sector of the free professions, the hypothesis does not change but is, rather, simplified. Especially during the earliest censuses, it is probable that individuals recorded as professionals in some or other sector (health, law, etc.) effectively practised that profession although they were not in possession of the necessary qualifications. The declining numbers of health professionals recorded by later censuses, as the reorganization of the professions got under way, seem to confirm this hypothesis. Again: it is likely (and this is at least partially documented) that respondents were recorded as practising certain professions although they had never actually done so (property-owners, etc.) or had ceased (for reasons of age, etc.). Lastly, in the sector of self-employed labour, too, the census figures tend to overestimate the size of the free professions.

Although these assumptions and arguments seem plausible (and have in part been verified), a possible objection – an important one since it would cast serious doubt on our conclusions (especially as regards the self-employed sector) – is that respondents may have been reluctant to give truthful answers to surveys which could also be used for fiscal purposes. Only on the occasion of the 1931 census, in fact, was the absolutely anonymous use of data guaranteed by the government, thereby allaying respondents' fears of fiscal investigation into their affairs.[14]

2. THE REFERENCE FRAMEWORK

In the aftermath of national Unification (1861), the physiognomy of Italy still inevitably replicated the features of the various states into

[14] See the survey form used by the *Censimento generale della popolazione 1931*.

which it had previously been divided. In order to account for this legacy, it seemed advisable to organize the data (mainly census-based) on a number of structural features which reflected the borders that marked out the old Italian states on the eve of Unification. This approach seems even more prudent if we bear in mind that the first population census was carried out on 31 December 1861, only a few months after the official proclamation of the Kingdom of Italy (Diagram 1.1). The uncertainty and approximations typical of the statistical data of the time suggest extreme caution; nevertheless, mention of some summary figures may prove useful as well as interesting.

Of the Italian population aged six and over, 75 per cent was illiterate (Table 1.1): 68 per cent of males and 81 per cent of females (Table 1.2). These figures, however, conceal significant geographical differences – especially between ex-Austrian Lombardy and the Kingdom of Sardinia (respectively 54 and 59 per cent) and, in maximum values, between the Kingdom of the Two Sicilies (87 per cent) and the Papal States (81 per cent). Moreover, a map of the country drawn according to the population's ability to read and write mirrors the differing educational policies adopted by the various states, which for many years sought to ensure social control either through *ignorance* or, later, through *education*.

In any event, one notes that the overall picture of Italy already reveals major disequilibria between the North, the Centre and the South, with their respective illiteracy rates of 60, 78 and 87 per cent.

But it is international comparisons, especially with the countries of central and northern Europe, which most starkly highlight the persistent educational backwardness of Italy (Table 1.3). Ten years after Unification, still 70 Italians out of every 100 were illiterate: the equivalent figure in France was 31 per cent, and in Prussia a low 12 per cent of the population aged over ten. In the early years of this century, 48 per cent of Italians were illiterate, while in Belgium, France and Austria the phenomenon was much more circumscribed.

The topic of educational attainment links with that of participation in political elections. In 1861, of every 100,000 Italians only 1,737 were eligible to vote; a figure much lower than those recorded for most of the countries of central and northern Europe (in Belgium there were more than 2,000 eligible voters per 100,000 inhabitants, in England more than 5,000, in Prussia almost 10,000, in Sweden more than 23,000, in France more than 26,000).[15]

---

[15] See the report accompanying the *Censimento generale 31 dicembre 1861*, vol. 1, Tip. Barbera, Florence, 1867, p. 67, and, on the electoral system, F. Cammarano in this volume.

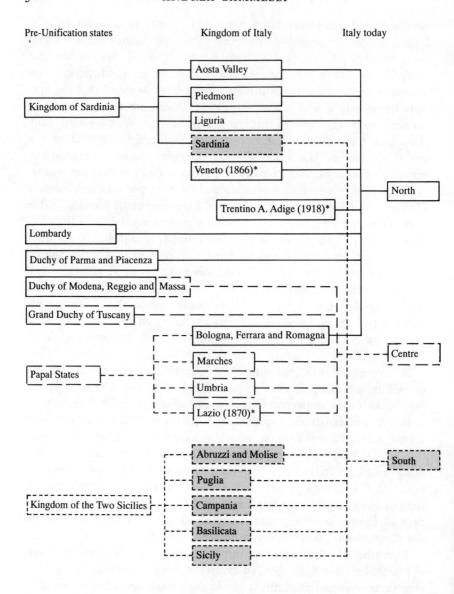

* In brackets the year of inclusion in the Kingdom of Italy

Diagram 1.1. Italy from the pre-Unification states to the Kingdom of
Italy to the present day

Table 1.1 *Illiteracy in Italy in 1861 (pre-Unification borders)*

Pre-Unification states	Illiterates aged 6 and over	
	absolute values	% of the population of the same age
Kingdom of Sardinia	2,106,669	59.2
Lombardy	1,436,473	53.7
Duchy of Parma and Piacenza	326,446	79.2
Duchy of Modena, Reggio and Massa	415,880	76.7
Grand Duchy of Tuscany	1,172,166	74.0
Papal States	1,709,260	80.8
Kingdom of the Two Sicilies	6,886,608	86.9
North	4,532,109	59.7
Centre	2,182,633	78.0
South and Islands	7,338,760	87.0
Kingdom (total population)	14,053,502	74.7

Source: Direzione Generale della Statistica del Regno, *Censimento Generale*, 31 December 1861, Tipografia G. Barbera, Florence, 1867.

Table 1.2 *Illiteracy of the population aged six and over (values relative to the population of the same age)*

	Males	Females	Total
1861	68.1	81.3	74.7
1871	61.9	75.7	68.8
1881	54.6	69.3	61.9
1901	42.5	54.4	48.5
1911	32.6	42.4	37.6

Source: Annuario statistico italiano, various years.

When one compares these figures against the Italian national average of 17.4 electors per thousand inhabitants, major regional differences emerge; differences which depended not only on educational conditions but also on the 'varying distribution of landed property' and on 'the differing systems of land registry and taxation'.[16] Achieving rates above the national average were the regions of the ex-Kingdom of Sardinia (the island of Sardinia in particular, with 36 electors per thousand inhabitants), Tuscany and the provinces of Parma and Piacenza; equal to the national average was Lombardy; while the ex-Kingdom of the Two Sicilies, the provinces of Modena, Reggio and Massa fell below

[16] Ibid.

Table 1.3 *Illiteracy in certain European countries, 1871–1911*

	Year	Population considered	Illiterates in population considered (%) Men and women	Women
Italy	1871	aged 6 and over	69	76
	1881	"	62	69
	1901	"	48	54
	1911	"	38	42
Austria	1890	aged 10 and over	29	30
	1900	"	23	25
	1910	"	17	18
Belgium	1880	aged 10 and over	31	34
	1890	"	26	28
	1900	"	19	21
France	1872	aged 6 and over	31	34
	1901	aged 5 and over	18	20
Prussia	1871	aged 10 and over	12	15
Spain	1877	all ages	72	81
	1887	aged over 10	61	73
	1900	"	56	66
	1910	"	50	59
Portugal	1890	aged 7 and over	76	84
	1900	"	74	82
	1911	"	70	77

Source: C.M. Cipolla, *Literacy and Development in the West*, Penguin Books, London, 1969.

it, and the lowest values were recorded in the regions of the former Papal States (in the Marches and Umbria, indeed, there was only one elector per 100 inhabitants).

The Italian economy, furthermore, was still closely dependent on agriculture (Table 1.4). According to the first census of 1861, 35 per cent of the total population was employed in the agricultural sector (with percentages ranging from 31 workers per 100 inhabitants in the Grand Duchy of Tuscany to 41 per cent in the Papal States). Overall, there were no significant differences between North, Centre and South. However, this was not the case of industry and crafts, a sector which employed just over 14 per cent of the labour force (9 per cent in the Kingdom of Sardinia, 17 per cent in the Kingdom of the Two Sicilies). A present-day observer, unaware of the conditions which favoured the mining and manufacturing industries in the *Mezzogiorno* prior to Unification (conditions which subsequently disappeared), may

Table 1.4 *Population by principal economic sectors in 1861*
(pre-Unification borders)

Pre-Unification states	Agriculture		Industry	
	Absolute values	% of the population	Absolute values	% of the population
Kingdom of Sardinia	1,501,106	*36.4*	376,955	*9.1*
Lombardy	1,086,028	*35.0*	465,003	*15.0*
Duchy of Parma and Piacenza	186,677	*39.3*	66,325	*14.0*
Duchy of Modena, Reggio and Massa	242,248	*38.4*	71,759	*11.4*
Grand Duchy of Tuscany	571,409	*31.3*	266,698	*14.6*
Papal States	987,902	*40.5*	288,697	*11.8*
Kingdom of the Two Sicilies	3,133,261	*34.1*	1,595,359	*17.4*
North	3,214,687	*36.6*	1,078,712	*12.3*
Centre	1,201,444	*37.3*	425,333	*13.2*
South and Islands	3,292,500	*33.7*	1,626,751	*16.7*
Kingdom (total population)	7,708,631	*35.4*	3,130,796	*14.4*

Source: Censimento Generale, 31 December 1861, (see Table 1.1)

be surprised to find levels of industrialization in the South (17 per cent of the overall population) which were higher than in the Centre (13 per cent) and in the North (12 per cent).

Italy's laggardly arrival on the international scene is well illustrated by the relative percentages of the working population employed in agriculture and in industry, as set out in Table 1.5.

Ten years after Unification, 61 per cent of the Italian labour force was employed in agriculture, which was a percentage between 11 and 17 per cent higher than in France, Germany and Belgium, and four times higher than in Britain, which had long before set off on the road to industrialization. In fact, whereas almost half the British active population worked in industry, not even one quarter of the Italian labour force was employed in industrial activities. France, Germany and Belgium registered intermediate values. Lastly, it is worth noting that a century would pass before Italy achieved Britain's 1871 rates of employment in the industrial sector — by which time, moreover, the tertiary sector had grown to unprecedented proportions.

The features briefly described above were part, as regards Italy, of a general trend whereby after two decades of post-Unification adjustment the country passed through a first phase of economic take-off in the 1880s (generated, amongst other things, by the first government orders to industry), followed by a period of recession provoked by the

Table 1.5 *Working population in certain European countries*
(absolute values in thousands)

Country	Year	Agriculture		Industry		Other activities		Working population	
		Absolute values	%	Absolute values	%	Absolute values	%	Absolute values	%
Italy	(1871)	8,700	61.0	3,325	23.3	2,237	15.7	14,262	100.0
Austria	(1869)	7,506	65.2	2,199	19.1	1,811	15.7	11,516	100.0
Belgium	(1866)	1,077	44.4	918	37.8	431	17.8	2,426	100.0
France	(1866)	7,536	49.8	4,237	28.0	3,370	22.2	15,143	100.0
Germany	(1882)	8,237	46.7	6,253	35.5	3,142	17.8	17,632	100.0
GB	(1871)	1,817	15.3	5,600	47.1	4,466	37.6	11,883	100.0

Source: B.R. Mitchell, *International Historical Statistics. Europe 1750–1988*, Macmillan, London, 1992 (author's calculations)

agrarian crisis of the end of the century. The true '*grande slancio*' (great spurt) of the economy (with a steady increase in industrialization) took place between the 1890s and the First World War.

The higher level of industrial employment in the South compared with the other regions of Italy is not the only feature that conflicts with the conventional picture of the conditions of many regions in the Italian *Mezzogiorno*. In the first years after Unification, the infant mortality rate in Italy was 22.6 per cent of live births: a rate lower than in Germany (29.8%) and Austria (26.4%) but much higher than in France (19.0%), England and Wales (15.3%), and Sweden (13.7%). And yet, internally to the country, the infant mortality rate was lower in all the southern regions of the ex-Kingdom of Italy (except for Basilicata), while it was highest in the regions of the North (26.7% in Veneto, 25.7% in Lombardy and Emilia-Romagna). It should be immediately pointed out, however, that this initial 'advantage' of the *Mezzogiorno* was only temporary:

> In the years that followed, infant mortality began to decline more rapidly in the northern regions until, at the beginning of this century and with increasing salience thereafter, a geographical classification emerged in which mortality in the first year of life became one of the most evident signs of the imbalances and disparities in the country's economic and social development.[17]

The average life expectancy at birth of the Italian population in the years immediately after Unification was 33.5 years. In the next decade the figure rose to around 37 years, although this was still 13 years lower

[17] A. Bellettini, *La popolazione italiana. Un profilo storico*, Einaudi, Turin, p. 180; see also Mitchell, *International Historical Statistics*, London, 1992.

than life expectancy in the Scandinavian countries (50 years), and around 8 years lower than in England, Belgium, Holland, France and Switzerland.

According to the self-declarations made during the first census to be carried out after Unification, the population of the Kingdom of Italy was served by just under 9 doctors and surgeons per every 10,000 inhabitants. In this respect, the regions of the ex-Kingdom of the Two Sicilies – with a rate higher than 10 – enjoyed a relative advantage. However, 'in none of our regions is medical science so poorly represented as it is in Belgium and England. France itself only has 7 doctors for every 10 thousand people. In this respect, we are surpassed, though only just, by Spain.'[18]

In the autumn of 1861 the academic year was inaugurated in nineteen universities and six institutes of higher education, with a total student population of more than nine thousand students (Table 1.6 and Diagram 1.2). One student for every 170 coevals attended university, and the rate of university attendance was 613 per 100,000 of the population aged 20 to 24, a figure equivalent to 43.3 university students per 100,000 inhabitants. However, on the assumption that student geographical mobility was much more restricted in those years, university attendance was not uniformly high in all the pre-Unification states: the six universities of the Papal States were attended by 37.8 students per 100,000 inhabitants, while at the five universities located in the Kingdom of the Two Sicilies the rate was 40.8. It was considerably higher in the less densely populated northern duchies of Parma and Piacenza (74.6) and of Modena, Reggio and Massa (70.5). Overall, better opportunities for university-level training were available in northern Italy (where the rate of university attendance was 48.4 per 100,000 inhabitants) than in the South (40.6) and, especially, the Centre of Italy (37.7). Ten years later, the rate of university attendance was 531 students per 100,000 young people aged 20 to 24 years.

In conclusion to this brief overview, it may prove useful to give a summary of the figures on the principal variables so far considered (see Table 1.7 and Diagram 1.3) as they emerge from the census of 1861 and according to the immediately post-Unification borders of the Italian state and its regions (which, as will be seen, in some cases coincided with the borders of the old pre-Unification states).

---

[18] *Censimento 1861*, vol. I, p. 98.

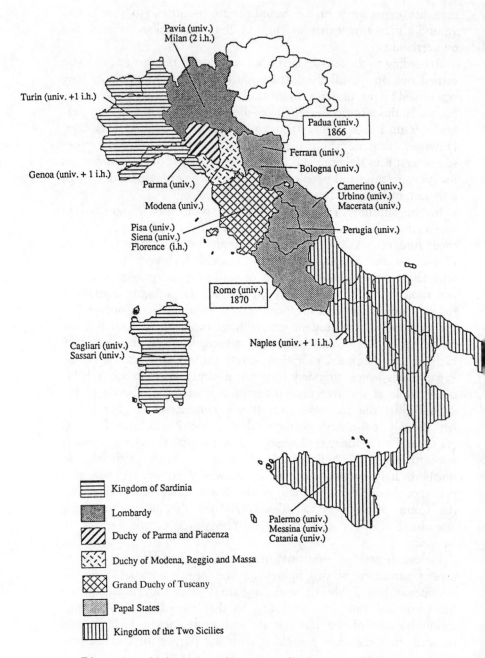

Diagram 1.2. Universities and institutes of higher education in Italy: 1861
(pre-Unification borders)

Table 1.6 *Universities and institutes of higher education and student enrolments*[a] *in 1861 (pre-Unification borders)*

Pre-Unification states	Higher education		Students enrolled in 1860–61	
	Universities	Higher institutes	Absolute values	Enrolments/ 100,000 in.
Kingdom of Sardinia	4	2	1,699	41.2
Lombardy	1	2	1,414	45.5
Duchy of Parma and Piacenza	1		354	74.6
Duchy of Modena, Reggio and Massa	1		445	70.5
Grand Duchy of Tuscany	2	1	856	46.9
Papal States	6		920	37.8
Kingdom of the Two Sicilies	4	1	3,748	40.8
North	7	4	4,255	48.4
Centre	6	1	1,214	37.7
South and Islands	6	1	3,967	40.6
Kingdom	19	6	9,436	43.3

[a] The figures on enrolments include both students and *uditori* (students entitled to attend lectures but not to sit for examinations). For the University of Naples only an estimate of enrolments in 1860–61 (2,500) is available.

Sources: Censimento Generale 31 December 1861; *Sulle condizioni della pubblica istruzione nel Regno d'Italia*, Stamperia Reale, Milan, 1865; Ministero di Agricoltura, Industria e Commercio, Direzione Generale della Statistica, *Statistica dell'istruzione per l'a.s. 1880–81*, Tipografia Elzeviriana, Rome, 1883.

3. THE PROFESSIONS AS MEASURED BY CENSUSES

3.1. *General aspects*

When census data are used in analysis of the professions, caution is obligatory. As Pietro Maestri, the eminent scholar who wrote the commentary report on the first Italian census, admitted:

> Let us not delude ourselves. Census returns are a less reliable source of information on the various professions of the country's inhabitants than special statistics [...] The census officers must rely by necessity on individual declarations and judgements, which may be erroneous [...] However, in spite of the inevitable imperfections in census procedures, the results obtained are extremely valuable, for they represent – in outline form, it is true, but with sufficient accuracy – the main groups of the professions practised by the population.[19]

The observations of the report accompanying the results from the

[19] Ibid.

Table 1.7 *Post-Unification Italy: illiterates, university students, sectors of employment – regions*

Regions	Illiterates 6 years and over		Enrolments at university		Sector of economic activity		
	Absolute values (in thousands)	%	a.v.	Enrolments per 100,000 inhabitants	Agriculture % inhabitants	Industry % inhabitants	total pop. a.v. (in thousands)
Piedmont and Liguria	1,654.5	54.2	1,480	41.9	38.0	9.8	3,535.7
Lombardy	1,436.5	53.7	1,414	45.5	35.0	15.0	3,104.8
Parma and Piacenza	326.4	79.2	354	74.6	39.3	14.0	474.6
Modena, Reggio and Massa	415.9	76.7	445	70.5	38.4	11.4	631.4
Romagna	698.8	77.4	562	54.0	34.4	12.5	1,040.6
Marches	636.8	83.0	211	23.9	43.3	13.2	883.1
Umbria	373.7	83.8	147	28.7	48.4	8.2	513.0
Tuscany	1,172.2	74.0	856	46.9	31.3	14.7	1,826.3
Continental Mezzogiorno	5,078.1	86.3	2,546	37.5	37.9	17.5	6,787.3
Sicily	1,808.5	88.6	1,202	50.2	23.6	17.0	2,392.4
Sardinia	452.2	89.7	219	37.2	27.1	5.3	588.1
Kingdom	14,053.6	74.7	9,436	43.3	35.4	14.4	21,777.3

Sources: *Censimento Generale* 31 December 1861 (see Table 1.1); *Sulle condizioni della Pubblica Istruzione nel Regno d'Italia*, Stamperia Reale, Milan 1865.

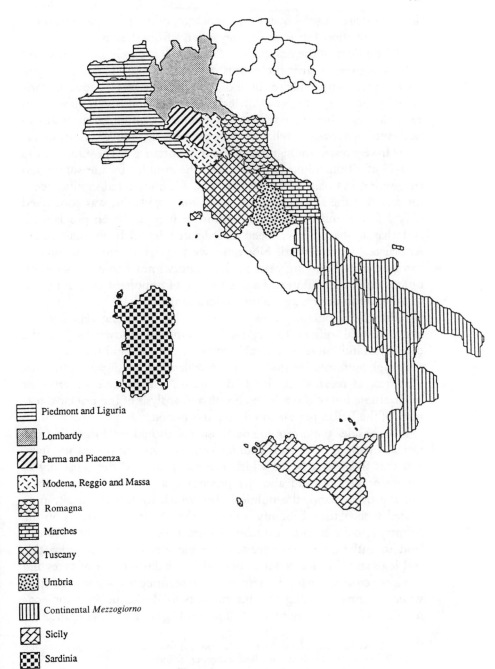

Diagram 1.3. Italy 1861 (Regions)

first census are a useful basis for presentation of the principal features of Italy's occupational structure as they emerge from the census data.

The purpose of the comparison (Table 1.8) is purely indicative, and especially so as regards the census of 1861, whose characteristics are only in part comparable to those of subsequent surveys, above all concerning the free professions, which were certainly overestimated in 1861 although they were subject in subsequent censuses to more analytical and increasingly reliable measurement. Moreover, historiographers have stressed the significance and importance of the effort by the post-Unification ruling class to 'assess' the country by measuring and analysing it in quantitative terms as well. Of undoubted significance is the fact that the first general census of the population was conducted only a few months after the Kingdom of Italy had been proclaimed, and that it should have been coordinated by such an outstanding scholar as Pietro Maestri. Nor must we forget the numerous surveys carried out in following years by the country's newly created statistical offices and which addressed a wide range of important economic and social issues (industry, agriculture, education).

Italian historiography views the efforts by the ruling class and the first statistical offices to accumulate statistical knowledge on the country as indicative of a notable sense of the state and the *res publica*. Although authoritative studies have revealed flaws and gaps in the data – at least as regards the first two censuses – they have nevertheless made ample use of them in discussion and analysis of the principal features of the Italian population during this period.[20]

Nor, besides these more general aspects, should we forget that statistical methods were still rudimentary in nineteenth-century Italy, and that this was a factor which inevitably affected the reliability of survey procedures and also the processing and analysis of the data. On the other hand, the political class which so enthusiastically promoted such statistical inquiry – in order to obtain information on the country's socio-economic situation from censuses and other surveys, 'and to gather the data necessary for the election of administrative and legislative bodies or for a more efficient distribution of taxes and services across the national territory'[21] – seemingly contradicted itself when it came to using this information to devise policies for economic and social development. The slow spread of basic education

[20] See R. Romanelli, *L'Italia liberale (1861–1900)*, Il Mulino, Bologna, 1979. See also P. Villani, 'Gruppi sociali e classe dirigente all'indomani dell'Unità', in *Storia d'Italia. Annali 1. Dal feudelesimo al capitalismo*, Turin, 1978, and Bruni, 'La realtà produttiva nei primi censimenti'.

[21] Bruni, 'La realtà produttiva nei primi censimenti', p. 3.

Table 1.8 *Economically active population by sector of activity*
(absolute values in thousands)

	Agriculture Absolute values	%	Industry Absolute values	%	Other activities Absolute values	%	Active population Absolute values	%
1871	8,700	61.0	3,325	23.3	2,237	15.7	14,262	100.0
1881	8,599	51.4	4,246	25.4	3,896	23.2	16,741	100.0
1901	9,666	58.8	3,990	24.2	2,798	17.0	16,454	100.0
1911	9,085	55.4	4,368	26.6	2,948	18.0	16,401	100.0

Source: Mitchell, *International Historical Statistics* (see Table 1.5) (our calculations)

N.B. The figures given here are higher than those presented by Vitali in *Aspetti dello sviluppo economico italiano alla luce della ricostruzione della popolazione attiva*, Facoltà di Scienze Statistiche, demografiche ed attuariali, Rome, 1970, except for agriculture. This is probably because Mitchell (drawing on Bairoch: cf. note 2) reconstructs only the working population, while Vitali only considers the working population in employment.

and the difficulties encountered in combatting illiteracy suggest that this is a topic that warrants further investigation.

The shortcomings of Italian census surveys were also apparent to the scholars of the time – scholars like, for example, Giovan Battista Salvioni (later professor of statistics at the University of Bologna) who roundly attacked the methods used to analyse the census data of 1871. Salvioni's criticism was certainly not restricted to issues of secondary importance, given that the calculations by the statistical offices rendered it impossible to distinguish – for the reference year – between the employees and owners of firms in sectors such as commerce, transport and industry. The census documentation of 1871 has been criticized for its flaws and omissions in recent times, too. Ornello Vitali concentrates his attention on the censuses carried out after 1881, which was the first year in which sufficiently detailed information was furnished at the sectoral and geographical levels.[22]

The census of 1861 reported with specific reference to the professions that 'if one relies on individual declarations, there is a risk of being taken in error regarding the position that each practitioner of a free profession occupies in the social hierarchy'.[23] Twenty years later Salvioni observed 'that certain professions are difficult to distinguish one from the other' and 'assigning them to this or that category is

[22] Vitali, *Aspetti dello sviluppo economico italiano alla luce della ricostruzione della popolazione attiva*, p. 3.
[23] *Censimento 1861*, vol. I, p. 97.

often questionable, since a citizen frequently practises several professions at once'.[24]

From 1901 onwards, information was gathered on each inhabitant of the Kingdom of Italy through the use of individual census forms,[25] and the government took considerable pains over the proper execution of census procedure. Because 'careful revision of the material received from the municipalities' revealed omissions and inaccuracies of various kinds, more than 75 per cent of municipalities were obliged to repeat the operation in order to complete the documentation required.[26]

For the purpose of this study, my analysis of the main professions naturally omits those subjects without a university-level qualification (*laurea* or *diploma*) but who were classified by the censuses of the time as health or legal professionals. This was the case, for example, of the '*maniscalchi*' (farriers or blacksmiths), whom the census of 1861 classified as health professionals; a category in which the 1871 census even included 'sellers of leeches', while it gave figures on 'dentists and chiropodists' in aggregate form – evidence that the professional function of the dentist had not yet been defined. Subsequent censuses are marred by similar inconsistencies. For example, 'ushers in local magistrates' courts and law courts' were included among the legal professions until 1901, while the 1911 census listed 'judicial officials' among professionals in the legal sector.

However, one fact is incontrovertible: although the practitioners of the principal professions did indeed increase numerically during the forty-year period considered by this study, in proportion to the rate of growth of the population as a whole there was no change in their position (Fig. 1.1). The 30 per cent increment in their numbers, in fact,

---

[24] 'Il censimento del 1881', *Annuario delle scienze giuridiche, politiche e sociali*, 2, 1881, p. 474.

[25] On the previous use of household forms and on the errors caused thereby, see *Censimento della popolazione del Regno d'Italia al 10 febbraio 1901*. Vol. v. *Relazione sul metodo di esecuzione e sui risultati del censimento, raffrontati con quelli dei censimenti italiani precedenti e di censimenti esteri*, Rome, 1904, especially pp. I–IV and LXXIV–CXI. See also M. Ceccotti, 'Censimenti della popolazione e delle abitazioni', *Annali di Statistica*, 1957, Le rilevazioni statistiche in Italia.

[26] 'Out of a total of 8,262 communes into which the territory of the Kingdom was divided at the time of the census, fully 6,347 had to have more or less large numbers of household envelopes returned to them, because the number of forms contained in these envelopes was not the same as the number of persons indicated on the cover as present in the household. Moreover, during the second survey stage, it was necessary to return packets of forms to 3,646 communes, because these forms lacked replies to one or more questions, especially those concerning age, civil status, education and profession.' *Censimento 1901*. Vol. v. *Relazione sul metodo di esecuzione*, p. IV.

was exactly equal to the increase in the overall population. Thus in 1911 there were 30 professionals for every 10,000 inhabitants, which was the same ratio as in 1871. And this, furthermore, was the case not only of the professions taken as a whole but of each individual professional sector (Table 1.9).

The stagnation of the health professions resulted from the combined effect of two opposing tendencies: the substantial fall (in ratio to the population) in the number of doctors and surgeons (until 1871) and especially of pharmacists – whose numbers continued to decline throughout the period in question – and the increase (almost imperceptible) in the number of veterinary surgeons and especially of obstetricians (Fig. 1.2). The decline in the numbers of doctors and pharmacists was probably due to the growing insistence that those who practised a profession should possess the appropriate educational qualifications, and also to the increasing precision of census survey methods. These two factors filtered out those respondents (undoubtedly numerous in 1861) who believed that they were entitled to declare themselves as effectively practising a profession although they did not possess the requisite qualifications or belong to an official professional association. It is perhaps no coincidence that this period saw a considerable increase – in relative as well as absolute terms – in the number of practitioners of 'other health professions' (see note 27), the number of whom in fact rose from 7,752 to more than 23,000 (from 2.9 per 10,000 inhabitants to 6.7). On the other hand, in confirmation of the disappearance of a wide range of health activities, the category 'other health professions' exhibits a steep rise in its proportion of nursing staff: already 60 per cent in 1871, the ratio rose to 74 per cent ten years later, then to almost 90 per cent at the end of the century, and fell only slightly in 1911.

However, there is another explanation, which relates to the relative overcrowding of the 'market' for doctors, and to the intellectual unemployment of graduates in medicine and surgery. This is a topic which I have linked elsewhere in this essay to the decline in enrolments at the medical faculties during the first decade of this century. But also the legal professions, when considered as a whole, exhibit distinctly different trends. Although attorneys and prosecutors were already the largest group of professionals in the population, their ranks continued to swell throughout the period in question. The notaries, by contrast, dwindled in numbers, mainly on account of the law of 1875 which (with subsequent additions and amendments) created the professional order and set quantitative limits on notarial

Table 1.9 *Evolution of the principal professions in Italy 1861–1911: absolute values and per 10,000 inhabitants*[27]

Professions	1861	1871	1881	1901	1911
Health	43,434 *(19.9)*	46,564 *(17.4)*	49,370 *(17.3)*	55,293 *(17.0)*	57,142 *(16.5)*
Legal	–	24,793 *(9.3)*	28,250 *(10.0)*	30,449 *(9.9)*	34,532 *(10.0)*
Engineering	–	8,942 *(3.3)*	10,883 *(3.8)*	9,590 *(3.0)*	12,125 *(3.5)*
Overall	43,434	80,299 *(30.0)*	88,503 *(31.1)*	95,332 *(29.4)*	103,799 *(30.0)*
Total population (in thousands)	21,777	26,801	28,459	32,475	34,671

(–) figure unavailable
Source: General censuses of the population 1861–1911 (author's calculations)

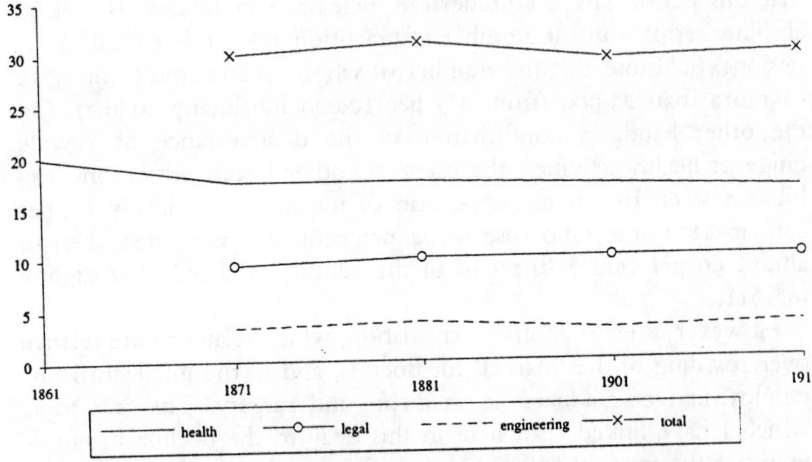

Figure 1.1. Evolution of the principal professions in Italy
(values per 10,000 inhabitants)

[27] The present survey of the principal professions omits certain categories which the original census documentation included among the health and legal professions. Table A1.1 in the appendix to this chapter gives the proportions of these other categories.

activity in each district (in 1911 the census figures still showed a slight surplus of notaries).[28]

3.2. The growth of the principal professions in the Italian regions

Given that the figures published on the occasion of the first Italian census of 1861 only concerned the health professions, I now discuss the distribution of doctors, pharmacists, veterinary surgeons and obstetricians in the various geographical areas of the country.

Immediately after Unification (Table 1.10), there was a greater proportion of doctors and pharmacists practising in the *Mezzogiorno* and the islands than in the rest of the country. As regards doctors in particular, this finding is probably accounted for by the already-mentioned bias introduced into the census figures by problems of statistical survey and by respondent self-perceptions of their professional status. On the other hand, the greater diffusion of pharmacists in the South was probably due to the particular geographical distribution of the population in those regions, especially in the period under examination here.[29]

Although, as far as the health professions were concerned, twenty years after Unification (Table 1.11) the gap between North and South had narrowed, the third census of the population (1881) revealed a distinctive feature of the occupational structure of the South and the islands with regard to the legal professions: a marked surplus of attorneys and prosecutors. I point out, by way of example, that of the country's 950 law graduates in the academic year 1880–81, fully 217 of them came from the University of Naples alone.[30]

As was to be expected, professionals in the engineering and architectural sectors were more numerous in the northern regions of Italy: a feature explained by the North's more advanced agriculture and, to a lesser extent, by its nascent industrialization.

Fifty years after Unification (Table 1.12), the overcrowding of the legal professions in the *Mezzogiorno* had become even more evident, although, of course, the census figures did not specify

---

[28] See *Censimento 1901*. Vol v. *Relazione sul metodo*.

[29] As Ernesto Ragionieri observes, 'the large town always ensured the presence of certain basic services like the school and the public offices, the pharmacy, the general practitioner and the midwife [...] Here lies the key to interpretation of certain findings yielded by the statistics which at first sight might appear disconcerting', and according to which 'there is a much greater number of towns in the South endowed with essential health services [...]' See 'La storia politica e sociale', in *Storia d'Italia*. Vol. iv, t. 3. *Dall'Unità a oggi*, Turin, 1976, p. 1718.

[30] See *Statistica dell'istruzione per l'anno scolastico 1880–81*, Tipografia Elzeviriana, Rome, 1883, p. 22.

Table 1.10 *Practitioners of the principal health professions in 1861: values per 10,000 inhabitants*

	North	Centre	South and Islands	Italy
Doctors and surgeons	7.7	7.0	10.2	8.7
Pharmacists	5.7	5.0	8.1	6.7
Veterinary surgeons	1.6	1.8	0.3	1.1
Obstetricians	3.7	3.0	3.5	3.5
Overall	18.7	16.8	22.1	19.9
Absolute values	16,433	5,416	21,585	43,434
Total population	8,787,141	3,222,426	9,767,767	21,777,334

Source: *Censimento generale 1861* (author's calculations)

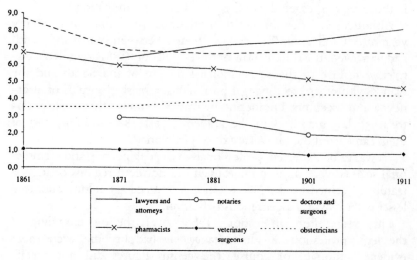

Figure 1.2. Health and legal professionals in Italy
(values per 10,000 inhabitants)

those practitioners (very numerous, according to contemporary observers) who only nominally exercised the profession of attorney or prosecutor. And also when one inspects the figures for the principal health
professions – those of doctor and pharmacist – one finds that the South
and the islands display higher values in relation to the total population.

Table 1.11 *Practitioners of the principal professions in 1881: values per 10,000 inhabitants*

	North	Centre	South and Islands	Italy
Doctors and surgeons	5.8	6.8	7.4	6.6
Pharmacists	5.2	4.8	6.9	5.8
Veterinary surgeons	1.4	1.7	0.4	1.0
Obstetricians	4.0	3.8	3.8	3.9
health professions	16.4	17.1	18.5	17.3
absolute values	20,725	7,902	20,743	49,370
Lawyers and attorneys	5.3	6.0	9.7	7.2
Notaries	2.2	2.0	3.8	2.8
legal professions	7.5	8.0	13.5	10.0
absolute values	9,441	3,714	15,095	28,250
Engineers and architects	4.2	3.9	3.4	3.8
absolute values	5,296	1,799	3,788	10,883
Overall	28.1	29.0	35.4	31.1
Absolute values	35,462	13,415	39,626	88,503
Total population	12,640,802	4,623,680	11,195,146	28,459,628

Source: Censimento generale 1881 (author's calculations)

Table 1.12 *Practitioners of the principal professions in 1911: values per 10,000 inhabitants*

	North	Centre	South and Islands	Italy
Doctors and surgeons	5.8	6.8	7.9	6.7
Pharmacists	4.3	4.0	5.4	4.7
Veterinary surgeons	0.9	1.1	0.6	0.8
Obstetricians	4.8	4.2	3.6	4.2
health professions	15.8	16.1	17.5	16.4
absolute values	24,582	9,326	23,234	57,142
Lawyers and attorneys	5.1	7.6	12.0	8.2
Notaries	1.5	1.4	2.4	1.8
legal professions	6.6	9.0	14.4	10.0
absolute values	10,268	5,222	19,042	34,532
Engineers and architects	3.9	3.7	2.9	3.5
absolute values	6,157	2,114	3,854	12,125
Overall	26.3	28.8	34.8	29.9
Absolute values	41,007	16,662	46,130	103,799
Total population	15,620,715	5,776,978	13,273,684	34,671,377

Source: Censimento generale 1911 (author's calculations)

3.3. The expansion of the public sector

The problem of the relationship between university studies and the intellectual labour market has often been tied, for various reasons, to the expansion of the civil service. Did the first fifty years of Italian history after Unification really witness such a major expansion? Was the phenomenon truly as large as various commentators have contended (both at the time and more recently)? The census returns – which list officials, clerks and attendants in public companies under the heading 'pubblica amministrazione' – show that the public sector grew only moderately in the period 1861–1911 (except for the decade 1871–81) in absolute terms, and that it indeed stagnated in relative ones (Table 1.13).

Omitted from these figures, however, are two important branches of the public sector – schools and the army – as well as other categories which, although quantitatively small in size, are highly relevant to our inquiry – the doctors, veterinary surgeons and obstetricians who worked for local government. It should be borne in mind that, according to estimates by Vitali, 20% of doctors, 40% of obstetricians and 78% of veterinary surgeons were (in the period 1881–1901) employed by the local authorities. It is therefore necessary to extend analysis to the total workforce in the public sector for the entire period 1881–1911.

As Table 1.14 shows, in the thirty-year period considered, employment in the public sector rose by 33 per cent in absolute value – an increase of 22 per cent with respect to the country's total labour force, but of only 10 per cent relative to the total population. From any point of view, these are values much lower than those so frequently described as 'abnormal'.[31]

As a matter of fact, it was during the period between the two world wars that the public sector in Italy grew to its most bloated proportions; and it was during this period, more than any other, that there was the greatest influx of graduates into the civil service and into the central or local government bureaucracies.

4. THE UNIVERSITIES

4.1. The situation at Unification

Immediately after Unification there were more than 9,000 students attending university in Italy, and by the end of the period considered

---

[31] In the mid-1910s a parliamentary deputy expressed alarm over the excessive growth of the bureaucracy between 1881 and 1914. See Abignente, *La riforma dell'amministrazione pubblica in Italia*, quoted in Barbagli, *Educating for Unemployment*, p. 45.

Table 1.13 *Public sector employees in Italy*

	Absolute values	Values per 10,000 inhabitants
1861	130,597	*60.0*
1871	136,929	*51.1*
1881	170,652	*60.0*
1901	178,241	*54.9*
1911	180,595	*52.1*

Source: Population censuses 1861–1911 (our calculations)

Table 1.14 *Working population employed in the public sector*

	Public sector employees	1881=100	Public sector/ total active population	1881=100	Public sector employees/10,000 inhabitants	1881=100
1881	403,025	100.0	2.7	100.0	*141.6*	100.0
1901	471,785	117.1	2.9	107.4	*145.3*	102.6
1911	537,154	133.3	3.3	122.2	*154.9*	109.4

Source: our estimates based on Vitali, *Aspetti dello sviluppo economico*, p. 331

their numbers had more than tripled (burgeoning to a total of 26,682 university enrolments in the academic year 1910–11). Carlo Matteucci, the Minister of Education in the first government after Unification, declared: 'If for at least ten or twelve years, Italy were to spend on popular education [...] the two or three million lire which, to the advantage of these studies, could be saved on the universities [...] and academies of fine arts, this would be a bargain and a deed well done.'[32] Matteucci's remark brings us to one of the principal problems (which we have already mentioned) that confronted Italian society in the second half of the nineteenth century: how to find a remedy for a situation in which levels of university education were below European standards and yet high when compared against the country's still rudimentary system of primary education.

This was a problem closely bound up with the relationship between education and economic growth: two phenomena which several distinguished commentators have stressed as closely interconnected, given that, in the historical experience of nineteenth-century industrialization, the presence of a sufficiently well-educated quota of the population was a decisive factor in a country's economic take-

[32] See 'Agli studiosi del migliore ordinamento delle scuole d'Italia', in *Raccolta di scritti vari intorno all'istruzione pubblica*, Vol II, Tip. Alberghetti, Prato, 1867, p. 10, cited in Barbagli, *Educating for Unemployment*, p. 45.

off.[33] In a classic study,[34] Cipolla observes that capitalist economies first arose in countries whose primary education systems had reached a satisfactory level of development; and the cases of mercantilist Holland and proto-industrial Britain prove his point. Although studies seeking to establish unduly close links (or better, an over-simplified dependence relationship) between education and economic growth have recently been disputed, still valid nonetheless is an interpretative scheme which posits education as one of the preconditions for the industrial revolution. However, one should not try to establish too close similarities between the countries which came late to industrialization in the nineteenth century and the developing countries of the twentieth century, although the latter have also had to cope with problems of (primary and secondary) education and the need to pursue an independent path of economic development.[35]

As regards Italy in the second half of the nineteenth century, besides the difficulties created by its recent unification, the country now entered a decisive phase of economic take-off attended by the disadvantages common to all the second-comers to industrialism. This was a situation which entailed the expansion not only of primary education but of secondary technical training as well, if the country was to benefit from the knowledge and experience acquired by the countries of early industrialization.

Italy had to train new and more highly skilled cadres of office-workers, managers, state officials, and also private and public professionals. The organization of an efficient public apparatus was of crucial importance to a country which had achieved national unity in such a short space of time, after centuries of political and administrative divisions and of foreign – direct or indirect – domination.

Nor was post-Unification Italy exempt from the more general requirement of developing a managerial class equipped with skills different from those possessed by the officials who had been trained and had worked in the previous political-institutional system. Obviously, the personnel inherited from the country principally responsible for the *Risorgimento*, the Kingdom of Sardinia, was not sufficient to cope with the new situation.

[33] See V. Zamagni, 'Istruzione e sviluppo economico in Italia 1861–1913', in G. Toniolo (ed.), *Lo sviluppo economico 1861–1940*, Bari, 1973, p. 199. The hypothesis proposed here originates from a study by M.J. Bowman and C.J. Anderson, 'Concerning the Role of Education in Development', in C. Geertz (ed.), *Old Societies and New States*, Glencoe, 1963, where the theory of the so-called 'educational threshold' is outlined.

[34] *Literacy and Development in the West*, London, 1969.

[35] See P. Bairoch, *Le Tiers-monde dans l'impasse*, Paris, 1971.

It does not transpire, however, that Italy had an abnormally high proportion of university students. Of course, there still remains the contradiction of a country which combined high levels of illiteracy with rates of university attendance close to those of the economically and socially more advanced countries. And as well as this feature, there is no denying that the fall in Italy's university population during the first decade of this century was in part due to the saturation of the intellectual labour market. However, I have already pointed out that the relatively high number of university students (as well as the large number of professionals with academic training) was an aspect that the young Kingdom of Italy had inherited mostly from before Unification. This latter observation brings us to the issue of 'points of departure' and their influence on subsequent socio-economic developments; an issue which has recently been given significant emphasis.[36]

4.2. Evolution of the university population

University education in Italy grew steadily between the mid-1870s and the beginning of this century; and this was growth that was part of a general European tendency caused, amongst other things, by the increasingly close relationship between university, access to public and private careers, and processes of professionalization.[37] Nonetheless, comparison with other European countries shows that at the beginning of the 1870s the newly born Kingdom of Italy with its 553 students per 100,000 young people aged 20 to 24 lagged behind all the countries for which the statistics are available (Fig. 1.3). Italy managed to close the gap in the last two decades of the century but then fell back again, reaching its lowest level in 1910.

This particular pattern assumed by the growth of Italian university education resulted from a number of features which were specific to the country. In the aftermath of Unification, Italy possessed a school and university system which was relatively 'open' and organized according to modern criteria.[38] However, it was a system which under-

---

[36] See V. Zamagni, 'L'Offerta d'istruzione in Italia 1861–1987'.

[37] See K.H. Jarausch, 'Higher Education and Social Change: Some Comparative Perspectives', in K.H. Jarausch (ed.), *The Transformation of Higher Learning 1860–1930*, Chicago, 1983, p. 17. For a comparison between patterns of university growth in Italy and Germany, another European state to achieve unification in the nineteenth century, see K.H. Jarausch, *Students, Society and Politics in Imperial Germany. The Rise of Academic Illiberalism*, Princeton, 1982, especially pp. 23–159. On the same topic see also H. Titze, 'Enrollment Expansion and Academic Overcrowding in Germany', in Jarausch (ed.), *The Transformation of Higher Learning*, pp. 57–88.

[38] See Barbagli, *Educating for Unemployment*, and V. Zamagni, 'L'Offerta d'istruzione'.

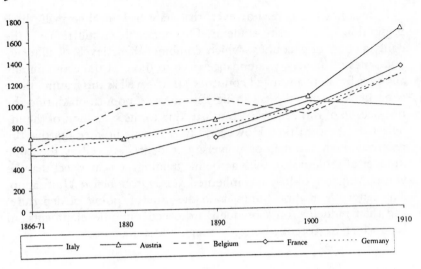

Figure 1.3. Enrolments at university per 100,000 inhabitants aged 20–24 years

went profound revision at the hands of the political class in subsequent decades. The growth of the student population and of the number of graduates between the 1880s and the end of the century, combined with the increased deprofessionalization of secondary-level schooling,[39] provoked considerable controversy in the country over the problem of intellectual unemployment. Increasingly broad sections of public opinion called for entry to the universities to be restricted, while pressure was applied for legislation to be passed that would radically increase university fees. Accordingly, at the beginning of this century, after an increase first in secondary-school enrolment fees and then in fees for the university faculties and schools, strict admission requirements were introduced for the schools of Pharmacy and Veterinary Science. At the same time, there was a distinct raising of the academic standards required of students already embarked on their courses of study.

This more stringent academic selectiveness was indicative of the progressive closure of the Italian higher education system – a process for which analysis of the academic performance by university students at the turn of the century provides convincing confirmation. Those statistics that are available can be used to construct a productivity index which, although it cannot be used for rigorous quantitative analysis,

[39] Barbagli, *Educating for Unemployment*, pp. 62–4 and 85–7. This phenomenon first began to appear in the quinquennium 1870–75. Ibid., p. 6.

nevertheless picks out a trend: namely, that in the Italian universities as a whole, the rate of university success – calculated as the ratio between graduates and matriculants five years previously – fell from 83.8 per cent of enrolments in the period 1881–88 to 71.9 per cent in the period between the academic years of 1904–5 and 1910–11.

All this throws substantial light on the attitude of the ruling class towards a relatively open educational system which it believed – especially in the last twenty to twenty-five years of the century – had 'dangerously' opened its doors to social strata other than the elite that had traditionally frequented the university lecture halls.[40] Recent research in numerous countries has shown that this attitude persisted in subsequent decades, and that it became manifest in marked social inequalities in effective access to education (access to university and university-level qualifications especially).[41]

The first fifteen years after Unification were a period of adjustment. In territorial terms, the entry of Veneto (1866) and the settlement of the *Questione Romana* (1870) finally established the borders of the Kingdom of Italy and thus drew the definitive map of its university institutions (the national university system, in fact, was enriched by the inclusion of Padua and Rome). And, furthermore, the statistical documentation was completed and brought up to date.

From the mid-1870s onwards, university enrolments steadily climbed, so that by the end of the century the university population had grown to 2.6 times its initial size: the 10,510 students enrolled in the academic year 1876–77 had risen, in fact, to 27,388 by 1901–2 (Fig. 1.4 and Table A1.2 in the Appendix to this chapter). After the anxious debate prompted by the expansion of the university population, after the steep increase in university fees, and following the onset of the phase of economic growth that Italy was to enjoy until the eve of the First World War, the beginning of the twentieth century was marked by a reversal in the previous trend and, for at least a decade, by a period of substantial stability.

The spread of university education assumed different patterns in different areas of the country according to socio-economic and demographic features, and also according to the geographical distribution of the country's universities. (The discussion that follows refers only to universities; it therefore excludes other institutions of higher education: the *istituti superiori* and the *scuole speciali superiori*.)

---

[40] See M. Rossi, *Università e società in Italia alla fine dell'800*, Florence, 1976, pp. 115–33.
[41] See H-P. Blossfeld, Y. Shavit, 'Ostacoli permanenti: le diseguaglienze di istruzione in tredici paesi', *Polis*, 6, 1, April 1992.

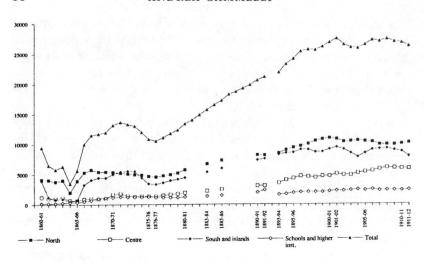

Figure 1.4. Students and *uditori* enrolled at universities in Italy

The surge in university studies was therefore a phenomenon which involved the various areas of the country to differing extents. In the period in question, according to our calculations, student numbers in the northern regions increased 4.8 times, those in the *Mezzogiorno* 2.4 times, while there was an almost fivefold growth of the university population in Central Italy. This means that, whereas immediately after Unification there were 40 students per 100,000 inhabitants in the South, 47 in the North, and only 37 in the Centre, in 1911 their numbers had grown to 63 per 100,000 inhabitants in the North, 65 in the South, and more than 100 in the Centre.

Predictably, these figures reflect to a considerable extent the role and weight of certain individual universities. An emblematic case in point is the University of Rome, which began its operations in the Kingdom of Italy with a student body of just over 700 (fewer than those attending the universities of Naples, Turin, Padua and Pavia) but in forty years had more than quadrupled its student body, thereby accounting for 56 per cent of the entire university population of central Italy and growing into the second largest university in Italy. In the *Mezzogiorno*, the University of Naples expanded to a similar extent.

Italy's university system was polarized among a restricted number of seats of learning (Table 1.15 and Table A1.2 in the Appendix to this chapter). Indeed, concentrated into nine of the twenty-one universities then in operation (see Diagram 1.2) were three-quarters of the university population. This situation – which was recorded in the

Table 1.15 *Students and uditori enrolled at the principal Italian universities*

	Turin (a)	Genoa (b)	Pavia	Padua (c)	Bologna	Pisa	Rome (d)	Naples (e)	Palermo	Partial total	% of main universities in total	Other universities	Inst. of higher education	Total
1860–61	1,136	285	1,353		454	653		2,500	603	6,984	74.0	2,276	176	9,436
1870–71	1,647	460	789	1,110	568	571	726	4,275	274	10,420	79.1	1,601	1,157	13,178
1880–81	2,008	648	763	1,079	754	576	831	3,346	532	10,537	78.7	1,593	1,257	13,387
1890–91	2,484	1,113	1,095	1,316	1,527	728	1,645	4,900	1,253	16,061	78.0	2,529	1,991	20,581
1900–1	3,505	1,351	1,328	1,460	1,949	1,095	2,440	5,989	1,082	20,199	75.5	4,434	2,128	26,761
1910–11	3,218	1,154	1,137	1,383	1,686	956	3,152	5,680	1,280	19,646	73.6	4,784	2,252	26,682

(a) Figures include enrolments at the *Scuola di Applicazione per gli Ingegneri*, which became a polytechnic in 1906–7.

(b) After 1870–71 the figures include the *Scuola Navale Superiore*.

(c) After 1908–9 the figures include the *Scuola di Applicazione per gli Ingegneri*.

(d) After 1880–81 the figures include the *Scuola di Applicazione per gli Ingegneri*.

(e) The figure for 1860–61 enrolments is an estimate.

Sources: *Sulle condizioni della pubblica istruzione nel Regno d'Italia*; *Statistica dell'istruzione per l'a.s. 1880–81*; Ministero di Agricoltura, Industria e Commercio, Direzione della Statistica, *Annuario Statistico Italiano*, Rome, various years; Ministero di Agricoltura, Industria e Commercio, Direzione della Statistica e del Lavoro, *Annali di Statistica*, C.P. Ferraris, *Statistiche delle Università e degli Istituti Superiori*, Rome, 1913.

academic year 1911–12 – in fact reflected long-term trends. Whereas in the North there was a broad spectrum of universities of major importance in quantitative terms (in 1911–12, in order, Turin, Bologna, Padua, Pavia and Genoa), the universities of Rome and Naples attracted many more students than the others in the centre and south of the country.

Of considerable interest are the dynamics of growth of the university population as regards each of the various sectors of academic study (Fig. 1.5).

It was the faculties of Law and Medicine – which offered degree courses preparing students for the most sought-after professions (the law and medicine[42]) – that attracted the largest number of enrolments throughout the period under examination. These faculties, moreover, were those with the greatest prestige and longest traditions, and on which the history itself of the Italian and European universities had been founded.

Already evident in the period immediately following Unification, the predominance of the medical and legal faculties was a constant feature of Italian university life in subsequent decades. There are, however, a number of distinctions that must be drawn.

Although enrolments in Law steadily expanded (rising from 4,459 in 1880–81 to 9,851 in 1910–11, which was an increase of 120 per cent), enrolments in Medicine reached their peak – almost 6,500 – at the beginning of the century, and then fell back to 4,500 enrolments during the academic year 1910–11. By the end of the first decade of this century, the numbers of students enrolled in the newly created schools of Engineering had outstripped those in the faculties of medicine. This increase in engineering enrolments (which quintupled over thirty years) was particularly marked during the phase of the 'grande slancio' of the Italian economy. Since the university schools are discussed later, for the moment I merely point out that the schools of Veterinary Science and diploma courses[43] in Pharmacy attracted significant numbers of students, and especially at the turn of the century.

[42] Ernesto Ragionieri regarded these professions as 'alternative [...] to a substantially identical cursus onorum' in post-Unification Italy. See La storia politica e sociale, p. 724.
[43] The course leading to the diploma universitario in a special subject area lasted (in the 1860–1914 period) for two, three or four years. The degree course leading to the diploma di laurea lasted for four, five or six years. Henceforth I shall use the terms diplomati for graduates from the corso di diploma and laureati for graduates from the corso di laurea.

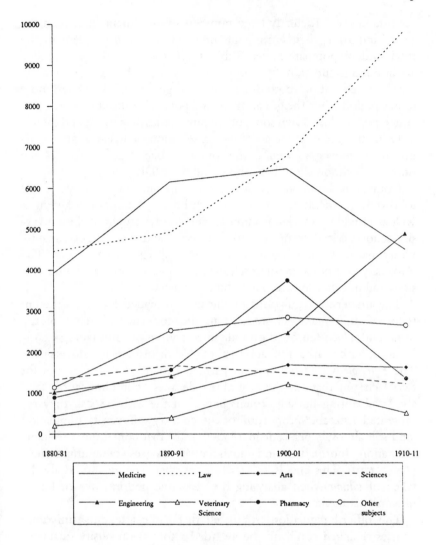

Figure 1.5. Enrolment in Italian universities according to main subject
area

4.3. The organization of teaching in the higher education system

The principal component in Italy's system of higher education consisted, of course, of its twenty-one universities proper; nevertheless this
period also saw the gradual development of other institutions of post-
secondary education (the *Istituti superiori* and *Scuole superiori speciali*).

Although the *Istituti superiori* and the *Scuole superiori speciali* never

accounted for particularly large numbers of enrolments (between the
1860s and 1911, their enrolments hovered around 9 per cent of the
total student population: see Table 1.16), they nevertheless fulfilled
an important function by completing the country's range of post-
secondary education (both didactically and geographically); even more
so in a period when the government and political authorities were more
concerned to close down some of the universities than to expand them.

From the point of view of the organization of Italian higher education, moreover, as well as the four main faculties, the role of the
university schools should also be mentioned (Diagram 1.4).

Courses in the university faculties lasted from four to six years and
followed a curriculum which was both broadly cultural in content as
well as providing specialist training. The courses taught in the university schools lasted from two to four years and were predominantly
vocational (and therefore gave training in specific occupations). The
university vocational training schools were located both at the universities and in other institutions of higher education.

The university regulations of the time provided for two different
types of undergraduate: students in the conventional sense of the
term, and *uditori* (enrolled on individual courses but not taking examinations, rather like the auditors of North American universities).
These *uditori* would not warrant particular mention if it were not for
two facts: (a) that, in the first three decades after Unification (and
above all during the adjustment period of the early 1860s), they represented a sizeable proportion of the country's university population
(and still almost 5 per cent in 1890–91); (b) that contemporary documentation (normative and quantitative) stresses their importance
(Table 1.17). This entails, as we shall see, that account should also be
taken of *uditori* when analysing the academic performance of Italian
university students.

The official regulations stipulated that those attending university
courses as *uditori* could not be awarded a formal university qualification. In reality, however, the chaotic situation of the Italian universities
immediately after Unification (well represented by the largest Italian
university, Naples, where enrolment on courses was not
compulsory),[44] as well as the statistics of the time, suggest that a rigid
distinction between student and *uditore* could not be drawn. Amongst
other things, a special measure was introduced in the mid-1870s which

---

[44] On the situation at the University of Naples, see S. Polenghi, *La politica universitaria
nell'età della destra storica*, Brescia, 1933, pp. 112–26. Except for the estimate for
1860–61 (2,500 students), figures on enrolments at the University of Naples are
available from 1865–66 onwards. See Table A1.2 in the Appendix to this chapter.

Table 1.16 *Enrolments at universities and other institutions of higher learning*

	Universities	Institutes of higher education		Total enrolments
	Absolute values	Absolute values	% of total enrolments	Absolute values
1860–61	9,260	176	1.9	9,436
1870–71	12,021	1,157	8.8	13,178
1880–81	12,130	1,257	9.4	13,387
1890–91	18,590	1,991	9.7	20,581
1900–1	24,633	2,128	8.0	26,761
1910–11	24,430	2,252	8.4	26,682

Sources: *Sulle condizioni della pubblica istruzione nel Regno d'Italia; Statistica dell'istruzione per l'a.s. 1880–1881; Annuario Statistico Italiano;* Ferraris, *Statistiche delle Università e degli Istituti Superiori.*

Diagram 1.4. *Faculties and university schools operating in Italy in the period 1860–1914 and the duration of courses*

Faculties	Schools
Law (4 years)	Notarial Studies (2 years)
Medicine and Surgery (6 years)	Pharmacy (diploma 4 years, degree 5) Veterinary (4 years) Obstetrics (2 years)
Sciences (mathematics, physics and natural sciences: 4 degree courses, 4 years)	Engineering (2+3) (a) Agriculture (4 years)
Arts and philosophy (2 degree courses, 4 years)	
Theology (4 years, abolished in 1873)	

(a) The engineering course was divided into a two-year course in mathematics and physics (at the faculty of sciences), successful completion of which was followed by a further three-year course of study at the *Scuola d'Applicazione per Ingegneri.*

allowed university students 'in arrears with their examinations relative to the immediately previous year' to be admitted to courses as *uditori*.[45] The auditorial system was therefore used to 'rescue' the many university students who had fallen behind in their studies during the difficult years of post-Unification adjustment.

In 1875, the Minister of Education, Ruggero Bonghi, attempted to impose some order on the situation by restoring the regulations in force (at least formally) in the period 1859–70. The university regulations that Bonghi introduced stated that *uditori* could enrol on one or

[45] See 'Circolare n. 317 del 1871', in *Annuario dell'Università di Bologna 1874–75*, p. 43.

Table 1.17 *Students and* uditori *enrolled at universities and other institutions of higher learning in Italy*

	Students	Uditori	Total	% uditori in total
1860–61	8,977	276[a]	9,253[a]	3.0[a]
1861–62	5,805	440	6,514[b]	6.8
1862–63	4,979	529	5,814[b]	9.1
1863–64	4,713	1,161	6,340[b]	18.3
1880–81	12,805	582	13,387	4.3
1885–86	16,892	348	17,240	2.0
1890–91	19,671	910	20,581	4.4
1900–1	26,496	265	26,761	1.0

[a] The figures do not include *uditori* enrolled at the *istituti superiori*.
[b] The figure for the University of Naples is unavailable.

Sources: Sulle condizioni della pubblica istruzione nel Regno d'Italia; Statistica dell'istruzione per l'a.s. 1880–1881; Annuario Statistico Italiano 1892; Ferraris, Statistiche delle Università e degli Istituti Superiori.

more courses of a particular degree programme, on completion of which they were awarded a simple certificate of attendance. Thus, studies pursued by *uditori* for the purpose of obtaining a diploma or degree once again became invalid.

It is very probable, though, that the *regolamento Bonghi* (like the other measures that followed it) was only laxly applied. At the beginning of this century, the education authorities reaffirmed that 'the studies or examinations of the *uditore* do not have and cannot acquire validity for the earning of a degree or other academic qualifications'.[46] This suggests that the distinction between student and *uditore* was still anything but rigid, and that in everyday university practice students who had fallen behind with their examinations continued to attend lectures as *uditori*. Not coincidentally, the registration of *uditori* ceased almost simultaneously with the registration of students '*fuori corso*' (those students still enrolled at university but not making normal progress towards their degrees).

It is also worth noting that the university statistics themselves (those produced both by the Ministry of Education and by the Minister of Agriculture, Industry and Commerce) distinguished between students and *uditori* in each university and by sector of study, and that they treated both categories as belonging to the overall population enrolled at institutions of higher learning.

A much clearer picture than that provided by the above summary

---

[46] See 'Regolamento universitario', *Annuario dell'Università di Bologna*, 1901–2.

table of the number of university *uditori* in the first years after Unification can be gained from the documentation included in the Appendix to this chapter (Table A1.3).

4.4. University fees

The various attempts to raise university fees again – after the already considerable increase of 1876 – did not come to fruition until 1903. The new rates were substantially more expensive, being now between one-third and three and a half times higher than those previously in force. For the purpose of comparison, Table 1.18 also sets out university enrolment fees immediately after national Unification. One notes that the increases did very little to take into account the existence and operation of laboratories and other academic facilities. Indeed, fees for enrolment at the faculty of Law were still the most costly (bearing in mind the length of the course).

University enrolment fees turn out to have been even more costly when compared against a number of base economic indicators for the period in which debate on the excessive number of university students was most heated. In 1876, enrolment for a year's attendance on the degree course in Law amounted to 215 lire; somewhat exorbitant if one considers that 100 litres of olive oil (a staple ingredient of the family diet in many parts of the country) cost 152.5 lire, while 100 kilos of bread cost 50 lire, and the price of 100 litres of wine was 32.9 lire. This means that university fees alone required a household to disburse the equivalent of 140 litres of oil or 430 kilos of bread or 650 litres of wine.

Reference to wages and salaries in the period in question completes the picture. Jobs in the upper echelons of the civil service carried salaries ranging between 2,500 and 9,000 lire per year. Subordinate and auxiliary staff earned respectively between 1,600 and 3,900 lire and 1,000 and 1,600 lire. Pre-university teachers never received more than 2,100 lire annually, while the wages of a factory worker (for 11 hours of work a day) exceeded 1,000 lire only at the higher-skilled levels and in the engineering industry.[47] Hence, if a director general in the civil service at the height of his career enrolled his son in the law faculty, he had to pay out one-third of his monthly salary. An official at the

---

[47] Istat, *Sommario di Statistiche storiche, 1861–1965*. At a cotton mill in the province of Genoa, a shop-floor worker earned between 624 and 1,092 lire in 1876. At the hemp-spinning factory in Casalecchio di Reno, on the outskirts of Bologna, the wage for the average worker ranged from a minimum of 673.9 lire to a maximum of 1,048 lire. See *Annuario statistico italiano 1895*, p. 487.

Table 1.18 *Enrolment fees at university faculties and schools*[a]

	1862	1876	1903
Law	410	860	1,145
Medicine and surgery	280	860	1,365
Sciences	240	450	845
Arts and philosophy	155	450	845
Engineering		860	1,175
Pharmacy (degree)		450	1,000
Pharmacy (diploma)	152[b]	200	560
Veterinary science	51	168	560
Notarial studies	63	200	685
Obstetrics		89	

[a] Fees for the entire course of study.
[b] The report *Sulle condizioni della pubblica istruzione nel Regno d'Italia* quotes this figure for a three-year course, without further specification.

Sources: Sulle condizioni della pubblica istruzione nel Regno d'Italia, p. 155; Polenghi, *La politica universitaria nell'età della destra storica*, p. 524; *Annuario dell'Università di Bologna*, academic year 1905–6.

lowest level of the public administration had to invest more than one month's salary, while a teacher had to pay at least a month and a half's income per year for his son's university education. For the son of a skilled factory worker (who had managed to complete secondary schooling), enrolment at university cost two months' wages. One thus immediately realizes the extent to which the further raising of enrolment fees at the beginning of the century rendered university entrance even more expensive and even more selective.

It has been rightly observed that

> in an essentially agricultural country where the majority of the population spent between 70 and 90 per cent of its income on food, attendance at university, and before that at high school, was a luxury inaccessible to young people of modest social extraction.[48]

It is evident, therefore, that it was only possible for the less well-off classes to attend university if they gained exemption from fees, either for economic reasons or for academic merit. Even before the increases of the beginning of this century, the level of university fees was such that investment in a son's university education was a formidable financial undertaking for a middle-class family. Nonetheless, growing sections of the petite and middle borgeoisie began – in the last fifteen years of the century – to stake their fortunes on university education.

[48] Polenghi, *La politica universitaria*, p. 231.

As for the working class, however, its participation in higher learning during this period was almost negligible.[49]

4.5. 'Laureati' and 'diplomati'

In absolute terms, the number of educational qualifications awarded by universities and higher institutes rose from 3,119 in the academic year 1880–81, to 2,669 in the following year (see note 6), to 4,624 in 1910–1911 (Table 1.19). Between the early 1880s and the mid-1890s (and therefore at the height of the debate on 'the graduate glut'), the number of qualifications awarded increased considerably and continued to grow until the first years of this century, shrinking somewhat thereafter. The universities were mainly responsible for this expansion, although the available figures (at least for the fifteen-year period 1881–96) show that extra-university institutions accounted for more than the 9 per cent estimated from enrolment statistics.

Just as the faculties of Law and Medicine recorded the highest number of enrolments, so too they produced the most graduates (see Table 1.20).

The disquieting problem (which also aroused the fears of experts on economic and social affairs) of growing intellectual unemployment was accompanied by anxious speculation on political-social issues. From Nitti to Ferraris, from Arangio-Ruiz to Baccelli, distinguished commentators warned against what they presumed to be the swelling ranks of the 'intellectual proletariat' (one of the first to use the expression was Francesco Saverio Nitti in a study of 1901 on *L'avvenire economico dell'Italia*).[50] This was why, together with the still urgent need to increase budgetary expenditure on primary education, numerous deputies and senators produced – above all during the 1990s – studies and proposals calling for a reorganization of higher education which would reduce the number of universities inherited from the pre-Unification states, introduce stricter admission requirements for degree and diploma courses, and substantially increase university fees yet again.

However, only the latter two measures passed into law, in the early 1900s. Moreover, as we have already seen, the first decade of this century saw a sharp fall in rates of university success, a phenomenon which may be interpreted as further evidence of closure.

Yet the topic of the surplus of graduates in Italy at the turn of the century can be addressed from a different perspective; one which

---

[49] See Barbagli, *Educating for Unemployment.*
[50] Now in *La ricchezza dell'Italia.*

Table 1.19 *Degrees and diplomas awarded by universities and* istituti superiori

	University	*Istituti superiori Scuole superiori*	Total	% *ist. sup.* and *scuole sup.* in total
1880–81			3,119[a]	
1881–82	2,210	459	2,669	*17.2*
1883–84	2,339	453	2,792	*16.2*
1885–86	2,679	488	3,167	*15.4*
1887–88	2,992	591	3,583	*16.5*
1889–90	3,208	528	3,736	*14.1*
1891–92	3,544	621	4,165	*14.9*
1893–94	3,757	641	4,398	*14.6*
1895–96	3,976	681	4,657	*14.6*
1904–5			5,085	
1905–6			4,811	
1906–7			4,950	
1907–8			4,621	
1908–9			4,628	
1909–10			4,724	
1910–11			4,624	

[a] see note 6

Sources: 1880–81: *Statistica dell'istruzione per l'anno scolastico 1880–81*, Rome, 1883; 1881–96: Nitti, *La ricchezza dell'Italia*, Laterza, Bari, 1966; 1904–11: Ferraris, *Statistiche dell Università e degli Istituti Superiori.*

Table 1.20 *Degrees and diplomas awarded by Italian university faculties and schools*[a]

	1880–81		1910–11	
	Absolute values	%	Absolute values	%
Medicine	661	*21.2*	663	*14.3*
Law	950	*30.4*	1,611	*34.8*
Arts	85	*2.7*	256	*5.5*
Sciences	68	*2.2*	155	*3.4*
Engineering	314	*10.1*	453	*9.8*
Agriculture	24	*0.8*	91	*2.0*
Veterinary science	103	*3.3*	176	*3.8*
Pharmacy (degree)	(b)		64	*1.4*
Pharmacy (diploma)	487	*15.6*	313	*6.8*
Notarial studies	140	*4.5*	164	*3.5*
Obstetrics	287	*9.2*	678	*14.7*
Total	3,119	*100.0*	4,624	*100.0*

[a] As well as universities, the figures also include the *istituti superiori* and *scuole superiori* offering university-level courses.
(b) The figures for degrees awarded in chemistry and pharmacy (for which courses began in 1876–77) are not available.
Sources: author's calculations on *Statistica dell'istruzione per l'anno scolastico 1880–81*, Rome 1883 and Ferraris, *Statistiche delle Università e degli Istituti Superiori*, Rome, 1913.

stresses the propulsive role of the relatively high availability of human capital in a decisive phase of the country's economic development. According to one interesting interpretation, the educated elites 'provided the basis for positive internal (and international) migratory flows which enriched the entire country with human capital. Italy as a whole was furnished with an abundant elite, the best members of which could easily rise to prominence and work to the advantage of the entire nation'.[51]

Whereas the first decade of this century saw an increase in the numbers of law graduates, the amount of degrees awarded in medicine and surgery declined in concomitance with the downturn in enrolments during those years. This was a decline that stemmed to a large extent from the already substantial unemployment among medical graduates, who tended to flock into a professional sector that was already overcrowded – in proportion to the total population – at the time of national Unification.

4.6. The university schools

The foregoing discussion has concentrated on the Italian university system as a whole. Certain specific features of the country's higher education system have been mentioned: its institutional distinction between universities, istituti superiori and scuole superiori speciali; and its didactic distinction between university faculties and schools. A further distinction has been drawn within the student body between students and uditori.

As regards the University Schools, the reader is referred to Fig. 1.6, which sets out the trend in enrolments by main subject on the national scale. Note, in particular, the surge in enrolments at the schools of Pharmacy and Veterinary Science at the turn of the century.

5. CONCLUSIONS

The essay has reconstructed the dynamics of the exercise of the principal professions in Italy in the period between Unification (1861) and the first decade of this century through the detailed analysis of census data.

The picture that has emerged demonstrates that the increase in the number of professional practitioners proceeded pari passu with the growth of the overall Italian population and thus, in relative

[51] See Zamagni, 'L'offerta di istruzione'.

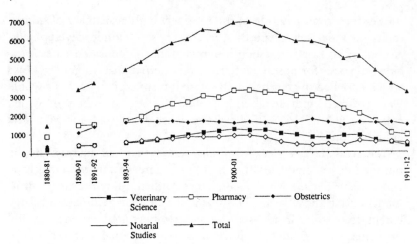

Figure 1.6. Students and *uditori* enrolled at the Schools of Veterinary
Science, Pharmacy, Obstetrics and Notarial Studies in Italy

terms, remained substantially stationary. (In 1879 in Italy, there were
30 individuals practising the principal professions per 10,000 inhabitants; forty years later the proportion was the same.) This more general
trend, moreover, is to be found in each of the professional sectors in-
vestigated (health, the law, engineering), although major differences
can be discerned internally to each of them. In the health sector, for
example, the decline in doctors, surgeons and pharmacists was
matched by an increase in veterinary surgeons and obstetricians. In the
legal sector, the increase in attorneys and prosecutors (which continued
throughout the period, especially in the *Mezzogiorno*) was offset by a
decline in lawyers.

In parallel, careful analysis of the same census data shows that, in the
period considered, the civil service was not characterized by a steep rise
in its staffing levels, as several commentators have instead argued.
Indeed, between national Unification and 1911, the numbers of civil
servants increased only slightly.

The expansion of university education in Italy during the same
period, as evidenced by comparative analysis of national and international statistical sources, was certainly large, but not as pronounced as
was once believed. Comparison among university enrolments in the
principal European countries, with respect to the population aged 20
to 24, reveals in fact that Italy lagged behind them, and even more
markedly in the first decade of this century.

The analysis conducted in this essay shows that the imbalance between the demand for and supply of professionally trained labour in the fifty years following national unity – an imbalance probably due to factors which exerted their influence prior to Unification – remained practically unchanged.

APPENDICES

Table A1.1. *Proportions of other categories included among health and legal professions in original census documentation*

	1861	1871	1881	1901	1911
Other Professions					
Health	7,752	7,837	10,347	14,620	23,121
Legal	–	1,193	–	3,297	3,013
Total professions not considered					
– Absolute values	7,752	9,030	10,347	17,917	26,134
– *% of all professionals*	*15.1*	*10.1*	*10.5*	*15.8*	*20.1*
(of which nurses)	–	4,712	7,648	13,110	18,084
Total professions	51,186	89,329	98,850	113,249	129,933

Source: General censuses of the population 1861–1911 (author's calculations)

Table A1.2 *Students and uditori enrolled at university in Italy and by individual university: 1860–61/1911–12*

	Turin[a]	Genoa[b]	Pavia	Padua[c]	Bologna	Ferrara	Modena	Parma	Siena	Pisa	Camerino	Macerata	Urbino
1860–61	1,136	285	1,353		454	108	445	354	193	653	71	102	38
1861–62	1,026	224	1,380		471	134	510	345	161	622	51	59	38
1862–63	1,004	200	1,173		464	100	532	326	162	593	55	68	8
1863–64	1,150	238	1,204		489	126	466	345	155	691	74	81	14
1864–65	1,220	308					475		109	506		67	
1865–66	1,205	312	1,120		559		443	283	92	485		78	
1866–67	1,283	323	1,055	1,444	460	84	405	257	92	517	44	87	50
1867–68	1,642	325	977	1,523	542	96	403	264	92	591	39	86	55
1868–69	1,581	330	840	1,259	623	87	383	297	100	456	29	101	69
1869–70	1,634	370	846	1,217	560	91	381	310	88	603	28	105	64
1870–71	1,647	460	789	1,110	568	102	354	304	97	571	22	101	83
1871–72	1,604	488	755	1,072	590	100	352	282	108	569	38	111	84
1872–73	1,476	510	718	1,121	577	113	315	270	118	503	46	115	83
1873–74	1,391	471	707	1,207	565	110	285	241	123	526	32	84	75
1874–75	1,477	456	619	1,217	557	88	278	205	113	532	31	106	71
1875–76	1,590	448	597	1,069	492	63	231	200	125	519	20	86	80
1876–77	1,529	454	652	974	511	67	223	184	141	470	25	52	60
1877–78	1,704	518	642	907	551	57	216	187	153	553	28	47	55
1878–79	1,758	565	672	948	569	46	195	194	181	586	43	82	60
1879–80	1,890	600	690	910	654	47	217	205	215	565	57	116	61
1880–81	2,008	648	763	1,079	754	49	238	208	195	576	65	118	76
1881–82													
1882–83													
1883–84	2,447	788	872	978	1,127	29	265	198	162	612	95	110	54
1884–85													
1885–86	2,541	882	1,005	1,052	1,286	39	274	210	162	605	100	109	86
1886–87													

1887–88													
1888–89													
1889–90													
1890–91	2,484	1,113	1,095	1,316	1,527	56	292	276	225	728	101	124	93
1891–92	2,434	1,094	1,123	1,269	1,470	79	346	313	218	742	101	160	67
1892–93													
1893–94	2,618	990	1,223	1,426	1,384	95	354	372	236	900	144	188	92
1894–95	2,762	1,010	1,272	1,603	1,457	84	412	408	229	972	162	264	76
1895–96	2,847	1,089	1,345	1,611	1,489	88	411	482	231	1,066	235	313	92
1896–97	2,923	1,132	1,345	1,568	1,633	96	412	519	262	1,132	206	369	92
1897–98	3,156	1,256	1,325	1,536	1,634	77	424	551	231	1,087	234	310	100
1898–99	3,344	1,297	1,385	1,495	1,812	101	450	584	220	1,068	228	196	126
1899–1900	3,424	1,326	1,307	1,518	1,933	123	525	564	213	1,089	250	197	140
1900–1	3,505	1,351	1,328	1,460	1,949	106	637	577	231	1,095	276	149	151
1901–2	3,500	1,330	1,347	1,401	1,873	127	577	585	233	1,059	297	230	155
1902–3	3,264	1,328	1,362	1,264	1,800	135	562	583	202	1,084	309	238	163
1903–4	3,400	1,293	1,363	1,312	1,638	153	565	675	213	1,068	314	267	184
1904–5	3,399	1,276	1,373	1,312	1,711	194	533	694	235	1,043	362	322	224
1905–6	3,386	1,193	1,339	1,323	1,729	226	474	695	225	1,083	355	357	267
1906–7	3,376	1,244	1,343	1,318	1,615	263	426	674	233	1,075	453	348	297
1907–8	3,178	1,122	1,302	1,267	1,644	316	422	565	233	1,065	505	379	301
1908–9	3,151	1,182	1,182	1,293	1,695	357	434	532	240	1,091	500	431	312
1909–10	3,152	1,138	1,153	1,343	1,762	410	422	392	242	1,051	442	412	311
1910–11	3,218	1,154	1,137	1,383	1,686	490	416	435	244	956	406	435	312
1911–12	3,205	1,390	1,100	1,432	1,629	513	419	410	257	902	420	387	310

Table A1.2 cont

	Perugia	Rome[d]	Naples[e]	Palermo	Catania	Messina	Cagliari	Sassari	Scuole and Istituti superiori[f]	Total
1860–61	147		2,500	603	469	130	139	80	176	9,436
1861–62	88			481	440	120	110	49	205	6,514
1862–63	99			304	275	127	76	46	202	5,814
1863–64	122		41	279	286	151	92	58	278	6,340
1864–65			46		315	134			333	3,513
1865–66	105		54	208	188	117	66	65	372	5,647
1866–67	109		2,660	228	152	83	86	71	500	9,986
1867–68	110		3,381	234	162	95	117	89	670	11,492
1868–69	95		3,754	280	148	64	113	90	1,000	11,714
1869–70	75		3,746	250	161	67	104	87	1,126	11,933
1870–71	81	726	4,275	274	183	91	103	86	1,157	13,178
1871–72	64	793	4,693	231	197	107	93	87	1,252	13,687
1872–73	60	534	4,719	306	233	112	88	71	1,234	13,326
1873–74	74	459	4,684	337	229	92	81	75	1,196	13,030
1874–75	74	470	3,694	340	191	94	62	66	1,222	11,963
1875–76	67	493	2,788	270	174	108	56	60	1,289	10,832
1876–77	63	559	2,683	333	152	79	54	70	1,171	10,510
1877–78	65	624	2,857	360	153	96	72	77	1,157	11,077
1878–79	73	648	3,039	449	168	128	95	93	1,163	11,747
1879–80	79	705	3,174	475	214	123	107	88	1,153	12,339
1880–81		831	3,346	532	239	141	103	82	1,257	13,387
1881–82										13,997
1882–83										14,870
1883–84	65	1,159	3,860	764	317	156	167	102	1,383	15,710
1884–85										16,531
1885–86	92	1,345	4,123	977	414	190	134	124	1,490	17,240
1886–87										18,257

1887–88										18,692
1888–89										19,261
1889–90										19,816
1890–91	179	1,645	4,900	1,253	584	329	147	123	1,991	20,581
1891–92	198	1,606	4,930	1,299	662	353	174	125	2,374	21,137
1892–93										
1893–94	226	1,762	5,205	1,488	748	456	191	139	1,633	21,870
1894–95	303	2,059	5,433	1,369	806	502	201	157	1,716	23,257
1895–96	298	2,084	5,370	1,343	890	551	223	166	1,899	24,123
1896–97	307	2,298	5,792	1,434	875	541	237	147	2,001	25,321
1897–98	320	2,300	5,888	1,222	906	602	246	146	2,047	25,598
1898–99	328	2,258	5,536	1,062	986	626	230	152	2,035	25,519
1899–1900	300	2,478	5,528	1,159	914	672	226	151	2,025	26,062
1900–1	307	2,440	5,989	1,082	925	692	235	148	2,128	26,761
1901–2	322	2,725	6,199	1,100	1,007	677	257	151	2,236	27,388
1902–3	318	2,532	5,953	1,038	996	642	260	162	2,206	26,401
1903–4	302	2,474	5,344	1,086	931	603	266	174	2,292	25,917
1904–5	326	2,630	4,745	1,083	891	597	254	200	2,397	25,801
1905–6	305	2,742	5,450	1,106	832	570	243	199	2,294	26,393
1906–7	355	2,725	5,850	1,277	828	572	224	229	2,427	27,152
1907–8	423	2,875	6,149	1,135	784	578	218	228	2,246	26,935
1908–9	345	3,072	6,332	1,209	842	356	245	198	2,296	27,295
1909–10	356	3,116	5,915	1,436	949	170	230	169	2,279	26,850
1910–11	350	3,152	5,680	1,280	1,048	229	243	176	2,252	26,682
1911–12	278	3,280	4,702	1,526	989	239	227	162	2,338	26,115

a The figures include enrolments at Scuola di Applicazione per gli Ingegneri, which after a.y. 1906–7 became a Polytechnic.
b After a.y. 1870–71 the figures also include the Scuola Navale Superiore.
c After a.y. 1908–9 the figures also include the Scuola di Applicazione.
d After a.y. 1870–71 the figures also include enrolments at the Scuola di Applicazione per gli Ingegneri.

[e] For the a.y. 1860–61 only an estimate of the number of enrolments is available; after a.y. 1863–64 the figures include enrolments at the *Scuola di Applicazione per gli Ingegneri* (the figures for the a.y. 1863–64/1865–66 refer only to this School).
[f] Included in the figures are: The university schools annexed to the lycées (Aquila, Bari, Catanzaro), the *Scuola di Ostetricia* (Milan, Novara and Vercelli, Venice), the *Scuola di Notariato* of Florence, the *Scuole di Veterinaria* (Naples, Milan, Turin), the *Scuole di Agraria* (Milan, Portici, Perugia), the *Scuola normale superiore* of Pisa, the *Regio Istituto Superiore* of Florence, the *Regia Accademia* of Milan, the *Regio Istituto tecnico superiore* of Milan, the *Scuola di Economia* (Bari, Genoa, Venice), the *Istituti superiori di magistero femminile* (Florence, Rome), the *Scuola di Scienze Sociali* of Florence, the *Museo Industriale Italiano* of Turin and the *Istituto Forestale* of Vallombroso.

Sources: *Sulle condizioni della pubblica istruzione nel Regno d'Italia*, Milan, 1865; Ministero di Agricoltura, Industria e Commercio, Direzione Generale della Statistica, *Statistica dell'istruzione per l'a.s.*, 1980–81; Tipografia Elzeviriana, Roma, 1883; Ministero di Agricoltura, Industria e Commercio, Direzione Generale della Statistica, *Annuario Statistico Italiano*, various years; Ministero di Agricoltura, Industria e Commercio, Direzione Generale della Statistica e del Lavoro, *Annali di Statistica*, C.F. Ferraris, *Statistiche dell'Università e degli Istituti Superiori*, Rome, 1913.

Table A1.3 *Students and* uditori *enrolled at Italian universities and percentage of* uditori *in overall student body: 1860–61/1911–12*

	Students[a]	Uditori[a]	% uditori in total enrolments
1860–61	6,477	276	2.9
1861–62	5,805	440	6.8
1862–63	4,979	529	9.1
1863–64	4,713	1,161	18.3
1880–81	12,805	582	4.3
1883–84	15,354	356	2.3
1885–86	16,892	348	2.0
1890–91	19,671	910	4.4
1891–92	20,588	549	2.6
1893–94	21,468	402	1.8
1894–95	22,836	421	1.8
1895–96	23,753	370	1.5
1896–97	25,025	296	1.2
1897–98	25,308	290	1.1
1898–99	25,289	230	0.9
1899–1900	25,861	201	0.8
1900–1	26,496	265	1.0
1901–2	27,093	295	1.1
1902–3	26,176	225	0.9
1903–4	25,690	227	0.9
1904–5	25,544	257	1.0
1905–6	26,080	313	1.2
1906–7	26,895	257	0.9
1907–8	26,650	285	1.1
1908–9	27,059	236	0.9
1909–10	26,622	228	0.8
1910–11	26,449	233	0.9
1911–12	25,884	231	0.9

[a] For the period between the academic years 1860–61/1863–64 the figures refer only to the universities. Values reflect the lack of information on enrolments at the University of Naples.

Sources: Sulle condizioni della pubblica istruzione nel Regno d'Italia, Milan, 1865; Ministero di Agricoltura, Industria e Commercio, Direzione Generale della Statistica, *Statistica dell'istruzione per l'a.s. 1980–81*, Tipografia Elzeviriana, Roma, 1883; Ministero di Agricoltura, Industria e Commercio, Direzione Generale della Statistica, *Annuario Statistico Italiano*, various years; Ministero di Agricoltura, Industria e Commercio, Direzione Generale della Statistica e del Lavoro, *Annali di Statistica*, C.F. Ferraris, *Statistiche dell'Università e degli Istituti Superiori*, Rome, 1913.

CHAPTER 2

A JURIST FOR UNITED ITALY: THE TRAINING AND CULTURE OF NEAPOLITAN LAWYERS IN THE NINETEENTH CENTURY

ALDO MAZZACANE

1. ITALIAN UNIFICATION AND THE CULTURE OF A CLASS

In Italy, unlike other countries, study of the legal profession in the nineteenth century is only in its preliminary stages.[1] The predominant interest of historiographers in legal doctrines and the history of legal scholarship in the universities[2] has induced them to neglect other networks and settings. Consequently, there has been a tendency to ignore the principal features of Italian legal culture in the nineteenth century; a legal culture, in fact, which was elaborated and diffused by centres other than the universities, which after a long and glorious tradition had by now largely fallen into decay and disrepute. Beginning in the Napoleonic period and for many years thereafter, reform of university legal studies and of the professionalization process was undertaken from outside the universities themselves. This, moreover, was a situation to be found in every state in the Peninsula.

Nevertheless, each of these states possessed a distinct heritage which impressed itself deeply on the new Kingdom of Italy. As a consequence, the nation which achieved political unification in 1860 was still a largely amorphous entity. The ancient traditions of the various parts of the young Italian state still stubbornly survived in its social structures and institutions and in its educational system. The emerging system of the professions, too, preserved the original features of arrangements in the country's previous regions. Only gradually, and

---

[1] See the collected essays in A. Mazzacane and C. Vano (eds), *Università e professioni giuridiche in Europa nell'età liberale*, Naples, 1994.

[2] A. Mazzacane, 'Neuere Rechtsgeschichte in Italien', *Zeitschrift für neuere Rechtsgeschichte*, 14 (1992), pp. 243ff.

then only incompletely, did the contrasts among the various areas of the country disappear.

It is evident, therefore, that analysis of the situation in Italy must make separate consideration of the various features that combined to constitute its many-centred, highly fragmented and often contradictory physiognomy. The ideologies, mentalities and customs which extended their roots into the deep-lying layers of the country's diverse municipal traditions were decisive in shaping the state and the system of the professions. As well as sociological surveys[3] and analysis of economic–social dynamics,[4] however, inquiry is also necessary into the formation and reproduction of Italian legal culture. It will thus become possible to specify one of the principal processes by which Italian lawyers were cemented together as a social class; a class, moreover, which buttressed its position as a central component of the Italian nineteenth-century bourgeoisie by virtue of its specialist knowledge. In Italy the *Bildungsbürgertum*, and the figure of the lawyer internally to it, asserted its function of societal government by deploying political skills and competences rather than by operating in the economic-productive sphere. The modernization of the country resulted, not from the industrial transformation of the economy but from the construction of a new juridical and administrative framework. In other words, political-institutional factors played a much more significant role than did socioeconomic ones.[5] Consequently legal professionals were the members of a bourgeoisie imbued with a rhetorical and humanistic culture who possessed the greatest expertise in politics and institutions, and they 'naturally' established a close relationship with the apparatuses of the expanding state – or indeed assumed control of them.

2. SOUTHERN LAWYERS: THE FRENCH MODEL AND ITALIAN UNIFICATION

Naples and its lawyers played a decisive role in the *Risorgimento* movement and in the building of the unified state. The Jacobean republic of 1799, the Napoleonic decade, the uprisings of 1820–21, the brief constitutional experiment of 1848 – these events marked

---

[3] See H. Siegriest, 'Gli avvocati nell'Italia del XIX secolo. Provenienza e matrimoni, titolo e prestigio', *Meridiana*, 14 (1992), pp. 145–81.

[4] Detailed treatment is given, for example, in P. Macry, *Ottocento. Famiglia, élites e patrimoni a Napoli*, Turin, 1988.

[5] M. Meriggi, 'Italienisches und deutsches Bürgertum im Vergleich' in J. Kocka (ed.), *Bürgertum im 19. Jahrhundert. Deutschland im europäischen Vergleich*, vol. 1, pp. 141–59.

crucial stages in the growth of the nation as a whole. The city of Naples stood at the forefront of the country's intellectual life, of which it was the 'epicentre of the underground communication of national and European culture';[6] and when Unification came in 1860 it acted as the focal point for progressive forces. Indeed, for more than a decade, southern lawyers exiled to the other regions of Italy, especially to Piedmont, disseminated a broad and non-provincial vision of what they deemed to be the most urgent task faced by the profession: building the 'edifice of a national jurisprudence'.[7] After Unification, these same lawyers were the first to design the architecture of this edifice. Legislative and administrative unification – 'steam-driven unification' as its critics called it because of the speed with which it was implemented – was also largely due to their efforts.[8] Lastly, the Federico II University of Naples – which was attended by more than half the students of the kingdom – trained a conspicuous number of the future members of the legal profession and of the new state bureaucracy.[9]

However, legal culture in Naples extended well beyond its regional boundaries. It was a crucial factor, first in the ideological preparation and then in the legal-institutional consolidation of the Kingdom of Italy. Both its backwardness and its innovative thrust had a profound impact on the entire institutional framework of post-Unification Italy. In other words, in legal culture, as in most other aspects of the *Risorgimento*, groups of intellectuals from the *Mezzogiorno* exerted considerable leverage over the ruling strata at the national level and often decisively conditioned government decision-making. Hence, the influence of the legal professionals, as an emerging stratum of the Italian bourgeoisie, and of their shared attitudes, cannot be understood without examining the world of Neapolitan jurists and their distinctive culture in the period prior to Unification. And the centre of this world was the Italian Bar or *avvocatura*.

Neapolitan legal practitioners long looked to France – until the

---

[6] L. Russo, *Francesco De Sanctis e la cultura napoletana*, Florence, 1959 (3rd edition), p. XIII; see also the collection of essays by G. Oldrini, *Napoli e i suoi filosofi. Protagonisti, prospettive, problemi del pensiero dell'Ottocento*, Milan, 1990.

[7] C. Vano, ' "Edifizio della scienza nazionale". La nascita dell'Enciclopedia giuridica italiana' in A. Mazzacane and P. Schiera (eds), *Enciclopedia e sapere scientifico. Il diritto e le scienze sociali nell'Enciclopedia giuridica italiana*, Bologna, 1990, pp. 15–66.

[8] See G. Astuti, *L'unificazione amministrativa del Regno d'Italia*, Naples, 1966; C. Ghisalberti, *Unità nazionale e unificazione giuridica in Italia*, Rome–Bari, 1979; *idem*, *La codificazione del diritto in Italia 1865–1942*, Rome–Bari, 1985.

[9] S. Cassese, *Questione amministrativa e questione meridionale. Dimensioni e reclutamento della burocrazia dall'unità ad oggi*, Milan, 1977.

1870s and also thereafter – as an extraordinary laboratory of juridical-constitutional theory and experiment.[10] Indeed, Neapolitan intellectuals showed a particularly keen interest in French political culture throughout the modern age.[11] At the beginning of the nineteenth century, the legislative, administrative and judicial reforms introduced during the 'decade' of Joseph Bonaparte and Murat[12] – most of which reforms were never subsequently rescinded – obliged the southern Italian lawyers rapidly to acquire detailed knowledge of the French system. Instead of the ancient instruments of *ius commune*, they now had to study the *Code Napoléon*, the sentences handed down by the French courts, especially the *Cour de cassation*, and the plethora of commentaries, reports and doctrinal works that rolled in from Paris.[13] This obligation imposed on students of law to master the new techniques developed beyond the Alps combined with more ambitious intellectual aspirations. It was now apparent that cultural renewal in Italy would only be possible if contacts were established and comparisons made with the more advanced European centres of learning. In agreement on this point – albeit for different reasons – were intellectuals of both politically moderate and radical persuasions. The 'decade' therefore saw the growth and consolidation of a corpus of knowledge and experience which would develop during the Restoration period – with abrupt shifts in direction, spurts and revivals – to become of profound importance for the building of the unified state.

3. NAPLES, A CITY OF LAWYERS

The Neapolitan lawyers, however, enjoyed a dubious reputation in Europe. Despite the close contacts of some of them with outstanding foreign jurists, and despite the positive reports of certain

[10] For further discussion see A. Mazzacane, 'Die italienische und deutsche Rechtskultur im 19. Jahrhundert: "Wege des Austausches"' in R. Schulze and A. Mazzacane (eds), *Die deutsche und italienische Rechtskultur im 'Zeitalter der Vergleichung'*, Berlin, 1994.

[11] R. Ajello, *Epistemologia moderna e storia delle esperienze giuridiche*, Naples, 1986, chs III and IV.

[12] A. De Martino, *Antico regime e rivoluzione nel regno di Napoli. Crisi e trasformazioni dell'ordinamento giuridico*, Naples, 1973; idem, *La nascita delle intendenze. Problemi dell'amministrazione periferica nel regno di Napoli*, Naples, 1984.

[13] F. Ranieri, 'Rezeption und Assimilation ausländischer Rechtsprechung, dargestellt am Beispiel des europäischen Einflusses der französischen Judikatur im 19. Jahrhundert', *Ius Commune*, 6 (1977), pp. 202–33. Interesting information is also given in M.T. Napoli, *La cultura giuridica europea in Italia. Repertorio delle opere tradotte nel secolo XIX*, Naples, 1987.

visitors to Naples,[14] it was Savigny's harsh judgement of them that prevailed. Savigny's was a criticism, moreover, which chimed well with the prejudice of many historians of the *Risorgimento* period against the Restoration, which they rejected out of hand as dominated by Bourbon obscurantism. Savigny visited Italy in 1825 and 1826–27 and on the latter occasion spent several months in Naples. On his return to Germany, he published a highly critical account of the teaching of law in the Italian universities, and at the University of Naples in particular.[15] The Neapolitan professor of Principles of Roman Law (*Istituzioni di diritto romano*), Francesco Avellino, otherwise apparently a man of considerable cultivation, had previously occupied the most disparate of professorial chairs and devoted most of his time to his legal practice. In this, however, he was no exception, because almost all the other professors in the faculty simultaneously practised as lawyers or magistrates. Attendance at the faculty was extremely poor, and since the doors to the lecture halls were always left open, students came and went as they pleased; as did the curious onlookers who roamed the corridors. Professors and students were largely indifferent to the university. Most courses were taught in the professors' own homes, and the entire syllabus was covered in a matter of two years – with obviously deleterious effects on the students' preparation. The aim of most students was to enter private legal practice on graduating: 'Naples is truly the city of lawyers', Savigny concluded, and their excessive numbers inevitably provoked a frenetic hustling for business by practitioners and attorneys. The most important trials were eagerly discussed at every level of society up to the intellectual milieu of the fashionable salons – with the frequent and well-informed participation of the ladies present.[16]

Although Savigny's description of legal education in Naples was largely accurate, it concentrated almost entirely on the city's university (and mainly on the teaching of Roman law within it). His point of view was entirely coherent with the mentality of a Berlin professor convinced of the lofty purpose of the university and actively engaged

---

[14] On legal culture see for example L. De Lavergne, 'Naples en 1841', *Revue des deux mondes*, 29 (1842), pp. 576ff.

[15] F.C. von Savigny, 'Ueber den juristischen Unterricht in Italien', *Zeitschrift für geschichtliche Rechtswissenschaft*, 6 (1828), pp. 201–28, later republished with additions in *Vermischte Schriften*, Berlin, 1850, vol. IV, pp. 309–42; translated into Italian in an abridged version by A. Turchiarulo and published in the anthology *Ragionamenti storici di dritto del Prof. F. C. di Savigny*, Naples, 1852, part IV, pp. 67–84. Savigny's critique also circulated in the simplified and inflexible form given to it by *L'Universel, Journal quotidien de la littérature, des sciences et des artes*, no. 126, 6 May 1829, p. 432; and by F. Lerminier, *Introduction générale à l'histoire du droit*, Brussels, 1829, p. 221.

[16] See *Vermischte Schriften*, pp. 328–36.

in bringing Humboldt's project to fulfilment.[17] His wholly negative view of the fact that legal studies in Naples were pursued almost entirely in private schools, and that the *avvocatura* was the focus of the city's legal life, is therefore understandable. The absence of reputable university studies must have struck him as the absence *tout court* of a genuine legal culture. However, by failing to conduct thorough inquiry outside the university, he overlooked significant personalities and accomplishments, and above all he misinterpreted the dynamics of an entire milieu. Savigny reports that he visited just one private school (perhaps that of Loreto Apruzzese). He took brief notes on the subjects taught therein – Roman law, natural and criminal law, and civil law – but he made no attempt to gauge the significance of the choice of disciplines, and nor did he grasp the manner in which they were linked together in the curriculum. This latter feature, however, was the novelty of an enterprise which transcended the indifferent quality of individual lessons. The programme of the school, in fact, closely followed the recommendations set out in the celebrated *Lettres sur la profession d'avocat* by Armand-Gaston Camus.[18] It is therefore possible to discern a relationship between the efforts, even the most modest, by the Neapolitan private schools and the transformation of legal systems then under way not only in Naples but in most of Europe. These efforts, however, Savigny ignored. Consequently given only secondary emphasis in his report, and never taken up by later commentators, were his most acute observations: the central importance in Naples of the legal professions, the primacy of the private school, and the very specific nature of their syllabuses.

The authority of Savigny's testimony proved crucial in fixing the enduring image of pre-Unification legal culture; an image which, in the course of the nineteenth century, was reinforced not only by observers indulgent towards the stereotypes of Naples and Italy then current, but also by jurists such as Mittermaier[19] and Jhering,[20] who strove to give a

---

[17] A. Mazzacane, 'Jurisprudenz als Wissenschaft' in F.C. von Savigny, *Vorlesungen über juristische Methodologie 1802–1842*, edited by A. Mazzacane, Frankfurt a. M., 1993, esp. pp. 15ff; *idem, Savigny e i suoi interpreti. Studi sulla scienza giuridica dell'età liberale*, Naples, 1994, ch. IV.

[18] This circulated widely in Naples in the expanded version edited by A-M. J-J. Dupin (Paris 1818 and subsequent editions).

[19] C.J.A. Mittermaier, *Italienische Zustände*, Heidelberg, 1844, pp. 264–5; and P. Balestreri, 'Mittermaier e l'Italia. Orientamenti politici e dottrine processualistiche in un carteggio di metà Ottocento', *Ius Commune*, 10 (1983), pp. 97–140.

[20] R. von Jhering, *Scherz und Ernst in der Jurisprudenz*, Göttingen, 1891 (4th edition), pp. 363–4; and C. Vano, 'Itinerari italiani di Rudolf von Jhering' in O. Behrends (ed.), *Rudolf von Jhering. Beiträge und Zeugnisse*, Göttingen, 1993 (2nd edition), pp. 121ff.

more balanced picture of the Italian situation but both of whom complained of the excessive influence exerted, entirely to the disadvantage of the university, by the *avvocatura*. In accounts and analyses produced in Italy, this judgement developed into something akin to a cliché.[21] During a period in which 'Germanism' held sway in the universities, however, there were still those who adhered to different traditions: eclecticism, the doctrines of Vico, comparative legislation, case law. In Naples after Unification, for example, Enrico Cenni and Emanuele Gianturco – both of whom were lawyers, professors and politicians – pointed to the experience of the southern '*avvocheria*' as the outstanding achievement of national legal culture.[22] Very different, though, was the opinion that finally prevailed and which drew on the prestigious canons of German doctrine. The professors of 'learned Germany' vigorously engaged in building *Deutsche Wissenschaft* and the university system corresponding to it[23] inevitably saw the primacy of the *avvocatura* and the neglect of academic studies in Italy as a form of backwardness and as indicative of intolerable confusion. The incomprehension therefore stemmed from an absolute diversity of experience. The Italian system had its own specific features which foreign observers were unable to grasp. The fluid boundaries among the legal professions, the confusion that reigned in public education, the weakness of the cultural institutions, and the lack of a project for higher education, disoriented European observers. And Naples displayed all these characteristics to an exceptional extent.

4. LAPSED KNOWLEDGE AND USEFUL KNOWLEDGE

The social and scientific decadence of the universities was a phenomenon common to all the European countries in the seventeenth and eighteenth centuries. Everywhere, higher education suffered from increasingly successful competition by private colleges, academies and institutes, which varied in nature according to their political and

[21] I have discussed elsewhere the reasons for these interpretations and their shortcomings: see A. Mazzacane, 'Die Rechtskultur in Italien und Deutschland nach der nationalen Einigung' in R. Schulze (ed.), *Deutsche Rechtswissenschaft und Staatslehre im Spiegel der italienischen Rechtskultur während der zweiten Hälfte des 19. Jahrhunderts*, Berlin, 1990, pp. 55ff.

[22] E. Cenni, 'Sulla importanza e sul merito delle allegazioni degli avvocati napoletani, massime nel secolo XVIII', appendix to *Studi di diritto pubblico*, Naples, 1870; F. Gianturco, 'Don Ciccio Correra' (1895) in *Opere giuridiche*, Rome, 1947, vol. I, pp. 209–10.

[23] P. Schiera, *Il laboratorio borghese. Scienza e politica nella Germania dell'Ottocento*, Bologna, 1987.

religious settings but all of which were quite distinct from the university.[24] This was equally true of Naples. Indeed, the dominant role occupied for centuries by the judiciary and the Bar in the city explains the poor regard in which its university was held. Teaching in the university was trapped in the mechanical transmission of an ancient 'culture of the cloisters' which was entirely irrelevant to professional problems and needs. In one of the most lucid pamphlets written in favour of the *avvocatura*, at the end of the seventeenth century, Francesco d'Andrea vehemently criticized his own academic training. And, in the same years, another celebrated lawyer, Giambattista De Luca, castigated his university professors for their failings.[25]

Like everywhere else, therefore, there was a longstanding tradition of substantial indifference to university studies in the Kingdom of Naples. It was a feature of the cultural landscape of the city and much of its province that was universally taken for granted. 'The best progress, as well as the most commodious, rapid and constant of studies, are to be had in private institutions not in public ones', admitted an official of the *Real Camera di Santa Chiara* in 1736.[26] Throughout the eighteenth century, legislative measures were introduced to eliminate abuses, to impose order on the schools, and to link their activities with university teaching. However, academic legal studies were never attributed any importance in preparation for the Bar. The *prammatica* (law) of 6 December 1780, entitled 'IV: De advocatorum neapolitanorum Collegio instituendo', insisted on the 'honesty and expertise' required of those who wished to exercise this 'sacred and jealous office', and it strove to halt the corruption of the profession caused by the 'ignorance and licentiousness' of the many 'intruders' who thronged the lawcourts. Legal practitioners were organized into a hierarchy of three categories, and special bodies were set up to assess their competence and 'exactness, honour and loyalty' in defending 'just suits and in expelling the pleaders of unjust ones'. Reference was even made to proper modes of dress, but the university was never mentioned: indeed, it was stipulated that lawyers should 'keep the schools open so that they

---

[24] The literature is enormous. See, in particular, L. Boehm and E. Raimondi (eds), *Università, accademie e società scientifiche in Italia e in Germania dal Cinquecento al Settecento*, Bologna, 1981; R. Stichweh, *Der frühmoderne Staat und die europäische Universität*, Frankfurt a. M., 1991.

[25] See A. Mazzacane, 'D'Andrea Francesco' and 'De Luca Giambattista' in *Dizionario biografico degli Italiani*, respectively vol. 32, Rome 1986 and vol. 38, Rome ,1990.

[26] Quoted in G.M. Monti, 'Le scuole private universitarie a Napoli dal 1737 al 1799', in G.M. Monti and A. Zazo (eds), *Da Roffredo di Benevento a Francesco De Sanctis. Nuovi studi sulla storia dell'insegnamento superiore a Napoli*, Naples, 1926, p. 95.

88   ALDO MAZZACANE

can provide training for young men', and that they should issue certification for such training.

The private schools were never seriously combatted, therefore, until the crisis that began in the 1790s and culminated in 1799; a turn of events, though, which ushered in radical change. The return of the Bourbons to the throne after the brief Jacobine republic dealt a severe blow to the private schools. The execution, persecution and exile of the leading members of the Neapolitan *intelligentsia* inaugurated a climate of suspicion towards intellectual circles which affected the universities and the private schools alike. Many of them were closed down, while the others were subjected to severe controls and censorship; surveillance by the police grew oppressive. The rift between the cultivated classes and the monarchy was irremediable, and it persisted into the nineteenth century as a constant feature of the Bourbon regime.

Under Joseph Bonaparte and Murat, the uncertainty and difficulties of culture were ameliorated only in part. However, the breadth and depth of the restructuring of the state and its institutions brought profound social changes. It generated increasing mobility in the bourgeois classes, and it involved wider social strata in the civil and political life of the country. The more progressive intellectual groups were allowed greater freedom of movement, and a number of leading proponents of late-Enlightenment reformism returned from exile and were appointed to influential positions. The rapid expansion of the civil service, the growing demand by the new legal and administrative apparatus for personnel with appropriate training, and the concomitant growth of the technical and professional cadres both at the centre and in the periphery, revived demand for private education. Thus, after an initial period of disorientation,[27] legislation came into force which gave definitive regulation to the private schools.[28] In Italy, and in Naples in particular, university reform was still to come: like England, but unlike France and Germany, Italy did not adopt a definitive model of higher education until well into the second half of the nineteenth century.[29]

[27] On 31 January 1801, the Superintendent of Santa Maria Capua Vetere urgently asked the Minister of Justice for instructions regarding an application submitted to him to open a school of criminal law: Archivio di Stato di Napoli (henceforth ASN), *Ministero degli Interni*, II inv., fasc. 2314.

[28] The relative decrees are those of 1 January 1812 and of 30 January 1813. In general see A. Zazo, 'Le scuole private universitarie a Napoli dal 1799 al 1860' in Monti and Zazo, *Da Roffredo di Benevento*, pp. 109ff; idem, *L'istruzione pubblica e privata nel Napoletano* (1767–1860), Città di Castello, 1927.

[29] I. Porciani (ed.), *L'Università tra Otto e Novecento: i modelli europei e il caso italiano*, Naples, 1994.

5. BETWEEN *IUS COMMUNE* AND CIVIL CODE

In the meantime, urgent measures were necessary in the legal and administrative spheres. The new system required the devising of new practices and the elaboration of new doctrines. The transition from the ancient *ius commune* to the new legal code prompted the most alert legal intellects to reconsider fundamental issues of juridical experience: What was the origin of the law and how did it become rooted in society? What was the relationship between jurisprudence and the law? There had been no change in the syllabuses taught in the university law faculties for centuries, and questions such as these were ignored unless they were couched in terms of theology and metaphysics. The most pressing need – that of investigating 'the spirit of laws' in order to establish, with the aid of critical analysis and historical comparison, a link between the past and present systems – was accordingly ignored. Niccola Nicolini, a lawyer and magistrate in the Murat period, and later a noted penalist and member of legislative committees, described the situation very clearly. In 1809 he published in Naples a speech delivered in his capacity as general prosecutor at the criminal court of Santa Maria Capua Vetere, which he significantly entitled *Del passaggio dall'antica alla nuova legislazione*. In 1812, as attorney general at the Court of Cassation, Nicolini returned to the issue in an oration on *La Corte suprema di giustizia nelle sue relazioni con le antiche istituzioni del Regno*, in which he analysed the relationship between the old legal system and the new one on the basis of the rational principles of jurisprudence and using a historical method drawn from his readings of Vico. Nicolini denounced as 'grave' the prevalent custom in the lawcourts of 'only treating the questions of law with the authority and decisions of the jurisconsults of France. Not that I do not have high regard for the names of Locré, Merlin and Sirey. But before the new laws were introduced, we were certainly not without our own laws or jurisprudence'. The task at hand, therefore, was not to 'break' every relationship between the old legislation and the new one, but to 'consider the latter as an improvement and a continuation of the former'.[30]

Theoretical analysis of the change in the legal system brought by the advent of the codes and the Napoleonic reforms therefore began early in Naples. It engaged not only intellectuals of the stature of Cuoco[31] but

[30] Quoted in F. Nicolini, *Niccola Nicolini e gli studi giuridici a Napoli nella prima metà del secolo XIX*, Naples, 1907, pp. XLV–XLVI note.
[31] On this topic see in particular F. Tessitore, 'Vincenzo Cuoco tra illuminismo e storicismo', in his collected essays *Storicismo e pensiero politico*, Milan–Naples, 1974, pp. 3–40.

legal 'practitioners' as well, since it was also necessary to create legitimation and consensus for the new legal system, to smooth the transition from the old to the new, and to direct jurists in the day-to-day
exercise of their profession. Nor was it solely out of abstract exigencies
of principle that such guidelines were necessary. Judges and lawyers
frequently found themselves having to cope with the normative gaps,
contradictions and inconsistencies produced by the lack of coherence
between the modern legislation and an enduring and deeply-rooted
tradition. The universities, still somnolently ploughing through
Roman and canon law or the natural law doctrine of the Scholastics,
were unequal to the task.

'What the state of jurisprudence was like at the time', Mancini later
wrote in his commemoration of Pasquale Liberatore,[32] 'can be conveyed in a few words'. The 'sum benefit of the new codes was that
they merely created conflict between the old jurists steadfastly loyal to
Roman law [...] and the young ones eager for novelty and progress'.
Conservative resistance was stubborn, 'and the use of Roman law in
the universities and lawcourts was preserved in order to hamper the
study and observance of the new legislation, which to assert its
authority had to prove itself the legitimate offspring of the old and
succour its faltering steps' by resorting to the authority of the Roman
jurisconsults.

With the greater or lesser awareness of their teaching staff, and with
varying degrees of efficiency, the private schools catered to these new
needs. Run by lawyers and by legal practitioners, or at any rate by in-
structors trained in the law, they were especially well adapted to transmitting knowledge of immediate relevance to the conduct of business.
And since the success of the private schools depended on the extent to
which they reflected the fusion of traditions and reforms, with caution
or enthusiasm they threw in their lot with the new, which they then
blended with the already tried and tested. According to the culture and
the ideology of the teacher, they examined the most delicate issues
raised by the new order. They furnished knowledge useful for practical
purposes, but they did not hesitate to address topics of ideological importance. They were thus perfectly attuned to the social dynamics of
the times. They did not cultivate abstractions, but nor did they refrain
from the construction of broad-gauge intellectual systems. An exemp-
lary case is provided by Domenico Furiati. In the *Monitore napoletano* of
30 October, the good abbot enthusiastically promoted his school and

---

[32] P.S. Mancini, 'Della vita e delle opere di Pasquale Liberatore', speech to the Accademia Pontaniana, in *Continuazione delle Ore solitarie ovvero Giornale di scienze morali,
legislative ed economiche*, 1842, fasc. II, pp. 124–5.

extolled the efficiency with which it instilled understanding of 'the spirit of the law' in its pupils. To this end he spelled out the connections between Roman law and the (French) civil law of the Kingdom. Furiati had an extraordinary following of students and was judged an 'admirable jurisconsult'. After the events of 1820–21 he was banned from teaching. But in 1825 he reopened his school, which he ran until 1843, 'and although his name was in the book of suspects, because he was a priest and of such affable disposition he was tolerated'.[33]

6. PRIVATE SCHOOLS AND POLITICAL OPPOSITION DURING THE RESTORATION

The case of Furiati highlights another distinctive feature of the relationship in Naples between the private schools and the Bar. With the advent of Restoration at the end of the Napoleonic decade, the entire educational system found itself subjected to the conditioning and restrictions imposed by Bourbon authoritarianism. However, one of the results of the court's offensive against the intellectual milieu was that the private schools sometimes performed a function which was not only educational but civil and political as well. Some of these schools were among the first centres of rebellion against the overwhelming conformism of the time. Liberal ideas circulated within their walls, albeit clandestinely, and they were among the few places where demands for cultural renewal and constitutional reform could mingle and fuse. Ferdinand IV (Ferdinand I as the sovereign of the Two Sicilies) returned to Naples in June 1815. In the early years of his reign, the 'amalgam' policy pursued by the minister Luigi dei Medici – the policy, that is, of reconciliation with at least some of the leading groups that had emerged during the French decade – persuaded the government to behave with relative restraint. The need to increase the efficiency of the state machinery prevailed over more repressive impulses and reactionary tendencies. Thus the principal reforms introduced under Murat were preserved, and substantial institutional continuity with the previous period was maintained.[34]

In actual fact, however, behind the facade of moderation a general climate of hostility towards the intellectuals was gathering strength. The gains achieved by reformist forces were abolished and the more liberal and progressive voices were silenced. A spirit of narrow-minded pietism took over, accompanied by sullen obsequiousness to every

[33] L. Settembrini, *Ricordanze della mia vita e Scritti autobiografici*, edited by M. Themelly, Milan, 1961, p. 23.
[34] A. Scirocco, *L'Italia del Risorgimento 1800–1860*, Bologna, 1990, pp. 35ff.

92 ALDO MAZZACANE

form of authority. The brief constitutional period of 1820–21 induced the monarchy to adopt openly reactionary policies. Oppressive controls were imposed on the university and on the private schools. The most conservative segment of the clergy tightened its grip on education. Taxes and censorship muzzled the press and obstructed the circulation of books, which a decree of 2 June 1822 described as a danger 'fatal to the tranquillity' of the state. For a considerable period of time the kingdom was 'a nation whose book trade seemed surrounded by the Great Wall of China'.[35] As the repressive measures proliferated, numerous academics were forced into exile. The lawyer Giuseppe Poerio, for instance, moved to Florence; Domenico Capitelli, who was also a lawyer and a teacher, retreated to Santa Maria Capua Vetere. For a decade, men of culture in Naples were hounded by police intimidation. The law faculties were now dominated by studies which celebrated, 'whether in the guise of erudition or as pure and simple edification', the ideology of the regime: religion, authority and monarchic despotism;[36] a dominance to which the works on public law published in those years eloquently testify.

With the universities and the lycées forced into submission, with even moderately liberal academics harried by persecution, it was the more mediocre and backward private schools that prospered in Naples and the provinces. These schools also profited from the scarcity of institutes of education and from the incomes they could offer to unemployed graduates in straitened economic circumstances who improvised as teachers. The schools provided a basic education, which in some cases also included a smattering of law. Culturally and politically ultra-conservative, bound by the straitjacket of rigid clericalism, they obtained authorization only at the price of submission to stringent surveillance.

In a context such as this, demands for cultural progress and for political reform were so closely linked that they became indistinguishable. Because of their repression – which combined with the intrinsic weakness deriving from their still fragile and narrow social base – the southern intellectuals could only feebly voice their grievances. They operated in small groups, in secrecy or under the cloak of dissimulation, and these were tactics which further weakened their impact. The boldest conversations were held in secret societies or at the private meetings of clubs and salons which were either tolerated or persecuted. An outstanding example was the literary 'academies' organized in the

[35] The expression is P.S. Mancini's in a letter to von Mohl of 1843 quoted in Vano, *Edifizio*, p. 41n.
[36] G. Oldrini, *La cultura filosofica napoletana dell'Ottocento*, Rome–Bari, 1973 pp. 47ff.

house of Basilio Puoti from 1825 onwards at which the classics were read and then followed by general discussion. Despite Puoti's narrow and conservative ideology, these meetings accomplished their own civil function.[37] The general topic of Italian language and literature acquired the importance of an educational issue of national significance. The most celebrated representatives of southern liberalism attended lessons at Puoti's house, especially after 1830 when it became a regular school.

7. THE ADVENT OF THE NEW IN THE LAW SCHOOLS

In 1830 the ascent to the throne of Ferdinando II brought a substantial relaxation of the government's repressive policies.[38] The new climate reinvigorated the private schools. Now directed by leading lawyers, they were able not only to provide training of immediate practical usefulness but also to adopt new approaches and to broach new fields of study. Economics, constitutional studies, comparative law, or even – according to Matteo de Augustinis – 'absolute and abstract law', the 'genesis of law' and the 'criticism of law',[39] appeared on their curricula. There were 48 of these schools operating in Naples in 1831,[40] but their numbers increased over the years and each of them was attended by hundreds of students.[41] They benefited from the 'interval of tolerance conceded by the Bourbon reaction to intellectual development'[42] which allowed ideas to circulate with a certain amount of freedom. Settembrini observed that the relative autonomy enjoyed by the private schools in deciding their study programmes encouraged their success; the deplorable state of the universities, however, persisted.[43]

At the end of 1829 the lawyer Domenico Capitelli reopened his school. The most authoritative proponent of the legal historicism founded by Vico, a campaigner for representative government, Capitelli was later a leading figure in the parliament of 1848.[44] As described by

[37] Ibid., pp. 92–4.

[38] Scirocco, L'Italia, pp. 149ff.

[39] M. de Augustinis, Considerazioni sul sapere e sugli studii della Sicilia citeriore dal 1801 al 1831, e della loro condizione da quest'epoca a tutto il 1842, Naples, 1843, p. 15.

[40] Notamento delle scuole private della capitale, in ASN, Min. Int., II inv., fasc. 4209.

[41] A list is given in Zazo, 'Le scuole', pp. 235–237n.

[42] F. De Sanctis, La letteratura italiana nel secolo XIX, edited by F. Catalano, Bari, 1953, vol. II, p. 115.

[43] Settembrini, Ricordanze, p. 58.

[44] P. Mari, 'Capitelli Domenico', Dizionario biografico degli Italiani, vol. 18, Rome, 1975.

one of his pupils, his approach consisted in treating laws as 'non-arbitrary facts' which corresponded to the moral and political conditions of the population that had produced them. Since the nature of mankind had developed gradually, Capitelli argued, the law must reflect this evolution.[45] Again in 1829, Tommaso Tagle (a lawyer unknown today)[46] was granted a licence to teach a syllabus – announced to the public in 1831[47] – which covered Roman law and civil code, criminal law, commercial law and procedure. Tagle's course also included discussions and practical exercises intended to encourage the comparative method and to enhance the teacher-pupil intimacy of seminar-based teaching, which was the great strength of private education in Naples.

Slowly, the offices of certain lawyers (significantly called *studi*, or studies, because of the scientific and didactic activity conducted therein) began to emerge as the power-houses of legal culture and southern liberalism. They became centres of civil education, as well as of technical training, delivered to students both young and not so young. In 1833 Giuseppe Poerio returned to Naples from Florence, armed with experience acquired as a member of Vieusseux's circle. Also employed in Poerio's *studio* were Capitelli and Savarese, Pisanelli, Paolo Emilio Imbriani (in 1861 appointed to the first Italian chair of comparative law at the University of Naples), as well as the Manna brothers, who later opened their own schools. Giovanni Manna, an expert on administrative law, published a historical work in 1839 in which he described the tradition of the southern Bar as a linking theme in Italian culture and as one of the greatest achievements of the country's civil history.[48] Between 1831 and 1837 – once the numerous obstacles against the granting of a licence to teach privately because of his political ideas had been overcome[49] – Pasquale Liberatore was granted authorization to operate his own school. He was among the first to use 'the beacons of philosophy and history' to illuminate the law in force.[50] As teaching materials for his courses, Liberatore wrote the three-volume *Introduzione allo studio della legislazione delle Due Sicilie ad uso della Scuola privata*,[51] the contents of which were organized ac-

[45] G. Pisanelli, *Dei progressi del diritto civile in Italia nel secolo XIX*, Naples, 1871, p. 19. See also E. Pessina, 'La scuola storica napoletana nella scienza del diritto' (1882), in *Discorsi varii*, Naples, 1913, vol. II, p. 127.
[46] ASN, *Min. Int.*, 1 inv., fasc. 792.
[47] It appeared in *Giornale delle Due Sicilie*, no. 233, on 17 October 1831.
[48] G. Manna, *Della giurisprudenza e del foro Napoletano dalla sua origine fino alla pubblicazione delle nuove leggi*, Naples, 1839.
[49] ASN, *Min. Int.*, 1 inv., fasc. 786.
[50] Mancini, 'Liberatore', pp. 14–15.
[51] Naples, 1832–34.

cording to the 'system' followed by his lectures. After a lengthy first section setting out the basic legal notions, and in which the name of Vico figured prominently, Liberatore's manual retraced the history of Roman, feudal and Neapolitan law. Extensive treatment was given to the principal strands of legal science, from Irnerio to the contemporary age, while its exegesis of contemporary law in the southern kingdom covered the judicial system as well as court procedures. The concluding section of the course described the improvements that should be made to legislation.

By the end of the 1830s numerous schools organized by lawyers were in operation, and they now pursued ambitious cultural goals. In 1836 Luigi Zuppetta, an authority on criminal law, began teaching private courses. The owner of a prestigious legal firm, a follower of Mazzini and a freemason, Zuppetta was forced into exile after taking an active part in the uprising of 1848 and then became a prominent politician after Unification.[52] In 1838 royal approval was granted to the school of Francesco Correra, a noted lawyer and collector of works on *ius commune* who taught Roman law and the history and philosophy of law; and also to the school run by Matteo de Augustinis, a lawyer and an economist.[53] The programme of de Augustinis' school was published in the journal *Lucifero* on 23 October 1839. From it we learn that the course lasted for two semesters and covered the principles of 'universal law', 'social economics', public and administrative law, Roman law and the 'ancient law of the Kingdom', civil code, procedures, commercial law and the laws in force. Between 1838 and 1839 the lawyers Roberto Savarese and Giuseppe Pisanelli were persuaded by Capitelli to open their own school, the programme of which Pisanelli set out in an announcement reflecting the teachings of Vico and Montesquieu but also bearing evident traces of Savigny's legal historicism.

'We must', wrote Pisanelli, 'portray the ideal history of every legal institution corresponding to the progressive development of the human intelligence', thereby 'revealing the origin of laws, their value, and their future'. When studied from this point of view, laws appear not as 'isolated and inanimate contingencies, with no connections among them, but as the living and continuing expression of human consciousness, and the Law emerges with increasing clarity as the perennial link among the human generations'.[54]

---

[52] See the proceedings of the conference *Luigi Zuppetta patriota – giurista – parlamentare*, edited by T. Nardella, Manduria–Bari–Rome, 1990.

[53] The administrative documentation regarding the granting of the licence can be found in ASN, *Min. Int.*, 1 inv., fasc. 797.

[54] Quoted in Pessina, 'La scuola storica napoletana', p. 134.

Although Pisanelli taught in the school for only a few years, Savarese continued until 1849, the year in which he was driven into exile. In 1848 Savarese also delivered a course of lectures in constitutional law which, from a moderate political viewpoint, illustrated the development of the representative institutions from their origins until the present day. These were lectures which were long remembered and admired in Naples.[55] His courses in civil law gave comprehensive treatment to Roman and pre-modern law, which was set against the background of the entire process of history. The law in force was then analysed in relation to the historical evolution thus described, of which it was hailed as the culmination. The doctrines of Vico and of the German historical school (sometimes criticized) were the central focus of Savarese's method, although he also dealt with economics and comparative law. Savarese was widely regarded as the most outstanding of the private teachers of law in Naples. One of his pupils described him as 'the perpetuator of the ancient school of Neapolitan lawyers' and as the model teacher and the 'perfect lawyer' – adding that 'one may say in general that the best of today's legal experts, professors, lawyers, magistrates, graduated from Roberto Savarese's school'.[56]

8. A SCHOOL FOR THE LEGAL PROFESSION

However, the relative freedom enjoyed by intellectual life in Naples during the 1830s did not mean that good relations with the Crown had been restored. Culture and the public institutions continued to diverge, and attempts at renewal were confined to small groups or individuals, whose activities were grudgingly tolerated when the regime did not actively suppress them. Hence derived the importance in Naples, too, of the private meetings and salons which had acquired such crucial social and political importance in the rest of Europe.[57] These circles generated the numerous journals which sprang up in those years, and the teaching imparted by the lawyers in the private schools was a further stimulus to the growth and organization of intellectual activity. Economics now occupied a position of unprecedented importance on the schools' curricula. *Laissez-faire* ideas were subject to intense debate and were the most evident sign

[55] E. Cenni, 'Della mente e dell'animo di Roberto Savarese' in R. Savarese, *Scritti forensi*, edited by F. Persico, Naples, 1876, pp. XL–XLI.
[56] Ibid., pp. XIxff *et passim*.
[57] U. Frevert, 'Il salotto' in H-G. Haupt (ed.), *Luoghi quotidiani nella storia d'Europa*, Rome–Bari, 1993, pp. 126–37.

that new cultural and political currents were maturing in the
Mezzogiorno.[58] The central importance accorded to economics in
legal and administrative discourse placed jurists at the forefront of
cultural renewal.

The cultural climate of the 1840s was epitomized by the activities
of Pasquale Stanislao Mancini. Numerous studies have been written
about him,[59] but only recently has sufficient attention been paid to
the profound roots of Mancini's thought in the 'struggles of ideological preparation for 1848' and to his action as an 'organizer of
culture'.[60] Mancini worked throughout his life in the publishing
trade, as the editor of journals, books and collected works, ranging
from the newspaper *Le Ore solitarie*, which he purchased in 1838, to
the *Enciclopedia Giuridica Italiana*, which he began writing in 1881. His
career sums up and underscores the most salient features of Neapolitan culture in those years. He was educated privately and never attended university. Indeed, he was not even required to sit the
obligatory examinations, from which he was granted special exemption when awarded his degree on 31 January 1844.[61] Mancini practised for many years as a lawyer after he had received his training in
the studio of Giuseppe and Carlo Poerio. The publication in 1841 of
his correspondence with Terenzio Mamiani on the foundations of the
right to punish[62] had already secured him the fame as an able and far-
sighted jurisconsult which accompanied him throughout his illustrious
career. His house was a meeting-place for Neapolitan intellectuals of
liberal leanings, and his wife, the poetess Laura Beatrice Oliva, presided over a literary salon.

With the characteristic energy that he devoted to all his enterprises, in 1842 Mancini, with the collaboration of two other
lawyers, Raffaele Tecci and Matteo de Augustinis, organized a 'complete' course in jurisprudence. The idea of 'combining Italian talents'
in order to build the new science of the nation, without prejudice
regarding their methods and approaches, while at the same time
uniting numerous 'classes of readers' (lawyers, professors, magistrates,

[58] Oldrini, *La cultura*, p. 115ff.
[59] See in particular E. Jayme, *Pasquale Stanislao Mancini. Internationales Privatrecht
zwischen Risorgimento und praktischer Jurisprudenz*, Ebelsbach, 1980 (Italian trans.
Padua, 1988).
[60] See G. Oldrini, 'La missione filosofica del diritto nella Napoli del Giovane
Mancini', in Oldrini, *Napoli*, pp. 58–75; and Vano, *Edifizio*.
[61] ASN, Min. Int. 1 Inv. Fasc. 795.
[62] The first Neapolitan edition was followed by others containing further letters by
Mamiani: see T. Mamiani–P.S. Mancini, *Intorno alla filosofia del dritto e singolarmente
del dritto di punire. Lettere*, Naples, 1844.

functionaries) around his publications, gradually developed into Mancini's overriding objective – as set out in writings, which ranged from his editorial for *Ore solitarie* in 1840 to his manifesto for the *Enciclopedia* written in 1881.[63] This conviction, moreover, matched the eclectic approach which he impressed upon his own school.[64] 'The reform of the teaching of law', he solemnly declared, 'can only consist in bringing about the happy conjunction of philosophy and history'. His school's curriculum therefore comprised courses on the rational principles of private and public law (Mancini) and on the principles of economic policy and the science of administration (de Augustinis). These courses were followed by studies in Roman law, which were supervised by Tecci. Modern law in the Two Sicilies was covered by the courses on civil and commercial law taught by de Augustinis, and by those on criminal law and the law governing judicial proceedings taught by Mancini. Tecci was responsible for the last course on the programme: civil procedure and the judicial system. Mancini also wanted the comparative history of legislations to be included on the curriculum, but this proved impossible, and instead monthly practical sessions were organized to examine practical cases. The school's seminar-based system of tutoring encouraged considerable intimacy between master and pupil: Enrico Pessina, who attended the school from 1842 to 1844, remembered how he would linger in Mancini's house after lessons to consult the books in his library.[65]

The school's courses commenced on 7 November 1842 with an inaugural lecture delivered by Matteo de Augustinis[66] which announced the aims of the school: 'civilization' and 'progress', de Augustinis declared, were to be its watchwords. In reaction to the inadequacy of traditional studies and to the one-sidedness of the French and German approaches, he proposed a 'middle way' for Italy which consisted of a 'school of progress', 'industrious and moderate', able to combine empirical examination of the *useful* with recognition of the *truthful*. 'Rational' and 'experimental' methods were to be unified in a single

[63] Vano, *Edifizio*.

[64] [Mancini], 'Studio di dritto de' professori de Augustinis, Tecci e Mancini. Programma per l'insegnamento di un corso completo di dritto', *Continuazione delle Ore solitarie ovvero Giornale di scienze morali legislative ed economiche*, 1842, fasc. I, pp. 343–7.

[65] The autobiographical note is in E. Pessina Jr, *Note sulla dottrina filosofica e pedagogica di Enrico Pessina*, Naples, 1928, p. 7n.

[66] 'Prolusione nell'apertura dello studio di dritto de' professori Matteo de Augustinis, Raffaele Tecci e Pasquale Stanislao Mancini', *Continuazione delle Ore solitarie ovvero Giornale di scienze morali legislative ed economiche*, 1842, fasc. II, pp. 19–30.

project where codification and respect for the tradition of *ius commune* were conjugated in pursuit of 'civil liberty'.

De Augustinis' address thus expressed the ideological doctrine of a 'happy medium' as the distinctive feature of the Italian 'genius'; a doctrine destined to enjoy extraordinary fortune after Unification although it was based on a theoretical eclecticism as fragile as it was efficacious. Mancini's school was among the first to disseminate these principles in a convincing and organized manner. The political crisis of 1848–49, however, put an end to his experiment and, more in general, to the 'interval of tolerance' from which the Neapolitan private schools had benefited. A new wave of repression – dubbed the 'negation of God' by Gladstone in 1851 – swept through the Kingdom of Naples.[67] Almost all the leading jurists, compromised as they were by their parliamentary and constitutional activities, suffered persecution and banishment. In their cities of exile most of them practised as lawyers and continued their political campaign for independence and national unity. Some were appointed to university chairs. Mancini, Pisanelli and Scialoja joined forces in Turin to publish a series of textbooks which provided a generation of lawyers with their legal training.

As a result of the diaspora of the southern intellectuals, the cultural and political ideas that later came to exert such a major influence on the *Risorgimento* movement radiated outwards from Naples to take root in numerous cities of Italy, especially Turin. There spread among jurists that most typical paradigm of the Neapolitan legal professional: the lawyer-professor-politician adept at switching from one role to the other and often combining all three of them in one person. The conviction that there was an indissoluble bond between cultural and political reform, the careful attention paid to institutional mechanisms and their influence on civil society, the close study of foreign developments in order to keep abreast of them, finally liberalism and *laissez-faire* economics: all these elements placed the Neapolitan exiles at the forefront of events during the 'decade of preparation' for national unity. And after the Unification of Italy they were among the principal artificers of the 'national legal science', and of the new state's institutions and ordinances.

---

[67] The literature on the topic is vast and is reviewed by a number of general works: see, for example, G. Candeloro, *Storia dell'Italia moderna*, Milan, 1956–86. For the repercussions of political repression on intellectual life in the capital and of the exiling of the Neapolitan intellectuals on national culture, see Oldrini, *La cultura*, pp. 273ff.

9. TOWARDS THE NATIONALIZATION OF THE LEGAL PROFESSIONS

What physiognomy did the Neapolitan *avvocatura* assume in the decades following national Unification? An answer to this question requires brief examination of certain characteristics of the political system and of higher education in unified Italy. In fact, removing the regional connotations from the lawyers' culture and day-to-day practice was a long process which was never entirely accomplished. It was implemented 'from above' and was driven by the centralizing impetus set in motion by the state. The nationalization of the legal professions was mainly the result of the government's determined efforts to bring the lawyers under its control.[68] The lawyers, for their part, asserted their autonomy more by defending their municipal privileges, or by exploiting the opportunities offered by the new legal system for corporative purposes, than by advancing any sort of innovative proposal. The link between the organization of university studies and the quality of the professions, so frequently stressed in the debates that initiated and followed the reform of the *avvocatura*, did not concern the lawyers to any great extent, given that their attention was most closely engaged by ongoing changes in the administrative institutions.

On the other hand – and this was only apparently a paradox – the rules and prerogatives ratified for the lawyers, and which they so often contested and criticized, were both a point of reference and an aspiration for the other professionals.[69] The law regulating legal practice – the first in Italy to govern the 'free' professions – was regarded favourably by the doctors, engineers and architects, although they themselves would have to wait many years before their own legal status was defined. As a result of the system adopted for the lawyers, the hierarchy of the bourgeois professions was fixed according to the extent to which they belonged to the public sphere – that is, to a state which was seeking to merge its identity with that of the nation.

The marked *étatisme* of Italian liberalism, in its origins as well as in its creation of the country's institutions following Unification, has frequently been commented upon.[70] On the assumption that the state was the 'engine' of modernization, the protagonists of the *Risorgimento*

---

68 H. Siegriest, 'Die Rechtsanwälte und das Bürgertum: Deutschland, die Schweiz, und Italien im XIX. Jahrhundert', in *Bürgertum*, vol. II, pp. 92ff.

69 M. Malatesta, 'Gli ordini professionali e la nazionalizzazione in Italia', in M. Meriggi and P. Schiera (eds), *Dalla città alla nazione. Borghesie ottocentesche in Italia e in Germania*, Bologna, 1993, pp. 165ff.

70 U. Allegretti, *Profilo di storia costituzionale italiana. Individualismo e assolutismo nello stato liberale*, Bologna, 1989.

often took the building of the state to be an end in itself, and they assigned an importance to it which overrode any other consideration – for example, reducing the economic and social disparities among and within the country's various regions. The consequence was a tendency to 'juridicize' problems; a tendency, that is, to address the great issues raised by conflicts and power relations in society by imposing rules and regulations, instead of changing the system after scrutiny of its contradictions. The large number of lawyers and jurists in parliament – as documented by another essay in this book[71] – both reflected and emphasized this phenomenon. Not infrequently, in fact, the great parliamentary debates on national policy took the form of a clash between opposing juridical points of view rather than between ideologies.

Several studies have examined the structural reasons for the contradictions and shortcomings of this behaviour and, more in general, of Italian liberalism.[72] The concept of the state embraced by the Neapolitan intellectuals under the influence of German philosophy and Hegelianism – namely that of the state as an entity which ordered and ruled civil society and directed it towards higher ends – was contradicted by the much more modest results achieved in actual practice. The *étatisme* preached by the Neapolitan intellectuals was enormously influential in the early years of the new nation, but in reality the institutions were employed to reach *ad hoc* arrangements which were often bereft of any coherent design.[73] The outcome of this interweaving between appeals to principle and a constant search for compromise was the rendering of the constitutional system into 'a weakened statocentric model'.[74] The state thus constructed, and in which such high hopes were placed, was inefficient, isolated, and based on inadequate consensus. The hasty 'Piedmontization' of the legal system, with the consequent penalizing of southern regional autonomies, further alienated the majority of the population from the institutions.

The milieu of the Neapolitan lawyers was particularly sensitive to these matters. It developed an acute awareness of the institutional issues to be addressed as the country moved towards Unification. These preoccupations were expressed in a variety of attitudes, ranging from outright demands for autonomy to the most conservative of pro-Bourbon nostalgia. Roberto Savarese was among the first to raise the alarm over the dangers of a too short-sighted annexation of the South.

[71] F. Cammarano, this volume.
[72] See R. Romanelli, *L'Italia liberale*, Bologna, 1990.
[73] R. Gherardi, *L'arte del compromesso. La politica della mediazione nell'Italia liberale*, Bologna, 1993.
[74] Allegretti, *Profili*, pp. 23 ff.

On 13 July 1861, immediately on his return to Naples from exile, he wrote as follows to his Florentine friends:[75]

> Place no trust, my dear Vieusseux, in the words of certain of our orators when they declare in parliament that here the concept of Italian unity has become paramount or that it has penetrated to the hearts of the people. This may come about in time. At the moment it neither happens nor could happen without a veritable miracle [...] Let us not be deceived by words. Italy, which for us is an end, is for the overwhelming majority of my fellow citizens a means to achieving good government.

This, however, was not the sort of government installed by the Piedmontese, who continued to compound their errors: 'If a gang of schoolchildren on holiday had come here to govern us, they could not have wreaked such havoc.' The decisions taken in regulating the army, the civil service and industry were unacceptable, 'and many conclude with these ugly words: they treat us like a conquered country!' The most crucial issue for Savarese, like Manna two years before him,[76] was the legal institutions:

> Every population has its self-respect, and we have ours. We have the third city of Europe, the noblest of civil histories, and laws and institutions which we believe to be better (and in large part they really are) than those of the other Italian provinces. It would be prudent to respect, indeed to cherish, this provincial vanity of ours, which arises from a good source and can stimulate us to work to noble ends. The government apparently does the opposite.

Savarese's strictures, however, were not dictated by any antipathy towards united Italy. His letter continues:

> I write as an Italian, not as a Neapolitan. I love Naples out of duty, having been born and bred there. But I have never liked its way of life, and after twelve years of absence I do not know if I shall ever get used to it again. I know our vices, the corruption that rules us, the coarseness and ignorance of the people. It does not anger me if they call us barbarians.

Lucidity was required if these 'barbarisms' were to be eliminated. Instead, the rapidity of unification, the gravity of the country's problems, and the government's scant knowledge of the regions annexed, encouraged the search for compromise. The need to mediate between the government and civil society in the *Mezzogiorno* and, at all costs, to

[75] The letter was published as an appendix to an article of 1921; now reprinted with other writings in A. Anzilotti, *Movimenti e contrasti per l'unità italiana*, edited by A. Caracciolo, Milan, 1964, pp. 299–303.
[76] Cf. his letter to Scialoja from Naples, 17 June 1859, in P. Alatri, 'Lettere inedite di Antonio Scialoja', *Movimento Operaio*, 1956, pp. 193–6; see also G. Manna, *Le provincie meridionali del Regno d'Italia*, Naples, 1862.

find a solution for its dramatic difficulties, considerably expanded the lawyers' market, given their traditional expertise in these matters. The new laws regulating relationships among citizens, and increased interference by central and local government in their affairs, enhanced the mediatory function that legal practitioners had always performed. In parallel, it became of increasing urgency to improve and control their legal training and professional practice. The reform of the universities and the adoption of a uniform legal statute governing exercise of the legal profession throughout the kingdom were therefore among the principal concerns of the liberals in power, the men of the so-called *Destra storica*.

10. THE UNIVERSITY QUESTION AND THE UNIVERSITY OF NAPLES

As well as exposing the backwardness of the economic and institutional structure of the South, the rapid collapse of the Bourbon monarchy in the summer of 1860 also revealed the chaos that reigned in its educational system; a state of anarchy which had produced deep-seated corruption, especially among legal professionals. In Naples, the social strata that should have shouldered the task of building the unitary state were dominated by a disorderly mob of lawyers of dubious morals and uncertain culture. 'In the capital', wrote Farini to Minghetti in November 1862, 'there are 12,000 *paglietti*, that is jackleg lawyers, pettifoggers, shysters, lawmongers, blackguards, scoundrels: these are the men who fix everything – in the streets, in the lawcourts, in the stock exchange, in the lobbies, in the theatres. What do you hope to achieve with material like this?'[77]

The immoral behaviour rife in the professional classes was generally blamed on the decay of the cultural institutions and the educational system. The situation had been denounced in polemical tones by a pamphlet published anonymously in August 1860 but which was in fact written by Francesco Del Giudice.[78] The rejoinders and arguments provoked by the pamphlet, however, were soon swamped by events when Garibaldi's troops arrived in Naples in September and the plebiscite on annexation was held. Nevertheless, the issue still remained on the agenda: in a letter of 5 January 1861, Nicola De Crescenzio described to Mittermaier the disastrous state of legal studies in both the university faculties and the private schools.[79] Energetic action in this

---

[77] *Carteggi di Camillo Cavour. La liberazione del Mezzogiorno e la formazione del Regno d'Italia*, Bologna, 1952, vol. IV, p. 56.

[78] *Le piaghe dell'istruzione pubblica napoletana*, Naples, 1860.

[79] Heidelberg, Universitätsbibliothek, *Heid. Hs.* 3468, pp. unnumbered.

area could no longer be postponed, he declared: the state should assume control over education as one of its principal tasks and convert the universities into the engine of civil renewal for the entire country.

As Director General of Education from 24 October to 8 November 1860, and the next year as Minister, Francesco De Sanctis was responsible for a set of measures designed, as he later declared in a letter to a relative, 'to make the University of Naples the first university of Europe'.[80] Like the other southern intellectuals, De Sanctis was convinced that educational reform was the first and vital stage in building the moral unity of the nation: 'The *Risorgimento* should be not only political but intellectual as well; it should be preparation for both the unity and the civilization' of Italy.[81] Numerous historians have described De Sanctis' project for the universities and the ideals that inspired it, and although they may have pointed out its flaws and shortcomings, they have always acknowledged its lofty ethical and cultural purpose.[82] De Sanctis began his reform of the University of Naples by dismissing those members of its teaching staff conspicuous for incompetence or for their evident hostility to the ideals of Italian unification, and he delayed the immediate application to Naples of Piedmont's Casati Law on the universities, which was intended to cover the entire country. The men appointed to the professorial chairs thus vacated were mostly exiles or teachers who had already distinguished themselves by their work in the private schools. Although De Sanctis's action occasionally resembled a political purge, it nevertheless achieved a twofold purpose: it restored to the universities the intellectual energies that the Bourbon regime had alienated or exiled; and it affirmed the primacy of public education by shutting down a parallel system that might have frustrated efforts to give greater efficiency to the state structures.

The brevity of De Sanctis' term of office meant that his programme of reform was never fully accomplished. Although for several decades the University of Naples was successfully transformed into one of the leading centres of learning in Italy, over the long period its peculiarities continued to be one of the greatest obstacles against solution of the country's university problems. Partial reforms, proposals and bills followed each other as the years passed, but none of these measures effectively dealt with the most serious flaws in the system.[83] It was

---

[80] Quoted in Russo, *De Sanctis*, p. XII.

[81] Atti Parlamentari, VIII Legislatura, *Camera, Discussioni*, 13 April 1861, p. 507.

[82] There is a vast body of literature on this topic: see especially the 'Introduction' by G. Talamo to F. De Sanctis, *Epistolario (1861–1862)*, Turin, 1969.

[83] See in general S. Polenghi, *La politica universitaria italiana nell'éta della Destra storica 1848–1876*, Brescia, 1993.

Ruggiero Bonghi, with a decree law of 30 May 1875, who finally brought the University of Naples under the aegis of a legal regime substantially fashioned by the Casati Law and which applied throughout the country. Bonghi's decree extended the obligation of student matriculation and enrolment on courses to include the University of Naples as well. It also decisively dealt with the problem of private education which had so vexed previous ministers and which, in 1872, still aroused the indignation of Settembrini: 'in Naples, anyone who so desires can teach university subjects privately, without a degree, without any qualification, and without interference by the authorities'.[84] The measure in fact recognized and protected the *pareggiati* (officially recognized) private professors: those, that is, who were entitled under the provisions of the decree to teach as *libero docente* (similar to the *Privat-Dozent* in the German universities). They were permitted to teach their courses in the university faculties and also to sit on the examination boards. The possibility was also envisaged, under certain conditions, that these private professors might conduct their courses extramurally. The qualifications of all the other private teachers were no longer recognized, and they were only allowed, on authorization by the rector, to give lectures with no official academic status.

Thus private teaching was neither eliminated nor obstructed; it was, however, brought under the control and the guidance of the academic authorities. Similar principles were applied in the other measures simultaneously adopted by Bonghi to regulate the educational system; measures which were later partly altered by the *Regolamento Coppino* of 1876. Bonghi's aim was to rationalize the relationship among the various forms and structures of education. He therefore took pains to safeguard the right to teach, but made higher education the exclusive province of the universities while giving more precise specification to the various functions of scientific research and professional training. He set the universities the task of furnishing a general education of humanist stamp, but this was to be flanked by more specific programmes providing training for professionals and which made no concessions either to trivialities or to excessive scientific specialization. During debate in the Chamber of Deputies – in which Bonghi had to defend his policies against the numerous attacks brought against them – he proclaimed that students must be provided with an education that equipped them to exercise a profession. Purely scientific research was to be confined to specific areas of the curriculum or else assigned to

[84] See Settembrini's letter to Sella of 3 July 1872, p. 451.

the other educational institutions connected in various ways to the universities.[85]

In actual fact, efforts to bring training for the higher professions under the monopoly of the state encountered major obstacles. The distinct improvement in the organization of the universities and the internal reform of the legal disciplines – which resulted mainly from the efforts of the universities themselves – failed to eliminate deeply ingrained habits. In Naples, private teaching continued to thrive by exploiting the system of *libera docenza*. In the mid-1880s the lawyer Emanuele Gianturco was still able to contrive an apologia for the private schools by criticizing the university faculties for their 'preoccupation with examinations' and for allowing their role to be reduced to that of the mere 'conferral of degrees as at the present University of London'. By contrast, he hailed the glorious tradition of the private schools in the *Mezzogiorno* as epitomized by prestigious lawyers whose example should be followed.[86] Moreover, the endeavour to bring professional training under the sole control of the universities aggravated a problem that had long preoccupied academics: the relationship between theory and practice. Intense debate developed on the link to be established between theoretical elaboration of the law and its practical application. Gianturco reflected long on this issue and sought to have courses on 'practical cases' included on the law faculties' programmes, although in this he was acting largely on his own.[87]

II. THE JURIDICAL REGULATION OF THE BAR

Beginning in 1865, besides the promulgation of codes which contained – especially those governing procedure – numerous provisions regulating on the legal profession, and together with the decrees on the judicial system and on free legal aid for the poor, preparatory work was in progress on a law which would impose a uniform set of regulations on the exercise of the professions of attorney (*avvocato*) and prosecutor (*procuratore*) in the country. These two professions were disciplined in ways that differed from one pre-Unification State to another, and the first measures to be introduced after the annexa-

[85] Atti Parlamentari, XII Legislatura, *Camera, Discussioni*, 20 May 1876. See also, for previous speeches on the subject, R. Bonghi, *Discorsi e saggi sulla pubblica istruzione*, Florence, 1876.

[86] E. Gianturco, *Relazione letta all'Associazione dei Privati Docenti con effetti legali, intorno alle condizioni della privata docenza in Napoli*, Naples, 1885.

[87] For a review of the topic see A. Mazzacane (ed.), *L'esperienza giuridica di Emanuele Gianturco*, Naples, 1988.

tions addressed only the most pressing problems created by this heterogeneous system.

A first bill was presented to the Senate by the minister De Falco in March 1866. Its progress through parliament, however, was an extremely tedious affair. Modifications and amendments piled up as the years passed, accompanied by repeated discussion in parliament – discussion which was never conducted on any broad-ranging basis but monotonously returned to a limited number of what were only purely formal issues. Nor did the professional associations and journals go much further than the stubborn defence of corporatist interests. This, for example, was the predominant attitude of the articles published in the *Gazzetta del Procuratore*, founded in Naples by a group of lawyers in 1866. The declared aim of the journal was to 'smooth the way' to a new normative order, or at least to 'clear paths' through the 'dense undergrowth' created 'in this vacillating period of transition, when various systems of laws and rulings for many years rooted in the habits and life of the nation have so abruptly given way to different laws and codes, and when this change has taken everyone unawares'.[88] The *Gazzetta* therefore closely monitored the government's efforts and kept its readers minutely informed, but it failed to propose measures that would decisively deal with the situation. The reform finally passed into law on 8 June 1874 accompanied by the rules for its implementation which were issued in July of the same year.[89] Its principal purpose was to unify the juridical regime of the professions of attorney and prosecutor in Italy, which still displayed marked differences from one region to another – although, since the Napoleonic period, the influence of the French system had reduced these differences. This objective was not immediately and fully achieved, however: because of the partial and mediatory nature of the measure, numerous previous customs, rules and institutions continued to be operative.[90]

The law did not stipulate any distinction between the two professions of attorney and prosecutor; it merely regulated their practice by

---

[88] 'Programma', *Gazzetta del Procuratore*, no. 1, Naples, 20 February 1866, p. 1.

[89] For a detailed technical description of the provisions of the law see A. Bianchi, *Sull'esercizio delle professioni di avvocato e procuratore*, Turin, 1885.

[90] A description of the restrictions on the Italian legal profession in united Italy, with historical and comparative analysis, technical and sociological assessment, as well as proposals for reform, is provided by G. Maroni, 'Avvocato e procuratore', *Enciclopedia giuridica italiana*, I, 5, Milan, 1905, pp. 871–976; and by C. Cavagnari and E. Caldara, 'Avvocati e procuratori', *Digesto italiano*, 4, 2, Turin, 1899, pp. 621–704. Because of the system used in publication of these encyclopaedias, the two entries were written some years earlier.

fixing admission requirements to each of them. This defect created considerable and serious uncertainty over crucial areas of the legal profession – legal counselling, for example – which the measure entirely ignored; and it heightened the confusion over the distinction between attorney and prosecutor by failing to specify whether they were two distinct professions, as prescribed by some pre-Unification systems, or one and the same, as envisaged by others. It was this ambiguous mingling of the legal traditions of the various Italian states that was responsible for the ambiguous wording of article 2: 'The two professions are distinct, but they may be practised jointly by those who possess the qualifications established by the law as regards the one or the other and who fulfil the obligations mandatory for both of them.' The only differences stipulated by the law between the two professions were external in character: two distinct professional registers were to be compiled by the respective Orders at the lawcourts of the Kingdom (it was, however, possible to enrol on both); the opposing parties in certain lawsuits were obliged to appoint a prosecutor rather than an attorney to represent them, except before the Court of Cassation. Prosecutors were authorized to practise only within specific geographical districts, but attorneys could plead suits in any part of the country as well as in the Courts of Cassation; a right which was denied to prosecutors.

Instead of clarifying and distinguishing the roles of lawyer and prosecutor, subsequent dispositions and exceptions only compounded the confusion between them. In fact, both professional categories were permitted to act as legal counsel and their specific functions consequently tended to overlap. It was therefore left to the jurisdiction of the courts and to jurisprudence to establish their respective spheres of competence, and in practice it was the legal traditions of the various regions that prevailed: in Lombardy the two professions were very rarely differentiated; in Piedmont, by contrast, they very rarely combined in the same practitioner. In the *Mezzogiorno*, where the theoretical distinction between them was confounded by innumerable abuses, the situation persisted and worsened. The immediate outcome, therefore, was the failure of the government's project for legislative unification and the appearance of alarming phenomena. The large number of pre-Unification traditions and the haphazard organization of university legal studies – together with the two-tier hierarchy of attorney and prosecutor, and the disparities in social prestige and income consequent upon it – meant that the profession of prosecutor came to be regarded as merely propaedeutic to that of lawyer. In 1881, there was a total of

17,649 lawyers in Italy (with densities reaching almost one per every thousand inhabitants in the larger cities of the South), as compared to only 2,705 prosecutors.[91] The overcrowding of the legal profession, especially in Naples, generated a veritable intellectual 'proletariat' to which the counterpoint was the swarm of *faccendieri*, or 'fixers', who fraudulently practised as lawyers. These hucksters turned the Palace of Castelcapuano, the Naples hall of justice, into what some commentators described as closely akin to a flea market with swindlers lurking on every corner.[92]

The problem of the fraudulent use of the titles of attorney or prosecutor long vexed the world of the professions. It provoked constant denunciations to the authorities, judicial rulings and much doctrinal discussion; none of which, however, ever produced any concrete results. Under the law, the titles of lawyer and attorney were awarded following enrolment on the professional registers compiled by the relative Order and kept at the lawcourts. Attorneys were required to possess a degree in order to qualify for enrolment, while prosecutors had to have passed certain examinations in a faculty of law. Also required was certification that the applicant had practised for two years, and that he had attended civil and criminal hearings. On completion of this period, the candidate was allowed to sit the admission examinations set by each profession and, if successful, apply to the Order for enrolment. Further provisions stipulated that a prosecutor was to be an Italian citizen, that he must have reached the age of majority, and that he should not have been convicted of a wider range of offences than those which debarred lawyers. Moreover, as has been said, prosecutors could only practise in their districts of residence.

Most of these provisions encountered stubborn resistance in every part of the country; resistance which was only eventually overcome by the 1926 law governing the legal profession. Complaints about irregularities therefore proliferated, as well as lawsuits, appeals to the courts and demands for intervention by the government.[93] Moreover, the question of whether women should be allowed to practise the professions, to which there was no legislative impediment, was postponed *sine die*.[94]

---

[91] ISTAT, *Sommario di statistiche storiche italiane 1861–1955*, Rome, 1958.
[92] C. Vano, ' "Avvocati innanzi all'Eccellentissima Corte". Una collezione ritrovata di allegazioni forensi', in *Università*.
[93] For an analytical description see the articles cited at note 90.
[94] On the opposing positions taken up on the issue see C.F. Gabba, *Le donne non avvocate*, Pisa, 1884 and E. Ciccotti, *Cause ed effetti. Note sulle presenti condizioni dell'avvocatura e su un nuovo ordinamento di essa*, Turin, 1889.

Against this background, one understands why – from Giuriati to Zanardelli[95] and many other authors besides – the emphasis was placed on the moral quality and culture that distinguished the lawyer and his 'mission' from the unscrupulous venality and the petty corruption of the legal impostors. The argument shifted back to the function of the universities[96] and to the ethical-political and intellectual training of legal professionals. This issue was still at the centre of lively debate in Naples at the end of the century: suffice it to mention the acute analysis conducted by Pasquale Turiello.[97] This, however, brings us to a new phase of Italy's social and political history, one very distant from the problems and ideals of the *Risorgimento* and the building of national unity.

[95] D. Giuriati, *Arte forense*, Turin, 1878; G. Zanardelli, *L'avvocatura. Discorsi*, Florence, 1879.
[96] Bianchi, *Sull'esercizio*, pp. 98ff.
[97] P. Turiello, 'Governo e governati in Italia' (1892), ed. by P. Bevilacqua, Turin, 1980, pp. 60; 190ff.

CHAPTER 3

OFFICIALS AND PROFESSIONALS. NOTARIES, THE STATE AND THE MARKET PRINCIPLE

MARCO SANTORO

The profession of notary in Italy is an ancient occupation with roots that extend deep into a long legal tradition. As A.M. Carr-Saunders and P. Wilson wrote in their classic study of the professions, 'In the ancient Roman Law and in systems derived from it, great importance is attached to the formal witnessing of documents by a notary. In those countries whose law is still largely based upon the Roman Code the notary remains generally speaking an important figure among legal practitioners.'[1] As both the cultural and geographical inheritor of Roman civilization, Italy was also the land in which the profession of 'notary public' first originated and then spread through the countries of Mediterranean and continental Europe between the eleventh and thirteenth centuries.[2] Officially appointed by the public authorities but independently organized into (often powerful) guilds, *societates* and

[1] A.M. Carr-Saunders, P.A. Wilson, *Professions*, Oxford, 1933, pp. 55–6. See also C.M. Cipolla, 'The Professions. The Long View', *The Journal of European Economic History*, 2, 1973, p. 39; M. Weber, *Economy and Society*, Berkeley: University of California Press, 1968. As Cipolla, p. 40, explains, 'in the South [of Europe] the notarial act was (and still is) received in evidence of a judicial matter and the certificate of a notary was (and is at present) probative of the facts certified'. The figure of the notary in Italy and other countries of continental Europe, however, cannot be compared to the Anglo-Saxon notary public, who is a public functionary and whose function is restricted to simple certification (in functional terms, the British legal professionals most closely resembling the Italian-style notary are the solicitor or the scrivener). See P.G. Stein, C.W. Brooks, R.H. Helmholz (eds), 'Notai pubblici in Inghilterra dopo la riforma', in C.R. Cheney, P.G. Stein, C.W. Brooks, R.H. Helmholz, *Notai in Inghilterra prima e dopo la riforma*, Milan, 1991, pp. 253–384. See also the analysis of the figure of the notary in E.N. Suleiman, *Private Power and Centralization in France. The Notaires and the State*, Princeton, 1987.
[2] On the notarial profession in England during the Middle Ages, see C. R. Cheney, *Notaries Public in England in the Thirteenth and Fourteenth Centuries*, Oxford, 1972.

collegi which controlled access to the profession and its practice, notaries were active from the Middle Ages to the modern age – and in certain cases almost until the end of the *ancien régime* – wherever and whenever it was necessary to give a legal and certain form to script.[3] Their task was not only to stipulate contracts and wills, but also to record jurisdictional deeds and documents. As clerks and secretaries, they also participated in a wide range of governmental and administrative activities of both a public and private nature. Subsequently, however, the ubiquitous role enjoyed by the notary in the system of social relations – political, economic and legal – became progressively confined to the drafting and authenticating of wills and private contracts.[4] Between the sixteenth and seventeenth centuries – in parallel with the transformation of the ancient and unitary *societas civilis* into the 'modern' (and soon solely ideological) distinction between 'state' and 'society' – the profession was subject to a twofold process whereby the 'privatization' of the notary's clientele, on the one hand, was counterbalanced by a simultaneous increase in the 'public nature' of his function on the other – in the sense that the state intervened with increasing vigour to legitimate and define both the notary's professional function and his day-to-day practice. The culmination of this process came at the end of the eighteenth century, and during the first decades of the nineteenth, when the various Italian states introduced policies which subordinated notaries to their own interests and to the exigencies of social control. Increasingly specific laws were passed which established criteria for access to the profession, set its standards, defined the number of notarial

---

3   There is a vast literature on the medieval Italian notary. See, for a general treatment, A. Petrucci, *Notarii*, Milan, 1958, and G. Costamagna, M. Amelotti, *Alle origini del notariato italiano*, Rome, 1975. Much sparser, however, is the bibliography on the notarial profession in the modern age: no works of synthesis exist, only local reconstructions. On the French notaries see, for the Middle Ages, R. Fédou, *Les Hommes de loi lyonnais à la fin du Moyen Age*, Paris, 1964, and for the contemporary age, J.P. Poisson, *Notaires et societé: travaux d'histoire et de sociologie notariale*, Paris, 1985; T. Zeldin, *France, 1848–1945*, ch. 3, vol. I, Oxford, 1973; E. Suleiman, *Private Power*. On the notarial profession in Spain, see D. G. Cruz, *Escribanos y Notarios en Huelva durante el antiguo regimen (1701–1800)*, Huelva, 1991, and J-M. Scholz, 'Katalanisches Notariat und Transformation des Juristischen Feldes im 19. Jahrhundert', *Ius Commune*, 15, 1988, pp. 135–97.
4   C. Mozzarelli, 'Strutture sociali e formazioni statuali a Milano e Napoli tra '500 e '700', *Società e Storia*, 1, 1978, pp. 431ff; U. Nicolini, 'Premessa' to G. Costamagna, *Il notaio a Genova tra prestigio e potere*, Rome, 1970. On the history of the notarial profession in the contemporary age the only available works examine juridical-legal matters: see F. Mazzanti Pepe, G. Ancarani, *Il notariato in Italia dall'età napoleonica all'unità*, Rome, 1983; P.H.M. Gerver, *Het notariaat in Italie*, Groningen, 1975, which describes the normative-institutional changes undergone by the Italian notariate between the Napoleonic period and the Law of 1913.

posts and sometimes also fixed their geographical distribution. The profession's corporatist independence was thus considerably restricted, although to an extent which varied according to local circumstances.[5]

It is with the final stages of this centuries-long process that our reconstruction and interpretation of the history of the Italian notarial profession begin. It is a history marked by two legislative events of profound importance: the 'Law for Unification of the Notarial Order' (*legge di unificazione dell'ordinamento notarile*) of 1875 and the Reform Law of 1913, which – with the additions and amendments made to it in subsequent years – still regulates the profession in Italy today.

1. `STATE-BUILDING´ AND PROFESSIONALIZATION: THE CREATION OF THE ITALIAN NOTARIAL SYSTEM

On the Unification of Italy in 1861, the notarial profession was highly diversified and bereft any social and economic, or indeed institutional, homogeneity. Ten different sets of *ordinamenti* (regulations) governed, and would continue to do so for several years, the profession in the new Italian state; a state which was nominally unified but whose institutional system was in fact still fragmentary. The unity achieved in 1861 consequently had no immediate impact on the social and demographic structure of the notarial profession: almost all the notaries in practice prior to Unification continued to be for some years thereafter.

But how many notaries were there in the new Kingdom of Italy? The information gathered and published by the first population census held in the new Kingdom (1861) does not answer the question, since, of the various free professions (*arti liberali*), it distinguished only those relative to medical practice (*sanità*) and to the clergy. When the second census was held ten years later, however, 7,746 citizens of the new kingdom declared that they were practising notaries, a figure that amounted to more than half that of respondents who reported themselves to be lawyers, *causidici* (unqualified advocates) and prosecutors. When the third census was carried out in 1881, these figures had

---

[5] The Law of Ventôse, which defined the new code for the notarial profession in post-revolutionary France, and its subsequent export to the countries which fell under Napoleonic domination, therefore dealt the final blow to a process of change already underway in Italy – particularly in the Savoy States and in Austrian Lombardy (see A. Liva, *Notariato e documento notarile a Milano*, Rome, 1979, pp. 176–7; E. Durando, *Il tabellionato o notariato nelle leggi romane, nelle leggi medievali italiane e nelle posteriori, specialmente piemontesi*, Turin, 1897) – during the 1770s. With the Restoration, the old *ordinamenti* came back into force almost everywhere, although they were emended to incorporate the key provisions of the Law of Ventôse. See on this, F. Mazzanti Pepe, G. Ancarani, *Il notariato in Italia*.

already increased: 7,896 notaries and more than 20,000 advocates were recorded under the heading of '*giurisprudenza*'. If one bears in mind that the new law of 1874 governing the legal profession allowed lawyers and prosecutors to occupy two offices – so that no reliable demarcation line can be drawn between the two professions – the minority position occupied by notaries in the broader category of legal professionals becomes even more evident (Table 3.1).

Despite the already reduced size of their profession, at least relative to other occupational categories, one of the demands most frequently advanced by notaries after the Unification of Italy – at their self-styled 'national' congresses, in petitions to parliament, in editorials and articles published in their professional journals (which appeared in increasing numbers in those first years of national unity) – was for a reduction in their numbers and for changes in their geographical distribution. In fact, almost 40 per cent of notaries were concentrated in Piedmont, Campania and Sicily, while 50 per cent of the notaries in the new kingdom of Italy lived and practised in southern Italy, mainly in the regions previously ruled by the Bourbons.[6] The 'rationalization' of the notarial profession swiftly became a priority for the government – an evident sign of the importance attached to it. However, only in 1876 – that is, fifteen years after the formal act of political unification, eleven years after the new civil code which partially changed the legal functions of the notary, and one year after the law on advocacy (*avvocatura*) had been passed – did a single and coherent normative-institutional system replace the piecemeal arrangement inherited from before Unification. With the '*legge di ordinamento del notariato e degli archivi notarili*' the new state defined the code of regulations governing the profession. This law set out the rules for admittance to the profession, educational qualifications, organizational structures, a code of practice, legal sanctions and pay scales. However, the notaries themselves played only a minor role in the drafting of this first law to regulate the Italian *notariato*. No notary sat in the Senate at the time, and the handful who were members of the Chamber of Deputies played no active part in discussion – a clear indication that their political-geographical identity predominated over their professional one. In fact, the law of 1875 was the outcome of a long process of legal wrangling and political bargaining to which the profession remained largely extraneous. As regards the manner of its formulation and its institutional and ideo-

---

[6]   See, for example, C. Gherardi, *Sulla necessità di limitare il numero dei notai*, Lucca, 1863; Collegio dei Notari di Genova, *Di alcuni articoli del progetto di legge sul notariato. Memoria*, Genova, 1865. For the figures quoted see the volumes of statistics on the professions compiled after the censuses of 1871 and 1882.

Table 3.1 *Number of notaries according to different sources, 1871–1923*

Year	Table of notarial posts	Census	Notarial Statistics	Cassa Nazionale del Notariato
1871		7,746		
1876	6,322			
1881		7,896		
1896			5,917	
1901		6,253	5,784	
1905			5,862	
1910			5,775	
1911		6,207	5,997	
1913	4,310		5,951	
1915			5,605	
1920				4,985
1921		5,480		
1923				4,258

Sources: Population Census, 1871–1921; Direzione generale della statistica, *Statistica giudiziaria civile e commerciale e statistica notarile per l'anno 1896. Parte seconda. Statistica notarile,* Rome, 1900; Ministero di Grazia e Giustizia, *Statistica notarile per gli anni 1901–1910,* Rome, 1915, and *Statistica notarile per gli anni 1914–1915,* Rome, 1921; Cassa nazionale del notariato, Rome.

logical contents, therefore, the new law seems to fit perfectly with that model of 'professionalization from above' which, according to some historians, distinguishes professional policy in continental Europe from that of the Anglo-Saxon countries.[7] The new law recognized the profession and provided it with specific legal safeguards. It

---

[7] See H. Siegrist, 'Professionalization with the Brakes on: the Legal Professions in Switzerland, France and Germany in the Nineteenth and Early Twentieth Centuries', *Comparative Social Research,* 9, 1986, pp. 267–98, and, by the same author, 'States and Legal Professions', *Università degli Studi di Macerata. Annali della Facoltà di Giurisprudenza,* 1989, II, pp. 861–86. Critical of the concept is C. McClelland, *The German Experience of Professionalization,* Cambridge, 1990, pp. 237–8, who writes: 'Only from a liberal-market perspective, in other words from a traditional Anglo-American bias, could one make the opposition of professionalization "from within" (successful manipulation of the market by group) and "from above" (domination of forces external to the group).' For more finely shaded and thorough analysis than that based on the opposition between two types of professionalization, one 'by the state', the other 'by the market', see A. Abbott, *The System of Professions,* Chicago, 1988, ch. 6. I note in passing that this distinction is reminiscent of the contrast between 'bottom-up' and 'top-down' models developed by political scientists in analysis of public policies: see, for example, C. Ham, M. Hill, *The Policy Process in the Modern Capitalist State,* Brighton, 1984.

required all notaries to enrol on special registers kept by the newly established *Consigli Notarili* (the local bodies regulating the profession which replaced the ancient *collegi*); it declared the deeds drawn up by subjects not so enrolled null and void; it set out a career structure which began with acquisition of a school-leaving certificate and culminated with the awarding of the full professional qualification; above all, it guaranteed the closure of the profession by instituting a 'table' of posts and of notarial offices (*Tabella delle sedi notarili*). The law thus satisfied at least some of the aspirations to professionalization that certain segments of the profession had expressed since the first days of Unification.[8] At the same time, by providing the government with broad discretionary powers in fixing the number and distribution of posts and in appointing notaries, and above all by subjecting notaries to a dense network of normative controls wielded by state functionaries (including magistrates), the law also reduced the notary to a sort of adjunct to the administrative machinery of the state. In no sense, however, could notaries claim that they were an integral part of the public bureaucracy. They received their training on courses of study defined and administered by the state and taught at the public universities. They were declared eligible for the profession on passing an examination before a board consisting mainly of magistrates, and then received their appointment from the Ministry of Justice. Nevertheless, notaries were neither employees nor stipendiaries of the state because their income derived solely from the market and from their clients.[9]

However, the notaries were not entirely uninvolved in the passage through parliament of the Law of 1875. A draft bill for the *ordinamento* of the notarial profession was prepared by a government-appointed committee which included nine notaries among its twenty-two members. Although never submitted for parliamentary approval,

[8]   On the notion of professional 'segment' frequently used in this essay, see R. Bucher, A. Strauss, 'Professions in Process', *American Journal of Sociology*, 66, pp. 325–34. Interesting proposals for reforming the notarial profession from within were made by F. Panciatichi, *Riforma radicale del notariato per tutto il regno*, Turin, 1861; L. Moscatelli, *Idee per un progetto di codice notarile in Italia*, Naples, 1863; D. Lissoni, *Progetto di legge per l'esercizio del notariato, con annotazioni, cenni storici e rapporti*, Milan, 1868.

[9]   Both in the years immediately after Unification and at the turn of the century, for many notaries, especially those practising in southern Italy, the bureaucratic option offered an escape from the restrictions of the market and a more reliable source of income than fees. Although the 'statization' of the *notariato* is a recurrent theme in post-Unification history, it had little impact either within the profession or within the state apparatus until after the First World War, and then moved back onto the agenda in the first years of the Fascist regime.

NOTARIES, THE STATE AND THE MARKET PRINCIPLE 117

this preliminary text influenced those that followed, all of which were drawn up by the government and the last of which eventually provided the basis for the law. Numerous reports, petitions and memoranda were submitted to the legislative assembly by notarial colleges and by individual notaries: heterogeneous in content and aim, indeed often incoherent, they had the effect of demonstrating more the manifold interests and cultural models of a fragmented occupational category than the dynamism and political and managerial abilities proper to a professional class. A Congress of Notaries organized in Naples in 1870 (the first to call itself 'national') with the aim of stimulating public discussion of the law then in gestation once again demonstrated, apart from the indifference of most practitioners, how difficult it was to aggregate people and ideas around a unitary design. Ancient geographical and cultural cleavages combined with differences in identity and conflicting personal and professional aspirations. This clash of interests and ideas reflected the concrete circumstances in which the notaries worked (the city and the countryside, for example, and the consequent distinction, then particularly marked although not institutionally recognized, between urban and rural notaries), as well as differences in social background and the various institutional models of reference. The distinct contrasts among various local notarial traditions – the Lombard *notariato* was different from the Neapolitan *notariato*, which again differed from the Piedmont *notariato* – were reflected in a diversity of cultural attitudes and social identifications.

Not surprisingly, therefore, it was the ideas and interests of the government on the one hand, and the Chamber of Deputies (with lawyers in the majority) on the other, that came to predominate. The central thrust of the new law – which stemmed directly from its pre-Unification antecedents – was to classify the notary as a '*pubblico ufficiale*'.[10] The ruling class of post-Unification Italy, with its overriding concern to strengthen the weak structure of the state and to invigorate an even weaker national culture, therefore based its reorganization of the *notariato* on the late seventeenth-century model

[10] Fundamental insights into the relationships between 'office' and 'profession' (*Beruf*) are provided by the pages on bureaucracy in M. Weber's *Wirtschaft und Gesellschaft* and O. Hintze's treatment in *Der Beamtenstand*, now in *Soziologie und Geschichte: Gesammelte Abhandlungen zur Soziologie, Politik und Theorie der Geschichte*, Göttingen, 1964. See also J.L. Berlant, *Profession and Monopoly*, Berkeley, 1975. On the use of this concept in the historiography of the professions, see H. Siegrist, 'Public Office or Free Profession?', in G. Cocks, K. Jarausch (eds), *German Professions 1800–1950*, New York, and also A. La Vopa, *Prussian Schoolteachers. Profession and Office, 1763–1848*, Chapel Hill, NC, 1980.

of the 'state profession'.[11] The ideological premise of the 1875 law (and of the debate that attended its drafting) was, not coincidentally, the notion of a state power – a *certifying power* – which the state itself delegated to private individuals after obtaining guarantees of their moral probity and expertise, and after ensuring that such individuals could be controlled. It cannot be said that the notarial class actively sought out an alternative source of legitimation for its institutional role. As the building of the new national state proceeded, the majority of notaries believed that their classification as '*pubblico ufficiale*' would enhance a professional status and a 'dignity' which they felt to be greatly undervalued. Those that disagreed remained a tiny minority.[12] The desire for status of most notaries chimed well with political interests of the government, which was more than willing to grant a formal title of dignity in exchange for guaranteed control over the agents of political-social integration and mediation that the notaries were likely to become. And it also matched the corporatist interests of the lawyers, who were now entirely integrated into the government and the state institutions, and who hoped that the complex but 'logical' institutional edifice erected on the figure of the notary-public official would protect them against the claims for status and access to the market advanced by the more competitive components of the rival profession.

2. CREDENTIALS AND THE PROBLEM OF NOTARIAL CULTURE

Among the various consequences of the classification of the notary as a public official, it was the fact that a university degree was not one of the qualifications required for appointment as notary that for long represented one of the most significant and evident limits to the 'professionalization' of the Italian *notariato*. Two years of university legal studies, for a total of seven examinations and without a final dissertation, was all that the law required of the aspiring notary. Once again, the legislative definition of the profession was dominated by a conservative mentality. Possession of a degree in order to practise as a notary had been stipulated by the pre-Unification regu-

---

[11] See H. Siegriest, 'Professionalization as a Process: Patterns, Progression and Discontinuity' in M. Burrage, R. Torstendahl (eds), *Professions in Theory and History*, London, 1990, pp. 177–202.

[12] Among the very few contemporary defences of the notarial profession against state legitimation is the article by G. Cantalamessa in the Neapolitan *Gazzetta de' notai*, a. II, 1872, pp. 500–12 and 534–41; and the pamphlet by Tommaso Spinelli, *Sulle presenti condizioni del notariato*, Brescia, 1876.

lations only in Lombardy-Venetia, where, since the end of the eighteenth century, both a sizeable annual income and a university degree had been required of those who applied for the office.[13] The government's concern that it would prove impossible to find graduates willing to live in small municipalities – which constituted the majority of the notarial offices established by the *Tabella* – was, however, largely unfounded. In actual fact, many notaries already possessed a degree when the new law came into force.[14] The disequilibrium in the labour market between the supply of and demand for university graduates, which was entirely to the disadvantage of the former,[15] should have been a clear indicator that the obligation to reside in a small or a very small commune would not have seriously dissuaded young law graduates from embarking on a career as notary. And, moreover, there were numerous cases of members of the rural petty bourgeoisie who, on earning their degrees, returned to the provinces to practise the profession of notary in placid obscurity.

The problem of the credentials required to qualify as a notary long persisted as one of the dominant issues of debate within the profession. Several factors were involved. As many notaries had complained since Unification, the few and simple qualifications required by the law in every Italian region was one of the chief reasons for the 'decadence' of their profession caused by the proliferation of incompetent and unscrupulous practitioners. The new *ordinamento* not only failed to solve the problem, indeed it exacerbated it. The university course in notarial studies (*corso di notariato*), in fact, soon became a convenient shortcut for those who wished to acquire a qualification in higher education – a highly sought-after status symbol both in the liberal period and subsequently.[16] Those who took advantage of this opportunity benefited from lower enrolment fees (the fees for the *corso di notariato* were fixed at one-third of those for the complete course in legal studies) and a lighter study load, given the indulgence customa-

---

[13] See Liva, *Notariato*, and F. Mazzanti Pepe, G. Ancarani, *Il notariato in Italia*. More ambiguously, a course in legal studies similar in terms of years of study to a degree course – although formally distinct from it – was instituted in the Duchy of Parma in 1844.

[14] Examination of professional registers reveals that 10% of the notaries practising in Turin in 1876 possessed university degrees, 24% of those in Novara (Piedmont) in 1877, 28% of those in Perugia in 1881, and 20% of those in Lucca in 1883: see M. Santoro, 'Notai e notariato in Italia', p. 207.

[15] M. Barbagli, *Education for Unemployment: Politics, Labor Markets and the School System. Italy, 1859–1973*, New York, 1982.

[16] See the ample testimony quoted in M. Barbagli, *Education for Unemployment*.

rily shown by the lecturers towards those of their students hoping to
qualify as notaries.[17]

It was therefore this unrestricted entry to the profession that lent
strategic significance to the demand for higher educational standards
advanced by so many notaries. More than this, however, it was the
desire to narrow the symbolic gap between the professions of notary
and lawyer (for the latter, possession of a degree was confirmed as obligatory by the regulatory law of 1874) which induced the most competitive and highly motivated (one might almost say 'professionalized')
segments of the profession to press for educational qualifications to be
raised.

However, the government's concern to create a network of public
officials as guarantors of property rights and representatives of the new
legal and political order, even in the most outlying areas of the
country, once again found its natural allies in the traditionally most privileged groups of the legal profession. Despite the demand by the notaries for restricted entry to their profession – perhaps the only issue on
which their conflicting interests and disparate aspirations converged –
it was the desire not to upset consolidated power relationships within
the legal professions, dominated as they were by lawyers and, to a
lesser extent, magistrates, that once again prevailed. The notary, as a
famous lawyer deputy said in Parliament, 'must know little and know
it well; he must not lose himself in the boundless ocean of the entire
science of law'.[18] And on another occasion, a parliamentary speech-
maker declared:

> The notary is not obliged to draw up the deed, to devise and to compose
> the contract; it is the lawyers, the consultants and similar who ordinarily
> attend to this task. Notaries are called upon only to receive the deed, to
> compile it and to give it legal form [...] This is the essential part of the
> notary's functions: to compile the deed with order, with clarity, with pre-
> cision, so that it gives rise to no doubts and raises no questions before the
> magistrate. Since the function of the notary is restricted to this, I believe
> it is excessive to demand a degree in jurisprudence, to oblige the young
> aspirant to follow an entire university course lasting a full four years, as
> well as courses at gymnasium and high school.[19]

This model of the division of labour derived from the history itself of
the two professions, the relationships between them, and above all the

[17] See G. Sacerdoti, 'Sul corso per il notariato nella facoltà di giurisprudenza', L'Uni-
      versità italiana, 1988.
[18] See Atti parlamentari. Senato. Discussioni. Sessione 1867–68. Tornata del 3/12/1868
      (Conforti).
[19] See Atti parlamentari. Camera. Discussioni. Tornata 26/5/1875 (Samarelli).

relationships of each of them with the university and the state. The problem of the status of notarial knowledge was of ancient origin. It had begun with the medieval classification of knowledge (the *ars notariae* was originally part of the university for artists, not that for jurists). Subsequently, between the sixteenth and eighteenth centuries, it ramified into the complex interprofessional relationships that obtained among *giureconsulti* (lawyers), *causidici* and notaries. And it culminated in the functional and social juridical hierarchy internal to the 'legal field' on whose lowest rung stood, as we have seen, the notary.[20] The system of the legal division of labour which had emerged during the two previous centuries (structured into a stratified hierarchy on the one hand, and a set of linked groups and tasks on the other) therefore constituted a formidable cultural legacy which the simple formal provision of higher credentials for entry to the *notariato* – proposed, among others, by the central committee of the Senate – was unable to dispel. To the extent that interests are conveyed by ideal universes, it would not be an exaggeration to assert that an entire cultural constellation was called into question by the demand that notaries should possess degrees.

However, the example of the Lombard *notariato* provided a precedent on which legitimate claims could be based.[21] It was therefore, of course, the notaries of the former Kingdom of Lombardy and Venetia who most vigorously campaigned for the legal requirements for admittance to their profession to be raised to include a university degree. But pressures on Parliament to increase the level of notarial credentials were applied by notaries in other regions of Italy as well, including the

---

[20] See C. Mozzarelli, 'Strutture sociali'; E. Brambilla, 'Genealogie del sapere', *Schifanoia*, 8, 1989, pp. 123ff; M.C. Zorzoli, *Università, dottori, giureconsulti*, Padua, 1986. Analytically important is P. Bourdieu, 'La force du droit. Elements pour une sociologie du champ juridique', *Actes de la recherche en sciences sociales*, 1, 1986, pp. 3–33, from which I draw my notion of 'legal field'.

[21] On the division of labour between notaries and lawyers in nineteenth-century Lombardy – as a significant exception to the rule resulting from recent social and institutional change – see A. Liva, 'Le professioni liberali e i loro collegi: gli avvocati', in C. Mozzarelli, R. Pavoni (eds), *Milano fin de siècle e il caso Bagatti Valsecchi*, Milan, 1991, pp. 319–33; N. Raponi, 'Il Regno Lombardo-Veneto (1815–1859/66)', in *Amministrazione della giustizia e poteri di polizia dagli stati preunitaria alla caduta della destra*, pp. 93ff. For historical precedents, essential reading are C. Mozzarelli, 'Strutture sociali', and E. Brambilla, 'Il "sistema letterario" di Milano: professioni nobili e professioni borghesi dall'età spagnola alla riforma teresiana', in A. De Maddalena, E. Rotelli, G. Barbarisi (eds), *Economia, istituzioni, cultura in Lombardia nell'età di Maria Teresa*, vol. III, Bologna, 1982. On the social figure of the lawyer in nineteenth-century Lombardy see also H. Siegrist, 'Gli avvocati nell'Italia del XIX secolo. Provenienza e matrimoni, titolo e prestigio', *Meridiana*, 14, 1992, pp. 145–81.

former Kingdom of Naples. In the absence of a course of higher study for a notarial career expressly envisaged by university regulations, it was a degree in law that was most frequently cited. But there were some who went further to urge that the notary should be recognized not just as a 'jurist', but as a jurist *sui generis*, and that the *ars notariae* – which in the early 1800s had entirely disappeared from university curricula in Italy[22] – should be recognized as an autonomous specialization in jurisprudence. In Parliament this opinion found an authoritative spokesman in the person of Giuseppe Sclopis, the eminent jurist and historian of law. But it soon came to coincide with the aspirations of those who campaigned for the notary to be granted professional autonomy and a specific, non-subordinate role in the 'legal field'.

In actual fact, as we have seen, many notaries were already graduates when the new law came into force, and graduate notaries grew in numbers in the years that followed (see Fig. 3.1). Two factors were responsible for this development. First, the market's reduced capacity to absorb university graduates obliged many of them to undertake careers for which a degree was not required; and of the various career opportunities available to the *dottore in giurisprudenza*, that of notary was one that closely corresponded to his academic studies.

Second, matching this external factor was an internal one determined by the same institutional mechanism that tied the university and professional systems together. The Law of 1875 set out a career structure for notaries divided into four basic stages: acquisition of the notarial diploma, a two-year period of practical training, a qualifying examination (success in which earned the candidate the title of notary, but not the right to practise), and, finally, an appointment following a public competition. However, many years could pass before a young diploma-holder obtained his appointment as notary, the chief criterion for which was chronological 'seniority of examination' (*anzianità di esame*). The incentive to continue one's studies while waiting for an appointment, however, was only one of the unforeseen consequences of this institutional mechanism.[23] A second, and in this case perverse, effect was that the notarial profession became a comfortable retreat for elderly lawyers, prosecutors or public functionaries, who were able to dust off a qualification as notary (the Law of 1875, indeed, eased the passage of lawyers and prosecutors by reducing their period of practical training to six months) and take up a post in congenial surroundings. Many of the graduate notaries, in fact, belonged to this category.

22 A. Anselmi, *Le scuole di notariato in Italia*, Viterbo, 1926. It was only in the universities of Modena and Pavia that the teaching of notarial law continued until 1859.

23 See for this concept, R. Boudon, *Effets pervers et ordre social*, Paris, 1977.

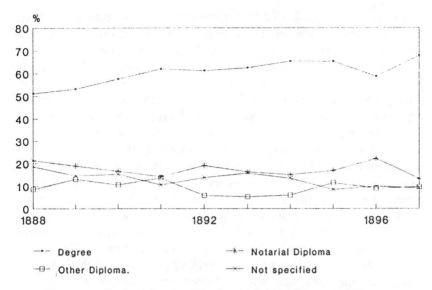

Figure 3.1. Credentials of notaries by year of appointment 1888–97

Very soon, however, this system of equilibria began to show signs of breaking down: a development which, in the next few decades, prompted certain segments of the profession to return with increasing insistence to the problem of credentials and to the question of their professional status. As both individuals and local associations, they vociferously stated their case at conferences and in protest action. Meanwhile, in 1906, the *Scuola Libera per il Notariato* was founded in Rome, the first professional training institute to be managed independently by the category.

3. SOCIAL BACKGROUND AND CRITERIA FOR RECRUITMENT

Although the 1875 law confirmed the practice of *numerus clausus* – as already stipulated by most of the pre-Unification *ordinamenti* – and thus granted the profession the privilege of a form of institutionalized closure, the number and especially the quality of practitioners of the profession were frequently a matter of heated controversy, both internally to the profession and between it and the public powers. As regards the number of notaries, the issue was institutional in nature. The table drawn up by the government on advice from the provincial councils, and which came into force jointly with the new *legge notarile* of 1875, had in fact considerably reduced the number of posts relative to the notaries then in practice, thereby creating the category of notaries '*in sovrappiù* (in surplus): that is, notaries confirmed as entitled to practise but in district offices which no longer officially existed. Of the 7,954 notaries confirmed, some 1,731 were '*in sovrappiù*', and of these 56 per cent practised in the southern regions of the country.[24] Although the Law of 1875 stipulated that the table was to be revised every ten years, no government took it upon itself to review the number and distribution of the notarial posts established by decree in 1876, and then again in 1882; and no attempt was made to adjust to the major social and economic changes sweeping through Italy in those end-of-century decades. Increased literacy reduced demand for the services of a notary, services which were once necessary for the drafting of even the simplest deed. The urbanization of broad strata of society altered the balance between city and countryside and therefore between demand for notarial services in rural areas on the one hand, and in urban areas on the other. Apart from these changes, in the first years of application of the new *ordinamento* it became obvious that many of the *sedi* established by the table were almost entirely unproductive, and that they could not guarantee even a minimal income for their incumbents. And now the notary's economic problems combined with the qualitative issue of his social status in post-Unification Italy.

But who became a notary? From what social strata did the notaries in practice at the turn of the century spring? Contemporary data on the social origin of Italian notaries are extremely sparse, but sources indicate that most of them belonged to the middle and lower landowning classes.[25] In a social structure still dominated by agriculture, the category of 'landowner' obviously comprised, in the large majority of cases, social actors tied to the land: and this seems confirmed, at least indirectly, by the high degree of 'rurality' that still characterized the profession in terms of the geographical provenance of its practitioners at the end of the nineteenth century. But the category also comprised sections of an upwardly mobile urban bourgeoisie whose links with the land were growing increasingly tenuous – although the weight of this social category of origin apparently decreased over time.

In Milan (Table 3.2), 19 per cent of the notaries practising in 1876 were the sons of landowners, and 13 per cent in 1893. The percentage was a little higher in less urbanized areas: for example in the district of Novara, in Piedmont (Table 3.3), 18.5 per cent of notaries active in the period

---

24 Of the 6,322 posts created by the new *tabella*, 100 were vacant because they were newly instituted. Although 56% of the surplus notaries practised in southern Italy, 70% of the vacant posts were situated in the North. See Archivio Centrale dello Stato, *Ministero di Grazia e Giustizia. Matricole notai. Elenco dei notai confermati.*

25 See, for example, *La Riforma del notariato*, 1902, p. 172.

Table 3.2 *Social origins of notaries in Milan, 1847–1911 (%)*

Father's occupation	Year of practice			
	1847/57	1876	1893	1911
Notary	14.2	8.4	6.6	11.6
Lawyer	14.2	1.7	1.6	6.6
Physician/engineer	–	13.5	11.6	5.0
Other profession	2.3	6.7	11.6	8.3
Landowner	16.6	18.6	13.3	13.3
Public official	4.7	11.8	10.0	10.0
Clerk	7.1	8.4	6.6	3.3
Merchant/shopkeeper	7.1	16.9	16.6	15.0
Manufacturer	2.3	–	1.6	3.3
Craftsman	–	1.7	1.6	3.3
Unknown	30.9	10.1	15.0	20.0
Total	100.0	100.0	100.0	100.0
N	(42)	(59)	(60)	(60)

Sources: Archivio Centrale dello Stato (Rome); Archivio anagrafico del Comune di Milano; Archivio storico civico del Comune di Milano; Archivio della Diocesi di Milano. For more detailed information see M. Santoro, 'Notai e notariato in Italia. Sociologia storica di una professione', unpublished PhD thesis, Università di Trento, 1993.

1885–91 came from landowning families, a proportion which increases further if one omits the notaries working in the city of Novara itself. In this same area, however, at the end of the eighteenth century the recruitment rate from the landowning class amounted to 28 per cent.[26]

The impact of this social change on the expectations and needs of late nineteenth-century notaries should not be underestimated. As a professional journal pointed out at the time:

> In the past, a village which was not a *sede notarile* could become one if a person possessing the appropriate qualifications applied for appointment as its notary. This individual was almost always a local landowner, and the practice of the profession enabled him to earn an income, even if a small

[26] These figures are taken from a survey (begun in January 1990 and still in progress) of the families of origin and arrival of a number of samples of notaries practising in the nineteenth and twentieth centuries, the sources for which are principally public records (household registers, population rolls, registers of births, marriages and deaths) and church records (baptism certificates). For a more detailed description see M. Santoro, 'Notai e notariato in Italia', chs. 7 and 11.

Table 3.3 *Social origins of notaries in the district of Novara (Piedmont),*
1826–91

	Year of practice			
Father's occupation	1826–44	%	1885–91	%
Notary	40	35.1	12	17.1
Lawyer/physician	10	8.8	8	11.4
Other profession	9	7.9	8	11.4
Landowner	11	9.6	13	18.5
Merchant/shopkeeper	4	3.5	11	15.7
Clerk	2	1.7	2	2.8
Farmer	–	–	2	2.8
Unknown	38	33.3	14	20.0
N	*114*	*100.0*	*70*	*100.0*

Sources: Consiglio notarile di Novara; Archivio di Stato di Novara; Archivio anagrafico del Comune di Novara; Archivio diocesano di Novara. For more detailed information about the sources see M. Santoro, 'Notai e notariato'.

one, without leaving his home district. Therefore, the applicant for the institution of the new *sede notarile* assured the state that he was economically self-sufficient, and when that same *sede* was offered to applicants on the death or retirement of the first incumbent, the state was obliged to guarantee the new aspirant a quantity of business at least sufficient to maintain a modest lifestyle.[27]

Although, at an aggregate level, it would be foolhardy to draw one-to-one connections between social origins and attitudes, and even more foolhardy to seek to document them, we may assume that it was precisely this social change that led to the greater 'professionalization' of the notary because it induced large sections of the profession to mobilize, even if they came from different cultural backgrounds and had different attitudes. (In any case, seeking to gain control of the market is different from claiming a salary from the state, although both behaviours stem from the same desire for a guaranteed source of income.)

Whoever these landowners actually were – *rentiers* in the strict sense of the term, or scions of the aristocracy or the offspring of wealthy bourgeois families – the term denotes a world of values and economic

[27] E. Duranti-Valentini, 'E' possibile la statizzazione del notariato?', *Gli Archivi Ita-liani*, 7, 1920, p. 55.

behaviour that had little in common with industry, trade and entrepreneurship. Nonetheless, also the world of business was amply represented by the families of origin of nineteenth-century notaries. In Milan, for example, 15 per cent of the notaries practising in the second half of the 1800s and the early 1900s came from families of shopkeepers and traders. A similar percentage was recorded in the district of Novara, a finding that confirms the close links between a profession which by its very nature engaged in economic and social affairs, and local society.

However, the majority of notaries – around 18 per cent of the samples analysed, with a tendency to increase over time – belonged to families of self-employed professionals: other notaries, physicians, and engineers, more rarely lawyers and surveyors. Analysis of kinship relations also reveals a complex pattern of interprofessional links and connections; and these, in their turn, reflect the operation of forms of extra-institutional social regulation based on a ramified system of alliances and closures. These relationships, which were familial and professional at the same time, underpinned systems of identity which are difficult to define but which certainly influenced behaviour.

To summarize the information at our disposal, we may therefore say that most nineteenth-century Italian notaries were members of families which belonged to the urban and rural middle class; families which often rode the crest of intergenerational processes of upward social mobility. However, cases of notaries from families belonging to the great property-owning or commercial class, or to the higher echelons of the civil service, were not uncommon. Only an extremely small proportion of Italian notaries, however, originated from the two extremes of the social scale: the nobility and the working class. Moreover, in the former case one discerns a fall in the numbers of new recruits to the profession, while there was a slight increase in the latter. A number of factors were responsible for this phenomenon: the relatively lower level of education required for entry to the profession, which, as we have seen, involved fewer years of study (and therefore of absence from the labour market) as well as considerably less expense; the relaxation of the census and status requirements imposed by pre-Unification legislation; the relative ease of access to the profession sanctioned by a law which set *anzianità di esame* as the most important criterion – which although objective was both professionally and socially controversial – for appointment as a notary. A situation thus arose in which individuals possessing a diploma or an equivalent qualification took the examinations required to qualify as a notary. But they only utilized their qualification after many years devoted to another occupation, in order to settle into the comfortable notarial business to which they were entitled by the seniority increments they had accrued on the basis of *anzianità di esame*. Indeed, some of them offered to sell the withdrawal of their candidature to the highest bidder among the other less 'qualified' candidates. Consequently, surreptitiously and illegally, a vein of corruption crept through the profession.

As regards the closure of the profession, the problem of the system of recruitment established by the Law of 1875 centred on the fact that entry to the career as notary was left 'entirely open to anyone who at any time possessed entitlement to practise as a notary',[28] regardless of their preparation and competence. The consequences were not only the gradual 'ageing' of the notarial profession compared with the others, but also the spread of a general climate of petty corruption, and above all – as the notaries themselves often stressed – lower standards of professional service.

From the point of view of collective action, this system generated formidable pressures which gradually gave a unitary collective identity to the manifold social orientations, career paths, expectations and individual identities which at the end of the century still seemed, in sociological terms, to form the majority of notaries into an 'amorphous group'. In actual fact, extra-institutional social mechanisms made the profession much less open than professional rhetoric claimed, although rates of professional self-recruitment progressively declined during the nineteenth century. In the college of Novara, for instance, they dropped from around 30 per cent to values between 10 and 20 per cent (Table 3.4). How far this was due to the lesser attractiveness of the profession or to the weaker resistance of forms of corporative closure is difficult to say. The introduction throughout Italy of public archives, in which notarial deeds and records were deposited on the death of the notary who had stipulated them, radically changed the parameters determining the calculation of the economic convenience of pursuing the paternal profession of notary; a choice previously strongly influenced by the fact (at least in the regions where there were no notarial archives, like Piedmont or the Kingdom of the Two Sicilies) that the notary's deeds and therefore his clients automatically passed to his heirs. This patrimonial practice whereby an office was handed down from father to son – sometimes from uncle to nephew – was deeply ingrained in the profession's culture, and the authorities (including the ministry of justice itself) were loath to obstruct it: as

[28] A. Moretti *et al.*, *Concorsi e nomine*, Milan, 1922.

Table 3.4 *Self-recruitment rates among notaries practising in Milan and in the district of Novara (Piedmont), as a percentage of notaries with a notary father, 1770–1911*

	Year of exercise						
	1770–1800	1826–44	1847–57	1876	1885–91	1893	1911
Milan			14.2	8.4		6.6	11.6
Novara (district)	28.6	35.1			17.1		
N	171	114	42	59	70	60	60

Sources: see tables 3.2 and 3.3.

witness the frequency with which the public authorities tolerated the delayed announcement of public competitions for vacant posts, and their promptness in approving transfers and exchanges among notaries of very different ages (often fathers and sons).

4. PROFESSIONAL MARKET AND JURISDICTIONAL CONFLICTS

Unlike medicine, which has acquired importance as an economic activity only in the past two centuries, by its very nature the notarial profession has always been enmeshed in market relations and structures. Long before the Great Transformation, notaries performed their clerical and legal services in circuits of economic and social exchange and received payment in return.[29] The close contacts between the profession and the world of business, trade and entrepreneurship reverberated through the tight network of kinship relations that united the two groups, and they induced notaries closely to monitor the economic aspects of their profession: from control over access to their market sector to the fixing of notarial fees. In more abstract terms, the principal problem for the profession was striking a balance between the largely autonomous occupational control ensured by the availability of a large clientele[30] and the preservation of the two advantages deriving from state control: the legal specification of the size of the profession (and

[29] See Cipolla, 'The Professions'; A. Petrucci, *Notarii*; M. Berengo, 'Lo studio degli atti notarili dal XIV secolo al XVI secolo', in Istituto Storico Italiano per il Medievo, *Fonti medievali e problematica storiografica*, Rome, 1976, vol. I; P. Jones, 'La storia economica', in *Storia d'Italia Einaudi*, vol. II, part ii, Turin, 1972.

[30] A.T. Johnson, *Power and Profession*, London, 1972.

therefore institutional control over supply), and obligatory recourse to notarial services (and therefore guaranteed demand).[31]

The birth of the unified state and the building of a national market had repercussions in every economic and social sphere, but two factors in particular influenced the notarial profession's market: the new tax system and the new legal codes.

The impact of the new fiscal measures on the notarial labour market was, in certain cases, traumatic. As a notary in the ex-Kingdom of Naples wrote concerning the so-called '*legge di bollo e registro*' (the law which introduced stamp duty in Italy):

> Since the law of 21 April 1862 was passed, the profession has been reduced to miserable economic conditions. The law has now been in force for three years, and in each of these years the number of notarial acts has fallen by more than two-thirds with respect to the number that used to be stipulated before 1862.[32]

According to figures compiled by notarial chambers and sent to the ministry – figures which provided the basis for discussion in Parliament on reforming the tax law – in the ex-Kingdom of the Two Sicilies the number of contracts and deeds had shrunk by almost half since the introduction of the new fiscal measures. Compared to the 1,646,000 registered in the three-year period 1857–59, public deeds amounted to only slightly more than 800,000 in the equivalent period 1863–65. Nor, moreover, was it solely the contingent fact of the *legge di bollo e registro* (which in any case was reformed in 1866 following the outburst of protest) that adversely influenced the work of the notary and altered its coordinates. It was the overall change in the institutional context that shook the set of social relations which time and 'accommodations' had gradually created. The de-

---

[31] Of course, a market in the abstract sense of a network of exchange relations governed solely by considerations of efficiency and utility has never existed as regards the notarial profession, and nor has it for any other profession. Like other markets – and perhaps more so, given the particular nature of the services exchanged – professional markets are social and institutional constructs whose forms and regulatory criteria can be identified. See M. Granovetter, 'The Old and the New Economic Sociology: A History and an Agenda', in R. Friedland, A.C. Robertson (eds), *Beyond the Marketplace: Rethinking Economy and Society*, New York, 1990; A. Abbott, *The System of the Professions*; E.M. Burrage, K. Jarausch, H. Siegriest, 'An Actor-based Framework for the Study of Professions', in M. Burrage, R. Torstendahl (eds), *Professions in Theory and History*.

[32] F. Noschese, *Idee intorno ad una riforma del notariato*, Salerno, 1865, pp. 10–11. For a detailed picture of post-Unification fiscal policy, with a wealth of data on its impact on economic transactions, see G. Alessio, *Saggio sul sistema tributario in Italia*, Turin, 1887, vol. II.

clarations made to the Committee of Inquiry on the Palermo Uprisings of 1866 by the president of the local notarial chamber graphically summed up the situation:

> The class of notaries is dissatisfied with the *legge del registro*, by the lack of public law and order, by the measure which attributes notarial practice regarding certain deeds to various functionaries who do not vouch for their quality [...] Contracts by public deed are replaced by bills of exchange, or other means are used for routine deeds of minor importance concerning the circulation of securities. The profession of notary in Palermo now yields less than half the income of 1859 [...] The profession has been ruined by the tax on contracts [...] The poor people refrain from having the appropriate deeds drawn up in order to avoid paying the tax.[33]

Unfortunately, reliable information is not available for systematic comparison between the situations before and after Unification as regards notarial practice in the south of Italy.[34] However, the statistics published from the 1890s onwards show that although the market may have collapsed immediately after Unification, it nevertheless revived in the decades that followed. In any case, in the South the number of notarial deeds relative to the population was systematically higher than in other regions of the country. The ratio is reversed, however – and thus demonstrates the economic weakness of the southern notaries compared with their counterparts in the rest of the country – when the size of the market is set against the number of practising notaries: for instance, in 1901, while 193 deeds per notary were recorded in northern Italy, the average was only 139 in the South (excluding Sicily). But it was above all the quality of the deeds drawn up that differed between North and South, not so much in terms of the *type* of acts as in terms of their *economic value*. The territorial structure of notarial income shows the geographical differentiation of notarial practice at the turn of the century very clearly. Again

[33] M. Da Passano (ed.), *Inchiesta sui moti di Palermo del 1866*, Rome, 1981, p. 207.
[34] Complete series of notarial statistics are only available for the post-Unification period. These statistical series have been published since 1896: first by the *Direzione Generale della Statistica*, then by the *Ministero di Giustizia*, and finally by Istat. However, figures on the amount of notarial work before 1896 can be derived from the financial statistics published by the *Ministero delle Finanze*. Comparative analysis of the figures relative to two base years – one before and one after Unification for a restricted geographical area (Piedmont, Liguria and Sardinia) – clearly show a downward trend with respect to the population (with the exception of Sardinia), but a *marked upward trend with respect to the individual notary*; a pattern obviously determined by the reduction in the number of notaries by the new *tabella*. See M. Santoro, *Notai*.

in 1901, the fees earned by notaries in northern Italy amounted to 2,066 lire per head, in central Italy to 1,745 lire, but in southern Italy only to 1,182 lire.[35]

A further factor influencing the size and structure of the market for notarial services was the new civil code. In 1865, the *Commissione per la Formazione del Codice* completed its work. No notary had been invited to sit on the committee: a clear sign of the scant legal expertise attributed to the notarial profession. The outcome – which was undoubtedly due to manifold ideological and political factors which went beyond the more circumscribed criterion of interprofessional competition – was a further restriction of the notarial function, with the same legal value attributed to contracts drawn up between private individuals as to the notarial act, and recourse to the latter made obligatory for only two kinds of transaction: gifts and marriage covenants (for the settlement of dowries). It was the *laissez-faire* conception of society and the notion of the free market that pushed in this direction, and one notes with interest that the 'bourgeois' liberalization of the goods market had the paradoxical effect of restricting other secondary markets, such as that for notarial services. Nonetheless, the notarial profession did not decline in following years, in fact, despite the gloomy forecasts of contemporary commentators.[36] Indeed, the overall number of notarial deeds had risen to one million by 1896. Notarial work, moreover, continued to ramify through a broad range of sectors and gave rise to a wide typology of deeds: from mortgages to proxies, from agrarian contracts to contracts for the sale of real property, from settlements of estates to contracts of hire, etc.

Statistics on business taxes also show signs of growth in the latter years of the 1880s. Despite these positive indicators, however, the notaries continued to complain about the decline in notarial work provoked by the processes of 'social modernization' which were changing

---

[35] See Ministero di Grazia e Giustizia, *Statistica notarile per gli anni 1901–1910*, Rome, 1915. Sicily recorded the highest average level of fees: 1,850 lire. Note that the notarial statistics refer only to fees '*di rogito*', i.e. those earned for the attestation of documents. In order to calculate notaries' total incomes, the figures should be doubled. See V. Frugis, 'La riforma economica del notariato', *Il Filangieri*, 1914, p. 55.

[36] Among the factors usually cited are increasing literacy, urbanization, the widespread use of bills of exchange. See, for example, the introductory pages to A. Garetti, *Manuale del notaio*, Milan, 1893, and, as an example of reactions external to the profession, the report presented by Ettore Pistoni to the *Commissione per la Statistica Giudiziaria* and published in *Annali di statistica. Atti della Commissione per la Statistica giudiziaria e notarile*, s. IV, Rome, 1906, pp. 105ff.

the face of Italian society.[37] The fact is that the notaries were not the only category, and certainly not the first one, to benefit from this revival of business caused by an increase in transactions and contracts (an upturn also due to the fact that, twenty years after the introduction of the new tax regime, the population had by now grown accustomed to it, and because the circuits of domestic trade were now progressively expanding). It was on the *distribution* of work, in fact, that the grievances and claims of the notarial profession came to focus in the last decades of the century.

Having long lost its *monopoly* over documentation and certification, the nineteenth-century *notariato* fought to protect its few remaining functions and to regain some of the jurisdictions it had lost to other occupations. The protests by notaries against the 'usurpation' of their functions by clerks (in particular, those working in the municipal and provincial administrations), by mayors, by clerks of the court, by bailiffs, rose to a crescendo. That it was mainly economic interests which induced the notaries to press for the 'restoration' of their functions seems difficult to refute. But the foundation of the notaries' jurisdictional claim, they argued, was that it was in the public interest. The scant legal expertise of the clerks, whose only qualification was a licence obtained on leaving secondary school; the role they played in transactions, where they naturally promoted the interests of the body that employed them; their lack of caution, which the law instead imposed on the notary: these features, according to the notaries, demonstrated their 'moral' and juridical superiority over the clerks. However, the radical change in the administrative apparatus that had begun earlier in the century and which was now accelerating in those final decades aborted any chance of success that the profession's attempt to recover the jurisdictional area now occupied by the clerks might have had.[38]

Less inevitable in its outcome was the notaries' conflict with their other great rivals: the lawyers. Although numerically and politically (and also often socially) more powerful, the lawyers enjoyed a situation of advantage that had its roots less in the present (or in the

---

[37] During the 1890s the professional press underwent a significant change: from periodicals of a principally technical-legal character, the notarial journals (notably *Bollettino notarile* of Turin, *Rolandino* of Florence, *Il Giornale de' notari* of Rome, *Il notariato italiano* of Palermo) increasingly became arenas for debate on the institutional and economic problems of the profession.

[38] On the history of the municipal clerks in post-Unification Italy, see R. Romanelli, *Sulle carte interminate*, Bologna, 1988.

future) than in the past. The relationship between the work of the notaries and that of the lawyers had for long been a matter of controversy. Indeed, only in recent years has a solution to the problem been found in an equable division of labour: in the last century, the situation was very different. Innumerable and invariably tedious protests appeared in the professional press denouncing the weak and exploited situation of many notaries (especially in certain regions) vis-à-vis the lawyers: a sort of mix between subordination and what Abbott would call the lawyer's 'intellectual jurisdiction'[39] over all legal matters, with only routine tasks being delegated to the notary. The consequences of this subordination of the notary to the lawyer, which on occasion reduced the former to a sort of paid hireling of the latter, were numerous, and the notaries were not always entirely aware of them. Not only were the notary's professional image and dignity damaged, and legal obligations flouted (for example, that of conserving the original copies of deeds in the notary's office), but compliant notaries (disparagingly known as 'bollatori', or stamp-lickers, since their principal function was to affix the stamps to documents drawn up by the lawyer) were in illicit and damaging competition with other notaries. Moreover, although subordination to the lawyer could give the notary preferential access to clients (those of the lawyer) which would otherwise be difficult to find, the price was always a drastic reduction of fees, even to a third of that established by the tariffa (the table of notarial charges).

The jurisdictional conflict between the two professions had both ancient and recent origins. Chief among the latter was the marked imbalance between the demand and supply of labour which characterized the Italian legal profession in the first decades after Unification. Whereas the adult male population increased by 13.5 per cent between 1880 and 1913, the number of lawyers and prosecutors enrolled on the professional registers rose by 67 per cent. In the same period, moreover, the number of criminal sentences of major importance remained substantially the same, or almost, while civil actions actually diminished.[40] The competition between notaries and lawyers was therefore principally economic in character, although it was incorporated into a wider and more 'noble' rhetorical framework of cultural and political legitimation. The first blow against these old equilibria, which the Law of 1875 had helped to perpetuate, was delivered by the long-awaited reform of 1913.

[39] A. Abbott, The System of Professions.
[40] See P. Calamandrei, Troppi avvocati, Florence, 1921, p. 53.

5. FROM THE REFORM OF 1913 TO THE CREATION OF THE
CASSA NAZIONALE

The Reform Law of 1913 – the law which, although emended and supplemented, still today regulates the notarial profession in Italy – was the outcome of a long and difficult process, the origin of which dated back to the promulgation of the Consolidation Act on the *notariato* in 1879 which collected together the first and minor alterations made to the Law of 1875 when the Left came to power. Shortly afterwards, in 1882, a further Congress of Notaries (the third to proclaim itself 'national') was organized in Milan to discuss the additional problems for the profession created by application of the law. It was on this occasion that the issue of professional freedom was first seriously discussed by notaries – although the general conclusion was to confirm the hybrid situation decreed by the law. This Congress was followed six years later by a Conference in Bologna attended by representatives of the *Consigli Notarili* (numbering about forty, they represented a quarter of the *Consigli* then in existence); and subsequently, in 1891, a further Congress was held, this time in Turin.

Only in the next decade, however, were the social and political conditions ripe for the systematic mobilization of large sections of the profession. This mobilization took concrete form in the convocation of another Congress in Naples on the initiative of the notaries Michele Fava and Giuseppe Romano – the former since 1903 the editor of a new journal, *La Riforma del Notariato*, whose political programme was manifest in its title, and the latter a parliamentary deputy. The Naples Congress was the occasion of the founding of the *Federazione Notarile Italiana* – the first organization for the *notariato* to be created on a national scale after the failure of more limited attempts at association in the first years after Unification. The appointment by the Minister of Justice, Finocchiaro-Aprile, of a ministerial committee to examine reform of the *notariato* – a few months after the Congress and under pressure by a delegation from the *Federazione* – crowned the initiative with success.

The Congress of Naples undoubtedly marked a turning-point in the strategy so far pursued by the profession. The distinguishing features of this earliest form of notarial trade-unionism represented by the *Federazione* were the priority given to the profession's conditions of practice and its organizational forms, an emphasis on concrete action rather than on doctrinal elaboration, and a language inspired more by the class culture of the workers' movement than by the 'refined' dis-

136

MARCO SANTORO

course of academia and scientific conferences.[41] For the segments of
the profession belonging to the Federation, the 'questione notarile' was
essentially economic in nature: unrestricted competition, the reduction
of fees, disparities in earnings, were its main ingredients. The institutional remedies took either the form of local economic associations
patterned on mutual benefit societies, with the profits distributed
among the notaries belonging to the college, or the radical transformation of the notariato from the partially 'free' profession – which despite
everything it still continued to be – into a salaried public appointment.
In the latter case the 'professional freedom' of the notary would have
been annulled, but also in the former it would have been substantially
restricted: the compulsory association stipulated by the law was, in
fact, indispensable if the new institutional system was to function
properly.[42]

Between 1904 and 1906 the short life of the *Federazione Notarile
Italiana*, whose membership, in fact, had been almost entirely restricted
to notaries practising in southern Italy, came to an end. After two years
of sporadic action, of proposals advanced college by college, and of
local protests, it was the *collegi* of Rome and Milan which finally
managed to give systematic organization to the profession and to coor-
dinate its actions. In 1909 in Rome, under the 'benevolent protection'
of the then minister Orlando, the *Comitato Notarile Centrale Permanente*
was born. A Congress, not of notaries but of representatives from the
Consigli Notarili of the Kingdom (fully 127 out of 128), officiated at the
baptism of the *Comitato* which, despite its unorthodox beginnings,
could thus describe itself as the official representative body of the
Italian *notariato*. The 'notarial proletariat', whose 'redemption' Michele
Fava and his *Federazione* had sought to achieve, laboured to find organized expression. Thereafter it was no longer the democratic and radica-
lized spirit that had distinguished the Naples Congress and the
Federazione which imbued the movement of the *notariato*. It was now
the notaries practising in the big cities (with their greater volumes of
business and greater opportunities for profit) together with the
members of the *Consigli Notarili* – in short the elite of the profession –
who took over. And the composition of the *Comitato*, which was reflected in its executive committee, inevitably conditioned the professional policies which, between 1909 and 1912, it came to manage in
conditions of quasi-monopoly.

[41] See the *Atti del Congresso di Napoli*, Naples, 1905.
[42] *Voluntary* notarial associations modelled on mutual benefit societies appeared in the
early years of this century, especially among notaries belonging to colleges in
southern Italy. However, they were few in number and generally short-lived.

With the law of 1913 the aspirations of this elite segment of the notarial profession were satisfied. Confirmation and reinforcement of the 'free' nature of the profession, a broadening of functions, compulsory possession of a degree, merit and length of service as the principal selection criteria, an increase in fees and in the items on the *tariffa*, a relaxing of compulsory residence after the abolition of the obligation of permanent abode, the perpetuation of the district as the geographical ambit of the legitimate practice of the profession (as opposed to its further restriction to the borough that the supporters of the compulsory associations urged), a further reduction and redistribution of *sedi* according to the needs of the population and to the volume of business and without consulting the local administrations, increased collegial supervision of professional practice (without the creation – solicited by a number of ministerial plans – of the new bureaucratic body of the *ispettori del notariato*): with these and other measures, the manifest aim of the reform of 1913 was to propel the notarial system towards what sociologists and historians of the professions call the *professionalization* of an occupational group.

And yet it is only in certain respects that the central theme developed in this chapter can be identified as the 'history of the professionalization' of the Italian *notariato*. In actual fact, features of 'professionism' (such as the notion of public service, social closure, collegial autonomy, monopoly of the market, and to a certain extent its academic basis) had for long characterized the Italian notarial occupation in its centuries-long existence, albeit with certain variations in time and space. These features then merged during the nineteenth century into a hybrid structure with undefined boundaries, subject to ministerial and judicial control, endowed with (limited) powers of self-management and self-discipline, which however were rarely used, devoid in any case of a solid academic and cognitive basis, and almost everywhere dominated by the *avvocatura*. The reform of 1913 at least partly changed this situation. It was, however, only one stage in a broader process of socio-institutional transformation which, in 1921, led to the creation of a national notaries' fund, the *Cassa Nazionale del Notariato*, a public body established by law and under the direct tutelage of the ministry; and then five years later to a law which by establishing a nationwide competitive examination fixed uniform criteria for entry to the profession. The dramatic economic consequences of the First World War were the decisive factor in the former case, the centralizing policies of the new Fascist regime in the latter.

The *Cassa Nazionale del Notariato* – the first professional benevolent fund in Italy, soon to be imitated by other professions – was promoted by a new *Federazione Notarile* founded in 1918 on the initiative of the journal *Il Notaio* edited by Giuseppe Russo Ajello, a notary in Rome. It was then tenaciously advocated in Parliament by notary Giuseppe Micheli, a key figure in the Catholic movement and therefore in the *Partito Popolare* of Don Luigi Sturzo. The outcome of the high-level social and political relations manipulated by this leading exponent of the notarial profession (Micheli became Minister of Agriculture in 1920–21, and of Public Works in 1921–22), the creation of the *Cassa* was also and simultaneously the result of a complex game of 'political' mediations and trade-offs between the elite of the profession, firmly entrenched in its position of economic power and professional hege-mony, and that notarial 'proletariat' which had seen its hopes that the Reform Law of 1913 would improve its members' economic situation almost entirely dashed. Italy's entry into the First World War inevitably triggered new protest by this segment of the profession, which was the first to be affected by the economic consequences of the conflict. It was the creation in 1917 of a mutual fund to provide for the needs of the wives and children of notaries fighting at the front which led to the widespread recognition that some form of economic protection, long urged by the more disadvantaged members of the profession, was ne-cessary. The *Cassa* was a fund managed by a committee on which sat notaries elected by the members and representatives of the ministry, and it consisted of *compulsory* payments made by *all* notaries in propor-tion to their earnings. The institutional mechanism underpinning the *Cassa* reflected the delicate balance which had been achieved in those years among the various segments of the profession. On the one hand, it served to guarantee for all notaries a minimum income established by the law instituting the *Cassa*; an income revised upwards in subsequent years. This therefore provided a first solution to the so-called '*questione economica*' of the Italian *notariato*. On the other hand, and simultan-eously, it performed a crucial function of internal social control, both over the subversive and *étatist* aspirations of the most extremist fringes of the profession, and over more ostentatiously market-oriented forms of behaviour (competition, bargaining over fees) deleterious to the dignity and prestige of the profession. Above all, however, by linking the well-being of the socially and economically weaker segments of the profession to the earning capacity and power of its more dynamic ones, the *Cassa* was a force which unified and gave 'political synthesis' to the interests of all members of the category.

   The building of a collective professional identity was further stimu-lated by the 1926 Fascist law which reformed procedures for recruit-ment to the profession. Inspired by the entirely political goal of administrative centralization and rationalization pursued by the Fascist regime, this law introduced a national competitive examination as the new system of selection. This brought about the change from a localized and haphazard form of recruitment to that standardization of the 'production of service-producers' which Larson places at the heart of 'professionalization' processes.[43] But to what extent and in what sense can one speak of the 'professionalization' of the Italian *notariato* since Unification?

6. THE PROFESSIONALIZATION OF THE ITALIAN NOTARIAL PROFESSION?

As Burrage has pointed out in describing the French notaries, and anticipating the probable objections of his readers, 'to Anglo-American eyes the notaries are hardly a profession at all, since they are, in part, state functionaries'.[44] Suleiman, for his part, has shown how these same notaries have been able to prosper and defend their interests precisely because they operate *within* the state.[45]

The history of the Italian *notariato* demonstrates in effect that the 'state' (which is in fact a complex of forces symbolically united in the fiction of an alleged 'general interest' and, more recently, in the fiction of its legal 'personality') has always performed an important role in the definition of the social and institutional statutes of the profession. But the state's role has never been exclusive, since its action – with an assertiveness varying in time and space – has been mediated by broader social configurations of which the notaries, public functionaries, other professional groups, political parties and economic groups have been part.

The idea that 'state' and 'profession' are entities in antithesis to each other, the former seeking to exert control and the latter to apply pressure and to manipulate, stems from the crystallization of an ideological formula which the sociology and historiography of the professions are apparently still reluctant to recognize: the strict separation of 'state' and 'society'. It is only on this basis that the antithesis between 'professionalization from above' and 'professionalization from below' acquires significance. Social and political historiography, and their most influential

---

[43] M.S. Larson, *The Rise of Professionalism*, Berkeley, 1977.

[44] M. Burrage 'Introduction: The Professions in Sociology and History', in M. Burrage, R. Torstendahl (eds.), *Professions in Theory and History*, p. 13.

[45] E. Suleiman, *Private Power and Centralization*, and by the same author, 'State Structure and Clientelism: the French State Versus the "Notaires" ', *British Journal of Political Science*, 17, 1987, pp. 257–79.

practitioners, on the contrary, today recognize that the processes of state centralization, far from following a unitary and coherent logic, have been the outcome of an uninterrupted sequence, both arduous and fortuitous, of bargaining and compromise between the state apparatus and the centres of economic and social power.[46] A wholly similar pattern has been followed by the processes whereby those political and economic centres which are the 'professions' have been constructed. Institutions, both 'political' and 'economic' and therefore also 'professional', do not arise automatically in response to needs, nor do they follow the dictates of some sort of 'natural history'. On the contrary, they are constructed by individuals whose action is at once helped and constrained by the structure of the social networks to which they belong and to whose resources they have access.

Thus, by exploiting the change in social equilibria brought about by the advent of the Giolitti government, by tenaciously pursuing a strategy of pressure and negotiation *within and without* the state apparatus, a small elite centred on a nucleus of professional entrepreneurs in Rome and Milan conquered new 'jurisdictions',[47] greater collective autonomy, improved economic conditions, and a non-subordinate role in the legal hierarchy.[48] However, it is clear that the principal motive behind the vigorous action taken by the elite of the *notariato* was the desire − by now the necessity − to halt the excesses perpetrated by the mass of practitioners, that notarial 'proletariat' which had found its first form of aggregation in Fava's *Federazione*. With its tendency to collectivize and to create precarious profit-sharing associations, the 'proletariat', indeed, was now even ready to resort to strike action in order to resolve what was its most pressing problem: the *'problema economico'*.

The category of 'professional project' proposed by Larson[49] seems therefore to fit the case of the Italian *notariato* rather well. The 'professionalization' of an occupational group, however, is a phenomenon more complex than its collective action alone.[50] Far from being simply the outcome of systematic pressure applied by a social group, the stipulation of a university degree as a necessary qualification for entry to the notarial profession resulted from a long process of persua-

---

[46] See L. Ornaghi, ' "Crisi" del centro statale e "disseminazione" di centri politici. Note su un indice di trasformazione dello Stato moderno', *Quaderni sardi di storia*, 4, 1983–84, and by the same author, *Stato e corporazione*, Milan, 1983.

[47] A. Abbott, *The System of Professions*.

[48] P. Bourdieu, *La force du droit*.

[49] M.S. Larson, *The Rise of Professionalism*.

[50] A. Abbott, 'The Order of Professionalization', *Work and Occupation*, 1991, pp. 4, 355–84.

sion and mediation among contrasting forces and interests. The principal reason for the mobilization – albeit sporadic and disorganized – of certain sections of the profession, the degree requirement was also urged by academics, experts and reformers of the educational system, and by certain institutional bodies (such as the *Consiglio Superiore dell'Istruzione*) preoccupied by the element of irrationality introduced into the university legal curriculum by a course leading to a diploma in notarial studies.[51] The new law thus also satisfied the need for rationalization that was now manifest in society and in the administration. Secondly, raising the level of the profession's credentials (and even more so the assigning of new responsibilities to it) had the effect of curbing the power of the *avvocatura* by dismantling the often perverse system whereby the members of the lawyer elite could accumulate a variety of roles: political (the *avvocati deputati*, lawyer deputies), academic (the *avvocati giuristi*, the lawyer jurists) and professional (the *avvocati procuratori*, the lawyer prosecutors).[52] At the same time it provided an apparent, but politically effective, solution to one of the many cases of intellectual unemployment generated by the difficult relationship between the university system and the labour market in liberal Italy. Raising the credentials of the *notariato* to include a degree, in fact, gave symbolic legitimacy to the position of those graduates who had been obliged to 'settle for' a post as notary – 60 per cent of the new appointments in the 1890s – but who would never have accepted the subordinate role to the lawyers that public opinion attributed to them. But was it, in fact, the organizational effort of these actors that made the reform possible, marking an important milestone in the professionalization of the nineteenth-century Italian *notariato*? Or, instead, was it forces endogenous to the political-administrative system itself that prepared the ground for decisions that required little prompting?

The cultural and symbolic character of these processes should not be underestimated. In actual fact, no Italian in the first years after Unification would have seriously argued that the *notariato* was not a 'profession'; or even that it had once been a profession but now was one no

---

[51] See, for example, G. Sacerdoti, *Sul corso per il notariato nella Facoltà di giurisprudenza*; F. Martini, C.F. Ferraris, *Ordinamento generale degli istituti d'istruzione superiore*, Milan, 1895.

[52] This purely political need to restrict the legal profession had already been stressed by the report of the Senate central committee during discussion on the law of 1875; to no avail, however. The extent of the lawyers' concern about the effects of the new notarial law on their professional power emerges clearly from the speech made by Enrico Ferri to the Chamber of Deputies on 8 February 1913 and published in *La scuola positiva*, a. XXVIII, s. III, vol. IV, 1913, pp. 103–8.

142   MARCO SANTORO

longer. In specialized journals, in speeches to parliament, in official
documents, the notary was referred to as a public official and as a free
professional: the idea of 'public official' apparently was not in conflict
with that of 'profession'.[53] Thus, to contend that in those years at the
turn of the century the Italian notaries were struggling to professional-
ize their trade is, from this point of view, somewhat unwise.

In the last years of the nineteenth century and the first decade of
the twentieth, however, the idea that the two concepts were incompatible gradually took shape, although it was never given explicit
and thoroughgoing expression. 'Office' and 'profession' became the
symbolic objects around which were constructed the two principal
'collective action frames'[54] that cognitively and ideologically structured the movement of the notaries by coupling it to the cycles of
protest that broke out first during the Giolitti period and then after
the First World War. The first of these action frames, which stressed
the market components of the notarial function and the personal
and symbolically efficacious qualities of the figure of the notary (typically, competence and trustworthiness), indicated professional
freedom tempered by respect for public service as the key to the
historical development of the *notariato*. The second, which pivoted
on the idea of public interest, of duty and of dignity, tended to
attract greater attention from the government; a government which
imposed tighter discipline on professional practice in order to curb
competition *internal* to the profession and thereby resolve the economic problem of the *notariato*[55] or else guaranteed the standardization of selection and recruitment upon which the professional
aspirations of the *notariato* converged.[56]

By contrast, the hopes of those who pressed for the creation of a
state notarial service (*notariato di stato*) were invariably frustrated. The
bureaucratic option, apart from the costs that it incurred for the state,
appeared counterproductive for the management of the notarial function, an important element in which was still *personal* trust between

[53] In 1917, it was pointed out in the columns of a respected legal journal that the
notary 'according to our legislation is in no respect a professional, although this has
been too frequently repeated in official documents and in speeches made to parliament'. See A. Assisi, 'Il notaio nella storia e nella nostra legislazione', *Rivista di
Diritto Pubblico*, November–December 1917, part II, pp. 46–7.
[54] See D.A. Snow, R.D. Benford, 'Ideology, Frame Resonance and Participation
Mobilization', in B. Klandermans, H. Kriesi, S. Tarrow (eds), *From Structure to
Action: Studying Movement Participation across Cultures*, Greenwich, 1988,
pp. 197–217.
[55] See V. Frugis, 'Il problema economico'.
[56] See A. Anselmi, *Le scuole di notariato*.

notary and client.[57] Beyond professional rhetoric and ideological construct, the figure of the notary-bureaucrat was incompatible both with the interests of the elite of the profession, for whom the market was a conspicuous source of income, and with those of the elite of the notaries' clientele; a clientele which now increasingly consisted of banks and large and medium-scale entrepreneurs who would not have tolerated a situation in which their activities were directly subjected to the bureaucratic control of the state. During the Fascist period, not only did the notaries not become 'statized', they also made significant progress towards professionalization by skilfully transforming the impulse to administrative rationalization typical of Fascist totalitarianism into a strategy for the 'symbolic construction' of their professional status.

Around these two cultural models – 'free professionism' and the 'public function' – the professional status of the *notariato* was symbolically constructed during the inter-war period and thereafter, with the emphasis shifting between them according to the economic and political, ultimately historical, conjuncture. Assuming one model rather than the other as the key to understanding and interpretation of the history of the notarial profession would be misleading: indeed, it is within the space marked out by both of them that the social development of the twentieth-century Italian *notariato* unfolded.[58]

In the final analysis, the problem is not one of establishing whether and how the Italian *notariato* has been professionalized in the past hundred years, or whether it really constitutes a 'profession'; nor that the notaries have not yet achieved the 'purity' embodied in the idea of a 'free profession' to which many of them still aspire. The problem, instead, is that the history of the Italian notarial profession is evidently

[57] See, as an example of this professional rhetoric constructed on the idea of personal trust, S. Sandrucci, *Appunti sull'evoluzione del notariato in Toscana*, Florence, 1932, p. 67. See on the trust–profession nexus the remarks by J.B. McKinlay, 'On the Professional Regulation of Change', in P. Halmos (ed.), 'Professionalizations and Social Change', *The Sociological Review Monograph*, XX, 1973, pp. 62–84, and, more in general, those by L. Roniger, 'Fiducia: un concetto fragile, una non meno fragile realtà', *Rassegna italiana di sociologia*, 3, 1988.

[58] Thus interpreted, the history of the Italian notarial profession between Unification and Fascism apparently confirms that, from a comparative-historical perspective, 'professions' are not phenomena *sui generis* but a variant of a wider phenomenon which *also* includes the Weberian bureaucracy: 'the rise of expertise and certification as specifically middle-class techniques for advancement and for legitimizing privilege, rank, and power (*vis-à-vis* aristocratic resistance and democratic pretensions alike), intertwined with ideologies of "culture", science, and public service that function in a context of all-pervading instrumental rationality, specialization and secularization'. See C.W.R. Gispen, 'German Engineers and American Social Theory', *Comparative Studies in Society and History*, 1988, pp. 564–55; see also R. Collins, *The Credential Society*, New York, 1979.

the contingent outcome of a plurality of structural processes which (at a pinch) can be summed up by the only apparently technical term 'professionalization' – as a concise and therefore convenient formula used to describe a set of interrelated changes affecting an occupation in a specific period of time. In this sense – but only in this sense – one may say the Italian *notariato* professionalized itself between Unification and Fascism, thereby referring to a series of transformations which changed the features of an ancient profession, in certain respects 'modernizing' it, in others reintegrating it into a corporatist framework, in yet others '(neo)patrimonializing'[59] it: from the introduction of the degree as an obligatory qualification to the standardization of the entry criteria to the profession, from the creation of the first professional association on a national scale to the first beginnings of a collective professional identity, from the conquest of higher rates of remuneration to the achievement of greater autonomy from the state on the one hand and from other socio-professional groups on the other.

[59] See for this concept, G. Roth, 'Personal Rulership, Patrimonialism and Empire-Building in the New States', *World Politics*, 20, 1968, pp. 194–206. One of the most widespread notions of the contemporary Italian *notariato*, in fact, concerns precisely its 'patrimonial' character: in the sense of a public office which tends to pass from father to son, or in any case from one relative to another. However, there are no reliable data available with which to verify the extent of this phenomenon.

CHAPTER 4

BETWEEN THE STATE AND THE MARKET: PHYSICIANS IN LIBERAL ITALY

PAOLO FRASCANI

I. HEALTH-CARE AND PUBLIC EMPLOYMENT

Comparison between the situation of Italian doctors in the first half of the nineteenth century and that of their counterparts in the rest of Europe reveals two particular features of the medical profession in Italy: its surplus of practitioners, and the large number of physicians who worked as municipal employees. The first detailed survey of medical personnel carried out in 1876 reported, with ill-concealed pride, the high concentration of doctors in the country. In the 1870s there were 6 doctors for every 10,000 inhabitants in Italy (the same proportion as in England), compared with 2.91 in France, 3.21 in Germany and 3.41 in Austria. Of the slightly more than 18,000 doctors surveyed, only 4,679 lived in the 69 provincial chief towns, while a large proportion of the rest (8,903) were employed, although on a non-permanent basis, as *medici condotti*, or general practitioners, by the municipal authorities.[1] Socially, Italian doctors belonged to the middle and lower-middle classes: to the urban and rural property-owning bourgeoisie in the North;[2] to the rural lower-middle class anxious to improve its lacklustre social position in the South.[3]

Current Italian historiography regards the *medici condotti* as typifying the difficulties that afflicted the medical profession in the last century, but also the capacity which they shared with other marginal sectors of the intellectual middle class – elementary schoolteachers and priests –

---

[1] E. Raseri, 'Il personale sanitario in Italia e all'estero', in Ministero di Agricoltura, Industria e Commercio, *Annali di Statistica*, 1878, series 2, vol. II, pp. 177–8.

[2] A.L. Forti Messina, 'I medici condotti e la professione del medico nell'Ottocento', *Società e Storia*, 7, 23, 1984, p. 104.

[3] G. Moricola, 'Aria sana e corpi malati', *Quaderni del Dipartimento di Scienze Sociali* of the Istituto Universitario Orientale, Naples, 1993, p. 56.

to embed themselves deeply in the fabric of Italian agricultural society. If one considers the health services of Lombardia and Veneto, the *medico condotto* system seems to have been an adequate response to Italy's health-care needs in the nineteenth century, with a level of efficiency not to be found in other European countries. Indeed, two university degrees were required even of those intending to work for the poor people's health service – a requirement unique to Italy.[4] However, on closer inspection, the situation of the *medici condotti* appears rather more precarious: they could not rely on the municipalities to renew their three-yearly contracts automatically, and they were subordinate to a rural notability which was largely indifferent to sanitation and to public health-care.

There thus emerges a more dramatic and turbulent picture; one confirmed, moreover, by the compassionate terms with which nineteenth-century literature described the typical *medico condotto* of the time.[5] Neither did the physicians who worked in the cities find it any easier to share in the prestige and affluence enjoyed by other professional categories. These benefits only accrued to the small elite of doctors practising in the clinics and hospitals, who ministered to an exclusive clientele of aristocratic and high bourgeois patients; they never attached to the humbler opportunities for employment offered to the majority of the city-dwelling doctors by the religious institutes and hospitals.

The social 'weakness' of the Italian physician was certainly not an isolated case in the overall panorama of the evolution of the medical profession in Europe,[6] but its scant recognition was symptomatic of a more general problem which stemmed from the backwardness of the country. One notes in particular the substantial inability of Italian medicine to take advantage of the scientific progress brought by the 'medical revolution' of the beginning of the century, which accounts for its failure to accomplish any profound revision of the diagnostic methods then employed. In those years, and especially in the northern regions, medical students were still trained in methods inspired by the Brawnian paradigm, although the situation was somewhat different in the other medical training institutions. As Maria Luisa Betri writes,

---

[4] A.L. Forti Messina, 'I medici condotti', p. 158.
[5] G. Cosmacini, 'La famiglia e il medico tra Ottocento e Novecento', *Sanità scienza e storia*, 1–2, 1988, pp. 379ff.
[6] See for example M. Ramsey, 'Medical Power and Popular Medicine: Illegal Healers in Nineteenth Century France', *Journal of Social History*, 10, 1976–77, p. 560; R.W. Lee, 'Medicalization and Mortality in South Germany', *Abhandlungen zur Geschichte der Medizin und der Naturwissenschaften*, 39, 1980, p. 85.

In the rest of Italy, clinical practice was largely based on the principles of experimentalism and of close observation at the patient's bedside. At Florence, the teaching of Maurizio Bufalini rejected the dependence of medical theories on philosophical doctrines and their abstractness of terminology, while the Neapolitan school remained substantially faithful to the Hypocratic tradition.[7]

However, in general, newly qualified doctors had only scant familiarity with medical equipment and with the principles of anatomy. Their training consisted mostly of abstract disquisitions of a form (lectures were delivered in Latin) and content which rendered the physician's relationship with his patient unsatisfactory, and poorly appreciated. Medical students enrolled at the university faculties and the schools of medicine – the *Collegio Medico Cerusico* of Naples was more prestigious than the university faculty[8] – to pursue courses of study which led to the awarding of qualifications with differing levels of official recognition. Moreover, the restrictions on the practice of medicine introduced before Unification were flouted by the other health workers in competition with doctors. These practitioners, armed with various forms of medical training, had managed to acquire *de facto* recognition and to build up their own clienteles.

As in the rest of Europe, therefore, the medical profession in Italy was traversed by fierce internal conflict among its various components, and especially between graduate doctors and the more numerous and better-regarded unofficial practitioners. The image of the profession furnished by systematic studies of the subject does not display that wilful determination which drove the social ascent of English medicine during the course of the nineteenth century;[9] nor does it reveal the social and institutional processes which were beginning to consolidate the status of the physician in bourgeois France.[10] However, the difficulties which beset the profession in Italy should also be framed in the context of socio-economic backwardness in which the country's doctors were obliged to work. Their range of professional action was restricted to a constant battle against the widespread endemic diseases – malaria, typhoid and pellagra – provoked by poor sanitation, pollution and dietary deficiencies, and periodically exacerbated by the outbreak

---

[7] M.L. Betri, 'Il medico e il paziente: i mutamenti di un rapporto e le premesse di un'ascesa professionale (1815–1859)', in F. Della Peruta (ed), *Storia d'Italia, Annali*, 7, Turin, 1984, p. 211.

[8] V.D. Catapano, *Medicina a Napoli nella prima metà dello Ottocento*, Naples, 1990, pp. 15ff.

[9] N. Parry, J. Parry, *The Rise of the Medical Profession*, London, 1976.

[10] See J. Léonard, *La médecine entre les savoirs et les pouvoirs: histoire intellectuelle et politique de la médecine française au XIX siècle*, Paris, 1981.

of ineffectually controlled epidemics of, for instance, cholera.[11] A high
overall mortality rate – and an extremely high infant mortality rate in
particular[12] – are evidence of how far behind Italian medicalization
lagged at the time of Unification. At the same time, however, they
also induced medical practitioners to reflect on the relationship
between the country's nosological geography and its economic and
social backwardness. It was the failure of their prodigious and un-
stinting efforts to halt the recurrent epidemics of cholera,[13] in fact, that
persuaded many leading members of the medical profession – mostly
outside the universities, however – to heed the advice of mainstream
European medicine of the early 1880s concerning the deep-lying
causes of Italy's *questione sanitaria* (as the country's public health agenda
was known at the time). Accordingly, the meetings and conferences of
Italian doctors began to call for comparative epidemiological studies to
be conducted among Italy's various regions, and for the creation of a
nationwide health-care plan.[14]

In calling for a change in the health-care policies so far adopted by
the pre-Unification states, the doctors unhesitatingly threw in their lot
with the liberal-democratic movement of the *Risorgimento*. They
began to project the outward image of a profession closely involved in
the construction of new and modern institutional arrangements, and
they stood in the vanguard of the demand for national unification. Not
surprisingly, therefore, when unification was effectively achieved, the
physicians made a major contribution to analysis and solution of the
questione sanitaria – which was viewed as a decisive test for the policies
of the elite running the country during the crucial phase of nation
building. The thirty-year period between the birth of the nation and
the creation of a modern health-care system was marked by a long sequence of hopes and struggles in which the dream (or indeed the
utopia) of the medical profession as protagonist of the country's
health-care renaissance – as the interpreter of an advanced programme
of reform – inspired many of the initiatives undertaken by doctors

[11] There is by now a substantial body of literature on the nosological evolution of the
    Italian population during the nineteenth century. For a number of points of refer-
    ence, see *Il genocidio pacifico*, a special issue of the journal *Classe*, 15, 10, 1978; M.L.
    Betri, *Le malattie dei poveri*, Milan, 1981; M.L. Betri and A. Gigli Marchetti (eds),
    Salute e classi lavoratrici in Italia dall'Unità al fascismo, Milan, 1982; F. Della Peruta
    (ed.), *Storia d'Italia, Annali*, 7.
[12] E. Sori, 'Malattia e demografia', in F. Della Peruta (ed.), *Storia d'Italia, Annali*, 7.
[13] P. Sorcinelli, *Nuove epidemie, antiche paure*, Milan, 1986, and P. Frascani, 'Medicina
    ed epidemia nella Napoli ottocentesca', in A. Musi (ed.), *Dimenticare Croce?*,
    Naples, 1991, pp. 165–76.
[14] See G.C. Marino, *La formazione dello spirito borghese in Italia*, Florence, 1974.

both individually and through their professional associations. The principal objective of the campaign waged by the *Associazione Medica Italiana* and the *Associazione dei Medici Condotti* was to improve the still fragmented and inefficient health-care system created in 1865. Its specific aim was to strengthen the role of technicians at the system's various levels – municipality, province, ministry of the interior – so that they could become decisive actors in the bureaucratic structure of the state, empowered to intervene independently and authoritatively in municipal health-care matters as the sole representatives of civil society, and to the exclusion of other health workers.[15] As Giacinto Pacchiotti, professor at the University of Turin, put it in 1875:

> The government, almost like terrestrial providence, must always do good, it must never do evil. It must wisely lead the people to high destinies ... by the same token, an almost divine function is performed in the social body by the physician, not only when he saves someone's life by the miracle of his art, but especially when his counsel and example educate the masses to live wisely, or when he attends to the well-being of workers of every trade. This is the ideal man. The government is the brain of the social body, the doctor is its heart.[16]

These were objectives that extended well beyond an agenda endorsed by some or other professional assembly. They gradually developed into proposals for official legislation, thanks mainly to the efforts of doctors like Agostino Bertani, Mario Panizza, Luigi Pagliani and such leading left-wing politicians as the prime ministers Agostino Depretis and, especially, Francesco Crispi, who steered the comprehensive reform of the health-care system through parliament at the end of the century.[17] In demanding the strengthening of the public health system, moreover, the doctors gave voice to a proposal which, by reviving the enthusiasms of the *Risorgimento* years, was enriched by more solidly based knowledge of the relationship between the environment and the causes of disease. In their pursuit of sanitary-environmental reform, the doctors also took part in the various surveys conducted by the government to assess the effective state of the country's socio-sanitary conditions. In the first thirty years after Unification, the activism of the liberal elites led to a series of statistical and social surveys which re-

[15] M. Soresina, 'Associazionismo e ruolo dei medici nel primo trentennio dello Stato unitario', *Società e storia*, 8, 27, 1985, pp. 85–118.

[16] G. Pacchiotti, *Il programma dell'avvenire della medicina*, Turin, 1875, p. 54.

[17] The literature on social legislation in liberal Italy is enormous and concentrates mainly on health policy in the Crispi period (see F. Della Peruta, 'Sanità e legislazione sanitaria dall'Unità a Crispi', *Studi Storici*, 21, 1980, pp. 713–60; L. Mantegna, 'La legge sanitaria del 1888: una soluzione di compromesso?', *Sanità scienza e storia*, 1–2, 1988, pp. 157–88).

corded causes of death, drew up a map of the country's sanitary geography, analysed the working and living conditions of the peasants, and described urban hygiene and housing conditions.[18] On all these occasions, the tightly knit network of the municipal medical service was a crucial source of knowledge which, although still approximate, enabled a first reliable picture to be compiled of the country's health and sanitation.

In 1885, in the aftermath of the disastrous cholera epidemic of 1884 and shortly before the reform passed into law, a survey of the sanitary conditions of Italy's communes revealed that only 33% of municipalities possessed underground water mains, that only 50% of them had sewage systems, and that 47% of the population lived in dwellings entirely without, or with inadequate, solid waste disposal. Further evidence of the primitiveness of hygienic conditions was provided by surveys on the siting of cemeteries, while the sparse information gathered on the Italians' dietary habits revealed a low level of calory intake by the peasant and working classes.[19] This research highlighted the socio-economic aetiologies that provided the backdrop to the *questione sanitaria*, and it reinforced the ideological stance of the medical profession, which viewed 'the development of medical knowledge as the essential condition for the management of health-care policy'.[20]

This attitude corresponded to a more profound desire among physicians to improve their professional status, bearing in mind the scant resources available to them in a country which was still largely underdeveloped. Finding that they had to practise their profession in the conditions typical of an agricultural society slowly moving towards modernization, doctors saw public employment as an opportunity to enhance their status and to fulfil their professional aspirations. This strategy was grounded in awareness of the dynamic and propulsive effects of the phase of nation-building on Italian society. The public sector, in the absence of a market, enabled the doctors to acquire the resources and recognition which they needed for broader legitimation.

The reforms of 1888 fulfilled these expectations only in part. Although they established a health-care system better equipped to deal with the country's most pressing health problems, they did not extend the range of recognized health-care services to public medicine. The acknowledgement of the central importance of the *medici condotti*, and

---

[18] P. Frascani, 'Statistica e medicina nella formazione del sistema sanitario italiano', *Quaderni storici*, 45, 15, 1980, pp. 942–65.

[19] Ibid., p. 962.

[20] G. Panseri, 'Il medico: note su un intellettuale scientifico italiano nell'Ottocento', *Storia d'Italia, Annali*, 4, Turin, 1981, p. 1153.

the guarantees offered them in terms of stable employment and improved remuneration, thus brought their thirty-year dispute with the local administrations to an end. Yet it did not usher in a new era of state medicine. In submitting for approval by parliament a bill based largely on a proposal drafted by the radical deputy Agostino Bertani, Prime Minister Crispi definitively put an end to the government's dream of a health system run by the doctors. The role of technicians was curtailed at all levels of the administration: although assigned important consultative functions, they were still subordinate to the decisions taken by mayors, prefects and ministers of the interior. The powers granted to the newly created technical bureaucrats – the health officer (the *medico provinciale*), the director of health (who was not necessarily a doctor) – belonged to a centralist bureaucratic vision which sought to bring the *questione sanitaria* back into the realm of the defence of public order.[21]

The increase in employment opportunities in the health sector, therefore, amounted to a few dozen extra jobs, for which competitive examinations were announced at the various levels of the health system hierarchy. However, no form of career structure was introduced whereby the mass of doctors working as *medici condotti* or as municipal health officers could rise through the intermediate and higher levels of the administration. When the difficult decade of economic crisis of the 1890s came to an end, the doctors were forced to explore other avenues, and to pursue the much more difficult objective of professional upgrading.

2. CHANGES IN MEDICAL KNOWLEDGE

The doctors' persistent search for institutional points of reference which would help them to gain full professional recognition went beyond their demand for more modern health legislation. During the years that passed as the new law made its slow progress through parliament, profound and significant changes occurred in another sector of the public sphere, one which was crucial to the professional renaissance of Italian doctors: university education. As a result of the efforts of the *Destra Storica* (the party in government from Unification to 1876), in just fifteen years major improvements were made to the quality of medical training. The contents and form of medical science were profoundly altered as the followers of medical positivism gained control over the universities. Salvatore Tommasi at the University of Naples

[21] See L. Mantegna, 'La legge sanitaria', p. 162.

and Jacob Moleschott at Turin – to mention the names of only two outstanding representatives of the movement – introduced their students to new clinical methods and mobilized them against the custodians of a scientific paradigm hidebound by idealist assumptions and reluctant to define the object of its research according to rigorous quantitative principles. As a result of the power accumulated and wielded by a small group of doctors, professional training spread through public education as the younger generation moved into the country's principal seats of learning. The university regulations promulgated in 1862 and 1876 established administrative criteria which applied to all the medical faculties. The number of examinations required and the qualifications awarded were fixed according to an educational design which gave priority to the experimental approach of positivist medicine, and therefore to the training of medical students in the clinic and in the laboratory.[22] That this standardization process was neither straightforward nor painless has been documented by Forti Messina as regards the central-northern regions of the country,[23] while Catapano has described the resistance raised against it in Naples by the lobbyists for the private medical schools.[24] In any case, concrete implementation of the project – new buildings, more equipment and more financing, closer links with the hospital system – encountered major obstacles. The long inventory of the facilities required seems to have discouraged the promoters themselves of the programme for renewal. Indeed, in his lecture inaugurating the course in medicine at the University of Turin, Giacinto Pacchiotti declared:

> There is a lack of normal and pathological histology laboratories of suitable size; there is a shortage of large and commodious operating theatres in the clinics; there are insufficient instruments, apparatuses, specially equipped surgeries, electrical machinery, laryngoscopes, ophthalmoscopes, microscopes, thermometers, reagents for uroscopy, and orthopaedic devices – everything required for the systematic study of disease.[25]

Despite these difficulties, significant advances were made in the medium and large-sized towns. As Cosmacini pointed out, 'by re-

22 'The centre of medical activity', writes Cosmacini, 'having already slipped from the anatomical-clinical to the experimental clinical level, moved increasingly into the laboratories whence the clinic's diagnoses and prescriptions were issued' (see G. Cosmacini, 'Medicina, ideologie, filosofie nel pensiero dei clinici tra Ottocento e Novecento', Storia d'Italia, Annali, 4, Turin, 1981, p. 1165).
23 See A.L. Forti Messina, 'La formazione professionale dei medici in Italia dopo l'Unità. Appunti per una ricerca', paper presented at the conference on 'Università e scienza nazionale', Certosa di Pontignano (Siena), April 1991.
24 D. Catapano, Medicina a Napoli, p. 17.
25 G. Pacchiotti, Il programma dell'avvenire della medicina, p. 87.

moving the backwardness and the prejudices which continued to retard medical science in Italy, compared with the situation in advanced countries like France and Germany, the new regulations undoubtedly represented progress';[26] progress which was most apparent in the relatively rapid adoption of a new approach in which the central focus of medical training was the histological and anatomical changes exhibited by diseased organs. Twenty years after Pacchiotti's gloomy appraisal, the scientific vision inspired by medical positivism had become so well established as to engender a period of major scientific advance led by doctors working together with social scientists.[27] In Turin, medical positivism 'was taking shape as one of the historical growth phases in a culture of health, defined as a complex of structures, of services, of relationships, of knowledge ... developed in response to the social problem of disease'.[28] In Bologna, the leading figures in academic medicine vied with the municipal authorities to implement schemes for the improvement of public sanitation.[29] Although further examples of this resurgence of Italian medical science could be cited, this is an appropriate moment to turn to the effects of what was effectively a cultural revolution in the universities, as they endeavoured to secure a strategic role for themselves in the evolution of the Italian medical profession.

In examining the specific nature of Italian medicalization, and in insisting as I have done on the propensity of medical professionals to enter the bureaucratic apparatus of liberal Italy, there is a tendency to overlook the fact that the faculties of medicine were producing an ever-increasing supply of doctors during the last decades of the nineteenth century. In the absence of surveys conducted in a sufficiently large number of universities, however, it is difficult to specify the features of this process in Italy's various regions. Nevertheless, some indication of its importance is provided by the most crowded faculty of medicine in the country: that of the University of Naples, which in 1885 employed fifty-eight doctors in various capacities. Twenty years later their number had almost quadrupled: in 1905, the faculty yearbook listed 195 tenured lecturers employed at the various levels of the

[26] See G. Cosmacini, *Storia della medicina in Italia*, Bari, 1987, p. 369.
[27] See G. Pancaldi, 'Scienziati e filosofie del progresso (1860–1880)', in *Scienza e filosofia nella cultura positivistica*, Milan, 1982, pp. 193–212.
[28] D. Simon, 'Scienza medica e cultura della salute a Torino (1875–1910)', *Sanità scienza e storia*, 2, 1985, p. 42.
[29] A. Alaimo, 'I medici e la cultura dell'igiene a Bologna dopo l'Unità', *Storia urbana*, 44, 1988.

university hierarchy.[30] Members of the wealthy, landed, mostly provincial bourgeoisie, or else the sons of professionals, white-collar workers or tradesmen, the doctors working in the universities frequently exploited an efficient network of kinship relations, and they congregated in the clinical institutes where the most prestigious Neapolitan academics worked and taught.[31] I shall return to the importance of these mechanisms for the operation of the professional labour market later; for the moment, I merely point out that the creation of improved conditions for teaching and research triggered a process of professional upgrading which, over two generations of university graduates, profoundly changed the Italian physician's attitude towards disease.

Compared with the age of 'romantic' medicine, which was only vaguely aware of the existence of close relationships between the environment and nosological aetiology, and then called for measures to deal with them, after 1885 those doctors who kept abreast of advances in bacteriological research were able to address problems of sanitation and health in a manner that was much more scientific. Commenting on the results of the inquiry into the sanitary conditions of the Italian municipalities, published in 1886, the physician Antonio Vallisneri warned that henceforth an 'idyll of hygiene' would no longer be sufficient to counteract infectious diseases;[32] indispensable instead, he argued, were epidemiological studies which identified the pathogenic agents of each form of disease. And other, even more authoritative, voices were raised to announce the advent of a new age, one which would witness the disappearance of the doctor-bureaucrat closely involved in the political life of his town or commune as he struggled to secure the most basic standards of sanitation and diet for the inhabitants of a vast agrarian periphery.

3. THE CONQUEST OF PROFESSIONAL MONOPOLY

During the twenty years that followed the Crispi reforms of 1888, the predictions made at the moment of their promulgation were borne out. And during the subsequent, more liberal government of Giovanni Giolitti, too, the liberal political class made no secret of its determination to maintain its control over health policy, which it delegated to

[30] P. Frascani, 'Medicina e società nella Napoli post-Unitaria', Quaderni del Dipartimento di Scienze Sociali dell'Istituto Universitario Orientale, v, Naples, 1991, p. 184.
[31] Ibid., pp. 186–7.
[32] A. Vallisneri, 'Ancora della statistica sanitaria in Italia', Rassegna delle scienze mediche, Modena, 1888, p. 478.

the ministerial bureaucracy while 'technicians' were restricted to routine consultative functions. The onset of industrialization rendered health policy-making even more complex, since it was now obliged to deal with the further problems raised by the country's industrialization, and consequently had to regulate workplace safety and expand hospital facilities.[33] These were all matters addressed by substantially inadequate policies which rarely coincided with the principles of social medicine frequently proclaimed in parliament. In the event, the health system created in 1888 proved incapable of bringing coordinated change to the country's environment and to its nosological structure, mainly because of the limited financial resources allocated to the central administration. The main burden of health spending was shouldered by the municipalities, which paid the *medici condotti*, bought medicines for the poor, and reimbursed their hospital expenses. The funds of the ministry of the interior were much more meagre, and they were earmarked for a few minor items in the budget.[34] Measured by the yardstick of this limited spending capacity of the central components of the health system, the solution that the liberal ruling class sought to give to the problems raised by the medicalization of the country was inadequate; and it ignored, as we have seen, the option of increasing the number of doctors working in the public sector.

Rather than promote measures which diverted resources to the health-care system, Italian social policy during the Giolitti period undertook a series of sectoral initiatives (often not fully realized) which were implemented in a spirit of cost-cutting and substantially at odds with the measures which were creating new demand for health services in other countries.[35] These initiatives were only weakly contested by a medical class laboriously in search of an identity and whose demands for legitimation had not yet been fulfilled. Although a special disposition of the Crispi reforms recognized the pre-eminent role of graduate doctors, the law left the situation of other health workers, like foreign doctors and pharmacists, vague and undefined, while the sanctions introduced against quacks and unauthorized practitioners were entirely ineffectual. Thus, although the *medici condotti* were accorded greater recognition, which combined with the already-mentioned improvement

[33] L. Dodi, 'I medici e la fabbrica. Prime linee di ricerca', *Classe*, 15, 10, 1978, pp. 21–66.
[34] S. Sepe, 'Amministrazione e mediazione degli interessi: il controllo sugli istituti di pubblica assistenza e beneficenza', Istituto per la scienza dell'amministrazione pubblica, Archivio, no. 3, *L'amministrazione nella storia moderna*, pp. 1707–66.
[35] For a rapid comparison see P. Frascani, *Finanza, economia ed intervento pubblico dalla unificazione agli anni Trenta*, Naples, 1988, p. 36 and p. 42.

in their conditions of employment, the liberal professionals once again saw their institutional progress towards full legitimation frustrated, and they found themselves trapped in a substantially ambiguous position. By the end of the century, in fact, the traditional demands advanced by medical associationism no longer corresponded to the multiple interests and needs of a professional community which had greatly diversified since the years following Unification.

The strategies that doctors deemed most likely to achieve professional monopoly, therefore, were not those pursued by the declining *Associazione Medica Italiana*.[36] Rather, they were strategies which exploited the professional opportunities created by the law of 1888 and enhanced by the doctors' ability to form alliances with other strata of the intellectual middle class occupying crucial positions in the state apparatus. The first device employed by the doctors was to create professional associations in the country's various provinces. Doctors in Milan, Bologna, Naples and Rome set up official professional bodies composed of university graduates and led by small groups of distinguished practitioners. The Milanese professional association set itself the task, amongst other things, of 'constituting a voluntary tribunal to conciliate those questions which not infrequently arise between the medical practitioner and the authorities, the public and even his colleagues'.[37] However, the profession's principal concerns were to combat unauthorized practitioners and to organize initiatives which clearly demonstrated the difference between licensed physicians and quacks. These aims were vigorously pursued by the *Ordine* of Naples, founded in 1890, whose statute declared the order's intention 'to sustain the prestige of the profession and to defend its material interests before the authorities and the public, ...to report names and facts concerning the illegal exercise of the profession to the health authorities and to the judiciary, and ... to improve the economic conditions of physicians who belong to associations of any kind'.[38] Indeed, the range of associative action was then extended to include the manifold and delicate ethical issues that doctors had to grapple with as they came into contact with the first ambiguous expressions of health-care economics. These initiatives shifted the problem of gaining recognition of professional monopoly to the concrete terrain of winning better professional conditions for the physicians who practised in the large cities. But they were still unable to achieve the goal of complete legitimation for the medical

[36] M. Soresina, 'Associazionismo e ruolo dei medici', pp. 110ff.
[37] M. Soresina, 'L'ordine dei medici della provincia di Milano dalle origini al fascismo 1887–1926', *Storia in Lombardia*, 2, 1985, p. 61.
[38] Ordine dei Sanitari di Napoli, *Progetto di statuto*, Naples, 1890, p. 9.

profession. On reading the reports by the local associations printed in the various bulletins issued by the medical orders, one realizes that this objective was gradually achieved through ratification of the physician's primacy over other health workers backed by recognition of the practitioner's relative responsibility for acts committed during the exercise of his profession. The doctors' acquisition of monopoly was greatly helped by the readiness of the magistracy to safeguard their position in legal matters, but it was also imposed, over the twenty-year period following the Crispi reforms, by the prestige and esteem that accrued to the doctors from the quality of their professional service.[39]

By granting institutional authority to the medical orders, by fixing norms of professional self-government, by regulating the number of foreign doctors, and by proscribing every form of unauthorized practice, the law of 1910 on the medical profession formalized a state of affairs already ratified by a judicial system which, over two decades, had defended doctors' rights by relieving them of responsibility in dozens of lawsuits brought before the courts. However, although this development signalled the emergence of a class solidarity among distinct sectors of the intellectual middle class, it also revealed the previous acquisition of a solid social status – the expression, as a speaker in parliament declared, of 'the capacity of the doctors to equal in importance and merit other professional categories'.[40]

4. TECHNOLOGICAL RENEWAL, PROFESSIONAL FIGURES AND ROLES

> The range of functions of the charitable hospitals has expanded with extraordinary rapidity – because of the growth of the population, because of the lesser reluctance of the working class to enter them, because of the better conditions in which the patients are treated, and lastly because of the rapid progress of surgery, which can only be performed in hospital where it finds the necessary guarantees for its success owing to the exigencies of medicine which requires special conditions not easily fulfilled in the patient's home.[41]

This assessment of the hospital service in Emilia – one of the regions of the Po Valley – by a local administrator adequately sums up the complex transformation undergone by the medical profession in the

[39] See A. Lonni, 'Medici, ciarlatani e magistrati nell'Italia liberale', in F. Della Peruta (ed.), Storia d'Italia, Annali, 7, pp. 801–21; idem, I professionisti della salute, Milan, 1994.

[40] Camera dei Deputati, leg. XXIII, sess. 1909, doc. n. 173, presented at the sitting of 8 June 1909.

[41] A. Tonelli, Per carità ricevuta, Milan, 1991, p. 65.

early years of this century. The changed attitude of the ill towards hospitalization was caused by a set of external factors which, in Italy as in
other European countries, made the poor increasingly confident in the
health-care institutions.[42] The archaic but close-knit structure of the
charitable institutions had also undergone a transformation which,
from the mid-years of the nineteenth century onwards, rendered them
increasingly dependent on changing conditions in the agricultural
labour market, and therefore able to handle the new distribution
among the various members of the peasant household of the costs and
responsibilities involved in caring for the sick. Industrialization had
already accentuated this trend by placing the hospitals, especially those
in the Po Valley, at the centre of a more diversified system of health
services which the law on charitable institutions of 1890 brought under
the control, albeit indirect, of the municipal administrations.[43] Apart
from these external factors – which today are rightly regarded as decisive in the transformation of the Italian hospital service at the end of
the nineteenth century – a further feature was the ability of these institutions to acquire at least some of the technological innovations
already introduced into the university clinics, especially as regards
surgery. The modernization of health-care facilities in Italy, however,
was not comparable to that of countries with greater resources and in
the fortunate position of being able to build a network of modern hospitals from scratch, under the aegis of the medical profession.[44]

This modernization, therefore, was neither profound nor broad. It
was distributed unevenly over the national territory and proceeded
largely beyond the control of the doctors. However, as Cosmecini has
written, the passage of the hospitals from 'pious works' financed by
voluntary donations to 'public welfare services supported by planned
allocations and financing interlocked with further advances in bacteriological and physiopathological science and with the first important
applications of antiseptic and anaesthetic medication'.[45]

Thanks to the extensive and close-knit structure of the hospital
network, the period of renewal in the Italian health-care system left
visible traces. Not though in methods of management, from which
doctors were still excluded, but in its outward image and most notably
in the specialization of the system of roles and functions, which tended
to transfer from the clinics and hospitals to certain sectors of profes-

[42] P. Frascani, *Ospedale e società nell'Italia liberale*, Bologna, 1986, pp. 159ff.
[43] Ibid., pp. 124–32.
[44] See also *Studien zur Krankenhausgeschichte im 19. Jahrhundert*, Götingen, 1976.
[45] G. Cosmecini, *Storia della medicina*, p. 416.

sional practice in the large cities, which were ready to receive and pub-licize them by means of advertising and promotion in the press.

But let us proceed in order. Compared with the undifferentiated and rudimentary health-care system of the old *ospedale ricovero* – the reposi-tory of medical knowledge and practice phenomenologically extra-neous to the body of the patient – the restructured hospital system was geared to therapeutic ends, and as such it was 'organized' according to a division of labour unknown before the middle years of the nineteenth century. Its articulation into specialist departments comprising specific competences and roles – the surgeon, the anaesthetist, the specialist in infectious diseases, the paediatrician, the oculist, the radiologist – had no precedent in the former hospital system.[46] As the young doctors moved into the renovated wards of many hospitals – the temporary sites of post-graduate specialization – the content of health-care delivery was strengthened and enhanced by the introduction of work procedures unknown to nineteenth-century medical training. As one reads in a clinical report from the hospital of Cremona,

> (t)he routine examination of each patient today takes much more time than it did in the past, and if we move from diagnosis to therapy, here too we find a surprising increase in the amount of work that the state today re-quires of doctors. Hypodermic and intravenous injections, hypodermo-clysis, stomach pumps, massage, electrical and radiographic appliances which were previously not part of therapeutic apparatus, today urge them-selves on doctors for the effective treatment of certain diseases.[47]

An array of technical equipment such as this was certainly unfamiliar to the small infirmaries which, in 1902, constituted 89% of Italy's hospitals and employed 55% of its doctors, but it came into general use in the other 11% employing the remaining 45% of hospital personnel.[48] It was these professionals who experimented with forms of work organi-zation and the coordination of functions which, as Waddington has observed regarding Victorian England, 'encouraged shared experiences with other students and, by so doing, facilitated the development of a common professional identity and sense of professional community'.[49]

[46] For analysis of this process from a sociological point of view, see: I. Waddington, 'The Role of the Hospital in the Development of Modern Medicine', *Sociology*, 7, 1973; M.L. Costantini, 'Struttura e formazione della clinica universitaria: un contri-buto teorico all'analisi sociologica', *Studi di sociologia*, XI, 1973, fasc. III.

[47] Ospedale Maggiore di Cremona, *Memoriale sulle riforme nei servizi e miglioramenti eco-nomici*, Cremona, 1907, p. 9.

[48] Ministero dell'Interno, *Rilevamento statistico-amministrativo sul servizio degli ospedali e sulle spese di ospedalità*, Rome, 1906, p. 31.

[49] I. Waddington, *The Medical Profession in the Industrial Revolution*, Dublin, 1984, p. 202.

This was matched in Italy by the rapid creation of a professional association of hospital doctors which proudly declared its intention to distinguish its members from both their university colleagues and the
'swarm of private practitioners who, if their numbers continue to
grow, will become a veritable plague on society for obvious reasons,
compromising the function and dignity of our noble mission'.[50] Apart
from the corporatist forms that this process might take, it gave major
impetus to the legitimation of official medicine, which had no difficulty in asserting its authority over the other health practitioners. At
the same time it recast and redefined the hierarchical relationships
which had long predominated within the professional community.

By the eve of the First World War, the role of the doctor in the university or hospital clinics had changed profoundly. The exchange
between the free service provided by the young graduate and his acquisition of knowledge and prestige, to be subsequently exploited in
private practice, was incorporated into a more complex and diversified
network of professional relations. The clinical-hospital elites centralized the mechanisms of the selection and control of doctors intent on
moving up the hierarchy of the professional community. Criteria were
adopted which were increasingly based on the candidate's scientific
production and on his ability to support himself financially during a
long career of poorly paid academic activity. Seen from within the hospital system, and compared with the more generic and less closely controlled practices of previous decades, these increasingly widespread
changes were highly selective and brought radical innovation to professional conduct.

In the view of the *Associazione dei Medici Ospedalieri*, at the end of
the first decade of this century, it was already 'imperative for young
doctors swiftly to exploit clinical material and to adapt themselves to
the environment by seeking with every means to render their careers
more certain and more rapid', because 'only those endowed with sufficient economic means can undertake a long, onerous and difficult hospital career, while those deprived of such means cannot'.[51] Of course,
distinctions must be drawn between one situation and another, and
between one city and the next. In Milan, during the early years of this
century, the energies and resources of numerous exponents of academic medicine embracing democratic socialist principles led to the
creation of a chain of hospitals – the *Istituti Clinici* – designed to
combine the highly scientific specialization of modern medicine with

---

[50] *Atti Ufficiali del II Congresso Nazionale dei Medici Ospedalieri d'Italia*, Rome, 28–30
October 1907, p. 38.
[51] Ibid., p. 42.

the disinterested provision of health-care to the subordinate classes.[52] In the same years, in Naples, academic medicine rested on an efficient system of power relations which extended into the wards of the city's many hospitals and distributed honours and responsibilities among the members of the Neapolitan faculty.[53]

5. TECHNOLOGICAL RENEWAL AND PROFESSIONAL ROLES

Those wishing to analyse the professional situation of the physician in liberal Italy outside the framework of the prevalently 'public' character of the health service must concentrate on the urban transformation of the country brought about by industrialization. From the 1880s onwards, the reconstruction of many city centres, improved housing conditions, and the increasingly widespread introduction of communal sanitary services – water mains, sewers – brought a general improvement to the country's health.

The overall mortality rate – one of the highest in Europe – fell; and the geography of Italian urban morbidity showed a decline in the recurrent epidemics of those contagious diseases like cholera and typhoid which had long since been brought under control in the great cities of the rest of Europe.[54] These developments generated demand for health-care which was not restricted solely to emergencies and which adhered more closely to a trend in medicalization which by now included health protection among the goods consumed by late nineteenth-century society.[55] Nevertheless, it was a process, albeit one part of a more general European trend, which was markedly slower and less extensive in Italy. Given the progress achieved by medical science, and given increased and more confident awareness of its role, the professional community of medical practitioners was forcibly reminded of the gap between an over-abundant supply of medical services and still inadequate demand for health-care.

The selection imposed on the multitude of young medical graduates by the greater specialization required of the professional practitioner

[52] L. Mangiagalli, *L'insegnamento della medicina a Milano nel passato e nel presente*, Milan, 1912.

[53] P. Frascani, 'Medicina e società', pp. 188–9.

[54] L. Faccini, 'Tifo, pensiero medico e infrastrutture igieniche nell' Italia liberale', in F. Della Peruta (ed.), *Storia d'Italia, Annali*, 7, p. 709–40.

[55] E. Shorter, 'Il crescente consumo di assistenza sanitaria da parte delle classi medie dell'Europa centrale, 1880–1930', paper presented to the conference on 'L'economia domestica nell'età contemporanea: Italia ed Europa', Rome, 28–29 October 1992.

was regarded by the older doctors as 'ill-conceived and badly implemented',[56] and it widened the already considerable social distance between the clinical elite and the rank-and-file. Nonetheless it also seemed to enhance the profession's power of attraction. In absolute terms, the number of doctors rose from 18,043 in 1876 to 23,361 in 1911,[57] although this increase was mostly among private practitioners. Between 1885 and 1905 (the year of a systematic survey of health-care provision for the poor), private practitioners increased by 39%, while the number of *medici condotti* rose only by 20%. The growth in the number of self-employed practitioners occurred mainly in towns, with communes of more than 20,000 inhabitants accounting for more than 66% of the total. Even higher concentrations were to be found in the large cities, given that (excluding the special case of Naples) 13% of professional doctors worked in Turin, Genoa and Milan, cities which comprised 3% of the country's population. It is not easy to delineate the social status and economic conditions of this small but important component of the Italian intellectual stratum. Barbagli has stressed its membership of the middle classes during the period immediately prior to the First World War, and he highlights the problem of 'intellectual unemployment' that afflicted the sector as a whole.[58] Contemporary commentators reported a marked tendency for self-recruitment by the profession in cities like Milan and Rome,[59] although no systematic comparative studies have yet been carried out. The extent of professional success in economic terms, compared with other categories of professionals or in inter-regional terms, is difficult to measure. A survey of the medical profession in Naples during the 1870s and 1880s shows that great fortunes were amassed, although its findings cannot be generalized on account of the peculiar conditions that governed practice of the profession in the ex-capital.[60] What is certain, however, is that despite the fortunate careers of a small clinical elite, the medical press constantly dwelt on the theme of the hardships suffered by doctors in their day-to-day practice in what was still a small professional market which did not easily fit the categories of health-care economics. The reluctance of the poorest and most numerous classes to use the health-care system was certainly due to the economic backwardness of the country, but it should also be viewed in the light of the political

[56] See *Atti Ufficiali del II Congresso Nazionale dei Medici Ospedalieri*, p. 43.
[57] See Ministero dell'Interno, *L'assistenza sanitaria ai poveri*, Rome, 1906, pp. 268–73.
[58] M. Barbagli, *Disoccupazione intellettuale e sistema scolastico*, Bologna, 1974.
[59] A. Contento, *Le professioni nelle grandi città italiane*, Venice, 1906; F. Chessa, 'La trasmissione ereditaria della professione', *Studi senesi*, XXVIII, 1912, fasc. 5.
[60] See P. Frascani, 'Medicina e società', p. 187.

choices and cultural attitudes that hampered the process of medicalization. I refer in particular to Italy's failure to build a modern system of
social welfare; to the indifference, that is, shown by the ruling liberal
class and by a large part of the workers' movement to the reformist policies which in those years were accelerating the professional ascent of
medicine in other European countries. Compared with the results
achieved elsewhere – but also when set against the range and long-
sightedness of the proposals for Italian social medicine – the measures
actually introduced as the initial basis for a modern health-care system
in Italy were timid and inadequate, at least until the end of the First
World War. Thus the concept of 'health' suggestively defined by
Labisch with reference to Germany, as the means whereby the proletariat could be 'introduced into the scientifically organized, industrial
world',[61] did not provide a frame of reference for the welfare policies
of the Italian liberal state. Having said this, however, it should be
pointed out that those who interpret Italy's situation in terms of political or ideological immaturity fail to grasp the deep-lying reasons for
the country's laggardliness, which, more concretely, was due to the
survival of an ancient and still functioning system of social guarantees
and solidarist values at odds with the modern model of exchange on
which the professional market was based.[62]

The success of Italian medicine in the decades between the end of
the nineteenth century and the First World War should therefore be
measured not solely in terms of the pace and quality of the country's
medicalization and urban renewal; it should also be set against the persistence of institutions and bodies which had long governed the
demand for health-care. Operating within this system – which took
concrete form in the many charitable institutions and mutual benefit
societies that continued to survive in the Italian cities – were a large
army of professionals. Accustomed to competing for the few resources
allocated by these institutions to the care of the sick, doctors now only
paid lip service to an ideology which emphasized the generosity and al-
truism of the physician – his willingness to shoulder, out of religious
principle, the burden of mankind's ills and suffering.

In Naples – the city which contained the largest number of physicians – in the 1880s demand for medical treatment still took the form

[61] A. Labisch, 'Doctors, Workers and the Scientific Cosmology of the Industrial
World: The Social Construction of "Health" and the "Homo Hygienicus"', Journal
of Contemporary History, 20, 4, 1920, p. 610.
[62] For explicit reference to the need to take account of this survival in the historical
study of the Italian health system, see Cavallo's criticisms of the book edited by
F. Della Peruta, Storia d'Italia, Annali, 7, (see Quaderni storici, 61, 1986, pp. 251–9).

of a myriad confraternities, associations and guilds which paid physicians for services minutely defined by their statutes. The *Confraternita del Santo Rosario nella Chiesa della Speranza*, formed by *'fratelli'* who were 'artists, notaries or people of lower social extraction', stipulated that

> should some brother fall ill with a fever due neither to tuberculosis nor to syphilis, the guild shall provide not only a doctor but five *carlini* per day of which three will be paid by the same and two by the brothers who go their daily rounds visiting the said infirm, and this for the space of one month; should the illness persist for another month and again with fever, the assistance of a doctor must be given, and three *carlini* per day, of which one shall be paid by the guild and two by the brothers who visit the sick.[63]

This relationship between doctors and corporations, households and parishes, reveals the existence of a parallel health-care system which wove the doctor into a network of constraints and obligations which the instruments of medical knowledge – still unable to cope with the great diseases of the time – proved largely unable to dismantle. For the physicians, this behaviour was obligatory if they were to accumulate the prestige they needed to beat off increasingly fierce competition. However, the process of specialization and the proliferation of medical practitioners described above brought considerable change during the Giolitti period. In Milan at the beginning of this century, even the creation of a modern network of scientific institutes – the pride of the city's hospital system – aroused criticism and protest among the medical rank-and-file.

One reads, for example, in a report published by a medical journal of the time,

> When the hospitals lower their tariffs to fee-payers to an absurdly low level using the assets of the poor; when, as at the *Istituto dei Rachitici*, they lump all their expenses together in order to off-load those of the rich onto the poor; when special operating theatres are built for fee-payers at enormous cost, as if sterilization and disinfection can be neglected when treating the poor; when, as at the *istituti clinici* and various other hospitals, fees are truly competitive with those charged by private doctors – then the situation of those who already work for free becomes unbearable indeed.[64]

This scenario reveals the survival of a system of cultural values which

63 See Archivio di Stato di Napoli, *Opere pie*, s. 1°, f. 132 II, 'Statuto e regolamento della veneranda R. Arciconfraternita del SS. Rosario'.
64 See F. Ferrari, 'Le condizioni attuali dei medici di Milano', in *Il progresso sanitario*, Rome, 1907, p. 36.

emphasized, not without a dash of sophistry, the altruistic vocation of the medical profession. It was a system which induced the doctor to believe

> that he could serve both the public and himself by anticipating the expense of the sanitary and health reforms. But as soon as the public had accepted this advance, it did not respond as it should have done but instead convinced itself that it was entitled to it by right, and demanded philanthropic, that is gratuitous, work by the doctor.[65]

Hence the dramatic surrender by an entire generation of professionals schooled to obey a scientific code of knowledge which 'could not be transgressed' but who were now obliged to choose between continued service in the public health service and entry into a professional market which, although free, was constrained by old inertias and new ambiguities. Although these voices expressed a position probably in conflict with the general political and ideological stance of Milanese medicine,[66] they were echoed in the smaller towns, and they highlighted both the crisis of status which afflicted physicians in their day-to-day work and the incompatibility between the construction of modern professional practice and the inherited culture of solidarism. This was a culture which still persisted beneath the religious trappings of the old romantic medicine – or under those, more ideologically in keeping with the positivist scientific paradigm, of socialist medicine – although it seems to have taken more shallow root in other areas of the country.

In Naples, resistance to the principle of health-care for payment stemmed principally from the profound cleavages which split the professional community. The renewal of the Neapolitan hospital service, although restricted in scope, had quantitative and qualitative effects on a demand for health-care which had traditionally been large. The constant flow of migrants from the agrarian periphery of the *Mezzogiorno* into Naples, whence they departed for the New World, swelled the numbers of non-Neapolitans treated in the city's hospitals.[67] This inflow was accompanied by a simultaneous increase in the number of private patients who did not belong to the city's wealthier classes. The beds-for-payment wards and the private clinics accommodated a growing number of paying patients from a provincial bourgeoisie increasingly willing to be treated by a medical profession whose successes in surgical therapy had further enhanced its traditional prestige. Thus, the professional sphere of the luminaries of Neapolitan medicine

[65] Ibid., p. 27.
[66] For analysis of the relationships between medicine and politics in Milan at the beginning of the century, see M. Soresina, 'L'ordine dei medici'.
[67] M. Pietravalle, *La questione ospedaliera in Napoli*, Naples, 1908.

spread from the aristocratic-bourgeois districts of the city to the rich farmlands of Puglia and to the small villages of Calabria and Lucania. By contrast, there was no change – or perhaps a further deterioration due to the surplus of practitioners – in the conditions of the multitude of doctors who had first trained in the only faculty of medicine in the *Mezzogiorno* and then stayed on in Naples to compete for the limited opportunities offered by a scant clientele often reluctant to pay for the doctor's services.

By the beginning of this century, the service provided to the guilds and confraternities was no longer the obligatory first step in a successful career, but entry to the 'free market' was obstructed by forms of competition which the doctors' association did not hesitate to denounce as 'unfair'. In 1903 the newsletter of the Naples doctors' association complained about 'the soliciting on a large scale in Naples of clients at the railway stations and docks by go-betweens who, by exploiting the good faith of the sick, direct them to doctors of execrable quality'.[68] More than this was at stake, however. The newsletter set out very clearly the matters most keenly debated by the professional community during this difficult phase of transition. Principally at issue were the question of *perizie cliniche* (clinical reports by expert witnesses), which compliant judges always assigned to the same specialists; recurrent concern over the responsibilities attributed to doctors by the criminal code in a period of uncontrolled 'operational' activity; and the doctors' difficult and often subordinate relationships with other health professionals – like the owners of private clinics or pharmacies who inveigled the weakest and poorest practitioners into business ventures which frequently landed them in the lawcourts.

These are incidents which highlight the substantial similarity between the mechanisms which governed, in Naples and Milan alike, free exercise of the profession, marring its quality and restricting its scope. However, the drive for professional legitimacy – which the expectations created by advances in medical-scientific knowledge had provoked – was thwarted by the scarcity of health-care demand in a country still in large part agricultural. And it was also hampered by the illegitimate use frequently made of new technology by the clinical-hospital elite.

6. THE FORMATION OF THE PROFESSIONAL MARKET

In the background to the arduous progress of Italian physicians towards

[68] *Bollettino dell'Ordine dei Sanitari di Napoli e provincia*, 1901 and subsequent issues.

official recognition of their functions and prerogatives stands the subtle and more complex evolution of the ethical values that regulated their relationships with colleagues and patients. This is an area which has been little explored – especially as regards the procedures adopted in professional service and the doctors' attitudes towards their work.[69] In an excellent essay, Cosmacini has emphasized that study of these matters should be conducted from within the context of certain concrete historical situations. The principal advantage of this approach is that it yields a clearer picture of the perennial conflict between the doctor and the unauthorized practitioner.

> Until at least midway through the nineteenth century, in the rural world and also outside it, from an anthropological point of view (that is, in terms of interpersonal human relations) the bond between 'care-giver' and 'care-receiver' was more easily established between families 'of the people' and those persons 'of the people' traditionally regarded as the dispensers or brokers of health. These persons were felt to be kinsmen by social extraction and by virtue of their lifestyles, patterns of thought, expression and behaviour.[70]

The second advantage of this approach is that it illuminates the links between the world of the family – the point at which delicate economic and social equilibria intersect – and the changing ability of doctors to respond to demand for health-care. In my above discussion of hospitalization, I mentioned the influence on this relationship by the demographic and economic variables which regulated the organization of work in peasant and working-class households. Cosmacini reports that the popular classes accepted the doctor only belatedly and with reluctance, and that this acceptance largely coincided with outbreaks of epidemic disease. This, though, was not the behaviour of middle-class families. 'Their frequent recourse to the doctor as a *human* interlocutor with whom joys and sorrows could be shared and the crucial problems of life confronted'[71] was the outcome of deeper affective awareness; it stemmed to a lesser extent from the 'increased scientific prestige of the profession' brought about externally by changing tastes and patterns of consumption. Nonetheless, it should be stressed that apart from the resistances and pressures affecting the doctor's relations with the external environment, one discerns a distinct evolution in the doctors' relationships with their patients; an evolution that

[69] For comparison with the United States, see Barrington Moore Jr, 'Historical Notes on the Doctors' Work Ethic', *Journal of Social History*, Summer 1984, pp. 547–71.
[70] G. Cosmacini, *Il medico e la famiglia*, p. 362.
[71] Ibid., p. 384.

derived directly from the way in which these professionals conceived their role and projected it to the exterior.

The search for an ethical or prescriptive frame of reference, as conducted in the columns of the medical press and the bulletins issued by the medical associations, gave rise to worried discussion of the ethical and economic implications of a redefinition of the doctor's role and function. This anxiety was in part due to the fragmentation and heterogeneity of the professional categories operating within the Italian national health system, but it also resulted from the different forms assumed by demand for health-care. The social distance between the peasant users of the health service and the prosperous clientele in the towns and cities created a first cleavage among heterogeneous models of professional practice. Health-care in the countryside was part of a paternalistic culture which viewed the poor as being in need of protection, and it was entrusted to a practitioner aware of his limitations but also the proud proponent of social and political values which raised him above the common herd of the bourgeoisie. In the cities, however, matters were different. As the city-dwelling physicians struggled to cope with the difficult transition from the romantic phase of pre-Unification medicine to that of positivist naturalism, they were forced to revise the unwritten rules that had long governed the doctor–patient relationship.

There were substantial differences between the two periods. In the former, the health professional was careful to define, if timidly, the form and content of his relationship with the patient, whom medical etiquette still considered the principal party to the transaction, to be soothed by serious and dignified behaviour, but who could not be relied upon to pay his or her fees. 'I have never been able to understand', declared the doctor hero of a best-selling novel by Camillo De Meis, 'why, when I have done my duty as a man and perhaps as a friend, and feeling inwardly satisfied and content, people should then be obliged to pay me'.[72] And his words were echoed by the advice given by another doctor to young medical graduates: 'regarding the emoluments you receive, make it your custom not to solicit them, nor to refuse them, nor to dispute them. Ours is an intellectual as well as a humanitarian commodity; as such it should always be granted with a certain and apparent disinterest'.[73] These were attitudes, though, which began to change with the spread of the new naturalistic paradigm.

As a Neapolitan physician declared shortly after Unification,

[72] C. De Meis, *Dopo la laurea*, Bologna, 1868, p. 18.
[73] M. Sogliano, *La condotta del medico pratico*, Naples, 1874, p. 19.

the position of today's doctor with respect to the patient differs from that of any previous period ... he must reproduce in his mind the morphological changes in the body's innermost organs. But this is not enough: the eye of his mind must penetrate to the paramount secret of the living forces; he must think physically and chemically in the presence of the sick person.[74]

There thus began to coalesce an image of the doctor 'as a minister of nature', armed with knowledge and prestige unknown to the old school of Rasori or to that of Hippocratic inspiration, and determined to upset the still unfavourable power relations that tied him to wealthy clientele. We have seen how slowly this process unfolded in the social and cultural reality of liberal Italy. And there is no doubt that its ethical implications were swiftly recognized by those reluctant to rise to (sometimes passionate) defence of a scientific model which underpinned an ancient and enduring vision of the doctor–patient relationship.

Already shaken by the effects of the scientific revolution, the doctors of post-Unification Naples were now faced by the ethical implications of the naturalistic paradigm: 'Today', observed a leading member of the old medical elite, 'the cult of materialism which has invaded all the social classes regards men as nothing but bones and nerves, cartilages and muscles. The soul, and religion with the soul, are creatures extraneous to medicine. And yet mental illnesses are the most fatal, and there is no other remedy for them but religion.'[75] Similar sentiments couched in the language of idealist philosophy are expressed by Camillo De Meis's fictional doctor when, disillusioned by his positivist training, he declares: 'It is always the brain which verifies outward forms and never the soul which penetrates inner substance ... it is always classification and explanation, never reason.'[76] This resistance to the positivist model of scientific knowledge, moreover, was accompanied by concern that the very foundations of professional ethics were being undermined. 'Given that the entirety of the doctor's faith is summed up in nothing', wrote a professor at the University of Bologna in 1863, 'by which I mean that his studies of matter lead him to believe that the entire work of Creation can be encapsulated in the theory of fungi, for what purpose, then, will he exercise the profession? Will he speak in his heart of charity or of selfishness?'[77] No immediate answer was forthcoming to these questions, because they were stifled by en-

---

[74] R. Maturi, *Galateo del medico*, Naples, 1873, p. 35.
[75] *Difesa dei dottori in medicina*, Naples, 1875, p. 44.
[76] C. De Meis, *Dopo la laurea*, p. 18.
[77] G. Franceschi, *Prolusione letta all'università di Bologna*, Bologna, 1863, pp. 19–20.

thusiasm for the scientific theory which, in a few short years, conquered the entire academic world of Italian medicine. They nevertheless reappeared in different form as a cultural change which affected the professional figure of the doctor as the new century began. In claiming an independent and contractually defined relationship with the patient, and in shedding the altruistic and solidarist values that conflicted with the essential agnosticism of his scientific training, the doctor of the early 1900s looked with greater detachment on the conditions of the sick, and thus re-established the social distances that had seemingly narrowed in the course of the nineteenth century. At the beginning of this century, there cannot have been any significant improvement in the conditions of hospital patients, given that the association of hospital doctors itself denounced the fact that the invalid 'becomes practically a clinical subject for study and experiment, almost for vivisection, when one considers the long lists of surgical operations which candidates today must submit with their applications for employment'.[78]

7. DOCTOR AND PATIENT

My reconstruction of the development of Italian medicalization has often overlapped or merged with the better-known and more readily identifiable pattern displayed by the political and ideological evolution of the medical class during the liberal period. The first detailed analyses of the history of this class emphasized its strongly ideological bent and its contribution during the *Risorgimento* years to the Italian democratic movement; a contribution – like that of the intellectuals, priests and municipal schoolmasters – made in the difficult conditions of the country's agrarian periphery and in direct contact with the peasant classes.[79] More recent research, less constrained by political and ideological considerations, has stressed the central role of professionals – as an essential component of the intellectual middle class – in maintaining a social and political equilibrium which lasted for more than sixty years.[80] Less attention, however, has been paid to the fact that the political history of the doctors during the last decades of the nineteenth century, like that of the lawyers or the engineers, would be highly im-

---

[78] *Atti Ufficiali del II Congresso Nazionale dei Medici Ospedalieri*, p. 35.

[79] See G. Panseri, 'Il medico: note su un intellettuale scientifico'; T. Detti, 'Medicina, democrazia e socialismo in Italia tra '800 e '900', *Movimento operaio e socialista*, 1979.

[80] See P. Macry, 'Sulla storia sociale dell'Italia liberale: per una ricerca sul "ceto di frontiera"', *Quaderni storici*, 12, 35, 1977; P. Frascani, 'Les professions bourgeoises en Italie à l'époque liberale (1860–1922)', in *Mélanges des l'Ecole Française de Rome*, 1985; M. Meriggi, 'La borghesia italiana', in J. Kocka (ed.), *Borghesie europee dell'800*, Venice, 1989, pp. 161–86.

plausible if not carefully framed by the process of professionalization that I have sought to describe in these pages.

Even cursory examination of the relationship between medicine and politics reveals an apparently linear progression: from political commitment to disaffection, from democratic and socialist militancy to ill-concealed sympathies for fascism. The history of medical professionalization provides a number of indicators with which to conduct more satisfactory analysis of the doctors' political ascent that cannot be explained simply in terms of the restlessness and vulnerability of the intellectual middle classes. It is probable that the twin phenomena of the doctors' 'status inconsistency' and the contradiction between their imagined role and the one that they actually occupied in Italian society at the beginning of this century, provoked disillusionment and resentment among the many practitioners who found themselves impoverished and exploited by the new national health system. This frustration inevitably led to rejection of the altruistic role, either real or imagined, of democratic-socialist medicine. But it is also true that this evolution, or maturation, cannot be understood unless one takes account of the influence of a model of professional practice which increasingly distanced itself from the hegemonic and totalizing pretensions of nineteenth-century medicine; a model which was better suited to the scientific paradigm of the doctor scientist and naturalist who, in the sheltered surroundings of the clinic and laboratory, cultivated a taste for detachment and for political 'neutrality' previously unknown in the tradition of Italian medicine. More in general, it should be added that if analysis of the medicine–politics relationship is to be conducted correctly, it should also address the capacity of doctors to render political choices functional to professional ones – and vice versa – and to exploit their professional success in order to gain political power.

But let us proceed chronologically. After Unification, local political networks were enriched by the presence of 'technicians' – the doctors who, as the leaders of the professional community, made a crucial contribution to the reorganization of the sanitary-health systems of the country's ancient towns.[81] However, there is no doubt that the already-mentioned correspondence between service in the municipal health-care system and political militancy in the socialist party was the most striking feature of the doctors' participation in Italy's political life. The geographical area of reference is principally the agrarian periphery of central-northern Italy; and here it is possible to make adequate assessment of the doctors' contribution to the history of Italian socialism

[81] P. Alaimo, 'La cultura dell'igiene', p. 147.

during the course of the last decades of the nineteenth century.[82] In assessing these matters, however, one should also bear in mind the role of local political institutions in creating and shaping these attitudes. That is, we must ask ourselves to what extent the adoption of a particular political position – which in many communes of the Centre-North corresponded to municipal socialism – was 'conditioned' by pragmatic adjustment to local political circumstances. This therefore means that analysis of political participation must also examine the attraction exerted by an administrative political system which, through the rigid control of the labour supply, was able to interfere unduly in the doctors' ideological choices. When considering political journalism and contemporary testimony by members of the profession concerning the controversies that inflamed relations between the public institutions and doctors at the end of the period considered,[83] one should at least mention the problematic nature of a relationship which cannot be conveniently explained away as convinced commitment to socialist ideology.

Different considerations are prompted by the less well-known political history of rural medicine in the *Mezzogiorno*. In the southern regions of Italy – with certain exceptions such as those recently studied by D'Antone, who emphasizes the role of the doctor-socialist in the anti-malaria campaigns mounted in Puglia at the beginning of this century[84] – the doctors' membership of the agrarian notability meant that their co-option into the local administration, according to the traditional patterns of familial or clientelistic recommendation, was well-nigh inevitable. Nevertheless, a number of recent studies have shown that the early affirmation of the profession's status enabled certain members of the agrarian bourgeoisie to enter and to circulate among the elites of liberal Italy.

This process therefore included a professional career among the range of strategies available to the agrarian notability.[85] On a broader scale, it offered them opportunities to combine profession and politics in a lucrative ascent to parliament and the national government. This was the path followed by various members of the Neapolitan clinical elite of the beginning of this century. By operating, as we have seen, on the broad professional scale of the entire *Mezzogiorno*, and as members of the lower and middle ranks of the southern agrarian bour-

[82] T. Detti, 'Medicina, democrazia', p. 35.
[83] See for example *Ordine dei Medici Chirurghi della Provincia di Bologna, Relazione della commissione d'inchiesta nominata nelle assemblee ordinarie dell'ordine*, Bologna, 1921.
[84] See L. D'Antone, *Scienze e governo del territorio*, Milan, 1990, pp. 58–69.
[85] See for example G. Civile, *Il comune rustico*, Bologna, 1992.

geoisie, these doctors ably exploited – with the help of an efficient system of 'academic' cooperation – the power that accrued to them from their monopolistic control of Naples' health institutions, converting their successes among a clientele appreciative of the new hospital technology into electoral consensus. Analysis of the route followed by certain doctors as they rose from the restricted milieu of the provinces to a seat in the Senate or the Chamber of Deputies reveals how professional success provided the doctors, like other professionals, with unprecedented access to political power.[86]

8. CONCLUSIONS

My analysis has revealed a path of development more complex and more ramified than that described by Ramsey.[87] There is no doubt that the model of the predominantly public nature of the professional evolution of Italian medicine is still of help in construing its salient features. But the doctors' propensity towards public-sector employment should be set against Italy's 'typical' inability to reorganize a centuries-old public health service into at least the embryonic form of a modern welfare state. The ascent of the Italian medical profession was perhaps hampered less by the difficulties encountered by the physician in gaining the upper hand over the multiform practitioners of a deeply entrenched popular medicine, than by the profession's inability (widespread in civil society) to rid itself of the economic and cultural legacy of a pre-existing welfare system. The determination of doctors at the beginning of the century to eliminate the solidarist-altruistic values which, in the eyes of the patient, continued to legitimate the professional's behaviour may thus explain why the liberal ruling class and the more progressive political forces were reluctant to embrace the principles of the free market.

Considered in as much detail as has been possible in the space available here, the professional development of Italian doctors throws light on the growth, during the liberal period, of a small but exceptionally competent sector of the Italian intellectual bourgeoisie. Its advance, at least until the First World War, was identical with the ongoing process of Italian medicalization, and it largely coincided with the difficult construction of a professional market in the country. Although frustrated by the gap between demand and supply, the free and authorized exercise of the profession challenged a mentality and set of values di-

[86] P. Frascani, 'Medicina e società', pp. 188–9.
[87] M. Ramsey, 'Medicina e politica di monopolio professionale nel XIX secolo', *Quaderni storici*, 16, 1981, pp. 959–1011.

rectly at odds with the principle of service in exchange for remuneration. It substantially altered the political attitudes of a profession which had traditionally allied itself with the forces of progress and social renewal. Because of the delay with which the Italian doctors converted to the rules of a modern health service, and because of the frustrations provoked by the mismatch between their real social status and the prestigious image that they had cultivated of their profession, they succumbed to disillusionment and political neutrality, attitudes which continued to spread after the First World War. The effects of this 'conversion' inevitably conditioned the process of Italy's medicalization in the long term. They were manifest not only on the occasion of the abrupt political *volte-face* of the fascist years, but also, more recently, in the demonstrable inability of the Italian medical profession to commit itself to a more modern and advanced national health service.

CHAPTER 5

THE ENGINEERING PROFESSION
1802—1923*

MICHELA MINESSO

I. THE NAPOLEONIC WIND

The profession of the modern Italian engineer is still profoundly influenced by the Napoleonic period – a significant turning-point in its history and the phase with which detailed analysis of the engineering profession in the nineteenth century must necessarily begin. It was the Napoleonic years, in fact, that saw the introduction in Italy of important measures which disciplined – under state control and according to principles which subsequently applied throughout the nineteenth century – both technical training and entry to the profession. This was legislation that therefore broke the monopoly exercised by the corporations of the Old Regime. And training which had previously been practical in character and based largely on the apprenticeship system was replaced by a formalized and highly theoretical culture. Significant

---

* Abbreviations used in the notes for this chapter:
    ACS, MPI, Dir. Gen. Istr. Sup., f. Pers. Univ., I o II vers. = Archivio Centrale dello Stato, Ministero della pubblica istruzione, fascicoli del personale universitario, I o II versamento;
    ACS, PNF = Archivio Centrale dello Stato, Archivi Fascisti, Partito Nazionale Fascista, fascicoli personali dei senatori e dei consiglieri nazionali;
    AUP, SA, Cart. = Archivio dell'Università di Padova, Scuola di applicazione, Carteggio;
    DBI = Dizionario biografico degli italiani;
    Acf = Atti del Collegio degli ingegneri e architetti di Firenze;
    Acm = Atti del Collegio degli ingegneri e architetti di Milano;
    Acn = Atti del Collegio degli ingegneri e architetti di Napoli;
    Acp = Atti del Collegio degli ingegneri e architetti di Palermo;
    Acr = Atti del Collegio degli ingegneri, architetti ed agronomi di Roma;
    SIAI = Annali della Societa' degli ingegneri e architetti italiani;
    Acv = Atti del Collegio veneto degli ingegneri;
    legisl. = Legislature;
    b. = busta;
    Sess. = sessione.

precedents had already been set in the State of Milan and in the Kingdom of Sardinia; but it was not until the arrival of the Napoleonic armies that the 'French model' of higher technical education with the *Ecole des Ponts et Chaussées* at its apex – a model already widely copied by other countries of continental Europe – became definitively installed in Italy as well. The new legislation created two distinct training and career paths for the aspiring engineer: either the free profession or employment in the public sector. The principal stages in this transformation were, as regards entry to the free profession, the restructuring of the curriculum of study in the universities and the introduction of a state examination; and as regards public-sector employment, the creation of the Corps of Waterway and Road Engineers (*Corpo degli Ingegneri di Acque e Strade*) and the setting up of special training schools for its members. Of course, these changes did not affect all the regions of Italy in equal measure, but they were nevertheless indicative of a trend which would consolidate in subsequent decades.

At the beginning of the nineteenth century, specific syllabuses for engineers were introduced in the physics and mathematics faculties of the Napoleonic Kingdom of Italy's universities: these being Pavia, where attendance was already compulsory for Lombard engineers, and Bologna and Padua (after 1806). Possession of 'a degree and therefore entitlement to practise [...] the profession of architect, civil engineer, hydraulic engineer'[1] thus became obligatory. The university engineering course – which initially lasted for four years but was then reduced to three in 1808 – established a disciplinary framework for the training of technicians which remained substantially unchanged for the first fifty years of the nineteenth century. The course consisted of pure and applied mathematics, physics, geology and agronomy, techniques of construction, and legal studies. Theoretical preparation at university was followed by a four-year period of probationary training under the supervision of a 'licensed' engineer. This aspect of the engineer's training closely resembled the previous apprenticeship system and it probably paid homage to, and was a legacy from, tradition. But it was also and certainly a contrivance to retrieve the young engineer from the exclusively theoretical preparation imparted by the universities.

---

[1] 'Legge della Repubblica italiana del 4 settembre 1802', *Bollettino delle leggi della Repubblica italiana*, I, pp 295–308; 'Piani di studio e di disciplina per le università nazionali', *Foglio ufficiale della Repubblica italiana*, II, 1803, pp. 155–216; On Pavia in particular see: I. Ciprandi, D. Giglio, G. Solaro, *Problemi scolastici ed educativi nella Lombardia del primo Ottocento*, vol. II, *L'istruzione superiore*, Milan, 1978. On Padua: M. Minesso, *Tecnici e modernizzazione nel Veneto La Scuola dell'Università di Padova e la professione dell'ingegnere (1806–1915)*, Trieste, 1992.

The engineering degree awarded on passing the state examination was valid throughout the *Regno Italico*. And its holder could then choose from a range of careers which encompassed the design and construction of buildings, topography and land surveying, and hydraulics. The functions of the engineer, therefore, also comprised tasks normally within the competence of the architect and the land-surveyor.[2]

This marking out of a career profile based on university-level instruction heightened the social prestige of the engineering profession; prestige which was further enhanced by the recognition accorded – by the creation of the *Corpo degli Ingegneri di Acque e Strade* – to the engineers' prominent role in the new state. The corps of engineers was created in 1806, and it was responsible for the construction and maintenance of roads, navigable canals and seaports, as well as for the upkeep of waterways. It was overseen by the General Directorate of Waterways and Roads with its headquarters in Milan. The corps was organized into a hierarchy consisting of general inspectors, chief engineers, ordinary engineers, and *aspiranti* or junior engineers. Some of the general inspectors liaised between the head office and the technicians at work in the regional Departments. They visited the various areas of the Kingdom, supervised work in progress and conveyed the plans drawn up by local engineers to the central management. Other general inspectors formed the Board of the General Directorate.

The chief engineers directed all the public works undertaken in their districts and supervised their execution. Measurements, soundings, levelling work – but also the drafting of projects, estimates, designs, budgets and reports – were the responsibility of the ordinary engineers. The *aspiranti* worked solely as assistants to the general inspectors and to the chief engineers. Within a few years the personnel working for the *Corpo* increased in numbers from 114 individuals to 224. Access to the civil service was reserved for the most outstanding graduates from the universities and from the Army Engineering School, although the creation of a special School of Waterways and Roads was envisaged. Intended to be an integral part of the university, under the direction of an inspector of waterways and roads, this school would have provided specialized training for graduates in the mathematics and physics faculty.[3] Although for various reasons the school was never opened, the project is nevertheless worth men-

[2] *Bollettino delle leggi del Regno d'Italia dall'1 gennaio al 30 giugno 1805*, 1805, pp. 552ff.
[3] *Bollettino di leggi, regolamenti e discipline ad uso de' magistrati e del corpo degl'ingegneri d'acque e strade*, Milan, 1806, vols I–II, especially vol. I, pp. 105–12; 218–36; 261–3; 267–83.

tioning because it is indicative of the complexity of the Napoleonic project for higher technical education, and its similarity to initiatives in another large area of French influence in Italy: the Kingdom of Naples.

In the southern regions of Italy, corresponding to the two careers available to engineers – the civil service and the free profession – were what effectively amounted to two distinct curricula of studies. In the South, too, entry to the liberal profession was restricted to those with a degree in sciences followed by postgraduate studies in architecture at the Royal Institute of Arts. A Corps of Bridge and Road Engineers was created under the jurisdiction of the Director General of Bridges and Roads – who also presided over the Higher Council of Public Works. Those aspiring to a career in the civil service, and who were groomed for the post of assistant engineer (*ingegnere aggiunto*), received their training at the School of Applied Engineering opened by Goacchino Murat in 1811.[4] Entry to this school, which was attached to the Corps, was by public examination, and the training course was rigidly selective according to merit. Students failing any of the written examinations – and success in all of them was obligatory for passage from the first to the second biennium – were expelled. Those who passed were entitled to occupy the vacant posts of assistant engineer, but this was an entitlement which they lost as soon as the next year's crop of students had graduated.

Hence, amid similarities and some differences, the years of French domination were a period of prodigious efforts to develop the engineering profession; years of profound change, therefore, the fruits of which came to maturity in the Restoration period. After 1815 the legacy of French domination proved indelible, with a continuity that was perhaps most evident in the territories directly ruled by Austria and in the regions of the South. In Lombardy-Venetia, trainee engineers still had to follow a three-year curriculum of university studies. Those intending to enter the free profession then spent the customary period of probation in an engineering firm, on completion of which they sat the state examination for their licence to practise. Those who instead opted for the public sector entered the technical branch of the civil service as trainee engineers.

Austria replaced the Napoleonic Directorate of Waterways and Roads with the General Directorates of Public Construction of Milan

---

[4]   F. De Mattia, F. De Negri, 'Il corpo di ponti e strade dal decennio francese alla riforma del 1826', in A. Massafra (ed.), *Il Mezzogiorno preunitario. Economia, società e istituzioni*, Bari, 1988; *Decreto per lo stabilimento di una Scuola d'applicazione nel Corpo degli ingegneri di Ponti e strade*, Napoli, 1811.

and Venice, and also established regional offices of public construction.[5] The most significant innovation brought by the Austrians, however, was the suppression of the managerial autonomy that the Corps had previously enjoyed under the French. The General Directorates and the provincial offices, in fact, were now subject to interference by the political powers. And if we also bear in mind the low salaries paid to the public engineers in those years, then the widespread disaffection with public-sector employment and the preference for the free profession become understandable. This is not to deny, however, that outstanding engineers – the names of Pietro Paleocapa and Elia Lombardini immediately spring to mind – spent many years in government service and reached the pinnacles of their careers in the public sector.

In the Kingdom of the Two Sicilies, the engineering profession developed in these years along the lines already laid down during the Murat period. Entry to the free profession was still conditional on possession of a university degree, while public service employment was reserved for graduates from the *Scuola di Ponti e Strade*. Now administered, together with the engineering corps, by the recently created Ministry of Public Works, this school gradually developed its own teaching programme, and it acquired an excellent reputation thanks to its outstanding academic staff. The school was directed by such eminent engineers as Francesco Carpi (during the French period), Luigi Maleschi (1815–17), Francesco de Vito Piscitelli (1818–24), Carlo Afan de Rivera (1825–52) and Bendetto Lopez Suarez (1853–60), all of whom had served as directors general of bridges and roads. Unlike in Lombardy-Venetia, a public-sector career in the Neapolitan region acquired increasing social prestige during the Restoration period – greater, indeed, than that of the free profession. One notes in evidence for this that, when the professional register of judicial architects-engineers was created, the credentials required of free professionals included specialist examinations as well as a degree; but members of *Ponti e Strade*, by contrast, were enrolled simply on presentation of their diplomas. Presumably, the public-sector career drew its prestige in the South from the dominant role performed by the state in all sectors; a state which was the protagonist, given the absence of alternatives, of the transformation of the territorial and economic-productive system in which the engineers operated.

In the years following the French domination, therefore, the engi-

---

5 *Manuale delle leggi, regolamenti e discipline intorno alle strade, alle acque e alle fabbriche*, Milan, 1845 and subsequent additions.

neering profession evolved along largely similar lines in the various parts of the country. Differences still persisted, of course, owing to the diverse economic and political contexts to which the engineers belonged; nevertheless the cultural foundations of the profession, as well as its areas of competence, were subject to a pronounced process of standardization. The Papal States created their own corps of waterway and road engineers in 1817. And in this case too, there was a significant precedent: the *Bureau des ponts, arges et travaux publics*, an executive body of engineers created by the French in 1809. The serious deterioration of roads and waterways in the papal territories meant that regulation of the sector could be postponed no longer, and a technical service with special powers was accordingly created. Part of a centralized structure, this new corps was administered from 1833 onwards by the General Prefecture of Waterways and Roads until the creation of the unified Ministry of Public Works in 1850.[6] A School of Waterways and Roads was also established, which offered a three-year course[7] to graduates from the universities of Rome and Bologna who had also attended an Academy of Arts. The best pupils entered the *Corpo*, while the others were awarded a licence which entitled them to practise as free professionals. Here too, as in the southern states, public-service employment seems to have enjoyed greater prestige than the private sector. Because of the economic and social backwardness of the papal territories of central Italy, private construction firms which relied on private commissions could provide only a meagre source of income. Consequently, they were an unattractive career option for the young engineer.

The modernization of the engineering profession also proceeded apace in the Tuscan territories, where a state engineering corps presided over by a Council of Engineers was created in 1826. The corps was responsible for the planning and construction of the king's highways, as well as supervision of work on the provincial main roads. It had no jurisdiction over the construction of minor roads, however, and it almost entirely neglected the maintenance of waterways.

In sum, the revival of public works was a phenomenon manifest in every area of Italy during the Restoration period. Involved in the

---

6 R. Santoro, 'L'amministrazione dei lavori pubblici nello Stato pontificio dalla prima restaurazione a Pio IX', *Rassegna degli archivi di Stato*, 1, 1989, pp. 45–94; *Motu proprio della santità di nostro signore Papa Pio VII in data 23 ottobre 1817 sul regolamento dei lavori pubblici di acque strade*, Rome, 1818.

7 *Regolamento della Scuola degl'ingegneri istituita col motuproprio di Nostro Signore del 23 ottobre 1817*, Rome, 1818.

process were the small states like the Duchy of Parma, Piacenza and Guastalla, which regulated the sector by an ordinance issued in 1821, and also larger states like the Kingdom of Sardinia, where a technical branch of the administration was established by the royal patents of 14 March 1816. First to be created in Sardinia was a General Office of Bridges, Roads, Waterways and Forests, which administered a *Corpo d'Ingegneri di Ponti e Strade* comprising both military sappers and civil engineers. Two years later the civil engineering corps was split off from the *Corpo* and placed under the authority of the Ministry of the Interior. In 1825 it was given the definitive title of Corps of Civil Engineers. In 1847 the Ministry of Public Works replaced the General Office and consequently assumed responsibility for the engineering corps. Once again, entry to the corps was open only to applicants possessing a university diploma. The regulations of 1825, in fact, provided for the establishment of a triennial school of applied engineering run by the *Corpo* itself, although subsequent amendments in 1833 abolished this provision.[8]

The first half of the nineteenth century, therefore, saw a major resurgence in the engineering profession which was then followed by a phase of stabilization. The theoretical principles for the training of engineers were formalized, and the central role of engineers in the state created out of the Old Regime was affirmed. However, this should not give the impression that the process was a straightforward one; on the contrary, it was beset by numerous uncertainties and difficulties. A bewildering plethora of rules and ministerial instructions delayed creation of the government's new technical structures. And this was within a civil service dominated by the suspicion typical of the country's more general climate of repression. Because of their obstinate belief in the superiority of humanistic culture and abstract knowledge, the universities – which provided training not only for free professionals but sometimes also for state-employed engineers – resisted the creation of professorial chairs in technical subjects. The situation changed to some extent in the 1840s, when a generation of younger and more able academics moved into the universities; but the renewal of university curricula still proceeded slowly, and higher engineering education was still constricted by the disciplinary framework established at the beginning of the century: hydraulics, agronomy and techniques of construction. An evident factor at work here was the economic

---

[8] *Bollettino delle leggi, regolamenti, istruzioni e circolari*, Turin, 1859, vols I–II.

backwardness of the country, exacerbated by political divisions and the overwhelming predominance of agriculture.

Some attempts were made to introduce courses in mechanics or chemistry. Nevertheless, apart from Piedmont's dynamic programme of public works, including railways – although these were built at the end of the period between 1849 and 1859 – and the economic growth achieved by Lombardy, the other areas of Italy stagnated. They were therefore inhospitable terrain for the growth of more specialized branches of engineering. Moreover, even the apparently strict controls on the free profession showed signs of breaking down. Some engineers never took the state examination; others indeed, at least in the first decades of the century, did not attend university but received their training at privately run professional schools. Nonetheless, the engineering profession made enormous progress in the first fifty years of the nineteenth century. And Italian engineers, united in awareness of their shared expertise, began to recognize themselves as a professional group even in regions where there was no previous tradition of professional associationism. In Venetia, for example, a mutual benefit society for engineers came into operation in the 1850s and survived until the end of the century.[9] These were still not solid and powerful institutions, and they bore little resemblance to the great foreign organizations like the Institution of Civil Engineers, founded in 1818, the *Société des Ingénieurs Civils de France* (1848) or Austria's *Oesterreichische Ingenieur und Architekten* (1848). Nevertheless, they signalled the presence of a professional category whose voice would be heard with increasing insistence in the liberal climate of post-Unification Italy.

2. THE ENGINEER IN THE NEW ITALY

Following the proclamation of the unified state in 1861, the young nation-state made prodigious efforts to overcome its profound regional differences and to accomplish effective national unity. The objective was to create a civil service which was both economically and administratively cohesive. It was also necessary to reorganize the engineering profession, which was of evident 'strategic' importance if Italy was to be modernized by restructuring its industrial system and imposing administrative control over a vast territory with only a rudimentary network of communications.

The first important change to the engineering profession came in

[9] M. Minesso. *Tecnici e modernizzazione nel Veneto*, pp. 33–4.

the field of professional training. The foundations of higher technical education[10] were laid by the law on education promulgated by Gabrio Casati in 1859.[11] The first step was the creation of a School of Applied Engineering in Turin and a higher technical institute in Milan, soon to be renamed the *Politecnico*.[12] In the early 1860s, between the drafting of the *legge Casati* – the law which regulated the education sector in Italy until the passing of the *legge Gentile* in 1923 – and the founding of the Milan Polytechnic, precisely which model of higher technical education was most appropriate to Italy was a matter of considerable debate. The educational systems of the major European countries were scrutinized as regards both their didactic features and the role assumed by the state. In this latter respect, there were essentially two models available elsewhere in Europe: on the one hand, the British system with its reliance on private initiative; on the other, the state-controlled system of countries like France and Germany. As regards the organization of technical training in particular, there were further alternatives. In Great Britain engineering training was still largely based on the apprenticeship system and continued to be so throughout the nineteenth century. In France and Germany, by contrast, formalized instruction predominated, although it was organized on a different basis in each country. French engineers received their general training at the *Ecole Polytechnique* and then enrolled at the special schools, the best known of which in terms of prestige and tradition was the *Ecole des Ponts et Chaussées*. In the German states, the most reputable institutions were the Polytechnics, with their distinctive emphasis on experimentation, on specialization, and on study of the most innovative branches of engineering geared to industrial development.[13]

[10] C.G. Lacaita, *Istruzione e sviluppo industriale in Italia (1859–1914)*, Florence, 1973.
[11] Still an essential reference is the essay by G. Talamo, *La scuola dalla legge Casati all'inchiesta del 1864*, Milan, 1960.
[12] G.M. Pugno. *Storia del Politecnico di Torino dalle origini alla seconda guerra mondiale*, Turin, 1959; *La formazione dell'ingegnere nella Torino di Alberto Castigliano. Le Scuole di ingegneria nella seconda meta' dell'800*, Turin, 1984; F. Lori, *Il Politecnico di Milano*, Milan, 1940; *Il centenario del Politecnico di Milano*, Milan, 1963; *Il Politecnico di Milano. Una Scuola nella formazione della società industriale 1863–1914*, Milan, 1981; *Il Politecnico di Milano nella storia italiana 1914–1963*, Roma–Bari, 1986.
[13] G. Ahlstrom, *Engineers and Industrial Growth. Higher Technical Education and the Engineering Profession During the Nineteenth and Early Twentieth Centuries: France, Germany, Sweden and England*, London, 1982; T. Shinn, *Savoir scientifique et pouvoir social. L'Ecole polytechnique 1794–1914*, Paris, 1980; K.H. and L.W. König (eds.), *Technik, Ingenieure und Gesellschaft. Geschichte des Vereins Deutscher Ingenieure 1856–1981*, Düsseldorf, 1981; K. Gispen, *New Profession, Old Order. Engineers and German Society, 1815–1914*, Cambridge, 1989; D.S.L. Cardwell, *The Organisation of Science in England*, London, 1957; P. Alter, *The Reluctant Patron. Science and the State in Britain 1850–1920*, Oxford, 1987.

In the event, the model of higher technical education chosen by the Italian ruling class was a compromise which mediated among the systems developed in the rest of Europe, the requirements of the Italian economy (still largely based on agriculture), and the experience, as we have seen, accumulated in the first half of the nineteenth century by the pre-Unification states. The system selected was shortly afterwards given definitive ratification in the form of the *Regolamento Generale sulle Scuole di Applicazione* enacted in 1875.[14] Higher technical education, as well as almost the whole of the educational sector, was to be directly administered by the state. Specific institutes were created, and diplomas in engineering were awarded after a five-year programme of study (comprising a preparatory biennium in the faculties of mathematics followed by a three-year course of applied study in the higher institutes of engineering). Graduates with qualifications from these institutes were guaranteed entry to both the private and the public sectors. The post-university probationary period and the state examination were abolished.

Administratively and didactically, the new university system of technical education was now standardized throughout the country. Nevertheless an evident split at the level of curricular content soon became apparent. On the one side of the divide stood the Schools of Applied Engineering, which emulated the French model and trained civil engineers with more traditional academic backgrounds. On the other side stood the Milan Polytechnic. Modelled on the German higher technical institutes, and also awarding diplomas in mechanical engineering, the Polytechnic's curriculum was designed to provide the specialized personnel required by infant industry. Rather similar in structure and curriculum to the Milan Polytechnic was the School of Applied Engineering in Turin which, after 1879, worked closely with the Industrial Museum and obtained authorization to organize a course for industrial engineers. In 1896, the School of Applied Engineering of Turin became the Turin Polytechnic.[15]

In the years following Unification, therefore, the reorganization of

---

[14] 'Regolamento generale universitario per le regie Scuole di applicazione approvato con r.d. 3 ottobre 1875', *Bollettino ufficiale del Ministero della pubblica istruzione*, 1876, pp. 37–9; *Regolamento per le regie Scuole di applicazione per gli ingegneri approvato con regio decreto 8 ottobre 1876*, 1877, pp. 44–8.

[15] 'Legge 8 luglio 1906 n. 321 per la fondazione del regio Politecnico' and 'Regolamento interno del r. Politecnico', *Annuario del r. Politecnico di Torino*, 1906–11, pp. 89–123.

Italian higher technical education led to the creation of a nationwide system of applied engineering schools.[16] With the advent of the Polytechnic, the engineering courses at Pavia ceased, and schools of applied engineering were opened in Padua, Bologna, Rome, Naples and Palermo. However, it should be borne in mind that these new institutions were created in places where, as we have seen, a tradition of study and teaching in technical subjects was already well established. In short, they were not created *ex novo*. At Padua (where the school of applied engineering became a full-fledged faculty in 1875–76), at Bologna (which began teaching technical subjects in 1875 and whose engineering curriculum was completed in 1877), and at Palermo (founded in 1860 but unable to begin its teaching activities until 1866), technical subjects were being taught in faculties of physics, mathematics and natural sciences created in the first half of the century. At Rome and Naples, it was instead two independent institutions – the Schools of Bridges and Roads founded during the Restoration period and which trained engineers for the civil service – which provided the basis for new faculties of engineering. The Rome school had already been incorporated into the Papal University earlier in the century; its new courses began in 1872–73. The Naples school was taken over by the University of Naples and removed from the authority of the Ministry of Public Works in 1863.[17]

The schools of applied engineering were closely linked to the universities. Independent in administrative, disciplinary and academic matters, they were regulated by the universities' self-governing bodies and funded by the Ministry of Education. This was a further feature which differentiated these schools from the Milan Polytechnic, which could rely on substantial financial support from local government and from private organizations. The Milanese institute increased its independence in 1875 when it obtained sufficient funds to launch a two-year preparatory course in engineering. However, the broad autonomy enjoyed by the Milan Polytechnic was counteracted by the *Regolamento Generale* of 1875–76, which allowed the schools of applied engineering to revise their study programmes. This equipped the more adroit directors and lecturers of the individual schools with a weapon which they wielded to good effect, and they sometimes also involved local power-groups in the process.[18]

---

[16] For an overview of the various Italian schools of engineering during the liberal period see Ministero della Istruzione Pubblica, *Monografie delle Università e degli Istituti superiori in Italia*, Rome, 1911–13, vols I–II.

[17] 'Leggi istitutive e regolamenti interni', *Annuario della r. Scuola di applicazione per gli ingegneri in Napoli*, 1890, pp. 1–20.

[18] C.G. Lacaita, 'Il Politecnico di Milano', in *Il Politecnico di Milano 1863–1914*, pp. 14–15; *Regolamento per le regie Scuole di applicazione*, p. 45.

Broadly speaking, the faculties of engineering performed both national and local functions. At the national level, in something akin to a tacit division of labour, the Milan Polytechnic and the Turin School of Engineering concentrated on the training of engineers for industry – the modernization of which had become a matter of concern after the industrial survey of 1874 and the first protectionist tariffs of 1878.[19] The task of the schools of applied engineering was instead to prepare engineers for employment in government service. At the local or regional level (which for the Polytechnic came increasingly to coincide with the national level, given the industrial growth of Milan and Lombardy), the tasks of the faculties of engineering were markedly different, for they had to cater to the diversified needs for specialized technical personnel in the country's various and economically heterogeneous regions. The changes made to the schools' study curricula, although they still adhered to a common set of principles, are evidence of the considerable efforts made to adjust to these needs.

Applied studies were preceded by a two-year course of basic training which was substantially similar for both students attending the Polytechnic (after 1875 in loco) and those attending the Schools of Applied Engineering (at the faculty of mathematics). Once the future engineer had completed this preparatory biennium, he was equipped with background theoretical knowledge in physics, mathematics and chemistry.[20] The core subjects taught at the Schools of Applied Engineering were agronomy, hydraulics and techniques of construction – subjects which the schools had taken over from the pre-Unification faculties of mathematics and then gradually expanded. The growth of university courses in rural economics and surveying obviously stemmed from the overwhelming economic weight of agriculture in

[19] See L'imprenditorialità italiana dopo l'Unità. L'inchiesta industriale del 1970–74, Milan, 1970; V. Castronovo, 'La Storia economica', in Storia d'Italia, vol. III, tome I, Turin, 1975, pp. 72–99; V. Zamagni, Dalla periferia al centro. La seconda rinascita economica dell'Italia 1861–1981, Bologna, 1990, p. 145–54.

[20] The information that follows on courses, syllabuses, laboratories, study journeys and students has been gathered from systematic examination of the yearbooks of the various Schools: Programma della r. Scuola di applicazione per gli ingegneri in Torino, 1880–81/1905–6; Annuario del r. Politecnico di Torino, 1906/1916–17; Annuario del r. Istituto tecnico superiore di Milano, 1863–64/1922–23; Programma della r. Scuola di applicazione di Padova, 1876–77/1915–16: Annuario della r. Scuola di applicazione per gli ingegneri di Bologna, 1877–78/1922–23; Annuario della r. Scuola di applicazione per gli ingegneri di Roma, 1873–74/1915–16; Annuario della r. Scuola di applicazione per gli ingegneri in Napoli, 1867–68/1904–5; Annuario del r. Scuola superiore politecnica in Napoli, 1905–6/1922–23; Annuario della r. Scuola di applicazione per gli ingegneri di Palermo, 1890–91/1922–23.

post-Unification Italy, and this was an area in which the engineer-agronomist was of key importance. Especially in the fertile lands of the Po Valley, now being converted to capitalist methods of agriculture, engineering expertise was essential for rationalization of farm management and assessment of the compensation to be paid to outgoing tenants for the increased value of land.[21] The Milan Polytechnic, in its determination to extend the range of its courses aimed at boosting industrial development, not coincidentally laid especial emphasis on rural economics and surveying. These courses were considerably expanded in the mid-1880s. On the urging of the Ministry of Finance – preoccupied by the difficulties that obstructed the general land survey, chief among which was the inadequate training of the personnel involved – the schools of engineering now introduced courses in cadastral surveying.[22]

Agronomy was flanked, of course, by courses in hydraulics: the science, that is, of water control, irrigation systems and land reclamation. However, now that rivers and canals had lost their importance as communication routes, interest in their maintenance correspondingly dwindled. Other subjects appeared on the university syllabuses – notably land drainage and reclamation, since these were closely bound up with the capitalist transformation of agriculture. And courses in hydraulic constructions were also expanded. Engineering training placed increasing emphasis on techniques for the pressurized piping of mains water, on the design of large-scale harbour installations, and on dam building. All this was in synergy with the transformations undertaken by a country which, amid a host of difficulties, was modernizing itself, whose cities were equipping themselves with sewage systems and mains water supplies, and whose industries were converting to water-powered technology.[23]

Until the 1890s, the construction sector was the most dynamic of the traditional engineering disciplines. Courses in road, bridge and tunnel building as well as in civil building accordingly developed and grew more specialized. The greatest expansion, however, occurred in railway engineering. Here there was an evident connection between the development of the building sector in general

---

[21] M. Malatesta, *I signori della terra. L'organizzazione degli interessi agrari padani 1860–1914*, Milan, 1989, pp. 114–24; idem, 'La Società' agraria di Lombardia e le élites fondiarie milanesi', in R. Finzi (ed.), *Fra Studio, politica ed economia: la Società agraria dalle origini all'età giolittiana*, Bologna, 1992.

[22] AUP, SA, Cart., 1886–87, Coppino alla Scuola, Rome, 5 November 1886.

[23] C. Giovannini, 'Italy', in R. Rodger (ed.), *European Urban History. Prospect and Retrospect*, Leicester and London, 1993.

and that of the railways in particular, with the creation of a nationwide network of infrastructures to link Italy's various regions together. Not by chance, when the 'railway unification' of the
country was finally achieved in the 1890s, this area of study lapsed
into neglect.[24] The same pattern can be discerned in the civil
building sector, which boomed during the urban reconstruction of
the large cities: in Rome especially, as it adjusted in the 1870s to
its newfound role as the capital. Courses in civil and rural building
and in technical architecture nevertheless still retained an important
place on the syllabuses of the engineering faculties in the years that
followed, because they provided training in the principal activities
of a free profession which, throughout the liberal period, and also
thereafter, provided engineering graduates with most of their opportunities for employment.

However, the curricula of the Schools of Applied Engineering
gave secondary importance to mechanical technologies – the
'engine' of the industrialization process – despite the presence of
such outstanding teachers as Enrico Bernardi, the pioneer car man-
ufacturer, at Padua or Jacopo Benetti, an expert in machine construction and later director of the School of Applied Engineering at
Bologna.[25] Although courses in agricultural machinery, hydraulic
and heat engines, often flanked by machine design, were taught in
all the schools, they were paltry affairs compared with the range
and depth of the specialized courses for industrial engineers offered
by the Milan Polytechnic (after 1863) and the Turin School of
Applied Engineering (after 1879). These institutions responded to
the needs of infant industry by promoting specialist courses in mechanical technology, industrial mechanics, machine construction,
heat engines, technological chemistry, metallurgy and mining. In
1887 and 1888 both Milan and Turin introduced compulsory attendance on courses in electrical engineering – which had started as
lectures or optional courses some years previously, simultaneously
with the opening of Italy's first electricity generating stations and
the founding of the first Italian companies in the electricity sector.
In 1883, in fact, the power station at San Radegonda near Milan

---

[24] L. Bortolotti, 'Viabilità e sistemi infrastrutturali', *Storia d'Italia. Annali*, 8, Turin,
1985, pp. 287–366.
[25] On Benetti: ACS, MPI, Dir. Gen. Istr. Sup., f. Pers. Univ., I vers., Benetti Jacopo;
M. Medici, 'Jacopo Benetti', DBI, vol. VIII, Rome, 1966, pp. 481–2. On Bernardi:
AUP, *Registro del personale universitario per gli anni 1867–1885*, p. 131; Comitato nazionale per le onoranze ad Enrico Bernardi. *Enrico Bernardi pioniere dell'automobi-
lismo*, Padova, 1927; M. Medici, 'Enrico Bernardi', DBI, vol. IX, Rome, 1967,
pp. 156–7.

came into operation and in 1886 the *Società Edison* was born.[26] Within a few years, specialist courses in electrical measurement, dynamoelectric machinery and electrical installations completed the gamut of engineering training delivered by the polytechnics.

Courses in engineering were taught by means of formal lectures *ex cathedra*, laboratory practice and educational visits. However, poorly equipped university laboratories – which in those years were hardly adequate for teaching purposes let alone research – prevented students from putting the theoretical knowledge acquired during lectures into practice. The pupils of Milan and Turin were better off than their counterparts at the other schools of engineering because of the financial independence enjoyed by the Milan Polytechnic, which opened laboratories of electrical engineering (in 1887) and applied mechanics (in 1895), and because of the Turin Polytechnic's association with the Industrial Museum.

However, at the Milan and Turin Polytechnics, like the engineering schools in the rest of the country, most students received their practical training in the form of study visits, for which they were obliged to pay a special fee. Educational tours were arranged for each year of the course, but the most interesting were reserved for final-year students. The itineraries covered most of Europe and were travelled by pupils from both the Schools of Applied Engineering and the institutes of Milan and Turin. Indeed, graduands from different faculties often made part of the journey together. They visited historic cities, modern farm businesses, major projects in railway engineering, large-scale harbour installations, and the most technically advanced factories. The itineraries changed as syllabuses evolved, so that they initially concentrated on more traditional engineering projects and then shifted their emphasis to industrial installations.[27]

The rationalization of the engineering curriculum, which now concluded with a final degree examination, led to the gradual disappearance of the apprenticeship system still in operation during the 1850s. The engineering faculties turned out increasing numbers of graduates, and they were attended by students who regarded a degree as a passport to social advancement: not a few of them were the sons of the petite bourgeoisie, although of course substantial numbers belonged to the medium-high bourgeoisie and some

[26] R. Bisazza, 'La Società Edison e il suo gruppo', in *Lo sviluppo della Società Edison e il progresso economico di Milano*, Milan, 1934, pp. 133–67; B. Bezza (ed.), *Energia e sviluppo l'industria elettrica italiana e la società Edison*, Turin, 1986.

[27] Detailed descriptions of these study tours can be found in the yearbooks listed at note 20.

indeed to the aristocracy.[28] Until the end of the century, moreover, a degree in engineering was, predictably enough, a strictly male preserve.

At the helm of higher technical education stood some of the most outstanding engineers in the country. The directors of the various schools were men of indubitable eminence; an eminence which stemmed, of course, from their academic distinction or technical expertise, but also and especially from their key role in the complex interweaving of profession, society and politics. Often senior officeholders in the professional associations and leading members of the ruling class, they were the protagonists of the country's political life, both national and local. This first generation of directors of the engineering schools – a generation which disappeared with the end of the century – had numerous characteristics in common. Most of them had trained in the pre-Unification faculties of mathematics, and they embraced a culture of a markedly theoretical bent: mathematicians like Luigi Cremona in Rome (1873–1903), Fortunato Padula in Naples (1864–81), Giuseppe Albeggiani in Palermo (1866–80), scholars of hydraulics and mathematics like Prospero Richelmy (1860–89) in Turin, Francesco Brioschi in Milan (1863–97), Domenico Turazza in Padua (1875–92), Cesare Razzaboni in Bologna (1877–93), Michele Capitò in Palermo (1892–1909), professors of construction engineering like Ambrogio Mendia in Naples (1881–86) and Giovanni Curioni (1882–87) in Turin, of architecture like Filippo Basile in Palermo (1880–91)[29] – these were academics who had been closely involved in the *Risorgimento* and then emerged as authoritative members of the ruling political class of the new Italy. Brioschi, Cremona and Basile played a significant role in the uprisings of 1848, and Brioschi,

---

[28] See M. Minesso, *Tecnici e modernizzazione*, pp. 188–99 and the relevant tables. See also the essays by A. Banti, G. Montroni and F. Cammarano in this book.

[29] The biographical information on the academic staff at the various schools of engineering has been taken from their personal dossiers deposited at the *Archivio centrale dello Stato*, in the files of the *Ministero della pubblica istruzione, Direzione generale dell'istruzione superiore, fascicoli del personale universitario, I e II versamento*.

Interesting information is also available from C. Pintacuda, 'Giuseppe Albeggiani', *Annuario della Scuola di applicazione per gli ingegneri di Palermo*, 1892–93, pp. 3–6; Comitato per le onoranze al prof. G.B. Basile, *Giovan Battista Basile*, Palermo, undated; 'Prof. Comm. Cesare Razzaboni', *Annuario della r. Scuola di applicazione per gli ingegneri di Bologna*, 1893–94, pp. 109–22; C. Guidi, 'G. Curioni', *Annuario della r. Scuola di applicazione per gli ingegneri di Torino*, 1887–88, pp. 87–98; E. Paladini, 'F. Brioschi', *Atti del Collegio degli ingegneri ed architetti di Milano*, II–III–IV, 1897, pp. 105–28; idem, *Commemorazione di Domenico Turazza*, pp. 16–28; 'Michele Capitò', *Annuario della r. Scuola di applicazione per gli ingegneri di Palermo*, 1908–9, pp. 76–80.

Cremona, Padula, Curioni, Turazza and Razzaboni were subsequently elected to parliament. However, these academics are most notable for their power in the city and provincial councils, bodies in which they often exerted considerably more influence than they did in the Chamber of Deputies. Embedded as they were in the leading political and economic class from Turin to Milan, from Padua to Bologna, from Rome to Naples to Palermo, these leading representatives of the engineering profession presided over local public affairs, and especially over the decision-making activities of the municipal and provincial councils. Consequently they decisively influenced decisions concerning urban and rural planning and the development of industry in the country's various regions.[30]

3. BETWEEN THE CIVIL SERVICE AND PRIVATE EMPLOYMENT

Matching these significant changes in the training of Italian engineers in the period following national Unification were others, just as important, in the engineering profession – and in both its public and private sectors.

One of the first tasks confronting post-Unification Italy was the construction of a network of infrastructures which would link together the various areas of the country, encourage the growth of the newly created national market and integrate it with the international market. It was an undertaking, however, beset with numerous and major difficulties. The country's roads had fallen into a parlous state of disrepair. Its railway network was rudimentary, and its maritime ports were obsolete. Moreover, the country contained vast tracts of marshland which harboured malaria and other diseases, and these required a systematic programme of drainage and reclamation.[31] The figures are unequivocal. In 1865, for example, the average density of roadway in Italy was 300 metres per square kilometre, compared to 1.29 kilometres in France and to the 1.28 kilometres that England had been able to build as early as 1839. One should also bear in mind the marked disparity between the regions of the North, all of which had at least 500 metres of roadway per square kilometre, and the regions of the South, none of which had more that 100 metres per square kilometre. In contrast to the road network, the Italian port system systematically covered the whole of the nation's territory at the time of Unification, although the backwardness of its installations penalized it somewhat in international

[30] See the essay by L. Musella in this book.

[31] P. Morachiello, *Ingegneri e territorio nell'età della Destra (1860–1875). Dal Canale Cavour all'Agro romano*, Rome, 1977.

comparisons. The problem, therefore, was not so much to increase the number of ports as to develop those already in operation so that they could cope with the increase in maritime traffic.[32]

There was no mistaking, therefore, the magnitude of the tasks confronting the Ministry of Public Works and its technical branch, the Corps of Civil Engineers, which was responsible for planning and directing the works undertaken by the state, as well as supervising those contracted out to private companies. The civil engineering corps was not created *ex novo*: it inherited its personnel from the various technical corps run by the pre-Unification state administrations, which have been described above.

As Italy converted to the national state, the decision to adopt the French model for the organization of the engineers employed by the Ministry of Public Works was confirmed. Hence, the system created in the first half of the century was preserved, and it corresponded to those already operating in the principal countries of continental Europe. In emulation of the French system, the waterway and road engineers of Italy's various regions were gradually incorporated into the Corps of Civil Engineers in accordance with the dispositions of the law on public works enacted in March 1865 and which laid the basis for the organization of the Corps during the first twenty years following Unification. This meant, in fact, that no genuinely new legislation was passed in this crucial phase for the state-employed engineers, of whom (if one excludes the few engineers employed as railway surveillance crew) there were 674 in 1866. This number resulted from the unification of the state-employed engineers in the various parts of the country into a single corps, and it was criticized from some quarters as being too high; a criticism which was vigorously rejected by Stefano Jacini, the minister of public works.[33] With the Law of 1882, more systematic regulation was given to the public-sector engineering profession, and staffing levels were fixed with a view to the continuing and major expansion of public works. Only growing economic problems and the consequent curbing of state intervention in the sector led to a cutback in managerial technical personnel (by a series of measures issued in the mid-1890s). Engineers began their careers in the corps as trainees after passing an entrance examination open to all engineering graduates aged under thirty. They then rose through the various ranks of engineer, chief engineer and inspector. The chief engineer directed the

---

[32] For a survey of the state of the territories and infrastructures see A. Mioni, *Le trasformazioni territoriali in Italia nella prima età industriale*, Venice, 1988 (1st edn 1977).

[33] In a report presented to Parliament in 1867: see S. Jacini, *L'amministrazione dei lavori pubblici in Italia dal 1860 al 1867*, Florence, 1867.

office of the Corps of Civil Engineers operating in each province. The *compartimenti* or regions, which comprised several provinces, were administered by the inspectors. But the true local centres of the public works service were the provincial offices, in which the junior engineers were employed.

These offices were responsible for almost all the public engineering projects carried out on behalf of the state. In the early 1860s the Corps of Civil Engineers expanded its sphere of competence to include road and railway building, the running of the state railways, the policing and maintenance of waterways, installations for defence and navigation, the construction and maintenance of harbours, urban development, the construction and maintenance of public buildings, and even the telegraph service and the state-owned mines. This concentration of functions, however, soon severely impeded the efficient functioning of the technical corps, and several of its tasks were assigned to other technical apparatuses specially created for the purpose – namely, the Inspectorate for the Construction and Maintenance of Railways, the Corps of Miners (1871), the superintendency of monuments, and the land register offices. Employment opportunities for engineers in the public sector therefore increased considerably,[34] and they were further augmented by the jobs created after 1865 by local government – especially by the provincial administrations, to which the new legislation gave prime responsibility for public works and which consequently set up their own engineering offices. After Unification, there was also a significant expansion of the municipal technical offices, which were responsible for major projects in urban redevelopment (demolition of the old city walls, the rebuilding of entire districts around railway stations, as well as other schemes).

The state-employed engineers – who in this period still represented one of the most modern aspects of the profession – often collaborated closely with self-employed engineers (the largest group in the profession). Still performing an important role, moreover, were the engineer-agronomists, who worked as land agents and agricultural surveyors, and undertook land reclamation for both private customers and the government.

However, it was in the private sector that the most significant innovations occurred with the rise of two new specialized professions – those of railway engineer and industrial engineer – as a result of national Unification. The enhanced importance of the railway engineer

---

[34] R. Porrini. *I ministeri*, Milan, 1900; C. Melograni (ed.), *Legislazione sui lavori pubblici*, Rome, 1949.

was a direct consequence of the completion of the country's railway network, a topic already discussed. In 1861, there were fewer than 2,000 kilometres of railway line in Italy (as compared with ca. 16,000 in England and ca. 9,300 in France). As well as being inadequate, the Italian railway network was badly distributed geographically, for it was almost entirely concentrated in the Po Valley, the Arno Valley and the Naples area. The government was therefore faced with the task of building around 6,000 kilometres of railway as rapidly as possible, amid enormous technical and economic difficulties. The role of the railway engineer, designer and builder of new installations was crucial in this context, and it would remain so until completion of the national network in the early 1890s. It was the responsibility of the new schools of engineering to train these specialists, all of whom in the first years after Unification had to be imported from abroad. Italian technicians competed energetically for jobs in the large railway companies operating in the various areas of the country – the *Società delle Strade Ferrate dell'Alta Italia*, the *Meridionali* and the *Calabro-Sicule* – into which the national network was divided in 1865 and which were subsequently reorganized into the *Adriatica, Meridionali* and *Sicula*[35] companies in 1879. Employment in the railway companies continued to be highly sought-after even when the expansion of the railway system came to a halt in the last decade of the century.[36]

These years also saw the industrial engineer's rapid rise to an authoritative position in the profession. Italy started along the road to industrialization with the adoption in two stages, in 1878 and 1887, of a set of trade tariffs designed to encourage the growth of national industry within the free competition regime of the international market. Entrepreneurial initiative – vigorous in the northwestern regions since the middle years of the century, amongst other things because of the presence of foreign capitalists – now took root in other 'poles' of the country, notably the Venice area in the north-east; and a national entrepreneurial class began to grow and flourish. The engineers further increased their influence and prestige: as the founders and owners of firms, as company executives and directors, as managers at various levels, they and their work constituted one of the major factors in Italian industrial development. One could cite as examples such celebrated names as Giovanni Battista Pirelli (founder of the tyre company of the same name) or Vincenzo Stefano Breda (the engineer and finan-

---

[35] Ministero dei lavori pubblici, Regio Ispettorato delle strade ferrate, *Elenco delle ferrovie costruite a tutto aprile 1899*, Rome, 1899. For a survey of the reconstruction see Mioni, *Le trasformazioni territoriali in Italia*, pp. 74ff.

[36] See, for example, on Padua the documentation in AUP, SA, Cart., 1902–3.

cier who created the *Società Terni*). But exclusive emphasis on outstanding personalities such as these obscures the exceptional importance of the other engineers at the forefront of Italian industry since its beginnings. More indicative of this trend, therefore, is the large number of industrial managers who had graduated from the Polytechnics of Milan and Turin, or the many engineering graduates from the Padua School of Applied Engineering who managed important industries in the Venetian area but who have since lapsed into obscurity: Carlo Serafini, for instance, who worked for the *Società Veneta per la costruzione e l'esercizio di ferrovie secondarie* in Padua, or Pietro Pusinich, a mechanical engineer at the *Officine Néville* of Venice.[37] Of course, this new breed of engineer sprang up in the wake of industrialization, and it was concentrated in those northwestern regions of the country which constituted, and would continue to do so for many years, the industrial base of the Peninsula.

4. IMPOSSIBLE ASSOCIATION

The modernization of Italy was begun by the rightist political forces of the *Destra Storica*, amid the numerous difficulties and major social tensions that followed national Unification. However, it assumed more the form of the conversion or construction of new local infrastructures than an overhauling of the country's productive system as a whole, which still depended on a backward agricultural sector. This process considerably enhanced the status of the engineering profession in the social sphere (significant, for example, is the high percentage of technicians in the post-Unification period who belonged to the middle-upper classes), but it also increased its stature relative to the other liberal professions, those which had always enjoyed ascribed prestige. In the new political situation, which guaranteed the freedom of association, and in the climate created by the modernization of the country – a climate which encouraged greater professional self-esteem – the engineers founded numerous professional associations. The aims of these organizations now definitively shifted away from the mutual benefit schemes typical of those prior to Unification as they embarked on wider-ranging action.[38] By the mid-1860s, influential associations of engineers were already active in northern Italy and in Tuscany. In 1866 the Milan College of Engineers and Architects was founded, and in 1868 the Society of Engineers and Industrialists of Turin: two orga-

[37] M. Minesso, *Tecnici e modernizzazione*, pp. 31ff.
[38] Collegio degli ingegneri e architetti di Milano, *Statuto*, Milan, 1868.

nizations which flanked the Colleges of Engineers of Genoa and Florence, in operation since 1855, and the Mutual Benefit Society of Engineers of Venice (1858).

Despite their limited resources, these associations were patterned on the great engineering organizations that had been created in other European countries over the previous fifteen years. The structure of the Italian colleges, however, resembled more that of the *Oesterreichische Ingenieur und Architekten*, the *Société des Ingénieurs Civils*, or the *German Verein Deutscher Ingenieure* created in 1856, than that of the prestigious Institution of Civil Engineers. The Italian colleges modelled themselves on these societies by establishing a registered office and by creating their own governing bodies. Periodic meetings were convened by individual associations to discuss questions of importance to the profession. The debate on technical matters conducted by the leading colleges focused on two issues: on the one hand, whether or not to join the international technical-scientific community; on the other, whether or not to specialize in aspects more closely tied to the economic conditions of their respective regions (evidence of this concern is provided by the libraries created by each college). Like the principal associations of continental Europe, but unlike the British Institution of Civil Engineers, most of the Italian colleges did not require their members to be practising engineers: in Milan and Turin, in Florence, Rome and Naples, membership was also open to industrialists and to experts in technological subjects. As regards the aims pursued by the associations, these divided between two main areas: the study of the applied sciences and of technical issues in the public interest (given priority by the statutes of the Milan, Turin and Florence colleges); and the tutelage of the profession's interests (expressly stipulated by the statutes of the colleges of Rome and Palermo).[39]

The 1870s were years of substantial growth for Italian engineering. The achievement of national unity, especially after the conquest of Rome in 1870, opened up new areas of activity for engineers. A further outcome of the consolidation of what was still a relatively young profession was the development of associationism, a phenomenon which was closely bound up with the protection of professional credentials. Although there is no doubt that this protectionism was determined by corporatist interests, in this initial and expansionary phase it nevertheless combined with an evident need to give more precise

---

[39] Società degli ingegneri e degli industriali in Torino, *Statuto*, Turin, 1866; Collegio degli architetti e ingegneri in Firenze, *Statuto*, Florence, 1876; Collegio degli ingegneri, architetti ed agronomi di Roma, *Statuto e regolamento interno*, Rome, 1877; Collegio degli ingegneri e architetti di Palermo, *Statuto*, Palermo, 1876.

specification to the profession and to establish its code of ethics. Between 1870 and 1879 no fewer than ten new colleges, some of them of enduring prestige, were created in various parts of the country. In 1871 the *Circolo tecnico d'ingegneri, architetti e agronomi* was founded in Rome, to be subsequently transformed into the *Collegio degli ingegneri e architetti ed agronomi* in 1876. The college of Naples opened in 1875, followed in 1876 by the colleges of Bologna and Palermo. Again in 1876, the college of Florence renewed its statute. These new colleges were presided over by some of the most eminent members of the Italian engineering profession: Alessandro Betocchi was chief official of the Rome college jointly with Prince Emanuele Ruspoli; Federico Rendina was elected president in Naples, and Giovanni Battista Basile in Palermo; Felice Francolini ran the Florence college, whose honorary president was the count and engineer Ubaldino Peruzzi, a leading member of Parliament.

In the 1870s, the first national congresses of engineers began to meet, following the initiative of the Milan college of engineers which organized the first congress in September 1872. These years also saw issues raised which would be constantly at the centre of professional debate in the remaining decades of the liberal period. The first problem was strictly economic in nature and concerned the fixing of fees, since these varied considerably from one region to another. The suggestion that the colleges should draw up and apply fee schedules was shortly followed by a proposal to give them greater control over the labour market, in favour of graduate engineers, thereby regulating access to incomes deriving from the expert appraisals commissioned by the government, by the public authorities and by the lawcourts; and it was even proposed that the colleges should discipline recruitment by private firms.[40]

The Florence congress of 1875 unanimously approved motions calling for the constitution of the professional order and the compiling of professional registers at every appeal court, along the lines suggested by the college of Naples. It also approved the proposal by the Milanese engineer Emilio Bignami-Sormani for the creation of a national association of engineers.[41] However, the positions of the various colleges soon began to diverge and conflicts of opinion grew acrimonious. The proposal to establish professional registers sparked heated debate, principally over the criteria to be adopted in selecting candidates for enrolment. The second proposal was attacked as an attempt to undermine

---

[40] *Primo congresso degli ingegneri ed architetti italiani in Milano*, Milan, 1873.
[41] *Secondo congresso degli architetti ed ingegneri italiani in Firenze*, Florence, 1876.

the autonomy of the individual associations. Last-ditch efforts to agree on a united strategy were made at an extraordinary national assembly convened in Rome in 1877, and at the Third Congress of Engineers held in Naples in 1879. The Rome assembly was called to discuss the constitution of the order's councils (*consigli d'ordine*) and the professional register. A compromise was reached which mediated among the various proposals advanced as alternatives to the Neapolitan motion by the societies of Venice, Florence, Pisa and Palermo. The outcome was the obligation – which applied to the lawcourts and local administrations alike – to commission the services only of engineers enrolled on the professional register. However, at least for the time being, extremely elastic criteria were established for such enrolment.[42] At the 1879 congress, the college of Naples also submitted a scheme for a national association of engineers, once the Milanese proposal had been rejected. This plan envisaged broad autonomies for individual associations and proposed the setting up of a single representative body in Rome; however, it was roundly attacked by the delegates at the congress.[43]

The deliberations of the Rome and Naples meetings failed to produce any concrete results. And the periodic appeals of individual colleges for the government to resolve the confusion of credentials and functions received no response. The creation of a national association was postponed *sine die*, and the institution of the councils and of the professional register, urged once again at the Fourth Congress held in Rome (1883), was dismissed out of hand by the subsequent congresses of Turin (1884) and Venice (1887). This rejection was instigated by the northern Italian associations and especially by the Milan college, which now abandoned its mediatory role of the 1870s and supported the delegations opposed to the establishment of a national engineering council.[44]

Thus, the pioneering phase of engineering associationism and its attempts to forge a common policy on professional issues ended in substantial failure. A profound split opened up between the colleges of the North, which grew increasingly uninterested in regulating the profession, and the colleges of the South, whose members saw the government and private individuals as their principal source of income. Of course, a crucial role in all this was played by the economic and pro-

---

[42] Acn, 1876, pp. 79ff; Acp, 1877, pp. 65ff; Acf, 1877, pp. 112ff; Acr, 1877, pp. 10ff.

[43] *Atti del terzo congresso degli ingegneri ed architetti italiani radunato in Napoli*, Naples, 1880.

[44] *Atti del quarto congresso degli ingegneri ed architetti italiani*, Rome, 1884; *Atti del V congresso degli ingegneri ed architetti italiani*, Turin, 1885; *Atti del VI congresso degli ingegneri ed architetti italiani*, Venice, 1888.

ductive contexts in which the profession in the North and South operated. The engineers in the North enjoyed relatively high demand for their technical skills, the range of which extended as industry developed. In the more static conditions of the *Mezzogiorno*, as well as in certain areas of central Italy, gaining control over public and private commissions became crucial to the profession as the country's economy slid deeper into recession. Thus, during the 1880s, while on the one hand the College of Milan cited liberal principles in its opposition to the creation of the Engineering Council (*consiglio d'ordine*), which it viewed as bureaucratic and repressive, and the professional register, which it considered to be restriction of the customer's freedom of choice, on the other the colleges of central and southern Italy pressed for their introduction.

None of the proposals advanced in the 1870s ever passed into law; indeed, Parliament never even discussed the engineering profession's problems. Blame for this failure lay with the factiousness of the Italian engineers in advancing their claims, and above all with the contrariness of the Milan engineers, who were perhaps the most influential and certainly the most active of the technicians in parliament: already fewer in numbers than the other professional deputies, they consequently had less chance of gaining legalization for their credentials. Furthermore, the policy pursued by the Lombard technicians was coherent with their more general *laissez-faire* principles and the autonomy of that 'State of Milan' of whose ruling class they were a key component.[45]

After the expansionary phase of the 1870s, debate on legal protection of the profession's interests resumed with vigour at the beginning of the 1890s. But it did so in a context of major difficulties for the profession which forced it onto the defensive. The engineers, too, suffered from the grave economic depression now afflicting the country: the government cut back staffing levels in important technical apparatuses, such as the Corps of Civil Engineers, and the building industry stagnated. Furthermore, the completion of a number of large-scale infrastructures, the railway system for instance, reduced the amount of work available to young engineers in search of their first employment. Consequently, agitation for the defence of the engineering qualification – which also took the form of the student protests which erupted in several engineering faculties in 1889 – resumed with a vengeance. Also responsible for this change in climate was the vigorous revival of professional associationism and the proliferation of engineering societies, which aggressively set out to gain legal protection for the profes-

---

[45] F. Fonzi, *Crispi e lo "Stato di Milano"*, Milan, 1972.

sion's interests. Between 1894 and 1895, years in which the country's economic crisis was at its height, fully seven new colleges were created in various parts of the country.

An event of outstanding importance in this critical period was the national assembly of engineers convened in Rome in 1890 under the authoritative chairmanship of Alfredo Baccarini, one of the country's most brilliant engineers, an influential politician, and minister of public works. On the basis of motions tabled by the societies of Bologna and Rome (which in 1886 became the *Società degli ingegneri ed architetti italiani*), a set of principles for regulating the professions of engineer and architect were approved. The assembly voted for the creation of the order's councils, which were to be consulted by the lawcourts when fixing fees, or when examining the qualifications of candidates for enrolment on the professional register. It also became obligatory for the lawcourts and local government to hire the services only of professionals enrolled on the register 'for all commissioned tasks within the exclusive competence of engineers'.[46] Although approval of these proposals was also the result of Baccarini's skilful mediation, it was evident that the northern colleges (Milan and Turin) only agreed to the creation of the order's councils because their request to deprive them of disciplinary authority had been granted. Furthermore, the Milanese delegation's consent was obtained by couching the motion in deliberately vague language, so that not only were private individuals still at liberty to choose the professional they preferred, but also the public administrations retained the right to do so. In fact, the clause which established the obligation of the public administrations with the expression 'commissioned tasks within the exclusive competence of engineers' was ambiguous and difficult to enforce under the law.

The results of the initiative were disappointing, despite the efforts of the Rome engineers' association to persuade the government to approve the project. Although in 1897 the Minister of Justice drafted a bill designed to regulate judicial appraisals, it was never submitted for parliamentary approval.

The cleavages which split the Italian engineers manifestly weakened the profession's position in its dealings with the government. The fragile compromise reached in Rome collapsed on the occasion of the Seventh Congress held in Genoa in 1896. The delegate from the College of Milan, the distinguished engineer Cesare Saldini (also acting on behalf of the other Lombard colleges), tabled a motion of

---

[46] SIAI, 1890, f. I, pp. 110ff; SIAI, f. II, pp. 65ff; Acm, 1890, pp. 85ff; *Criteri fondamentali per una legge intesa a regolare l'esercizio delle professioni di ingegnere e di architetto*, Rome, 1891.

no confidence in the decision taken in 1890 to constitute the order's councils. The Congress, with an agenda which even included an item obliging private individuals to hire only graduate engineers, and which called for reform of the general building regulations (*rego-lamento generale edilizio*), thus broke up in disarray.[47] There was obviously never much likelihood, in a context such as this, that the decision (taken unanimously) to create the national representative body proposed by the colleges of Naples and Florence would be implemented. The only concrete outcome, in fact, was the election of a committee composed of such eminent engineers as Giovanni Cadolini (president of the College of Engineers in Rome), Giuseppe Colombo (the Lombard engineer and businessman) and Giovanni Pini (representative of the college of engineers and architects of Rome); a committee, however, whose activities were soon paralysed by the opposition of the very same associations that had voted for its creation.

Nevertheless, it was precisely in these last years of the century that the engineers finally began to take concerted action. Responsible for this change of behaviour were not the geographically based colleges but the sectoral organizations. These years, in fact, saw the creation of the National Association of Land Survey Engineers and the National College of Italian Railway Engineers. The differences among regional colleges, closely tied to their specific local economic contexts, were attenuated, if not eliminated, by the shared problems created by belonging to the same occupational structure, whether public or private. And this was especially so if this structure was subjected to reorganization which affected staffing levels and/or career advancement. In this connection, it is worth mentioning that the National Association of Land Survey Engineers came into being at precisely the moment when the service was being restructured and a bill to this end was being debated in parliament: a development which provoked alarm among the engineers that their status would be downgraded by their fusion with the surveyors, who also worked for land survey.[48] The National College of Railway Engineers was created at the end of the century, in November 1899. The building of the national railway network was now complete, and the railroad companies were therefore unable to offer further employment. As their franchises approached their expiry dates – with all the uncertainty provoked by their rumoured non-renewal – the railroad com-

---

[47] *VIII congresso degli ingegneri ed architetti italiani in Genova*, Genoa, 1897.
[48] *Bollettino dell'Associazione nazionale fra gli ingegneri del catasto*, 6, 1900, 6, pp. 35ff.

panies began to reduce their costs, of which one easily predictable outcome was the laying-off of redundant personnel.[49]

5. HIGHER TECHNICAL EDUCATION IN THE GIOLITTI PERIOD

In the new century, the Italian economy and its productive system underwent profound changes, which created new roles and new specializations in the engineering profession. The country was passing through the phase of industrial 'take-off' generated by the growth of the steel, engineering and chemicals industries and by the rapid expansion of the electricity industry, which furnished a country as poor in raw materials as Italy with a crucial source of energy.[50] Higher technical education, too, changed in this new economic and productive context. A number of the leading engineering schools began to reorganize their curricula and to give priority to specialization. Indicative of this development was the growth of degree courses in industrial engineering. In 1901 the Naples School of Applied Engineering opened a special industrial section. In 1905 it was reorganized into the *Scuola Superiore Politecnica*, and the course for industrial engineers was split between electromechanical and chemical engineering.[51] The year 1906 saw the inception of the Turin Polytechnic. Thus the fragmentary engineering curriculum at Turin – which had been divided between the propaedeutic two-year course in the mathematics faculty, the School of Applied Engineering and the Industrial Museum – was now unified and streamlined. Simultaneously, Turin's core courses in industrial engineering were flanked by specialist modules in mechanical and chemical engineering. Postgraduate courses in electrotechnics, electrochemistry and mining engineering also appeared on the curriculum. Another industrial engineering section was opened at the Palermo School of Applied Engineering in 1907. The Milan Polytechnic, however, which had always offered a course in industrial engineering, now organized specialist modules in electrotechnics and chemistry. In 1902 the Polytechnic expanded its school of electrotechnics (founded in 1886) and opened a school of electrochemistry to flank its laboratory of applied mechanical engineering, the first to be established in Italy (in 1895). The range of training for industrial engineers was further expanded by

[49] Collegio nazionale degli ingegneri ferroviari italiani, *Statuto*, Milan, 1900.
[50] G. Mori (ed.), *Storia dell'industria elettrica in Italia*, vol. i, *Le origini: 1882–1914*, Rome–Bari, 1992.
[51] The relative provisions are in *Annuario della r. Scuola superiore politecnica*, 1905–6, pp. 3ff. See also R. Scuola superiore politecnica, *Nella ricorrenza del primo centenario*, Naples, 1911.

the founding of the school-laboratories for the oils and fats industry (1906), for the paper and textiles industry (1908), and by the opening of the industrial engineering laboratory (1908).

The reorganization of university technical education brought several other innovations as well. In 1904 the Naval Engineering School of Genoa, founded in 1870, was transferred from the Ministry of Agriculture, Industry and Trade to the Ministry of Education. In 1913 another School of Applied Engineering was opened in Pisa, where a first-year course in engineering had been on the curriculum since 1875. And in 1908 a five-year course in engineering with two specialist modules in general and hydraulic engineering was instituted at the University of Padua. Nevertheless, the outstanding feature of the period was the growth of courses in industrial engineering, and especially in the electrical disciplines – the 'engine' of industrialization. After Milan and Turin, which some time previously had introduced a wide range of specialist courses (in electrotechnics, electrical measurement, electrical installations, electrodynamo machines), and Rome and Naples (which in the 1890s already had chairs in electrotechnics[52]), other courses got under way at Padua (1903), Bologna (1903), Palermo (1909) and Pisa (1913).

However, the expansion of industrial engineering within the more general framework of the greater specialization of engineering studies did not eliminate the dichotomous nature of Italian higher technical education, which, as we have seen, had been its constant and distinctive feature. The conversion of the Turin faculty into a Polytechnic reinforced the privileged position in the training of industrial engineers that it shared with the Milan Polytechnic. Designed to perform a similar role was the reorganized faculty of engineering at the University of Naples, which now no longer provided training solely for civil engineers. However, given the simultaneously 'national' and 'local' functions performed by each school of engineering, Naples could never have successfully competed against Turin and Milan. At the national level, the narrower range of industrial engineering courses offered by the Neapolitan school (which in fact had no propaedeutic biennium) meant that aspiring engineers continued to attend the two northern polytechnics. At the local level, the creation of an industrial section at Naples was deliberately intended to promote industrialization in the area (not by chance, the new institute was provided for by the 1904 law on the economic development of the city). At Turin and

[52] With Gugliemo Mengarini in Rome, Luigi Lombardi in Naples, Ferdinando Lori in Padua, Luigi Donati in Bologna, Alberto Dina in Palermo.

Milan, by contrast, the new specialist courses were introduced to meet the needs of local society. The events at the Padua School, which specialized in hydraulic engineering, confirmed the division of roles at the national level between Milan and Turin on the one hand, and the other faculties of engineering on the other. And they also highlighted the 'local' function of the various schools, which forged technical skills that differed significantly from one regional economic context to another.

A first attempt to standardize higher technical education in Italy was made towards the end of the Giolitti period, with the introduction between 1913 and 1914 of a new set of general regulations.[53] The aim was to impose greater uniformity on the syllabuses of the country's now numerous engineering faculties. Courses were to be more closely linked with the propaedeutic two-year programme, and core subjects were to be the same in all schools and also obligatory. Final examinations were to be oral. Further evidence of the dynamism of industrial engineering in the Italian universities was the steady increase in enrolments on degree courses in the subject. In the early years of the century, matriculations in industrial engineering grew in numbers until they almost equalled enrolments on courses in civil engineering, and they stayed at this level until the First World War.[54] One significant sign of ongoing change in the profession was the graduation of the first female students of engineering (Emma Strada at Turin in 1908, and Gaetanina Calvi at Milan, both of whom were awarded degrees in civil engineering).

By the early decades of this century a 'second generation' of academics had moved in to occupy the topmost posts in higher technical education. The protagonists of the pioneering phase of the schools of engineering – many of whom had received their university training before Unification – departed in the first decade of the new century. Their places were taken by engineers and scientists who had graduated from the post-Unification faculties – except for Milan and Turin, where a number of older academics, like Giuseppe Colombo and Enrico D'Ovidio, remained in charge. The members of this 'second generation' had numerous characteristics in common, both with each

[53] 'Regolamento per le scuole di applicazione degli ingegneri', Annuario del r. Politecnico di Milano, 1914–15, part I, pp. 34ff.
[54] C.G. Lacaita, 'Ingegneri e scuole politecniche nell'Italia liberale', in S. Soldani, G. Turi (eds), Fare gli italiani. Scuola e cultura nell'Italia contemporanea, Bologna, 1993, pp. 241–2. On enrolments see also the statistics set out in C.F. Ferraris, 'Statistiche delle Università e degli Istituti superiori', Annali di statistica, vol. 6, s. VI, Rome, 1913.

other and with the generation that had preceded them. Almost all of them came from a theoretical and traditional academic background. With the exception (apart from Colombo) of Cesare Saldini, professor of engineering technology, and Luigi Zunini, professor of electrical measurement at Milan, and Ferdinando Lori, professor of electrotechnics at Padua, the other directors were all mathematicians, theoretical physicists, hydraulic engineers, or lecturers in construction science. This meant, therefore, that with the exception of Milan and Padua the growth of higher technical education would still proceed under the aegis of traditional knowledge. A second feature shared by this generation of academics and its predecessor was the brokering role between profession, society and politics which many of them performed as municipal and provincial councillors, deputies in parliament, leaders of the professional associations, and as actors at the centres of economic power – industrial as well. One recalls, for example, Colombo's role in the creation of the Edison Company, and the career of Lori, first as director of the *Società Forni Elettrici* of Rome, and after 1901, as member of the board of directors of the *Società Veneziana di Elettrochimica*, where one of his fellow board-members was the Venetian deputy, Count Pietro Foscari, who shortly afterwards founded the company which built the industrial port of Marghera.[55]

6. THE CRISIS OF PUBLIC-SERVICE EMPLOYMENT

The economic take-off of Italy in the Giolitti period propelled the industrial engineer to the summit of the profession. And this was particularly true of the engineers working in the electricity industry, which now developed to an extraordinary extent and not just in the northwestern regions of the Peninsula. This expansionary phase was at its height in the first twenty years of the century.[56] It was engineers, therefore, who founded or directed the leading companies in the electricity generating and supply industry. Cesare Saldini, a professor at the Milan Polytechnic, headed the *Società Lombarda per la Distribuzione di Energia Elettrica*. The *Società per Imprese Elettriche Conti* was directed by the engineer Ettore Conti, the able and enthusiastic promoter of the electrification of the country. And managing the *Società Adriatica di Elettricità* – which with the *Società per l'Utilizzazione delle Forze Idrau-*

---

[55] M. Minesso, *Tecnici e modernizzazione*, pp. 53–4.
[56] The process is graphically described in a celebrated diary kept by one of the protagonists: E. Conti, *Dal taccuino di un borghese*, Cremona, 1946. For a general picture see L. De Rosa (ed.), *L'industria elettrica in Italia*, vol. II, *Il potenziamento tecnico e finanziario 1914–25*, Rome–Bari, 1993.

liche del Veneto came to monopolize the sector in the north-eastern area of the country – was Amedeo Corinaldi, a member of the Giuseppe Volpi financial group, and the Bellunese engineer Achille Gaggia.[57] In short, the new economic path being pursued by the country gave the engineers, many of whom were leading members of the ruling class and key players in the dominant financial-entrepreneurial groups, a role of major importance. But the engineers' accomplishments in the industrial field were only the most evident aspect of their profession's more general success in the private sector, at the expense of the state-employed engineers: a success which henceforth would be a constant and irreversible feature – with the exception of the career as state-employed manager beginning in the fascist period. One should bear in mind, moreover, that the prestige of that other great branch of private-sector engineering, namely the free profession, had never waned; indeed, during the Giolitti period it gained renewed vigour from the expansion of the building industry consequent on the economic boom.

Public-sector employment – especially for engineers pursuing the traditional career in the state civil service but also for those in the employ of the local authorities – entered crisis. This was a crisis, however, which did not affect the new professional specialization in industrial engineering created by the entrepreneurial activity of the provincial and municipal administrations in the distribution of basic services (water, electricity and gas) and of transportation. Especially after the Law of 1903,[58] the municipal enterprises offered new careers for engineers in the public sphere, and assigned them a crucial role as brokers among the interests of the public, of the enterprise and the pressures of local government, which was their employer. The crisis in public-sector employment came about despite the fact that the economic growth of the Giolitti period enabled the government to embark upon a major programme of public works. Legislation in favour of the *Mezzogiorno*, for example, inaugurated a new phase of road-building, after its interruption in the 1880s and 1890s. It was also necessary to restructure the railway network, which had been nationalized in 1905. Again in the field of communications, the country's principal ports were enlarged and modernized, while the repair of its waterways (for the purposes of reafforestation and the tapping of hydroelectric energy) opened up new sectors of activity for engineers. Further demand for specialized personnel was generated by the crea-

[57] A. Ventura, *Padova*, Rome–Bari, 1989, pp. 174, 248. ACS, PNF, b. 13.
[58] On the situation in northern Italy see A. Berselli, F. Della Peruta, A. Varni (eds), *La municipalizzazione in area padana. Storia ed esperienze a confronto*, Milan, 1988.

tion of new regional offices and bodies, notably the *Commissariato per la Basilicata*, and the *Magistrato alle Acque per le Province Venete* created in 1907. And then there was the development of branch railways and tramways, which required increased intervention by the public authorities and the presence of supervisory technical personnel. Further employment in the public sector was created by the direct state management of public services such as the telephone network, which was nationalized in 1903.

In short, the government's growing need for engineers was beyond question.[59] And yet public-sector employment was no longer as enticing as it had been in the years following Unification. Significantly, the Corps of Civil Engineers was frequently obliged to re-advertise its entrance examinations owing to a lack of candidates, and there was a similar lack of interest in the competitive examinations for entry to the mining corps of the Ministry of Agriculture, Industry and Trade. But the gravity of the problem became most apparent during the first decade of the century when even the entrance examinations for the Italian State Railways – always an eagerly sought-after source of employment – began to show a marked and worrying fall-off in candidates.

The reasons for this disaffection with public-sector employment lay with the structure itself of the Italian civil service, with its long-term features, and with the innovations introduced during the Giolitti period.[60] The causes of dissatisfaction had been in place for some time, but they probably now came to a head because in the new economic context the occupational alternatives grew more numerous and remunerative. The economic reasons were evident. Low wages were the principal source of grievance; and because of this, in a phase of economic expansion, the guaranteed job security of public-sector employment became less attractive. The situation created by the generally low level of salaries was further aggravated by the disparities in income among the various categories of state-employed engineer. The technicians of the Corps of Civil Engineers, indeed, who should have been the elite of the government service, were still campaigning in 1913 for the equalization of their salaries

[59] On the growing demand for engineers in the public administration see *Giornale del Genio civile*, 1907, pp. 350ff.

[60] C. Mozzarelli, S. Nespor, 'Il personale e le strutture amministrative', in S. Cassese (ed.), *L'amministrazione centrale*, Turin, 1984; S. Cassese, 'L'amministrazione dello Stato liberale-democratico', in *La formazione dello Stato amministrativo*, Milan, 1974; E. Rotelli, 'Governo e amministrazione nell'età giolittiana', *Costituzione e amministrazione nell'Italia unita*, Bologna, 1981.

with those of other engineers employed by the Ministry of Public Works.[61] Nor was poor pay compensated by satisfactory opportunities for career development. Indeed, probably because of the expansion of the state bureaucracy, these years saw the further subordination of technical staff to bureaucrats.[62] As the Milanese engineer Achille Manfredini wrote in 1908:

> The reason why so few young engineers sit the competitive examinations for posts with the state railway service [...] is the scant attractiveness today of employment in the civil service; where in general the individual is erased [...]; where personal qualities are in the great majority of cases ignored; where career advancement depends largely on seniority and protectionism [...] How, in such circumstances, can one expect young men to be induced to enter the service when private industry or the firms of free professionals can offer them much more rapid, better paid and morally satisfying careers?[63]

The increasing subordination of technicians to bureaucrats was a feature common to all the principal branches of public-sector engineering: the Ministry of Public Works, the state railways, and the land register. In the intermediate grades of the land register, surveyors were given priority over engineers by the law of 1886, which as regards technical operations made only generic reference to 'land appraisers'.[64] The higher grades of the service, which officially required technical qualifications, were dominated by administrative officials with legal training, as Giuseppe Colombo complained in his speeches to the Senate as spokesman for the Finance Committee in 1906 and 1910. The problem was less severe in the state railway administration, although the regulations introduced at the beginning of the century, which replaced the title of 'engineer' with the new title of 'inspector', prepared the way for the future downgrading of technical personnel.[65] The situation was most serious, however, in the Ministry of Public Works, which employed most of the public-sector engineers. At the profession's national congress held in 1906 in Milan, the engineer

---

[61] 'I Congresso dei funzionari del Genio civile', *Giornale del Genio Civile*, 1913, pp. 254ff.

[62] The essential features of the growth of the central administration in the following period (but with numerous references to the Giolitti years) have been analysed in an important essay by G. Melis, *Due modelli di amministrazione tra liberalismo e fascismo*, Rome, 1988 (see in particular pp. 110ff).

[63] A. Manfredini, 'La crisi degli ingegneri', *Il Monitore tecnico*, 1908, pp. 486ff.

[64] 'Ingegneri e geometri nell'Amministrazione della Finanza', *Il Monitore tecnico*, 1907, pp. 76ff.

[65] *Rivista delle strade ferrate*, 1902, pp. 129ff.

Antonio Dal Fabbro denounced the supplanting of engineers by legally trained bureaucratics consequent on the *de facto* elimination of any distinction between technicians and administrators and the removal of the title of engineer from the staff lists, a process made manifest in the equalization of qualifications and salaries.[66] Manfredini (who later led the offensive of the College of Milan against any attempt at the corporative defence of the profession), mounted a campaign for technical jobs in the civil service to become the exclusive preserve of graduates in engineering.[67]

7. STERILE ASSOCIATIONISM

The economic boom of the early years of this century considerably enhanced the status of the Italian engineering profession. Flushed with the success of their new careers in industry, the engineers confirmed their standing both in society and with respect to the other free professionals. The Italian engineers therefore concluded the first fifteen years of the century with a decidedly positive balance sheet as far as their professional activity was concerned. However, they were unable to match this success with equivalent progress in the area of professional associationism, and certainly not in proportion to the amount of effort made and the number of new initiatives undertaken. New and important colleges were founded, notably the *Collegio Veneto degli Ingegneri* (1903). And above all the organization of national sectoral associations, like the *Collegio Nazionale degli Ingegneri Provinciali e Comunali* (1911), continued apace. However, associationism failed to achieve its most ambitious objective, a legislative framework for the profession, even though the issue was keenly debated by the most important associations, was discussed at the national congresses and, for the first time, appeared on the parliamentary agenda. However, the engineers' apparent unity of purpose, achieved by constant mediation between the *'laissez-faire'* position of the College of Milan and the 'protectionist' stance taken up by most of the other associations, was in reality extremely fragile, and this was a factor that seriously weakened the impact of their demands. The first open clash came at the congress of Cagliari, when the College of Naples once again proposed the creation of the order's councils. Manfredini reaffirmed the opposition of the Milanese engineers to any rigid regulation of the profession, arguing that it would

[66] *XI congresso degli ingegneri ed architetti italiani*, Milan, 1907, p. 610 ff.
[67] *Il Monitore tecnico*, 1911, pp. 706ff.

hamper the industrial development of Lombardy.[68] The motion to create the councils was passed against the opposition of the Milanese engineers, and henceforth, despite their continuing hostility, the drive to regulate the profession gathered momentum. A new phase began on 9 June 1904, when the Neapolitan engineer Luigi De Seta presented a bill to the Chamber of Deputies which would act as the reference-point for the advancement of the profession's demands throughout the Giolitti period.[69] The bill's key provision was the creation of an Order of Engineers comprising graduate engineers enrolled on the professional register. Granted to these was monopoly of the expert appraisals conducted on behalf of the public administration or the judicial authorities. Temporary measures were also proposed to protect the position of engineers who had obtained their professional licences in the years before Unification. Although the bill never passed into law, one positive result was nevertheless achieved. The Milan College of Engineers, realizing that it had been isolated by its obstructionism and fearful that the bill would become law, announced that it was willing to support the bill in its final version drafted by De Seta, provided that the order's councils were not made compulsory. At the same time it declared its opposition to the more inflexible text of the bill drawn up by the offices of the Chamber of Deputies, which gave disciplinary powers to the councils and prohibited non-graduates from carrying out public works, for which approval by the local authorities was required.[70] This shift of position by the Milanese engineers paved the way for the compromise reached in December 1906[71] between De Seta and the leading colleges at a meeting convened in Rome. A new text for the bill was hammered out which made enrolment in the order optional, abolished the mandatory regulations on the council's functions, and gave private individuals full liberty in their choice of professional. Milan therefore lent its support to the campaign but emptied the bill of its more 'protectionist' content and bent it to its own policy line.

Although the support of the Milanese engineers in parliament was by now assured, gaining approval for the bill when it came before the Chamber of Deputies at the end of January 1907 was still an uphill struggle. The bill was now vigorously opposed by the architects. The regulation of their position, which was to come about simultaneously

[68] *Atti del X congresso degli ingegneri e architetti italiani*, Cagliari, 1903, pp. 148ff.
[69] Atti parlamentari, Camera, legisl. xxi, ii sess., *Documenti*, no. 583.
[70] Acm, 1906. pp. 12–15; pp. 27ff; *Il Monitore tecnico*, 1906, pp. 41ff.
[71] Acv, 1907, pp. 5ff.

with that of the engineers, posed the problem of the status of diploma-holders from the Institutes of Arts, who sometimes misappropriated the title of architect. This led to a further adjournment of debate on the bill which effectively amounted to its postponement *sine die*. Nor was Parliament induced to re-examine De Seta's bill by the general outcry provoked by a subsequent bill to reform the offices of antiquities and arts (in particular Article 32, which permitted professors of architectural design to sit the competitive examinations), discussed in the Chamber in April 1907, and the consequent demand for the protection of the engineering profession, accompanied by strike action in numerous schools of applied engineering.[72]

The colleges of engineers reacted to these difficulties by strengthening their links. March 1908 saw the foundation of the Federation of the Associations of Italian Architects and Engineers, to which belonged, apart from the *Società degli Ingegneri ed Architetti Italiani* (SIAI), some 23 other associations.[73] The principal aims of the Federation were tutelage of the profession, the fixing of standard fees, and the creation of mixed tribunals on technical matters which would eventually become engineering tribunals. However, the new organization was dangerously weakened by the complete autonomy enjoyed by the confederated colleges. Even at the moment of greatest difficulty, these had been unable to settle their longstanding differences provoked by the diverse economic and productive contexts to which they belonged. The Federation, with its headquarters in Rome, was directed by a board consisting of representatives from the confederated associations and presided over by a chairman, who in this period was Giuseppe Colombo. The compromise reached among the various associations was clearly reflected in the distribution of its executive offices. Colombo was flanked by three vice-presidents: Romanin Jacur, spokesman for the Venetian engineers, the marquis Gennaro Pepe representing the Neapolitan engineers, and Luigi Luiggi for the Rome association.

The first objective pursued by the Federation was the resumption of parliamentary debate on protection of the profession, and for this purpose it enlisted the support of Prime Minister Giolitti.[74] The Federation prepared the text of a new bill[75] which, once opposition in-

---

[72] Atti parlamentari, Camera, legisl. XXII, I sess., *Discussioni*, sitting of 23 April 1907.
[73] These were the councils of the orders of Rome, Turin, Naples, the Council of the Order of Engineers and Architects in Tuscany, the colleges of Turin, Milan, Venice, Verona, Padua, Bologna, Modena, Genoa (College, and College of Naval Engineers), Florence, Siena, Naples, Bari, Palermo, Catania, Parma.
[74] SIAI, 1908, p. 222.
[75] SIAI, 1909, pp. 311ff; p. 622; *XII congresso degli ingegneri e di architetti. Atti*, Prato, 1910.

ternal to the profession had been overcome, provided the basis for a
further bill which came before the Chamber of Deputies in July
1910.[76] In both its ministerial version and the version drafted by the
parliamentary committee (chaired by Edmondo Sanjust de Teulada,
then president of SIAI), the text of the bill established distinct professional registers for engineers and architects, and proposed – in compli-
ance with what was the now tacitly accepted principle – the non-
compulsory nature of the order's constitution. The committee also
stressed that, for minor engineering work, the local authorities could
use the services of non-graduates.[77]

Just as everything was apparently proceeding smoothly towards
approval of the bill, the amendments proposed by the Chamber of
Deputies (who wanted to reinstate the obligatoriness of the order's
constitution) broke the fragile unity achieved by the various associations. The College of Milan once again opposed the bill. And there
matters rested until April 1911, when the parliamentary committee
submitted yet another proposal,[78] which stipulated the non-obligatori-
ness of the order and permitted professionals responsible for projects of
'acknowledged importance' to enrol on the professional register, regardless of whether they possessed a degree. However, the precarious
solidarity among the colleges had been severely strained. The policy of
mediation between the 'laissez-faire' position of the Milanese engineers
and the 'protectionist' posture of all the other colleges – which
however depended crucially on support by the influential group of
Lombard engineers in parliament – no longer satisfied anyone. Eventually, however, common sense prevailed and the decision was taken
to support the bill during its discussion in parliament, which now
seemed imminent. The political elections called in the autumn of
1913, however, once again postponed the matter.

The solidity of the compromise established among the associations
was once again sorely tried in February 1914, when the new government presented the final version of the bill to regulate the profession
drafted during the Giolitti period. Its only significant difference from
the text of April 1911 was the removal of Article 4, which gave entitlement to those enrolled on the professional register to practise
throughout the country. The cancellation of this article implied that
the engineer could only exercise his profession in the district in which
he was enrolled.[79] Not only did this ambiguity inevitably provoke

[76] F. Agnello, Il titolo d'ingegnere spetta ai laureati, SIAI, 1911, pp. 373ff.
[77] Atti parlamentari, Camera, Legislatura xxiii, Documenti, no. 591.
[78] Atti parlamentari, Camera, Legislatura xxiii, Documenti, 591–a-bis.
[79] Atti parlamentari, Camera, Legislatura xxiv, Documenti, no. 74.

bitter wrangling both in the Federation and within the parliamentary committee, it also provided the 'protectionist' faction with the pretext to press for the overall revision of the text into a more restrictive form.[80]

On the outbreak of the First World War in 1914, the Italian engineers were still divided between two hostile camps, although new and original positions were being taken up which would later produce significant developments. In February 1915, Mario Beretta, the leader of the young engineers in the College of Milan, campaigned for both enrolment on the professional register and the constitution of the order to be made compulsory, thereby challenging the traditional policy of the Milanese association.[81] Italy's entry into the war shortly afterwards was a decisive factor in inducing the Milan College as a whole to align its position with Beretta's.

8. ENGINEERS AT WAR

The First World War upset long-standing equilibria in Italian society, and it also — but as a powerful unifying factor — brought significant change to the engineering profession. During the war, the problem of the relationship between the state and engineers arose in new forms. Even before Italy entered the war, on the urging of the National Federation[82] numerous engineers had presented themselves as volunteers to the Ministry of War, and most of their applications were accepted. However, already in 1915 the enlisted engineers were dissatisfied with their treatment, as regards both the military ranks allocated to them and the tasks they were required to perform. They complained that state employees (in the engineering corps, state railways, and so forth) had been assigned more senior ranks, and more in general that they were discriminated against compared to other graduates — doctors and lawyers, for example.[83] Their main demand for both themselves and the conscripted technicians was that they should be assigned to the Army Corps of Engineers or to the artillery, where their skills could be put to more appropriate use, rather than to the infantry divisions as was usually the case. The volunteer engineers also petitioned to be organized into a special unit, created *ad hoc*.[84]

Predictably enough, the issue was one of the main items on the

[80] *Il Monitore tecnico*, 1915, pp. 61ff.
[81] Acm, 1915, pp. 270ff.
[82] SIAI, 1914, pp. 541ff.
[83] Acm, 1916, pp. 25ff; SIAI, 1916, p. 148; *Il Monitore Tecnico*, 1918, p. 527.
[84] Acm, 1916, pp. 70ff; Acv, 1.4.1916.

agenda at the few meetings held by the colleges during the war, chiefly those in the North. However, the various associations applied pressure on the military authorities and, partly as a result of their insistence, measures were introduced in favour of the volunteer engineers. In the spring of 1916, for example, after three months' service engineers were promoted to the rank of lieutenant and not, as previously, to that of second lieutenant.[85] In the following year, the Ministry of War issued more precise directives to the commanders of the army engineering corps and the artillery concerning the use of engineers.[86] These were only minor measures, however, and the proposal for the creation of a special engineering unit was ignored. Presumably, the engineers' requests were frustrated by the hostility of the regular army corps to the creation of a rival unit which would compete against them for the most prestigious postings and promotions. In June 1917, the professional associations again announced their dissatisfaction with the army's treatment of their volunteer members, and the engineers in parliament now decided to take action. Paolo Bignami from Milan raised the issue in the Chamber of Deputies, and the engineer Goglio assembled a powerful pressure group of technicians in parliament.[87]

The treatment reserved for the engineers by the army is important, not only because it sheds interesting light on the relationship between the profession and the state, which was by now openly conflictual, but because it highlights the crisis that in those years afflicted professional associationism (and in particular the National Federation); a crisis which would generate new forms of professional solidarism. Although the Federation was directed in those years by an engineer of outstanding prestige (Riccardo Bianchi, ex-director general of the state railways and, after June 1917, minister of transport), it was accused of inertia by the most influential colleges. In the campaign to protect the interests of the army engineers, after 1917 the Federation was energetically supported, and then supplanted, by the *Società degli Ingegneri ed Architetti Italiani*. It was the Rome college, in fact, which drafted a memorandum setting out the engineers' principal demands (the promotion of engineers already of officer rank from lieutenant to captain, their transfer from the infantry to the army engineering corps or to the artillery, the relocation of engineers suffering from war fatigue to the technical services) which it presented to the minister Vittorio Alfieri in October 1917.[88] Moreover, after the Ministry of War created a corps

[85] Acv, 1916, pp. 33ff.
[86] SIAI, 1917, p. 172.
[87] SIAI, 1917, pp. 192ff.
[88] SIAI, 1917, pp. 357ff; SIAI, 1918, pp. 30ff.

of military justice, the *Corpo della Giustizia Militare* consisting of magistrates and lawyers, in January 1918 it was the *Società degli Ingegneri*, and
not the Federation, which applied pressure for a similar military technical corps comprising the volunteer engineers to be created: once
again without success, however.[89] It was not until the late spring of
1918 that the Federation shook off its inertia and made overtures to the
Rome college, with whom its relations had grown distinctly cool. In
July 1918 the two associations were able to resume their joint campaign in favour of the army engineers, applying directly to the Prime
Minister and mustering the support of the press and the most influential parliamentarians in the two Chambers.[90]

The cabinet reshuffle in the spring of 1918, when the minister of
war Alfieri, and the minister of arms and munitions Dallolio, were
replaced by Zupelli, meant that the engineers' hopes were once
again dashed. Alfieri and Dallolio had prepared a decree which
agreed to their demands, but Zupelli refused to approve it, and was
indeed distinctly hostile to the proposal.[91] Thus when the war came
to an end, the engineers still had nothing to show for their efforts.
Resentment at this failure was directed against the Federation,
which was accused of having missed opportunities and of having
only half-heartedly advanced the profession's demands. The dissatisfaction was general, and the idea began to grow of creating a different and more cohesive organization of engineers; an idea
endorsed by every sector of the profession, including the Milanese
engineers who had opposed it for so long.

9. THE POST-WAR CRISIS AND THE CREATION OF THE PROFESSIONAL ORDER

After the First World War, the Italian engineers' resentment against
both the government and the Federation (the former accused of
undervaluing their specialist skills, the latter of inefficiency) took
concrete form in a significant restructuring of the engineering organizations which reflected this new-found sense of unity. The economic
crisis bore down with particular severity on the engineers with fixed
incomes, especially those employed by the state, whose numbers had
increased considerably in the first two decades of the century. Only
the railway engineers, with their more tightly knit organization,

[89] SIAI, 1918, pp. 47ff; *Criteri di massima per la costituzione di un corpo tecnico speciale per i
servizi ausiliari di guerra*, SIAI, 1918, pp. 95ff.
[90] Acm, 1918. pp. 68ff; SIAI, 1918, pp. 274ff; p. 352.
[91] SIAI, 1918, pp. 305ff.

managed to wring a salary increase out of the government.[92] But the economic slump also depressed the building industry and therefore damaged the interests of the free professionals as well. The situation was aggravated by severe unemployment among both war veterans and the young engineers who had graduated during the war or immediately afterwards. The wartime regulations introduced to favour students at the schools of engineering, and the special measures which accelerated the academic studies of veterans on demobilization,[93] had provoked an explosive increase in graduates and consequently in unemployment. The Milanese engineer Cesare Chiodi had this comment to make: 'Emigration should be encouraged because of the overwhelming number of engineers. The ratio between the number of graduates ten years ago and the number now is 1 to 5'.[94]

There were therefore numerous and serious reasons for the malaise which had spread through the profession and was now exacerbated by a further powerful source of dissatisfaction. The authoritative (or at least responsible) role that many engineers had performed during the war in the various bodies and committees created to direct the country's war effort had made them keenly aware of the importance of their technical expertise for the economic and productive conversion of peacetime Italy. The engineers campaigned for a leading role in the development and transformations that awaited the country and, in the postwar political climate, their demands took on nationalistic overtones which on occasion prefigured fascist views on the engineers' role.[95] The idea therefore began to spread of creating a new national organization of engineers. Not coincidentally, its chief promoters were the younger members of the profession and especially the College of Milan, which had always been opposed to any 'corporatist' action in defence of the profession, which they regarded as hampering industrial and economic growth in Lombardy. But the grave economic and

---

[92] *Atti del convegno regionale toscano degli ingegneri ed architetti*, Florence, 1920, pp. 37ff.

[93] DD. LL. 23.9.1915, no. 1489; 1.10.1916, no. 1202; 2.9.1917, no. 1623 (automatic enrolment from one course-year to the next and exemption from fees for the needy, independently of the number of examinations taken, retroactive matriculations, abolition of compulsory attendance, special examination sessions); D.L. 23.2.1919, no. 341. R.D. 20.11.1919, no. 2498 (supplementary courses, free three-monthly courses, special examination sessions, which were maintained until 1923).

[94] Acm, 1921, pp. 21 ff. Cf. M. Barbagli, *Disoccupazione intellettuale e sistema scolastico in Italia*, Bologna, 1974.

[95] On the relationship between the engineering profession and fascism see G. Turi (ed.), *Libere professioni e fascismo*, Milan, 1994; *idem*, 'Le libere professioni nello stato fascista', *Passato e presente*, 31, 1994, pp. 61ff.

social situation consequent on the war, which afflicted even the most developed areas of the country, acted as a powerfully cohesive force which also united the engineering profession. The Milan engineers therefore accepted a single organization created with the specific purpose of protecting the profession, and indeed would later claim paternity for it.

The process that eventually culminated with the founding of the National Association began with reflection on the functions that awaited the engineers in post-war Italian society. The government's policy for the development of the country, and in particular the measures foreseen in the field of public works, prompted the engineers to bid for a leading role in the imminent transformation, one which occupied an intermediary position between capital and labour. It is possible to discern various stages in this process. The debate opened with the two lectures delivered in the spring of 1918 in Rome and Milan by engineer Calisse on the role of the engineer in Italian public life.[96] In November of the same year, engineer Angelo Forti took up and developed Calisse's theme, especially his contention that the time had come for technical expertise to be given the status it deserved. Forti called for the creation of a new Association of Engineers, which he justified as being 'in the nation's interest'.[97] The influence of the nationalistic mood of the times is evident. But it should not be forgotten that the reorganization of the engineers in order to defend their professional interests – and also in order to give them control of the country's economic development – was not a phenomenon restricted to Italy. It was a theme of international importance in those years in both Europe and the United States, where engineers were also subjecting their organizations to critical examination.[98] And the Italian engineers, forced to shift their ground by the economic and social changes in the country, revealed once again their links with the international engineering community.[99] That the time was now ripe for a truly national association was demonstrated by the unconditional support given to Calisse and Forti's proposal by Achille Manfredini, who on behalf of the College of Milan had previously always opposed any such idea.[100]

The committee of 'young but not too young' engineers created to

[96] Monitore tecnico, 1918, p. 82.
[97] Monitore tecnico, 1918, pp. 25 ff.
[98] T. Veblen, The Engineers and the Price System, now in Opere, Turin, 1969.
[99] A. Salsano, Ingegneri e politici. Dalla razionalizzazione alla "rivoluzione manageriale", Turin, 1987.
[100] Monitore tecnico, 1918, pp. 257ff.

draw up plans for the new association duly received the backing of the College of Milan, which convened an assembly to promote the new association on 19 January 1919. Convinced that 'the war [...] has emphasised as never before that the engineer is in one of the foremost positions in modern society to be its constructor [...] in the widest sense of the term' and that 'as for all the grave problems concerning the reconstruction of the countries destroyed by war, [...] problems which are nearly all of engineering, the class of engineers as such is not consulted', the assembly founded an association which was to pursue overtly class-based goals. The new organization, which was intended to replace the National Federation, was strongly unitary in character. The former colleges were to be transformed into sections and, although they preserved their autonomy, their statutes were to be standardized with the national one. The Society was directed by a board of directors and a general council, and its first president was Odoardo De Marchi. The Society's principal aims were identified in 'defence of the class' and action for constitution of the Order. Again in Milan, the constituent assembly for the *Associazione Nazionale degli Ingegneri Italiani* (ANII) met on 25 May 1919. The engineers declared themselves ready to resort even to syndicalist means in defence of their interests, convinced as they were that 'suggestions and prayers are no longer enough in this day and age'.[101]

An important event in the organization's early life was the congress held in Florence in the same year and attended by engineers from every part of the country, as well as by representatives from the Federation and the new Association. This congress came at a time when the various colleges were deciding whether or not to join ANII, and it was marked by the success of the new association – both because the majority of the former organizations pronounced in its favour, and because the conflict between the Federation and the new Association centring on the leadership of the profession was largely resolved.

The new organization steadily developed thereafter. In January 1920 nine sections were created. Those of Milan, Naples and Turin incorporated the former colleges, while in Florence, Genoa and Rome the fusion was imminent. A section was also created in Bologna, although it was in competition with the local college. In February, a corporation of the civil engineers joined the ANII, followed by the engineers working for the monopolies and by the municipal and provincial engineers. In the meantime, also, the National Federation had been dissolved. By July 1920, fifteen sections were in operation. Since the

[101] SIAI, 1919, pp. 144ff.

beginning of the year the president of ANII and the parliamentary group of engineers, headed by Paolo Bignami, had resumed the campaign for a law to protect the profession's interests. The new draft law on the professions of engineer and architect was presented to the Chamber of Deputies in May 1922. The authors of the text reiterated the main provisions of the bills presented during the liberal period, to wit: the title of engineer was to be used only by graduates and by those awarded degrees on the basis of the regulations in force before the creation of the schools of applied engineering; the qualification was to give entitlement to enrolment on the professional register; expert appraisals for the judicial authorities and the public administrations were to be executed only by engineers enrolled on the professional register (except in special cases); temporary rules were to favour engineers and architects who had practised without degrees. The bill was approved by a large majority on 10 February 1922. The wide spectrum of deputies who took part in the discussion – from Finocchiaro-Aprile (who proposed the bill in 1914) to Francesco Mauro (the new president of ANII), from Pestalozza to Bevione to Rosadi (the longstanding opponent of the law), from De Andreis to Romita to Giovanni Gentile himself (who spoke on the 10th) – underscored the broad consensus that had now formed in favour of the bill. An undoubtedly crucial factor in its approval was the resolving of the position of the architects by the creation of their own professional register and the approval for schools of architecture to be opened in Venice, Florence and Rome. Also decisive was the new political climate consequent on the advent of the fascist regime, which repeatedly declared itself in favour of an enhanced role for engineering. Giovanni Gentile, fascism's foremost expert on education, stressed the Camera's general agreement on the bill, and Romita, in announcing the socialists' vote in its favour, justified it as defending 'the interests of the collectivity, which by disciplining the producers coordinates production'.[102] On 17 June also the Senate approved the bill.

Thus, for the first time in its history the engineering profession in Italy was subject to institutional regulation. Regulation which was accompanied by the reform of higher technical education introduced, in September of the same year, by the Gentile Law on education. The decree issued by the new minister of education stipulated that it was no longer possible to enter university via the physics and mathematics sections of the technical institutes. And it also changed the admission

---

[102] Atti parlamentari, Camera, Legislatura xxvi, *Discussioni*, sittings of 9 and 10 February 1923.

requirements of the engineering schools, for which only diploma holders from the classical lycées and the newly created scientific lycées were now eligible. The new faculties were also given greater autonomy. Graduate engineers were to be awarded the title of 'doctor', but the degree diploma no longer constituted entitlement to practise as an engineer, since this now required, as in the other professions, the passing of a state examination. The regulation of university studies and of exercise of the profession imposed by the Gentile Law of 1923 would prove to be extremely long lasting; indeed, it is still substantially in force today. Different, however, was the destiny of the organization of the profession: in a political climate dominated by fascism, discussion began on the organization of engineers into syndicates, while the *Associazione Nazionale degli Ingegneri*, which now also included architects, very shortly afterwards began to disintegrate.

PART II

PROFESSIONS AND SOCIETY

CHAPTER 6

ITALIAN PROFESSIONALS: MARKETS, INCOMES, ESTATES AND IDENTITIES

ALBERTO MARIO BANTI

I. CONTEMPORARY JUDGEMENTS OF THE PROFESSIONS

In the period between 1861 and the First World War the liberal professions in Italy were the subject of frequent scrutiny by journalists, politicians and commentators. This close interest, however, was not stimulated solely by the fact that certain professions enjoyed special prestige among the general public, for this was nothing new. Indeed, the 'historic' professions (doctor, lawyer, notary) had been so prominent in the medieval and modern history of Italy that the importance attached to them was amply justified.[1] What intrigued these observers was another phenomenon: the *exaggerated* prestige that the middle classes of the various areas of the country attributed to these professions. Precisely when this process had begun was not a question that they found particularly interesting. What these commentators were instead concerned to stress was that the new Italy, the society that had arisen from the struggles of the *Risorgimento*, was overrun by a swarm of lawyers, attorneys, doctors and engineers.

It was an idea that gained widespread currency. Whether the commentators were historians or economists, journalists or lawyers, almost all of them declared that the well-being of the new state was jeopardized by an overwhelming surplus of professionals. In the early 1900s, two English scholars, Bolton King and Thomas Okey, observed that whereas in England many young men studied for educational qualifications which would gain them entry to the world of business, their Italian counterparts insisted on attending the most prestigious of the university faculties – law or medicine. The ranks of the professions became bloated as a result, intellectual unemployment increased, and many aspiring professionals fell back on the civil service as their only

[1] C.M. Cipolla, 'The Professions. The Long View', *The Journal of European Economic History*, 1, 1973.

ALBERTO MARIO BANTI

viable source of work. They and their parents applied ferocious pressure on deputies in parliament to procure them some sort of employment, and the ministers were fully aware that creating a certain number of unnecessary jobs would ensure them the loyalty of many electoral colleges.[2] This, however, was not enough to reduce the glut of professionals on the market, and differentiated market circuits were created as a consequence. As Calamandrei declared in writing about lawyers:

> (T)he unrestricted numbers of legal practitioners has gradually divided them into two broad categories: on top are those few who have leapt to prominence because of their skill and their learning, who work much and earn much; below them are the multitude who, unable to escape from mediocrity, are forced into drudgery to earn a living, and to fight tooth and nail to silence the rumblings of their bellies. The existence of this legal proletariat, which every year becomes more debased as its numbers increase, like a river in full spate which becomes the murkier the more it swells, is the wretched cause of all the evils of our profession.[3]

But what had brought this situation about? As Leone Carpi colourfully put it in 1878, on conclusion of his inquiry into elites in Italy:

> There is in Italy the regrettable custom that as soon as a farmer, a tradesman, a shopkeeper has painfully scraped together some money, he sends his sons off to study; not, though, to continue in their father's trade but to become lawyers, engineers, doctors, teachers, architects, men of letters and philosophers. Whence derives that turbulent swarm of deranged and pretentious men, that corrosive invasion of half-wits in so many public offices, the restlessness of all those who, because they cannot find employment adequate to their ambition, become troublemakers and sycophants, disposed to the most audacious social insubordinations and ready to substitute beguiling dazzle for the hot light of truth.[4]

---

[2] B. King and T. Okey, *Italy To-Day*, ch. XII, London, 1901.

[3] P. Calamandrei, 'Troppi avvocati!', in *Opere giuridiche*, vol. II, Naples, 1966, pp. 98–9. Piero Calamandrei (1889–1956), of liberal-democrat orientation, was one of the most outstanding Italian jurists. He played an active part in the reform of the code of civil procedure (1942) and in the work of the *Assemblea Costituente* (June 1946–December 1947). See S. Rodotà, 'Calamandrei, Piero', in *Dizionario Biografico degli Italiani*, vol. 16, Rome, 1973, pp. 406–11.

[4] L. Carpi, *L'Italia vivente. Aristocrazia di nascita e del denaro – Borghesia – Clero – Burocrazia. Studi sociali*, Milan, 1878, pp. 231–2. Leone Carpi (1810–98) was a freelance journalist of liberal-moderate leanings. He took part in the political struggles of the *Risorgimento*, and then, in the first decades after Unification, adopted a statist-protectionist position. See R. Romanelli, 'Carpi, Leone', in *Dizionario Biografico degli Italiani*, vol. 20, Rome, 1977, pp. 599–604.

Carpi's view of social stratification is very evident in his angry mor-
alizing against the upward social mobility that threatened to upset established social equilibria. Yet behind his self-indulgent attitudinizing
one discerns two recurrent themes of nineteenth- and early twentieth-century commentary on the professions: first that education
gave easy (too easy) access to the professions for ambitious young
men, and consequently bred an excessive number of practitioners;
second that this surplus was a threat to social stability because it
created a pool of marginalized intellectuals willing to go to any
lengths in order to fulfil the expectations of social and economic
success that they had nurtured at school and university. As Francesco
Saverio Nitti wrote in 1901:

> It is from this that derives the greatest revolutionary danger for Italy. A
> mob of displaced men, who have pursued studies of no service to them in
> life, who at school have translated the *Phaedo*, who at university have
> learnt how to conciliate nations in international law, men with studies
> which have nothing to do with what is required to produce, are forced to
> wage a daily battle against hunger and are thus inclined to every violence
> and to every aberration.[5]

There was another issue which aroused acute discomfiture among
commentators. The hierarchy of values most widely embraced at the
time seemed to prefer the professions deemed most prestigious,
although they offered highly uncertain economic prospects, to those
which were certainly just as risky but more profitable to the individual
and more useful to the community. Nitti placed particular emphasis on
this problem:

> Now that nobility of birth has passed away, the nobility of pronouns and
> predicates has been created: the lawyer, the doctor, the teacher the engi-
> neer have swelled bourgeois and aristocratic ranks more than the descen-
> dants of Charlemagne and Goffredo di Buglione, the counts, marquises
> and barons of the Middle Ages.

And the high social prestige of these professions was accompanied by a
pronounced indifference to economic activity.

[5] F.S. Nitti, 'L'avvenire economico dell'Italia. Le vie della resurrezione' [1901], in
Scritti di economia e finanza, vol. III, *La ricchezza dell'Italia*, Bari, 1966, p. 85. Francesco Saverio Nitti (1868–1953) was an economist and a politician. On the liberal
left, he was Minister of Agriculture, Industry and Trade (1911–14, Giolitti government) and Minister of the Treasury (1917–19, Orlando government). From
June 1919 to June 1920 he was Prime Minister. After the murder of Matteotti
(1924), he retired from political life and was forced into exile in France. For a
wide-ranging analysis of Nitti's life and thought, see F. Barbagallo, *Francesco S.
Nitti*, Turin, 1984.

I have tried many times to talk to young people about what a healthy bourgeoisie should be, namely a class of producers: I realised that I was speaking a new language. Why do they sacrifice so many thousands of lire to learn matters which they do not love? Why do they become doctors, lawyers, engineers, when becoming one of these things may mean embarking upon a life of wretchedness?[6]

But Nitti's wise counsel went unheeded, and year by year the ranks of what he called the 'intellectual proletariat' continued to swell.

One could, of course, persist with this survey of contemporary testimony: but this is perhaps an appropriate moment to ask to what extent these criticisms were actually justified. Were they bred by the prejudices of their authors, or did they describe, more or less accurately, the real socio-economic condition of the professions in those years? It is advisable to resort to other sources in answering these questions. And it is a good idea to begin by addressing the following specific problem first: were Italian professionals really as numerous as these commentators claimed?

2. MARKET AND SOCIAL ORIGINS

According to the second ten-year census of the Kingdom of Italy, on 31 December 1871 there were 52,153 free professionals (lawyers, attorneys, notaries, doctors, engineers and architects) active in the country. After that year – the first for which overall figures on all professions and for every area of the country are available – the total number of professionals steadily increased until it reached 70,018 individuals in 1911. The trend was not uniform, however, since numerical increases varied significantly from one profession to another (Table 6.1).

The notarial profession was the most striking exception, with its linearly regressive trend between 1881 and 1911; a tendency induced by legislation which expressly limited the size of the profession's market. Unlike the rules governing the other professions, for which there was no restriction on entry, the law on the *notariato* of 25 July 1875 established that the number of notaries in each notarial district was to be fixed by royal decree according to a table revised at ten-yearly intervals. This law significantly reduced the number of notaries, which shrank by more than 20 per cent in the period 1881–1911; and as a result of a further law regulating the *notariato*

---

[6] F.S. Nitti, 'L'avvenire economico dell'Italia', p. 87 (this is a quotation from A. Roncali, *L'istruzione commerciale in Italia*, Genoa, 1899) and p. 84.

Table 6.1 *Professionals from 1871 to 1911*[7]

	Lawyers and attorneys	Notaries	Doctors	Engineers and architects	Total pop.
1871	17,047	7,746	18,418	8,942	26,801,154
1881	20,354	7,896	18,950	10,883	28,459,628
1901	24,196	6,253	22,139	9,590	32,475,253
1911	28,325	6,207	23,361	12,125	36,671,377

enacted in 1913, it continued to decline during the years of the First World War.[8]

Engineers and architects varied in numbers according to the phases of the economic cycle. A first expansionary phase lasting from 1871 until the end of the agrarian crisis was followed by a substantial downturn caused by the depression of the last two decades of the century (− 12 per cent between 1881 and 1901). There was a distinct reversal of trend in the following decade (+26 per cent), when Italy's first phase of true industrial take-off altered the professional labour market by increasing demand for specialized services. Unlike the notaries and engineers, Italian lawyers and doctors constantly grew in numbers

[7] Figures taken from Ministero di Agricoltura, Industria e Commercio, *Censimenti* (various years). In 1891, the census was not carried out. Note that the census data overestimate the number of free professionals, especially lawyers and engineers. In 1881 a large proportion of lawyers (45%) were employed in the civil service, while 62% of engineers worked either in the civil service or in private firms. In the field of medicine, by contrast, the number of civil servants was very low (F.S. Nitti, 'L'avvenire economico', pp. 94–9). It is possible to obtain a precise idea of the quantitative trend in the legal profession from the judicial year-books, which reported the number of lawyers enrolled in the country's various *collegi*. Rodolfo Benini, who compiled these figures, showed that the number of free-professional lawyers increased from 12,885 in 1880 to 21,488 in 1913: the trend was homogeneous with that revealed by the census data, although the rate of growth was more accentuated (R. Benini, 'Alcune notizie statistiche su gli avvocati e i procuratori in Italia nel 1880 e 1913', in *Rendiconti della Reale Accademia dei Lincei, Classe di scienze morali, storiche e filosofiche*, fifth series, vol. XXVII, 1918, p. 92). Despite these shortcomings, I have decided to use these census data because they give a concise picture of the quantitative trend of all the professions, in the whole of the country, and for the whole of the period discussed in this essay.

[8] L. Frezzini, 'Notariato', in *Il digesto italiano*, vol. XVI, Turin, 1905–10. The even more restrictive norms introduced by the reform law of 16 February 1913 led to a further and major reduction in the number of notaries, which the census of 1921 put at 5,378 (− 13% in ten years). See A. Grassi, 'Notariato', in *Enciclopedia Giuridica Italiana*, vol. XI, pt i, Milan, 1937; and Presidenza del Consiglio dei Ministri − Istituto Centrale di Statistica, *Censimento della popolazione del Regno d'Italia al 1 dicembre 1921*, vol. XIX, *Relazione generale*, Rome, 1928.

228   ALBERTO MARIO BANTI

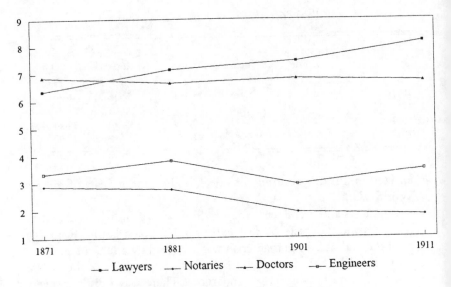

Figure 6.1. Professionals × 10,000 inhabitants, Italy 1871–1911

during the forty-year period considered: an increase of 66 per cent among lawyers and of 27 per cent among doctors. As the professions perhaps richest in tradition and prestige, the bar and medicine were invariably attractive to families and to young men, independently of the country's overall economic situation.

The change in the number of lawyers and doctors thus counterbalanced the erratic trend followed by the engineers and the decline in the number of notaries; and it was this pattern that gave the impression of a substantial rise in the numbers of professionals. However, the raw numerical data yield information that is by no means homogeneous. And it should also be added that the ratio between professionals and total population altered only to a very limited extent during the period (see Fig. 6.1). Indeed, the only increase of any significance regarded lawyers: whereas in 1871 there were 6 lawyers for every 10,000 inhabitants, in 1911 there were 8. The ratio instead remained constant for doctors and engineers, while of course it diminished for notaries.

Must we conclude, therefore, that the plague of intellectual unemployment in liberal Italy was a myth, an invention of contemporary pamphleteers and with no correspondence in reality?

The question can be addressed from another perspective. Comparison of the ratios between the leading professions and total population in the principal countries of Western Europe reveals certain features that are specific to Italy (Table 6.2).

Table 6.2 *Number of professionals per 10,000 inhabitants at the beginning of the twentieth century: France, Germany, England and Italy*[9]

	France	Germany	England and Wales	Italy
Lawyers and attorneys	2.7	1.9	5.9	8.1
Doctors	5.2	4.7	6.8	6.7

The most prestigious profession, the law, comprised four times as many practitioners in Italy than in France and Germany, and one-third more than in England. The case of doctors was different, however, since there were substantially more doctors per 10,000 inhabitants in Italy than there were in France and Germany, but almost the same number as in England. Overall, therefore, one discerns a marked difference between the markets for the professions in Germany and France on the one hand, and in England and Italy (with their similar rates for medicine) on the other. Obviously, however, these findings only make sense when the analysis is extended to include other aspects of the socio-economic systems considered. Without going into detailed comparisons, one may nevertheless state that the relative overcrowding of the Italian professional labour market emerges clearly when one observes the levels of wealth in the four countries. The figures for the years 1907–9 show that per-capita wealth in Italy amounted to only one-third of that in France and Germany and less than one-third of that in England.[10] This means that, compared with the professional markets of France, Germany and England, Italy's was not only more

---

[9] France: lawyers, year 1913, P. Calamandrei, 'Troppi avvocati!', p. 94; doctors, year 1906, C. Charle, 'Professionen und Intellektuelle. Die liberalen Berufe in Frankreich zwischen Politik und Wirtschaft (1830–1900)', in H. Siegrist (ed.), *Bürgerliche Berufe. Die Professionen und das Bürgertum*, Göttingen, 1988, p. 132; population, year 1911, B.R. Mitchell, *European Historical Statistics, 1750–1975*, London, 1980, 2nd edn, p. 30. Germany: lawyers, year 1913, M. John, 'Between Estate and Profession: Lawyers and the Development of the Legal Profession in Nineteenth-century Germany', in D. Blackbourn and R.J. Evans (eds), *The German Bourgeoisie*, London–New York, 1991, p. 179; doctors, year 1909, P. Weindling, 'Bourgeois Values, Doctors and the State: The Professionalization of Medicine in Germany 1848–1933', in *ibid.*, p. 212; population, year 1910, B.R. Mitchell, *European Historical Statistics*, p. 30. England, year 1911: lawyers, doctors, population, H. Perkin, *The Rise of Professional Society. England since 1880*, London–New York, 1989, p. 80.

[10] V. Zamagni, 'The Rich in a Late Industrialiser: The Case of Italy, 1800–1945', in W.D. Rubinstein (ed.), *Wealth and the Wealthy in the Modern World*, London, 1980, p. 141.

crowded from the point of view of supply but also obviously substantially poorer in terms of client spending power. The comparison seems to bear out the pessimistic view of contemporary observers on the state of the liberal professions in Italy; a view which received important confirmation from the figures published in 1898 in the appendix to the parliamentary report presenting the bill on *Autonomia delle Università, istituti e scuole superiori del Regno*.[11] Bodio compared the number of degree- and diploma-holders per year in various disciplines with the number of posts falling vacant because of the death or retirement of their incumbents in the years between 1887 and 1896, in both the private and public sectors (Table 6.3).

According to these figures, therefore, the disproportion was substantial in the legal and medical sectors, but much less so among engineers and architects on account of the fewer secondary-school leavers who entered the faculties of engineering.

As for the legal profession, a study carried out by Rodolfo Benini in 1918, using different indicators, confirmed the disequilibrium between supply and demand already noted by Bodio. Benini observed that, compared with the large increase in the number of lawyers between 1880 and 1913, the 'opportunities' for work remained the same or indeed diminished. In fact, minor civil suits brought before the justices of the peace declined in numbers from 567,000 in 1880–86 to 467,550 in 1910–13; cases adjudicated by magistrates in the same period fell from 193,122 to 145,495; in the period 1880–86 the law courts annually handed down 73,270 sentences, a figure which became 69,854 in the period 1910–13; sentences by the courts of appeal amounted respectively to 11,717 and 11,203, while in the courts of cassation they totalled 2,789 and 2,634. As for criminal proceedings, these advanced from 236,021 in the period 1890–92 to 300,000 per year and then fell back to 258,490 in the three-year period 1911–14. In the legal sector, therefore, professionals had to cope with a market which became increasingly crowded as the years passed, while professional opportunities at best remained the same and in many areas actually dwindled.[12]

Many graduates were thus confronted by a market which was strongly biased against them, and they faced a future of probable unemployment or under-employment. The threat was so manifest that radical and painful solutions had to be found. Between the last decades of the century and the First World War, the massive outflow

11 Published by F.S. Nitti, 'L'avvenire', pp. 93–104; see also M. Barbagli, *Education for Unemployment. Politics, Labor Markets and the School System. Italy, 1859–1973*, New York, 1982, pp. 21–2.
12 R. Benini, 'Alcune notizie statistiche', pp. 96–7.

Table 6.3 *Professional labour markets, 1887–1896*

	Number of posts available in a year		Average annual number of graduates	
Lawyers	500	(1891–92)	Law	1070	(1887–96)
Doctors	497	(1892)	Medicine	928	(1888–96)
Engineers and arch.	300	(1891)	Engineering and arch.	356	(1888–96)

of peasants emigrating from Italy was swelled by substantial numbers of aspiring professionals unable to find satisfactory employment in their home towns. In relative terms, indeed, the number of professionals who chose to emigrate was quite remarkable. Lumping together doctors, pharmacists, midwives, lawyers, engineers and teachers (and therefore including professions which fall outside this survey), the annual number of émigré professionals from Italy was 500–600 in the years immediately after 1876, 1,600 in 1891, with a maximum of 2,600 in 1903.[13] This means that in every year between 1881 and 1920 an average 35 per cent of graduates were forced to emigrate by a labour market which in the course of time had become totally saturated and impossible to penetrate (Table 6.4).

According to Marzio Barbagli, the principal factor responsible for the persistently severe imbalance in Italy between supply and demand in the professional labour market was the direct relationship between the country's delayed industrialization and the view of education as a

Table 6.4 *Average annual numbers of graduates and of emigrants practising a free profession (males in both cases)*[14]

Period	Emigrants	Graduates
1881–1890	772	2,912
1891–1900	1,278	3,681
1901–1910	1,950	3,951
1911–1914	2,095	3,955
1881–1920	1,315	3,791

[13] M. Barbagli, *Education for Unemployment*, p. 32.
[14] Table taken from Barbagli, *Education for Unemployment*, p. 32.

'solution-cum-refuge'.[15] Especially when economic growth grew slug-gish – as happened, for example, during the crisis of the last two decades of the nineteenth century – many parents believed that the employment difficulties of their children could be solved by keeping them longer in full-time education. This was a solution adopted in every part of the country, although it was more common in the southern regions than in the northern ones: in short, where economic growth was slower, there was greater pressure on the educational system and consequently on the professional labour market. Indeed, inspection of the growth rates of the professions in the four geographical zones into which Italy is conventionally divided (the North, the Centre, the South, and the Islands) shows that in the period 1871–1911 they were highest in the central–southern regions of the country (Table 6.5).

Although these figures confirm Barbagli's thesis – of an inverse ratio between economic development and increases in the numbers of free professionals – one should also remember that there were various cultural factors which induced individuals in the various areas of the country to choose one profession rather than another. Particularly striking from this point of view is the growth in the number of lawyers compared with the population increase in central–southern Italy. However, explanation for this variation is not to be found in a low initial ratio between lawyers and population, since the reality was precisely the opposite: in 1871 there were 5 lawyers for every 10,000 inhabitants in the North, 6 in the Centre, 8 in the South and 7 in the Islands. Forty years later there were still 5 lawyers for every 10,000 inhabitants in the North, while their numbers had risen to 7.5 in the Centre, 12 in the South and 11 in the Islands. Of course, figures for such large geographical areas conceal major differences among sub-regional zones. Nevertheless the overall pattern still remains, and it was an enduring feature of the social structure in cities like Naples, Palermo and Catania.

In these cities, structural constraints were reinforced by social prejudices. As early as 1876, for example, Giacomo Savarese, a Neapolitan politician and financier, wrote in a letter to his son Alfonso that a young man from a prominent family, with an income of 2,000 ducats,

> acquired aristocratic habits and could pursue no other career than that of lawyer or civil servant. And why? Because the careers of doctor, surgeon, architect, notary, etc., gave no standing in society. It would have been *déroger*, and in any case the sons of the well-to-do usually became civil

[15] M. Barbagli, *Education for Unemployment*, pp. 11–12.

Table 6.5 *Rates of growth of the free professions and of the population by geographical area, 1871–1911.*

	Lawyers	Notaries	Doctors	Engineers	Population
North	+30.9%	−16.4%	+26.7%	+34.7%	+30.5%
Centre	+68.3%	−5.7%	+30.8%	+42.7%	+29.9%
South	+82.8%	−23.0%	+28.5%	+30.2%	+21.9%
Islands	+113.5%	−29.0%	+15.9%	+37.4%	+40.4%

servants or magistrates. Entry to the other professions was sought by the provincials who came to Naples to study. As for commerce, this reduced one to shopkeeping because there were no more than three or four bankers, and there could not have been any more because of a lack of business.[16]

In Milan, however, in those years the families of entrepreneurs had no particular preference for the law; indeed, it was the engineering profession that began to acquire prestige and to attract larger numbers of students and practitioners.[17] The liberal professions occupied positions in an individual's hierarchy of values which varied according to the context; nonetheless, generally speaking and independently of specific choices and preferences, the free pursuit of academic studies up to a university degree in order to gain entry to a profession was a strategy adopted by the sons of 'bourgeois' families throughout the period between Unification and the First World War.

A study of matrimonial behaviour in nineteenth-century Naples has shown that, in 1831, the rate of professional self-reproduction was still very high: out of the twenty-nine professionals and senior civil servants surveyed on the act of marriage, more than half of them came from families of professionals and senior civil servants. Forty years later, however, out of eighty-nine professionals and civil servants, only 26% belonged to families with the same occupational background; 37% were sons of property-owners, 6% of high-ranking army officers, 14% of teachers, 10% of office-workers, and 5% of shopkeepers; only 2%

[16] Quoted by J. Davis, *Società e imprenditori nel Regno borbonico 1815–1860*, Rome–Bari, 1979, pp. 296–7. Giacomo Savarese (1817–84) was a councillor of state and minister of public works in the second Serracapriola ministry (1848) during the constitutional phase of the Bourbon monarchy. He was later director general of land reclamation under the Bourbon government. After Unification he was a councillor and municipal assessor in Naples.
[17] See C. Dau Novelli, 'Modelli di comportamento e ruoli familiari', in G. Fiocca (ed.), *Borghesi e imprenditori a Milano dall'Unità alla Prima guerra mondiale*, Rome–Bari, 1984, pp. 273–5.

234   ALBERTO MARIO BANTI

had fathers of low military rank while a further 2% had fathers in manual occupations.[18] In Florence in the period 1840–58, the majority of lawyers belonged to families in the aristocratic-bourgeois elite (approximately 60%) or to families of professionals (23.6%). Lawyers in Naples had slightly more varied origins in the same period, but none of them had a blue-collar worker or a peasant as a father.[19] The fathers of the engineers graduating from the school of engineering in Padua between 1875 and 1915 and whose professions are known (805 altogether) were property-owners (38.6%), engineers (15.9%), self-employed professionals (15.9%), office-workers (10.1%), but also artisans or tradesmen (6.2%); there were 7 factory workers (0.7%) and 4 peasants (0.4%).[20] Of the university students surveyed in Italy in 1911, 1% of those studying engineering had peasant fathers, 2% of those studying law did so, and 4% of those studying medicine; 5% of engineering and medicine students had blue-collar fathers, and 6% of law students; most of them had fathers who were proprietors (respectively, 40%, 42% and 24%), industrialists (1%, 2%, 5%) or professionals (24%, 26%, 30%); 12%, 7% and 14% had office-workers as fathers. Finally, 9% of law and medicine students, and 11% of engineering students, had fathers in trade.[21]

Thus, after the Unification of Italy, access to the free professions was open to young men from the broad spectrum of social groups to which office-workers, artisans and tradesmen by now effectively belonged. Dreams of a successful career, the desire to acquire prestigious credentials, 'refuge–solutions' adopted to cope with scant opportunities for employment or investment – these were the frequently overlapping motivations which steered these young men towards the free professions; and there is no doubt that their career choices were conditioned by an educational system which offered unrestricted entry to the university faculties.[22]

There were, however, no avenues of social mobility which led from peasant or working-class ranks to the free professions: despite everything, school and university studies entailed a financial commitment which was far beyond the slender resources of the urban and rural proletariat. At the other end of the social scale, the me-

[18] G. Laurita, 'Comportamenti matrimoniali e mobilità sociale a Napoli', *Quaderni storici*, 56, 1984, pp. 448–9.
[19] H. Siegrest, 'Gli avvocati in Italia nel XIX secolo. Provenienza e matrimoni, titolo e prestigio', *Meridiana. Rivista di storia e scienze sociali*, 14, 1992, p. 148.
[20] M. Minesso, *Tecnici e modernizzazione nel Veneto. La scuola dell'Università di Padova e la professione dell'ingegnere (1806–1915)*, Trieste, 1992, p. 190.
[21] M. Barbagli, *Education for Unemployment*, p. 127, table 5.4.
[22] Ibid.

chanisms of hereditary professionalism operated only for the few. Most young professionals confronted the market unable to rely directly on family support or on their fathers' clientele. And however strong the motivation that induced them to embark on university studies, and then a free profession, many of them wound up by being bitterly disappointed. The labour market for the free professions in post-Unification Italy was characterized by tensions and disequilibria between demand and supply which, although particularly marked in southern Italy, were evident in other areas of the country as well. This was a difficult situation, therefore, which had major repercussions on the socio-economic conditions of the Italian professional.

3. INCOMES AND ESTATES

Lack of information precludes analysis of the incomes of members of the Italian professions covering the whole of our period. We do have, however, one valuable albeit uncertain source: the lists of payers of income tax for 1889. The manner in which income tax was levied means that this is a precarious source of data: in the case of self-employed workers (a category which included the free professionals), taxes were paid on the basis of a declaration issued by the tax-payer, and this in a fiscal regime which, although it may have set relatively high rates, performed few and inefficient checks and controls. It is therefore probable that the under-declaration of income, or even total evasion, was extremely common – as those responsible for fiscal policy, the ministers or directors of the ministry of finance, themselves admitted.[23] For this reason, this source is wholly unsuitable for description of the real levels of income earned by professionals; and also because the incomes registered were net of the outlays required to earn them. Equally risky, moreover, are comparisons among different categories of tax-payer, since other groups of workers (civil servants, for example) were taxed according to a system of deductions at source; a method which precluded any form of under-declaration or evasion. However, despite its shortcomings, this documentation can be used to describe the distribution of incomes within individual profes-

[23] G. Parravicini, *La politica fiscale e le entrate effettive del Regno d'Italia 1860–1890*, Turin, 1958, pp. 245–9. This is confirmed by the fact that the number of professionals recorded in the tax registers was much lower than the number recorded either by the censuses, or by the rolls of the professional orders, or by the lists in the local administrative guides.

sional categories.[24] The analysis that follows is based on the hypothesis of a uniform distribution of evasion among the various bands of tax-payers; or else of particularly significant evasion in the higher tax brackets. This means that in studying the frequency distribution by category of income of tax-payers practising one of the liberal professions of interest to us, we must bear in mind that the information gained may be compressed downwards and may therefore underestimate the actual degree of income dispersion.

In order to analyse the effect of market conditions on the incomes of professionals, four cases were selected: two cities in northern Italy (Milan, an agricultural-industrial centre, and Piacenza, the chief town of an almost entirely agricultural province), one city from the sharecropping agricultural region of central Italy (Florence), and the largest city in the South (Naples).[25] According to the data gathered by the census of 1881, the density rates of the professions set Naples radically apart from the other three cities (Table 6.6).

One notes immediately the high density of lawyers and – to a lesser extent – doctors in Naples; a density even higher than in the other cities of southern Italy. Because of its university and above all because of its many opportunities for employment, Naples exerted a magnetic attraction on professionals from every area of the continental *Mezzogiorno*. However, although Naples was an extreme case of a pattern that, as we have seen, was common to the whole of the South, it was not a distortion of it. Corresponding to these differences among the city markets was a distribution of income which, in its turn, was highly differentiated (Fig. 6.2).

Naples stands out from the other three cities by virtue of its extreme concentration of professional incomes in the lowest range (0–999 lire), which is counter-balanced by the presence of certain professionals declaring annual incomes among the highest in Italy, and much higher than the top incomes in Milan, Piacenza and Florence. In these three latter cities, the average falls within the second income range of between 1,000 and 1,999 lire. Moreover, the overall dispersion of incomes in these three cities is wider than in Naples: in Milan, Piacenza and Florence, roughly equal percentages of professionals belonged to

---

[24] On this see P. Frascani, 'Per la storia della stratificazione sociale in Italia: i ruoli dell'imposta di ricchezza mobile', *Quaderni storici*, 39, 1978, who was the first to analyse and evaluate this source.

[25] Ministero delle Finanze. Dir. gen. delle Imposte Dirette, *Imposta sui redditi di ricchezza mobile. Elenco dei contribuenti privati delle categorie B e C, inscritti nei ruoli del 1889 (principali e suppletivi di 1a serie)*, Rome, 1889, *Province di Firenze, Milano, Napoli e Piacenza, categoria C.*

Table 6.6 *Professionals per 10,000 inhabitants, Milan, Piacenza, Florence and Naples, 1881*

	Lawyers and attorneys	Notaries	Doctors	Engineers and architects	Total
Milan	14.6	8.4	10.6	22.6	56.4
Piacenza	28.0	7.2	16.7	9.8	61.8
Florence	20.8	1.7	13.6	17.2	53.4
Naples	41.6	8.1	18.9	16.5	85.2

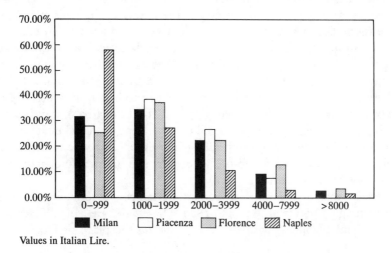

Values in Italian Lire.

Figure 6.2. Incomes of members of the professions, 1889

income brackets ranging from a few hundreds of lire to 8,000 lire per year. Lawyers, notaries, doctors or engineers declaring net annual incomes of 300, 400 or 500 lire were matched by others with incomes ten or fifteen times higher: a truly enormous gap with major repercussions on the social and political identity of professionals.

The nexus between market conditions and the distribution of incomes seems very close: the greater the density of professionals on the market, the lower their incomes. The ratios between average income and density rate give succinct illustration of this first conclusion: 2,326 lire in Florence, where there were 53.4 professionals per 10,000 inhabitants; 1,963 lire in Milan (56.4 professionals per 10,000 inhabitants); 1,822 lire in Piacenza (61.8 professionals per 10,000 inhabitants); 1,339 lire in Naples (85.2 professionals per 10,000 inhabitants).

The results of this analysis of income distribution coincide with the views of contemporary commentators; and they confirm the hypotheses that can be formulated from statistics on the numerical quantities of professionals and on the overcrowding of the market. As has been said, however, the nature of the source raises several doubts concerning the value of the results obtained. It is therefore advisable to compare these findings with those yielded by another source which is much more reliable than the lists of income tax liability: I refer to the probate records kept in the archives of the local tax offices and which itemize the nature and value of the property bequeathed on the owner's death. These records consist of a series of dossiers ordered according to date of presentation; and although they constitute documentation which, like income tax returns, is fiscal in origin, the nature of the register tax and the meticulousness with which checks were conducted mean that it is much more reliable. It can therefore be used for analysis of the distribution and the composition of wealth.[26] Examined here, of course, are items rather different from incomes earned from professional activity: these are assets accumulated not only as the savings from a lifetime of work but also as legacies (from parents or other relatives), dowries received on marriage, or as unearned income (rent from real estate or investment income). Although the relationship with the professional labour market is therefore more tenuous, it still has an influence on the distribution of wealth.

I was able to examine property inheritances in four cities and in years ranging between 1871 and 1879. These cities are Milan, Piacenza, Lucca and Naples,[27] with Lucca thus taking the place of Florence as

---

[26] On the nature of this source see A.M. Banti, 'Una fonte per lo studio delle élites ottocentesche: le dichiarazioni di successione dell'Ufficio del registro', *Rassegna degli Archivi di Stato*, 1, 1983. Also in Italy the tax is Napoleonic in origin; the source is similar to that reported for France by E. Labrousse (on which see A. Daumard (ed.), *Les fortunes françaises au XIXe siècle*, Paris–La Haye, 1973).

[27] The data on Milan have been kindly provided by Stefania Licini, and on Naples by Paolo Macry, to both of whom I am indebted. The legacies examined are contained, respectively, in Archivio dell'Ufficio del Registro di Milano, *Successioni – Milano*, vols 85–96, and in Archivio dell'Ufficio del Registro di Napoli, *Successioni – Napoli*, vols 63–72 (1876) and 443–64 (1906). The comprehensive data for Naples are set out in P. Macry, *Ottocento. Famiglia, élites e patrimoni a Napoli*, Turin, 1988, p. XXII, and *idem*, 'La città e la società urbana', in P. Macry, P. Villani (eds), *Storia d'Italia. Le regioni dall'Unità a oggi. La Campania*, Turin, 1990. The data on Piacenza and Lucca are kept in Archivio del Registro di Lucca, *Successioni – Lucca*, vols 48–75 (1876–79) and vols 277–326 (1902–5), and in Archivio di Stato di Piacenza, *Ufficio del Registro. Successioni – Piacenza*, vols 24–32 (1876–79) and vols 102–17 (1902–5). For comprehensive analysis of patrimonial patterns in these two cities see A.M. Banti, 'Ricchezze e potere. Le dinamiche patrimoniali nella società lucchese del XIX secolo', *Quaderni storici*, 56, 1984; and *idem*, *Terra e denaro. Una borghesia padana dell'Ottocento*, Venice, 1989.

the city representative of central Italy. The results are set out in Fig. 6.3.[28]

Once again, the figures reveal two patterns of distribution which are similar to those exhibited by the distribution of incomes. A particularly high proportion of the Neapolitan professionals who died in 1876 (69.05%) left no property at all to their heirs; in the other three cities the percentages are much smaller (23.53% in Lucca, 27.78% in Milan, 29.41% in Piacenza). Assets, of course, display a much wider distribution than incomes – especially in Milan and Piacenza, where estates ranged from a few hundreds of lire to fortunes approaching one million lire (in Piacenza), to others amounting to even five million lire (in Milan). The range is narrower in Lucca and Naples, cities in which assets never exceeded 500,000 lire. Although this pattern of distribution is strongly influenced by factors extraneous to the positions occupied by individuals in the professional market, the surplus of professionals described in preceding pages nevertheless leaves its mark – especially in the large share of Neapolitan professionals with no patrimonial estate.

This close relationship between market trend and economic situation is also revealed by comparison between the density rates of professionals in the overall population and the distribution of their wealth in Piacenza, Lucca and Naples when measured approximately twenty-five years after the first sample.[29] The relation is evidenced even more clearly by the anomalous trend in the density rate of professionals in Piacenza and Lucca compared with the overall trend (Table 6.7).

The consequence of the weaker pressure exerted by professionals on the market in the two provincial cities of central–northern Italy seems to have been an improvement in their financial position, as signalled by the disappearance of professionals dying without leaving an inheritance. In Naples, instead, an increase (albeit a slight one) in the density rate, which was already very high in 1881, is accompanied by

---

[28] The legacies concern only professionals who effectively exercised a profession during their lifetimes. In order to compile the list, the inheritance data were compared against the official lists of professionals and against the lists of names contained in the numerous administrative and commercial guides for the four cities. The first bar of the histogram relative to the number of professionals dying without leaving an inheritance is hypothetical, and has been calculated by applying the mortality rate estimated by Bodio, i.e. 20 × 1,000, to the number of professionals practising in the four cities in 1881 (F.S. Nitti, 'L'avvenire', pp. 93–104). The legacies were 26 for Milan (1871), 12 for Piacenza (1876–79), 13 for Lucca (1876–79) and 26 for Naples (1876).

[29] Inheritance data on Milanese professionals in the early 1900s are unfortunately not available.

Table 6.7 *Professionals per 10,000*
inhabitants, Piacenza, Lucca and Naples,
1881–1911

	1881	1911
Piacenza	61.8	42.3
Lucca	29.5	22.6
Naples	85.2	88.0

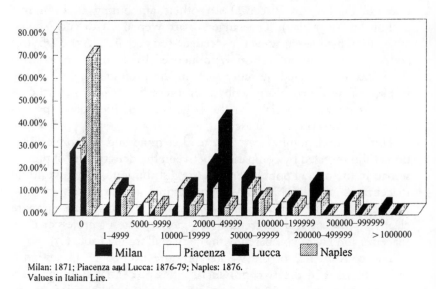

Milan: 1871; Piacenza and Lucca: 1876-79; Naples: 1876.
Values in Italian Lire.

Figure 6.3. Assets of professionals, 1871–79

a proportion of professionals possessing no patrimonial assets which is
even greater than it was in 1876 (Fig. 6.4).[30]

The features of the professional market do not seem, however, to
have influenced the patrimonial choices of professionals, which
broadly reflected the overall patrimonial pattern of their geographical
area. Nevertheless, there are two particular characteristics of these assets
that warrant mention. The share of real estate is invariably very high,
and sometimes even higher than the percentages of real estate in all the
property left as inheritance in the various cities. It would be over-hasty
to deduce from this a common, passive propensity towards rent, or an

[30] The legacies were 15 for Piacenza (1902–5), 16 for Lucca (1902–5) and 43 for
Naples (1906).

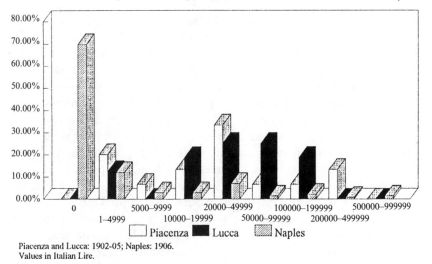

Piacenza and Lucca: 1902-05; Naples: 1906.
Values in Italian Lire.

Figure 6.4. Assets of professionals, 1902–6

attempt to imitate aristocratic behaviour. In reality, investment in real estate (whether buildings or land) changes radically in significance from case to case. In the Po Valley, professionals were frequently responsible for the economically more innovative agricultural ventures; and the purchase of land was an investment that brought not only substantial social prestige but also economic profit – especially if it was well managed. In Naples it was urban real estate that was most attractive to professionals with savings to invest. And although there was perhaps a speculative or parasitical element in their economic behaviour, these professionals paid close attention to the trend in property rents; they were quick to seize the best opportunities for profit, and they were adept analysts of shifts in the economic trend. The assets of the Neapolitan lawyers, as Paolo Macry has observed, displayed 'a strategy which preferred profitability to property as a status symbol'.[31] Of course, in both the North and South of the country, professionals were fully aware of the prestige accruing from property ownership; but their major concern was the yield on their investments, and only secondly its symbolic value. Moreover, the other particular feature of professional assets confirms this finding: almost everywhere in the 1870s, the amount of indebtedness by private individuals to members of the professions was very high – higher than that revealed by overall samples of assets (ranging from 12% in Piacenza to 33% in Lucca). This phenomenon stemmed from economic choices closely conditioned by profes-

[31] P. Macry, *Ottocento*, p. 210.

sional activity. Since the ablest professionals did business with a clientele that was extremely numerous and varied, they exercised virtually total control over the private credit market. Sometimes, and precisely because of the nature of the professional services they provided, lawyers, notaries or engineers had first-hand knowledge of their clients' economic circumstances and so could fix their interest rates accordingly.[32] This, of course, was not a particularly innovative form of investment; but it was nonetheless a rational strategy for those with ready access to information on the liquidity position of potential debtors. Nor was it an unwise investment from the point of view of profitability, since loan contracts, guaranteed by mortgages, yielded interest which in the central–northern cities ranged between 5% and 7%. In Naples, indeed, interest rates were as high as 7% and sometimes reached 8.5% or even 9%. However, during the last two decades of the century, the growth of efficient credit institutions reduced the clientele for private lenders, so that the percentage of credit in the professionals' personal estates began to diminish (by 3.27% in Piacenza, 17.18% in Lucca, 13.44% in Naples) and other investment strategies were adopted, some of them typically *rentier* in character: bank deposits, corporate stocks, but above all government bonds. The professionals' clienteles no longer served as they previously had done as financial markets. This is not to imply, though, that they did not still provide a solid relational basis for the building of fortunes which were not only professional but economic or political as well.

4. THE PROFESSIONAL EXPERIENCE

When one talks of credit networks, of real property, of investment in state securities, it is the assets of the most fortunate and wealthiest of professionals that are being referred to. It should be borne in mind that many legacies only consisted of the professional's home, some credit, at most a few small plots of land; and there were then the substantial numbers of professionals who were unable to bequeath even these few goods. If we take 10,000 lire as marking the watershed between affluence and indigence, and if we also take account of those who left no inheritance at all, then in the 1870s more than one-third of the professionals who died in Milan and Lucca, just under half of those in Piacenza, and a high 81 per cent of those in Naples, were in economic dire straits. Thus, from the

[32] It should not be forgotten that the engineers in the Po Valley carried out estimates, measurements and surveys for the institute of consignment (inventory of goods and equipment at the moment of consignment or restitution of rented land).

point of view of both income and property, socio-economic positions differed profoundly according to the ability of the individual
professional to secure an adequate share of a scarce clientele. But the
differences become even more striking when one considers the
marked segmentation of the various professional markets, which corresponded to further differentiations in the experience and identities
of the various professional groups.[33]

In one case – that of the law – the market was concentrated
mainly in the cities, in the sense that only a few lawyers chose to live
and practise in the small provincial towns. Richer markets and the location of the law courts in the large cities explain this particular
pattern of territorial distribution.[34] In 1911, the *collegi*, or professional
associations, of the eleven largest Italian cities had a total membership
of 11,226 lawyers and prosecutors, while the figure for the rest of the
country was 17,099. The ratio between lawyers and population was
14 for every 10,000 in the larger cities and 3.7 for every 10,000 in the
rest of the Kingdom. In the largest cities, the concentration grew increasingly dense as one moves southwards. Competition was so fierce
in the cities that many lawyers resorted to highly questionable practices in order to procure their clients. The Magaldi Report of 1907
on insurance services in Rome complained, for instance, that certain
lawyers

> have organized a sort of information service involving nurses in the hos-
> pitals, clerks or workers in factories or firms, and even the clerks in the in-
> surance companies, who inform them of accidents and the names and
> addresses of the workers injured. And an insurance company has reported
> that, on several occasions, it has noted individuals keeping watch at its
> front door who, as soon as they see someone who is apparently a worker
> heading towards the offices of the institute, stop him, ask him his busi-
> ness, and of course give him the name of a lawyer ready to plead his case
> and win him substantial damages.

[33] Considered here are only occupations available on the free market, excluding jobs
in the civil service or in private firms – which, for some categories (lawyers and engineers, for example) were very numerous. For estimates relative to the end of the
nineteenth century see F.S. Nitti, 'L'avvenire economico dell'Italia', pp. 94–9
(figures referenced in note 7); for the Veneto engineers see M. Minesso, *Tecnici e
modernizzazione*, pp. 179–88, which shows that in 1915 free professionals accounted for 55% of the total; office-workers in the civil service for 30%, and
office-workers in the private sector for 15%.

[34] This is also reflected in the difference between the average income of professionals
resident in the provincial chief towns and that of professionals living outside them:
for Milan, 1,712 lire against 1,166 lire; for Florence, 2,524 against 939 lire; and for
Naples, 1,302 against 617 lire.

Or:

> criminal lawyers who do not possess sufficient renown or enough
> decorum to be above these miserable practices, still today make wide-
> spread use of the services of so-called 'lawsuit brokers'. These noble gen-
> tlemen are versed in all the secrets of the underworld, and in exchange
> for a modest percentage of the profits they promote the professional re-
> putation of their recommended lawyer in the slums, and they hasten to
> places where a misdemeanour has been committed in order to offer this
> lawyer's services as defence counsel to the accused.[35]

Thus, added to disparities in income were differences in prestige,
image and social milieu: the disreputable lawyers, the pettifoggers,
were regarded with suspicion or outright contempt by the successful
lawyers and the celebrated barristers. As elsewhere, they were black-
balled by the gentlemen's clubs or excluded from the circle of friends
invited into their homes by the successful practitioners. There was
nothing strange in this, for similar things happened in Paris, Berlin,
London and Frankfurt; the difference was, however, that the number
of lawyers engaged in sharp practice was incomparably higher in Italy.

Competition among notaries, of course, was much less intense.
Although there were also marked differences of income among notaries, they reflected two geographically very distinct market circuits:
that of the notaries who practised in the rural districts, which were
much less prosperous and therefore much less sought after; and the city
notaries, to whose offices flocked a mixed clientele of landowners
(most of whom – in both the North and the South – lived in the
cities), tradesmen, bankers and businessmen. The differences among
the average incomes of notaries calculated on data from 1889 were
substantial: whereas those practising in the province of Milan earned an
average taxable income of 1,463 lire, their counterparts in the city of
Milan itself earned more than twice as much: 3,457 lire; in Florence
the ratio was 1,073 lire to 3,247; and even in Naples the difference was
sizeable: 777 lire compared to 1,871 lire.

The professional market of engineers in central–northern Italy was,
broadly speaking, similar to that of the notaries. In this case, too, there
was a marked difference between engineers working in rural areas,
who earned much lower incomes, and those with businesses in the
cities, who catered to a wealthier and more numerous clientele.[36] This

---

[35] P. Calamandrei, 'Troppi avvocati!', p. 105; see also G. Zanardelli, L'avvocatura.
Discorsi, Florence, 1879, p. 155; E. Ciccotti, Cause ed effetti. Note sulle presenti condizioni dell'avvocatura e su di un nuovo ordinamento di essa, Turin, 1889, pp. 10–11.

[36] Average incomes in the city and in its province were: Milan, 1,868 and 1,268 lire;
Florence, 1,688 and 580 lire.

difference, however, was also due to the fact that engineers specialized in specific areas: land and quantity surveying, civil engineering, and mechanical engineering. It is very likely that these differences were also reflected in income levels, although sufficient data are not available to quantify them. In Naples, by contrast, the market for engineers was almost entirely concentrated in the city, and here architects and civil engineers predominated.[37] Although the number of engineers in Italy was not particularly large (see Table 6.1), they had to compete with other professionals – the surveyors – who, although they were less well qualified, supplied similar services at lower prices. This explains why the engineers' incomes were modest, and in any case much lower than those of the notaries whose clienteles were similarly restricted (see Fig. 6.1).[38]

The market for the medical profession, too, was characterized by a wide disparity between the countryside and the city.[39] The distinction applied to two different categories of doctor. Operating in the rural market were the *medici condotti* (general practitioners), who were hired by the municipal administrations on (usually) three-year contracts which did not constitute permanent employment; they were therefore not municipal employees, and for this reason they paid income tax and were registered as free professionals. *Medici condotti* were among the most numerous of Italian professionals (they accounted for 49% of medical practitioners in 1885, and 45% in 1905), and they were also among those who earned the lowest incomes.[40] It is true that they could also rely on the payments in kind which they received from their rural clients; but even so they still had to battle to gain control of a market sector in which quacks and charlatans abounded:

> Towards the end of the century the quacks were more trusted in the Piedmontese countryside than were the men of science [i.e. doctors], who were summoned only *in extremis*. And it was the same in Sicily: 'The quack is preferred to the doctor. Spells are cast on children with worms ... those with back-pains consult the sorceress ... many do not

[37] Between 1881 and 1911 the architects and engineers counted by the census outside the municipality of Naples amounted to only 15% of the total. The average income was 1,183 lire in the city and 757 outside it.

[38] F. Bugarini, 'Ingegneri, architetti, geometri: la lunga marcia delle professioni tecniche', in W. Tousjin (ed.), *Le libere professioni in Italia*, Bologna, 1987, pp. 316–18.

[39] Average incomes in the city and in the provinces were: Milan, 1,989 and 532 lire; Florence, 2,197 and 485 lire; Naples, 1,487 and 513 lire, respectively.

[40] A. Forti Messina, 'I medici condotti all'indomani dell'Unità', in M.L. Betri and A. Gigli Marchetti (eds), *Salute e classi lavoratrici in Italia dall'Unità al Fascismo*, Milan, 1982, p. 681; T. Detti, 'Medicina, democrazia e socialismo in Italia tra '800 e '900', *Movimento operaio e socialista*, 1, 1979.

call the doctor but a friar, who reads a passage from the Gospel of St John
... or they rely on the prescriptions of midwives.'[41]

The city markets segmented into various distinct – though not
totally separate – circuits.[42] At the lowest level was the network controlled by the few *medici condotti* who worked for the local administrations, or the doctors employed by the confraternities and the charitable
institutions. The next level consisted of the free market for the lower
middle classes. Here the competition was ferocious, and doctors had to
resort to practices and behaviour not contemplated by their professional code of ethics.

> The brokerage system first arose at the beginning of the century as the
> method customarily adopted in the struggle for professional supremacy.
> As early as 1876 it was easy to identify the doctors who 'seek to boost
> their careers by frequenting coffee houses, casinos, clubs, and evening
> entertainments, where they meet hoteliers, doormen, hospital nurses'.
> With time the phenomenon changed in extent and form but not in
> content, so that, in 1903, the order of doctors had to adjudicate com-
> plaints concerning the brazen soliciting in Naples of 'clients from the
> provinces at the railway stations and at the docks by highly organized
> bands of go-betweens who betray the good faith of the infirm by taking
> them to doctors of execrable quality'.[43]

In the large urban centres, the hospitals provided a ready source of
employment. Internal hierarchies were very clearly marked out: in
mid-century Lombardy the scale ranged from the lowest rank comprising the junior doctor-surgeons, hired on two-year contracts and
with salaries varying between 300 and 500 lire, to that of head physician, a post which carried a salary of between 1,000 and 3,000 lire.[44] In
1875 there were 143 hospital doctors in Milan (42.6% of the total),
while self-employed professionals numbered 135 (40.3%).[45] However,
the most sought-after area and the one most difficult to enter and
control was the free market, since it was here that the richest clients
were to be found. Once in the private market, doctors were constantly
faced with the problem of charging fees commensurate with the prestige that they felt rightfully theirs because of their specialist knowledge

[41] Evidence gathered by the Inchiesta Agraria, 1883, quoted by A. Forti Messina, 'I
  medici condotti all'indomani dell'Unità', pp. 665–6.

[42] Some doctors working in hospitals or as *medici condotti* also ran private surgeries.

[43] P. Frascani, 'Medicina e società nella Napoli post-unitaria', in P. Frascani (ed.),
  Sanità e società. Abruzzi, Campania, Puglia, Basilicata, Calabria. Secoli XVII–XX, vol.
  v, Udine, 1990, p. 306.

[44] A. Forti Messina, 'I medici condotti e la professione del medico nell'Ottocento',
  Società e storia, 23, 1984, pp. 127–9.

[45] Ibid.

and technical expertise.[46] Episodes of the kind reported in 1891 by Enrico Russo, an assistant in the gynaecology clinic of the University of Naples, were therefore common. Having successfully treated a patient from whom he received 'the most enthusiastic manifestations of gratitude', and 'after polite and repeated requests' for payment of his fee, Russo received from the client's husband, a member of the nobility, a sum which was 'inadequate to the operation performed and injurious to my professional dignity in view of the prosperous financial position of the count, who lives in extraordinary luxury'.[47]

5. DIFFERENT IDENTITIES

Hence, from the point of view of both occupational trajectories and economic situation it is difficult to portray the world of the nineteenth-century Italian professions as a homogeneous and cohesive milieu. Certainly, medical progress, the new passion for science which began to spread in the middle years of the century, or the profession's solidarity against the criticisms or attacks brought against it by its clientele, were all elements which wove a shared fabric of convictions and forms of identity around the professional bourgeoisies.[48] Substantial numbers of professionals gathered to discuss scientific matters at the first conferences held in various Italian cities between 1839 and 1847; many of them frequented the recreational clubs which proliferated in Italy from the first decades of the nineteenth century onwards; numerous professionals also helped, in the 1880s, to create the *consorzi agrari*, or agricultural cooperatives, which played a vital role in the growth of capitalist agriculture in Italy, above all in the Po Valley. In short, the professionals were a leading component of a bourgeois world then in the process of formation. But it should also be stressed that those involved in these new forms of sociability – the importance of which for the consolidation of 'civil society' is too well known to require emphasis – constituted only a tiny segment of the universe of the liberal professions.

In 1891 in Milan, 370 professionals belonged to the city's most prestigious clubs, representing 26 per cent of total membership but only 20 per cent of all the professionals in the city. Moreover, an idealized rela-

---

[46] P. Frascani, 'Medicina e società', p. 309.

[47] From a letter from the president of the provincial council of health to the prefect of Naples, 1 September 1891, in P. Frascani, 'Medicina e società', p. 308.

[48] On the reactions by doctors to lawsuits brought by patients for damages and to the activities of quacks, see A. Lonni, 'Medici, ciarlatani e magistrati nell'Italia liberale', in F. Della Peruta (ed.), *Storia d'Italia, Annali 7, Malattia e medicina*, Turin, 1984.

tional map of the members of these clubs reveals a highly diversified pattern: not only did few professionals feel themselves obliged to pay their membership fees, only rarely did they belong to more than one association.[49] This is an aspect that goes beyond considerations of professional profile: the survival of status barriers and the influence of relational networks, both kinship- and friendship-based, external to the clubs were extremely influential in shaping the physiognomy of these associations, given that many of them only accepted new members through cooption.

Even smaller was the percentage of professionals who joined the agricultural cooperatives. In Piacenza – where the influential *Federazione Nazionale dei Consorzi Agrari* was created in 1892 – 20% of the members of the *Comizio Agrario* (chamber of agriculture) in 1879 were professionals, but they represented only 7% of the overall number of professionals in the province. Although the figure rose to 51% in 1912, this was still only 15% of the total.[50] The reasons for the discrepancy are obvious: only the landowning professionals were interested in joining associations whose main activity was promoting the most efficient agricultural methods and machinery.

The impression that this was a deeply divided social area increases when one inspects the data available on professional associationism. In 1915, only 15 per cent of the engineers practising in the Veneto region belonged to their local *collegi*. The membership rolls of the association of Bolognese engineers contained fewer than 50 per cent of the practitioners in the city.[51] In 1861, the Milanese doctors founded the *Associazione Medica Italiana* (the AMI) with the aim of defending the interests of the profession. In 1862 its Naples branch had around 200 members (22% of doctors in the province).[52] Despite its general aims (or perhaps precisely because of their over-general nature), in the year of its greatest success (1866) the AMI's total membership amounted to only

[49] M. Meriggi, *Milano borghese. Circoli ed élites nell'Ottocento*, Venice, 1992, p. 187.

[50] Comizio Agrario del Circondario di Piacenza, *Elenco dei soci*, 1879; and Comizio Agrario di Piacenza, *Elenco dei soci*, Piacenza, 1912.

[51] Several of these associations – whose purpose was not necessarily the defence of the profession's interests – used the same cooption procedure in recruiting new members as the elite clubs and recreational associations. See on this M. Malatesta, 'Gli ingegneri milanesi e il loro collegio professionale', in C. Mozzarelli and R. Pavoni (eds), *Milano fin de siècle e il caso Bagatti Valsecchi*, Milan, 1991, p. 308. The figures on the Veneto colleges are taken from M. Minesso, *Tecnici e modernizzazione nel Veneto*, p. 139; on Bologna from A. Alaimo, 'Società agraria e associazioni professionali a Bologna nell'Ottocento: una proposta di ricerca', in R. Finzi (ed.), *Fra studio, politica ed economia: la Società Agraria dalle origini all'età giolittiana*, Bologna, 1992, p. 314.

[52] P. Frascani, 'Medicina e società', p. 310.

4,000–5,000 associates, or 27% of all the doctors in practice. After the 1880s, the AMI broke up into numerous local committees comprising the medical elite of each district. In Milan in 1889 the provincial committee of the AMI had a membership of around 200 – that is, 25% of the medical practitioners in the province. In parallel with the *Associazione Medica Italiana*, there formed, or continued to operate, a number of mutual benefit societies for doctors. Locally organized and catering to the less economically fortunate professionals, these societies nevertheless attracted few subscriptions from doctors: in 1885, the mutual benefit society of Bologna had 126 members (33% of the total number of doctors in the city); the Rome society had 195 (22.7%); the Florence society had 129 (25.8%) and that of Lombardy 178 (29.1%, counting only the doctors in the province of Milan). To be stressed here is not just the exiguous memberships of these mutual benefit societies but also that they catered to professional groups other than those from which the prestigious provincial committees of the AMI recruited their members. Although this is a hypothesis that only detailed analysis can confirm, it is nevertheless coherent with what was the most important development in medical associationism at the end of the century: the founding of the *Associazione Nazionale Medici Condotti*. We have already seen that the deepest cleavage in the medical profession, in terms of status and income, was between the *medici condotti*, who worked mainly in rural areas, and the city doctors, especially the clinicians and successful consultants. This divide led, in 1874, to a split in the *Associazione* and the creation of a special association for the *medici condotti*, which was at first affiliated to the AMI but then later was entirely distinct from it.[53] Created with the intention of defending the contractual interests of the *medici condotti*, from 1906 onwards the association was administered by doctors with avowedly socialist beliefs. Although the association did not belong to the socialist trade union *Confederazione Generale del Lavoro*, and although not all its members were socialists, it was the *medici condotti* who – at the beginning of the twentieth century – provided the Socialist Party with a large proportion of its leadership and rank-and-file, and especially in the rural areas of central–northern Italy.[54]

In effect, therefore, economic, social and professional differences divided up the sector of the free professions as regards the political or-

[53] A. Forti Messina, 'I medici condotti all'indomani dell'Unità'; and M. Soresina, 'Ideologia e pratica della professione medica: il caso di Milano', in *Lavorare a Milano. L'evoluzione delle professioni nel capoluogo lombardo dalla prima metà dell'800 a oggi*, Milan, 1987.

[54] T. Detti, 'Medicina, democrazia e socialismo'.

ientations of their practitioners as well. As many nineteenth- and early
twentieth-century commentators feared, a large number of the marginalized professionals (but not only these) were attracted to the leftist
political parties – radical, republican and socialist – although the actual
forms of their political aggregation varied considerably from one area
of the country to another.

In central–northern Italy the pattern of political affiliation divided
into three segments. The upper layer of the professions provided
most of the parliamentary deputies belonging to the liberal centrist
parties – which held on to their majority in the Chamber of Deputies
from 1876 until the First World War and whose ranks also contained
a considerable number of lawyers.[55] Many of the doctors and lawyers
from the provinces, like some of the less successful urban professionals, also embraced centrist politics, sometimes in a manner entirely
at odds with their social and economic circumstances. Often, what
counted for these groups was more the creation of a network of personal relations granting them entry to the local notability than their
economic situation *per se*; for many of them, indeed, politics was a re-
source with which to avert impending economic marginalization, not
the outcome of a considered ethical–political choice.[56] At the same
time, however, in these parts of the country – and above all in the
rural areas of the Po Valley and central Tuscany – the leadership of
the leftist opposition groups remained in the hands of lawyers and
doctors, whose extremist politics stemmed from socio-economic circumstances which they either deemed unsatisfactory or denounced as
verging on proletarianization.[57]

A different pattern of political alignment can be discerned in

55 See on this P. Farneti, *Sistema politico e società civile*, Turin, 1971, and A. Mastro-
   paolo, 'Sviluppo politico e parlamento nell'Italia liberale. Un'analisi a partire dai
   meccanismi della rappresentanza', *Passato e presente*, 12, 1986. In some cases, in
   Milan for example, many engineers remained closely tied both politically and professionally to landowners and industrialists, and thus formed a central component
   in the city's liberal–conservative bloc (M. Malatesta, 'Gli ingegneri milanesi',
   p. 313; F. Cammarano, *Il progresso moderato. Un'opposizione liberale nella svolta
   dell'Italia crispina (1887–1892)*, Bologna, 1990, p. 142).
56 P. Macry has advanced this hypothesis as regards southern Italy in 'Tra rendita e
   "negozio". A proposito di borghesie urbane meridionali', *Meridiana*, 5, 1989. For
   examples of aggregation by marginalized professionals to the local socio-political
   notability in the Po Valley, see A.M. Banti, *Terra e denaro*, pp. 216–17.
57 In an important study of the Socialist Party, Maurizio Ridolfi has shown that,
   although in 1903 only 2.7% of the party's members were lawyers, they constituted
   27.6% of its governing body and 42.3% of the socialist delegation in parliament in
   1900. In Milan in the period 1906–20, professionals made up 10.3% of the party's
   membership (M. Ridolfi, *Il PSI e la nascita del partito di massa, 1892–1922*, Rome–
   Bari, 1922). See also T. Detti, 'Medicina, democrazia e socialismo'.

Southern Italy. Although the differences in income between the successful professionals and their marginalized colleagues were certainly just as wide as those in the Centre–North, they were offset by structures of political affiliation which were predominantly factional or clientelistic in character, and which operated through relational channels which were entirely independent of the individual's socio-economic position.[58] Indeed, the particular nature of the relationship between the professional and his clients reinforced, in this context, the clientelistic nature of political behaviour.

> The nexus between professional clientele and political activity became, not coincidentally, an unconscious element in popular opinion. 'He had accumulated a modest fortune and a clientele which loved him beyond belief', declared the obituary of a Casertan doctor who died in 1874, '*therefore* we always saw him seated on the city council'.[59]

But the chief protagonists were certainly the lawyers, whether in the large cities like Naples, Catania or Palermo[60] or in the small towns like, for instance, Pignataro in the province of Caserta:

> In the case of the lawyer [...], his professional service, tied as it was to the resolution of interpersonal conflicts which entailed trust and consensus in very large measure, was almost immediately transformed into an instrument of power and control. Not by chance, all the leaders of the factions which confronted each other in Pignataro in the 1880s and 1890s were lawyers.[61]

Of course, these structural features of the relational networks centring on the professionals had politico-clientelistic connotations in the Centre and North of the country as well: but in these areas political conflict stemmed principally from the 'horizontal' cleavages so conspicuous in professional stratification, whereas in the South it took

[58] See on this P. Macry, 'Tra rendita e "negozio" '; *idem*, 'La città e la società urbana'; L. Musella, 'Relazioni, clientele, gruppi e partiti nel controllo e nell'organizzazione della participazione politica (1860–1914)', in P. Macry and P. Villani (eds), *Storia d'Italia. Le regioni dall'Unità a oggi. La Campania*, Turin, 1990; G. Civile, *Il comune rustico. Storia sociale di un paese del Mezzogiorno nell'800*, Bologna, 1990; G. Gribaudi, *A Eboli. Il mondo meridionale in cent'anni di trasformazioni*, Venice, 1990. Among the classics, an essential reference is Gaetano Salvemini, 'La piccola borghesia intellettuale nel Mezzogiorno d'Italia' [1911], *Opere*, IV, vol. II, *Movimento socialista e questione meridionale*, Milan, 1963.

[59] P. Macry, 'La città e la società urbana', p. 155.

[60] Apart from the above-cited studies by Paolo Macry and Luigi Musella, see for Sicily, E. Iachello and A. Signorelli, 'Borghesie urbane dell'Ottocento', in M. Aymard and G. Giarrizzo (eds), *Storia d'Italia. Le regioni dall'Unità a oggi. La Sicilia*, Turin, 1987.

[61] G. Civile, *Il comune rustico*, p. 131.

mainly the form of clashes between factional coalitions which traversed the social sphere 'vertically'.[62]

Whatever the reason for these geographical differences, the many economic, social and political cleavages that split the free professions fashioned them into something that was very different from a uniform *Bildungsbürgertum*, or educated middle class, cohesive in structure and conscious of the prestige deriving from its academic training and from the acknowledged usefulness of its services.[63] These cleavages, instead, turned the professions into a fragmented and shifting constellation caught between awareness of its role and the bitter frustration provoked by a socio-economic situation radically at odds with dreams entertained at university. By income, social milieu and family origin, a country doctor and a successful city clinician, a pettifogger and a celebrated lawyer, a surveyor and a civil engineer, belonged to radically different social spheres, despite their common intellectual training and despite the similarity of their professional services. In the period of liberal Italy this deep and sharp segmentation was never knit together by political affiliations. Elsewhere in Europe, the driving force behind the political alignments which gained the support of the middle classes was their opposition to the socialist movement. In Italy, by contrast, the Socialist Party drew a large proportion of its membership from the professional bourgeoisie, and especially from its most economically and professionally marginalized sectors. The professionals belonging to the liberal groupings, moreover, had no difficulty in adapting to the mechanisms of clientelistic and localistic mediation which sustained the governments from the 1880s until the First World War. Consequently, it was sentiments of local belonging, rather than national socio-political solidarities, that predominated and therefore created a further deep line of cleavage. As Lombardo-Radice wrote in 1919, just before Italy entered the war:

[62] Examples of this diverse political morphology can be found in the studies cited at notes 56 and 58. Also worth mentioning is the varying behaviour of *medici condotti* in different parts of the country: whereas in the north they belonged in large numbers to the *Associazione Nazionale Medici Condotti* (55% of the total between 1907 and 1913), the proportion of affiliates gradually decreases as one moves southwards, with the lowest proportion of 4–8% in Sicily and Sardinia. Although not involved in trade-union struggles, the *medici condotti* in the central–southern areas of the country were never extraneous to the political arena, in which they often participated as leaders of factional groupings.

[63] On the concept of *Bildungsbürgertum* see W. Conze and J. Kocka, *Bildungsbürgertum im 19. Jahrhundert*, vol. I, *Bildungssystem und Professionalisierung in Internationalen Vergleich*, Stuttgart, 1985.

The ruling class lacked historical awareness, indeed it was entirely devoid of it, and consequently its political horizons were narrow. It was easier to find a mentality restricted to the constituency than one which encompassed the nation. The constituency was a closed world, riven by factional quarrels, by conflicts of local interest, by clientelistic feuding. And this world was the political horizon of the majority. For some, Italy was only a name; for too many, it was a pretext to flaunt their vanity; for too many political life was an arena of intrigue and machinations.[64]

Lombardo-Radice was arguing in general terms. Two years later, Calamandrei wrote in similar vein, more specifically about the Italian lawyers, who, although they had always enjoyed strong representation in parliament, never seriously worked for the judicial reform so earnestly and universally desired, because 'they allowed themselves to be guided not by national politics but by parochial politics or even by class politics' and attended to the interests of their constituencies or to those of their professional corporation. Furthermore,

> that shabby individualism, so characteristic of all Italian life, and because of which the individual enclosed in his selfish interests is indifferent to the overarching interests of the society of which he is part, and sees the State as only governed by thieves against whom he must defend himself and struggle, finds one of its most typical expressions in the mentality of certain lawyers, who to promote the individual interest of their client consider justice to be a matter of no concern to them, because it regards the state.

These were the various features of the crisis afflicting the Italian legal profession. A crisis, according to Calamandrei, which was provoked by a problem of a general kind: 'The pathological influx of the sons of the bourgeoisie into the legal professions has [. . .] its prime origin in that moral disorientation which, for some decades now, has been manifest in the so-called Italian ruling classes', and which the excessive numbers of professionals in the market, and their consequent unemployment and frustration so severely exacerbated.[65] It is doubtful, however, whether the hardships of the free professions were due to the sort of moral disease that Calamandrei described: they stemmed, rather, from the deep social, political and geographical divisions that fragmented the professional world, and these were a structural feature of liberal Italy as

---

[64] G. Lombardo-Radice, 'La difesa morale del soldato dopo Caporetto', in *L'educazione nazionale*, 15 June 1919, quoted in R. Vivarelli, *Storia delle origini del fascismo. L'Italia dalla grande guerra alla marcia su Roma*, Vol. II, Bologna, 1991, p. 81. An idealist educationist, Giuseppe Lombardo-Radice (1879–1938) worked on the educational reforms introduced by Giovanni Gentile. After the murder of Matteotti (1924) he resigned from his ministerial posts in protest against fascism.

[65] G. Calamandrei, 'Troppi avvocati!', pp. 116, 121–2 and 193.

a whole. The focus of Calamandrei's denunciation should therefore be adjusted, for it was precisely the depth of these cleavages – which neither political aggregations nor professional memberships were able to repair – that was one of the principal reasons for the ethical weakness which, in Calamandrei's view, and in that of so many other commentators, constituted the most distinctive feature of the bourgeois world during the first fifty years of post-Unification Italy.

CHAPTER 7

ARISTOCRACY AND PROFESSIONS

GIOVANNI MONTRONI

In 1963 David Spring noted in his *The English Landed Estate in the Nineteenth Century*[1] that the expansion of the professions had consequences of great importance for English society. Spring wrote:

> In the long run, it would lead to the destruction of the old order: an aristocratic society resting on hereditary privilege and personal ties had little in common with the personal ideals of professional excellence and effort.[2]

In this chapter I shall seek to show that in Italy, too, the old order was destroyed in the second half of the nineteenth century, and that in Italy, too, the professions helped to create an institutional framework and a cultural context which had no room for an aristocracy that had so little in common with them.

A substantial amount of printed documentary material, supplemented by more detailed information gathered from archival sources, allows assessment (though restricted to certain situations) of the extent to which the Italian aristocracy resorted to the professions for employment, or at least for partners in marriage. One reaches the conclusion that it is not possible to identify a uniform aristocratic attitude towards the professions. There are, in fact, settings in which, until the end of the First World War, the Italian aristocracy was still tied to social endogamy and service in the state bureaucracy. But there are other settings in which the aristocracy was much less loath to enter into marriage alliances with persons from the professional class, especially when these possessed substantial real estate or occupied important political and administrative positions.

For this conclusion to be framed with sufficient clarity, however,

[1] D. Spring, *The English Landed Estate in the Nineteenth Century: Its Administration*, Baltimore, 1963.
[2] Ibid.

there are certain characteristics of the Italian aristocracy that should be stressed, together with various processes with which it was caught up in the period from the abolition of feudalism at the beginning of the nineteenth century until the First World War.

1. After national Unification, the Italian aristocracy was granted official recognition of its titles. A *commissione araldica* was established to standardize the various regional aristocracies, while the new dynasty pursued a policy of ennoblement by bestowing titles on those families and individuals who had distinguished themselves during the *Risorgimento* by contributing, in the administration or in other sectors of civil life, to the difficult task of unifying the country. This new nobility, however, was not granted privileges, even less so was it accorded a specific role or function.[3] Even in the system of precedences at court and at the public ceremonies established by the new unitary state, the aristocracy, as a body, was entirely ignored. Nevertheless, the aristocracy did not disappear: it may have lost all its privileges of rank but it still kept, and in certain respects enhanced through its recognition by the new sovereign, the prestige that it enjoyed in Italian society.

Against this normative background, however, the notion itself of aristocracy requires substantial revision – beginning with the characteristics that, despite everything, it managed to preserve throughout the nineteenth century, and of which undoubtedly the most salient was its collective identity. Taken as a whole, the Italian aristocracy exhibited a set of commonly shared features: regardless of levels of wealth and power, it possessed a strong sense of identification with family affairs and prestige; it pursued a distinctive life-style; and, in more strictly economic terms, it showed a marked propensity to invest in land and, later, in state bonds. Although the nobility's tendency to give priority to forms of intra-class sociability and endogamic matrimonial alliances persisted until the First World War, it grew increasingly willing to integrate with other social groups. At the same time, more balanced familial relations with an egalitarian bias increased the number of aristocrats who decided to seek independent employment. These behavioural changes, however, were only apparently unproblematic, since the aristocracy's perception of itself did not necessarily coincide with the conception of it held by the rest of society.

For instance, the image that the southern aristocracy so enthusiastically promoted of itself as rural, paternalistic, thrifty and religious con-

---

[3] G. Rumi, 'La politica nobiliare del Regno d'Italia 1861–1946', in *Les noblesses européennes au XIXe siècle. Actes du colloque...*, Rome, 1988, pp. 577–93.

flicted with the fecklessness and frivolity instilled in the collective imagination by the society magazines of the second half of the century.

The second general aspect of the Italian aristocracy warranting revision concerns its economic interests. Like most of its counterparts in
Western Europe, the Italian aristocracy was long identified, and particularly in its feudal components, with landed property. Other components of the class, however, especially those belonging to the urban
nobility, were associated with other functions and other interests. The
interweaving of elements of collective identity and interests, as well as
their change over time, obliges us to disaggregate – or more precisely
to multiply – the notion of aristocracy. It is consequently more accurate to speak of Italian 'aristocracies' than of one single monolithic
'aristocracy'.

2. In the overall process of the modernization of European society in
the second half of the nineteenth century, a certain section of the
Italian aristocracy reinforced its closure towards other social groups
and, at the same time, in order to render this closure practicable, extended the range of its social relations beyond national boundaries to
every part of the continent. This created the paradoxical situation –
although only apparently so – in which a social group whose feudal
and patrician components had rooted themselves deeply in local contexts was perceived by the collective imagination of the *belle époque* as
highly cosmopolitan. Obviously, this is a phenomenon which cannot
be quantified even approximately; nonetheless a certain amount of information – albeit indirect – is available. In his well-known essay of
1964 on the demography of the English peerage,[4] Hollingsworth
stressed that, beginning with the 1850–74 age group, there was a
sharp decline in the rate of endogamy among the English nobility; a
fall which stemmed from the growing influence exerted by American
industrialists and millionaires on the English peerage.[5] Some years
later, Thomas returned to the topic and substantially confirmed this
marked decline in endogamic marriage within the ranks of the titled
nobility,[6] adding a number of observations which are of considerable
relevance to our purposes here. According to Thomas, endogamic
marriages within the aristocracy progressively decreased during the
course of the nineteenth century because more and more aristocrats

---

[4] T. Hollingsworth, 'Demography of the British Peerage', *Population Studies*, 1964,
supplement part 2.
[5] Ibid., pp. 9–10.
[6] D. Thomas, 'The Social Origins of Marriage Partners of the British Peerage in the
Eighteenth and Nineteenth Centuries', *Population Studies*, 26, 1972, pp. 99–111.

married the daughters of foreigners rather than commoners.[7] That this conclusion has recently been criticized by Montgomery, on the ground that many of those whom Thomas described as foreigners were also entrepreneurs, does not have a significant bearing on the matter.[8] It is a phenomenon which had evident and major consequences on the evolution of the social exclusivity of the English aristocracy, and it drastically reduced the importance of marriages between members of the aristocracy and the daughters of businessmen or industrialists. The statistics quoted by Thomas are also highly significant: 22.2% of exogamous marriages contracted by males – eldest sons or cadets – belonging to the English peerage in the years 1860–79 were with foreign women.[9] One should not forget, however, that the percentage of endogamous marriages was still very high, given that the figure, for the same age group, was 26.7% among eldest sons and 17.8% among cadets, with an overall average value of 20.8%.[10] Obviously, not all marriages were aristocratic alliances, but the statistics are nevertheless interesting, and especially in the light of Thomas's analysis. He suggests, in fact, the existence of an aristocratic group – not necessarily the richest but certainly the most prominent – which moved at the international level, whose sociability was entirely restricted to the most exclusive aristocratic circles of Europe, and which forged marriage alliances with noble families regardless of their geographical area of provenance. Simultaneously, though, this group was also ready to exploit opportunities to form alliances with foreign families which were wealthy but not aristocratic, because these were marriages which constituted less of a threat to the exclusiveness of the aristocracy than did those with partners who were just as wealthy but came from the same country. This section of the Italian nobility, in short, constituted something akin to an 'international aristocracy' whose nucleus was the families listed in the *Almanach de Gotha* and whose distinctive features – despite often highly diversified family histories and economic and financial backgrounds – were its exclusiveness and its impermeability to other social groups. Italian families like the Colonna, the Borghese, the Caetani, the Orsini, the Caracciolo, the Doria, the Boncompagni-Ludovisi, the Torlonia, and many others besides, looked on employment in the free professions (at least until

[7] Ibid., p. 104.
[8] M. Montgomery, 'Gilded Prostitution'. Status, Money, and Transatlantic Marriages, 1870–1914, London, 1989, pp. 87–90.
[9] D. Thomas, The Social Origins of Marriage Partners, p. 105.
[10] Ibid., p. 102.

the First World War) as a humiliating social comedown, and on marriage with that sector as a gross *mésalliance*.

Quantifying the number of marriages between different national nobilities is not an easy undertaking; but even when analysis is restricted to the genealogies of the Italian *Mezzogiorno*, numerous cases of foreign spouses are forthcoming: the Lucchesi Palli family, whose eldest sons assumed the title of Principe di Campofranco, provide a striking example of this cosmopolitan aristocracy so confidently at ease in the great cities of Europe. There were then the families with branches holding patents of nobility acquired in several countries. Of these a single example will suffice: the Acton family bore the title of lords of Aldenham in England and of patricians (*patrizi napolitani*) in Italy, and they were related to numerous aristocratic families in France and Germany. Furthermore, a diplomatic career – which seems to have been the preferred *métier* of the Italian nobility – helped to cement international relationships and to strengthen supranational vocations. By way of a minor but nevertheless illuminating statistic: of the 56 Neapolitans who embarked on diplomatic careers between 1861 and 1915, either in the consular service or in the diplomatic corps proper, more than half of them – specifically 57.1% – were noblemen.[11] One also notes that this 57.1% comprised members of the most prestigious families of the Neapolitan aristocracy; and, moreover, that some of them, like Marquis Camillo Caracciolo di Bella of the *principi* di Torella or Guglielmo Imperiali of the *principi* di Francavilla, had seats in the upper chamber of parliament.

Another component of the Italian nobility was the great landowning aristocracy of the kind that Anthony Cardoza has described in Piedmont.[12] Unlike its counterpart in the *Mezzogiorno*, the distinctive features of the Piedmontese aristocracy were a close correlation between antiquity of lineage and size of landed holdings and, until the First World War, an inflexible commitment to a policy of endogamous marriage.[13] Emblematic of the Piedmontese nobility's sense of separateness and exclusivity was the absolute social closure practised by the most aristocratic club in Turin, the *Società del Whist*, which barred even the most influential exponents of the city's entrepre-

---

[11] My calculation, based on information in *La formazione della diplomazia nazionale italiana (1861–1915). Repertorio bio-bibliografico dei funzionari del Ministero degli Affrai Esteri*, Rome, 1987.

[12] A. Cardoza, 'The Long Goodbye: The Landed Aristocracy in North-Western Italy, 1880–1930', *European History Quarterly*, 23, 1993, pp. 323–58.

[13] Ibid., pp. 326–8.

neurial bourgeoisie from membership.[14] Not surprisingly, therefore, the cadet sons of these families, whom manipulation of the rules of succession had deprived of assets, were largely uninterested in professional activities; they much preferred the upper echelons of the state administration, the diplomatic service, the senior ranks of the army, or even business and finance – although in the two latter cases they restricted themselves to capital supply and directorships, thereby avoiding the rigours of direct management.[15]

In the small and medium-sized towns of Italy – and this applied as much to the Centre–North as to those areas of the South not immediately overshadowed by Naples – the leadership and exclusivity of the landed aristocracy gradually declined. Its place was taken – most evidently in coincidence with the agricultural crisis of the last quarter of the nineteenth century – by a land-owning elite consisting of the titled nobility together with a patriciate and a bourgeoisie which had exploited every opportunity to extend their landholdings. In these areas, too, the real levels of social integration were lower than might first appear. In the town of Piacenza, as Alberto Banti has shown, many nobles practised as lawyers,[16] and the relationship between the aristocracy and the professions grew increasingly close over the course of the nineteenth century. The number of marriages between the offspring of the aristocracy and the bourgeoisie amounted to eleven in 1815–25 and twenty-four in 1890–1900; and although there were no families of free professionals among the former, there were fully nine among the latter.[17] In Piacenza, the two groups were brought into close contact by their common interest in landed property; an interest of extremely long standing for the aristocracy but of more recent origin for the bourgeoisie. In the landed elite which emerged from this alliance, it was the untitled rather than the titled nobility which was more attracted to the liberal professions and which was willing to marry into that social area – in order to reduce the distance that separated the two social extremes and to pursue its twofold interests in the political domain.

The situation described by Banti, however, was not peculiar to northern Italy; it was to be found, albeit with some specific local features, in most of the country's small and medium-sized towns, the

[14] A.L. Cardoza, 'Tra casta e classe. Clubs maschili dell'élite torinese, 1840–1914', *Quaderni Storici*, 26, 77, 1991, pp. 363–88.
[15] A. Cardoza, 'The Long Goodbye', p. 345.
[16] A. Banti, 'Strategie matrimoniali e stratificazione nobiliare. Il caso di Piacenza (XIX secolo)', *Quaderni Storici*, 22, 64, 1987, p. 157.
[17] Ibid., pp. 155–7.

Mezzogiorno included. The situation in southern Catanzaro, for instance, as described by Daniela Caglioti, was not markedly different.[18] In the South, too, the pattern of prevalently endogamous marriage within the aristocracy during the first half of the nineteenth century (63.3%) changed entirely in the second half, when it fell to 37%;[19] there too, the most prestigious and wealthiest stratum of the local aristocracy maintained levels of matrimonial endogamy that were still extremely high in the second half of the century; there too, the discovery of a landowning vocation by the professional bourgeois group buttressed a patrimonial elite in which the lesser nobility (where 'lesser' means less well endowed in resources and status) sought to bridge the divide between the two extremes of society; and there too, this mediatory role was performed in the political arena, considering that more than half the nobles on the city council of Catanzaro were qualified professionals.[20]

3. In some areas of the country – and here we may take Naples as our example – the aristocracy failed to establish itself as an interest group within a particular economic sector. It consequently laid more aggressive claim to honour, prestige and exclusiveness; and it adopted even more rigid forms and general codes of behaviour, thereby strengthening a collective identity which proved highly resilient but which, in fact, was grossly inflated in relation to the group's effective role in local society. In other areas, by contrast, the connections between the bourgeois world of the professions and the aristocracy – or better a certain aristocracy – grew closer and more frequent. In many respects, Naples and Milan represented the two extremes of a continuum along which a set of intermediate situations can be plotted.

When, in 1889, the *onorevole* Giovanni Codronchi was appointed prefect of Naples, one of the city's fashionable weekly magazines, *Fortunio*, expressed the hope that the newly appointed functionary would open the staterooms of the prefecture to Neapolitan high society. In the words of the writer of the article:

> A prefectural ball is more than merely a ball when it can bring together all those in Naples who think, strive and hope for the city's material and moral improvement; that is, when it can do something almost entirely new for Naples, where we are all divided into small groups and small circles of friends, unknown or almost unknown to each other.[21]

[18] D. Caglioti, 'Patrimoni e strategie matrimoniali nella Calabria dell'Ottocento', *Meridiana. Rivista di Storia e Scienza Sociali*, 3, 1988, pp. 97–128.
[19] Ibid., p. 111.
[20] Ibid., p. 103.
[21] *Fortunio*, no. 3, 20 January 1889.

GIOVANNI MONTRONI

And in fact, in a city where it is less easy than elsewhere to draw the boundaries of urban social geography, the absence of relations among the various social groups was striking. The metaphor of the oyster and the rock, originally used by Rocco De Zerbi to stress the physical contiguity and simultaneously the distance that separated the bourgeoisie from the general populace, has recently been revived by Paolo Macry.[22] However, the editor of *Fortunio* was obviously not referring to the subordinate groups, given his patently minimal interest in the *hoi polloi*: it was the distance that separated the representatives of big business and finance, of the professions, of the old and new (often bogus) city aristocracy that preoccupied him. Exchanges, unions and relations among these groups were, if not entirely nonexistent, rare or even isolated occurrences. The levels of social endogamy were extremely high. It has been stressed that, between the 1830s and 1870s, the choice of marriage partner in the city elite was made predominantly from within one's own social rank. As Giuseppina Laurita notes,

> The wives of high-ranking soldiers, of professionals, of magistrates were mostly the daughters of property-owners, with a consistency of pattern that remained unchanged from one decade to the next.[23]

In a context such as this, therefore, it comes as no surprise to find that the number of aristocrats who entered professional careers, and the number of marriages between the aristocratic and professional social strata, were both very small.

The general index of the commercial guide to Naples of 1881[24] – which gives all the names already included in the guide as well as 'more than 15,000 addresses of people notable by virtue of nobility and wealth' – lists 718 noblemen; or better, it lists 718 individuals attaching a noble title to their name. Setting aside for the moment the problem of the real nature of this nobility (a topic to which I return below, although by necessity only briefly), 626 of these individuals, i.e. 87.2% of the total, were described as 'property-owners'. The unreliable nature of this classification is notorious among all those who draw on contemporary archival or statistical material in order to study nineteenth-century social groups in Italy. Nevertheless, one may infer from the general information provided by the guide that these were individuals with no direct employment in any productive, professional or

---

[22] P. Macry, 'Borghesie, città e Stato. Appunti e impressioni su Napoli, 1860–1880', *Quaderni Storici*, 19, 56, 1984, pp. 339–83.

[23] G. Laurita, 'Comportamenti matrimoniali e mobilità sociale a Napoli', *Quaderni Storici*, 19, 56, 1984, p. 457.

[24] *Annuario napoletano. Grande guida commerciale, storico-artistica, scientifica, amministrativa, statistica, industriale e d'indirizzi di Napoli e provincia...*, Naples, 1881.

commercial sector, and that their incomes consisted mainly of rent from urban or rural estates or from gilt-edged securities, or, most commonly, from a prudent combination of both. Of course, there was no lack of aristocrats with employment in other sectors of the world of work. Together with five noblemen whom we may generically call entrepreneurs, one notes three stockbrokers, a director of an insurance company, two clerks in private companies, a journalist, and even two retail tradesmen and a forwarding-agent. There were, in addition, forty-four individuals (6.1% of the total) classified as professionals, as well as seventeen others listed as magistrates, army officers, diplomats and university professors, and a further sixteen listed as state and municipal civil servants.

Interestingly, this group of aristocrats includes a number of important political office-holders: sixteen senators, eleven deputies, and eighteen municipal and provincial councillors – as well as that year's mayor of the city, Count Girolamo Giusso.[25] And yet almost all these personages were *rentiers*. Of the twenty-one categories from which, according to the Constitution, the senators of the kingdom were to be appointed, no fewer than fifteen of the sixteen senators from Naples belonged to the twenty-first category: 'persons who for three years have paid three thousand lire of tax on their goods and on their industries'. In the specific case of Naples, this was a category which comprised the great landowning aristocracy, mostly of feudal origin, but which also included the families that had risen to noble rank in the early nineteenth century following the dissolution of the ecclesiastical mortmain and the dismemberment of certain great estates – a process which on occasion resembled landed cannibalism and which, after the abolition of feudalism, had brought profound changes to the ranks of the great landowning class. Conspicuous among the former were Luigi Caracciolo, Duke of Sant'Arpino, and Ernesto Dentice, Prince of Frasso; among the latter, Baron Alfonso Barracco.[26] The only senator not to belong to this twenty-first category was the already-mentioned Marchese Camillo Caracciolo di Bella: as a diplomat, he was appointed under the terms of the seventh category – 'extraordinary envoys after at least three years' – although he belonged socially to the twenty-first. The eleven deputies originated from the same social stratum as the senators appointed by the crown, with two exceptions: Baron Giuseppe

---

[25] I have considered only the most important appointments. Hence, senators or deputies holding offices in local government have only been calculated as senator or deputy.

[26] On the Barracco family, see M. Petrusewicz, *Latifondo. Economia morale e vita materiale in una periferia dell'Ottocento*, Venice, 1989.

264 GIOVANNI MONTRONI

Angeloni, the secretary general of public works, and Count Cesare di Gaeta, an architect. There was not one professional among the eighteen municipal or provincial councillors; indeed, *rentier* families enjoyed absolute monopoly within the aristocratic group. This finding is particularly interesting because it shows that although the Italian ruling class may have miscalculated by restricting itself to the landowning component alone, in Naples it sought to build an alliance with the group which more than any other was identified with the Bourbon monarchy. However, as regards the issue that most closely concerns us here, this phenomenon relates to the scant ability of the professions to satisfy the desire of the Neapolitan aristocracy to enhance its status. We may therefore conclude that, when aristocrats were called upon by the king or the collectivity to participate in the administration of the *res publica*, they would not accept what they regarded as *déclassé* employment in bourgeois occupations; and that the public powers were therefore better advised to resort to a thoroughly bourgeois group. The lawyers, for example, offered their services to the ruling class as the professionals of politics.

4. Of course, the aristocracy did not lump all the professions together indiscriminately. There was, in fact, not a single Neapolitan noble among the practitioners of the minor professions. My researches failed to find even one nobleman practising as a doctor or a dentist between 1853 and 1915, not one who practised as a pharmacist, a veterinary surgeon or a notary. The Neapolitan nobles who entered the professions did so solely as lawyers and attorneys or engineers and architects. Of the forty-four cases identified for 1881, thirty-four of them (77.3%) worked as lawyers or barristers, while nine were architects and engineers. The single exception to these two categories (though only a partial exception) was a land-surveyor, and he can be considered a minor member of the group of engineers and architects.

Although the attraction of engineering for the Neapolitan aristocrats is certainly of interest, it was not a feature specific to them. David Cannadine has recently described the same phenomenon among the English aristocracy:

Of all the 'new' late-nineteenth-century professions, engineering seems to have attracted the greatest interest from non-leisured notables. It was closely involved with the land, was an obvious choice for a patrician dilettante, and boasted unrivalled social prestige.[27]

[27] D. Cannadine, *The Decline and Fall of the British Aristocracy*, New Haven–London, 1990, p. 396.

In Naples, interest in engineering also stemmed from the tradition of analysis and intervention in the drainage and reclamation of the *Mezzogiorno*; a tradition revived by the energy and passion of Carlo Afan de Rivera, who after 1824 was general director of bridges and roads in the Kingdom of the Two Sicilies. Between 1881 and 1905 the number of nobles practising as architects in Naples and its province increased from 6.4 to 19.3 per thousand.

Although detailed research has not been conducted in this area, the link between the aristocracy and the legal profession can be taken as well established. As Paolo Macry has written:

> The lawyers handled the innumerable jurisdictional controversies that afflicted the noble estates before and after the abolition of feudalism. Through their hands passed the protracted litigations which split the landowning families, their quarrels over contested wills, unpaid dowries, and usufructs of difficult calculation, the conflicts between those who wished to keep the family estates intact and those who wished to break them up. And it was often the lawyers who attended in their daily routine to the public and market relationships between the great families and leaseholders, tenants, local agents, debtors and creditors.[28]

This, however, may not be an adequate explanation, given that the profession of the notary – an equally central figure in the aristocracy's relational network and in many respects its guarantor – did not attract the same interest, either in the country as a whole or, especially, in the *Mezzogiorno*. The difference (and it is this feature that makes the legal profession so interesting) is that the lawyer performed a public function; he acted on the public stage and thereby frequently acquired fame and prestige. The notary, by contrast, operated in a more private sphere and maintained a demeanour of service and subordination which the aristocracy found irksome. That these factors accounted for the differing fortunes of the two professions has also been suggested by Siegrist, who argues that if the sons of the aristocracy took up the law, 'they entered the profession of legal adviser and defence counsel, since this traditionally commanded respect, but not the office of attorney, because this was traditionally considered "*arte procuratoria*" and a petty-bourgeois occupation'.[29] In England too, for that matter, aristocrats only regarded the profession of barrister, not that of solicitor, as the occupation worthy of their station.

However, although the relationship between the advocacy and the aristocracy has been confirmed as significant, it was quantitatively a

[28] P. Macry, *Ottocento. Famiglia, élites e patrimoni a Napoli*, Turin, 1988, pp. 207–8.
[29] H. Siegrist, 'Gli avvocati nell'Italia del XIX secolo. Provenienza e matrimoni, titoli e prestigio', *Meridiana*, 14, 1992, p. 163.

phenomenon of very small proportions. In 1853, 17.6 per thousand of all legal professionals in Naples belonged to the aristocracy;[30] in 1881 the figure contracted to 8.6 per thousand; in 1905 it reached a peak of 23.4,[31] and then fell back sharply to 8.9 per thousand in 1915.[32] These are figures which almost entirely coincide with those set out by Siegrist,[33] who calculates that almost all the Neapolitan lawyers in practice between 1840 and 1860 belonged to families of property-owners (with all the ambiguity which surrounds that term), of shopkeepers, or of professionals. That their origins were therefore thoroughly bourgeois is confirmed by the small proportion (2%) of lawyers from the ranks of the aristocracy.[34] Nor did the ratio change to any significant extent in the period that followed, given that only 2 per cent of the lawyers who married between 1840 and 1860 – and were therefore economically active in the next thirty years – belonged to the aristocracy.[35] As regards the first years of the twentieth century, the figures given above again coincide with Siegrist's finding of a further reduction in the percentage of lawyers of aristocratic origins.[36] In Naples, moreover, as in the rest of the country, only an extremely small number of lawyers managed to marry into the aristocracy: indeed, only 2 per cent of lawyers' wives belonged to aristocratic families.[37]

This latter statistic requires some comment. It would be wrong to believe that the position of women remained entirely unchanged throughout the nineteenth century. Already in the early decades of the century, in fact, more and more women were being allowed to select their marriage partners: only under certain conditions, though, as the Duke of Terranova explained to his son in 1837:

> the girl's choice should concern sympathy, physique, and mode of behaviour, however little time there is to ascertain this latter; whatever concerns matrimonial convenience in terms of property, and much more so the moral qualities of the groom and his family [...] pertain to those responsible for her, who must show the greatest discernment possible.[38]

Paradoxically, it was precisely this degree of independence granted

30 La guida. Ossia libro d'indirizzi de' negozianti, commercianti, banchieri, professori, artisti..., Naples, 1853.
31 Indicatore generale dei professionisti di Napoli, Naples, 1905.
32 Guida annuario dell'industria, commercio e professionisti, Naples, [1915].
33 H. Siegrist, 'Gli avvocati nell'Italia del XIX secolo', pp. 145–81.
34 Ibid., pp. 148–9.
35 Ibid., p. 161.
36 Ibid., p. 165.
37 Ibid., p. 164.
38 Archivio di Stato di Napoli, Archivio Serra di Gerace, vol. 90.

to women which restricted – perhaps directly against the wishes of their fathers – the social area of provenance of their husbands. The 'mode of behaviour' to which the Duke of Terranova referred was not, of course, any specific ability; it was the generic capacity to move with self-assurance through the relational world of Neapolitan high society, to adopt a set of codes and manners which were inevitably of aristocratic character in the young nobleman, but which the young professional did not always find easy to acquire.

Of the forty-four aristocratic professionals identified, none of them had a seat in the Senate in 1881, and only Alfonso Vastarini sat in the Chamber of Deputies. To these should be added the lawyer Matteo Mazziotti of the Barons of Celsio, who was elected a deputy in 1882 and, after a long political career, became a senator in 1919. Like Mazziotti, Vastarini belonged to a typically bourgeois family of recent ennoblement: his father, in fact, had acquired the title of Marquis of S. Antonio *maritali nomine* on marrying the Marchioness di S. Antonio. And it is certainly significant that both men represented provincial constituencies where it was easier, compared with Naples, for them as professionals and aristocrats to gain recognition as leaders of local society. The fragility of the alliance between professions and the aristocracy in a context such as Naples is further confirmed by the absence of municipal and provincial councillors in the sample.

5. I have so far used the expression 'aristocratic' to refer to individuals who appeared in the commercial guides and professional lists with some sort of noble title affixed to their names. Yet an analysis of the relations between professions and the nobility which takes solely the parade of a title as constituting membership of the aristocracy is inevitably misleading. Consequently, Siegrist's conclusions regarding nineteenth-century lawyers – conclusions which are based entirely on this criterion – not only overestimate the relationship but fail to give clear specification to those areas of the aristocracy in which it was particularly close.

In the specific case of Naples and the *Mezzogiorno*, analysis must begin with a number of general considerations concerning the aristocracy. The first of them is prompted by the preamble with which, in 1891, Francesco Bonazzi began his *Elenco dei titoli di nobiltà concessi o legalmente riconosciuti nelle provincie meridionali d'Italia dal 1806 al 1891*:

By one of those strange contradictions which occur not only in the lives of individuals but also in those of populations, never has there been so much talk of the aristocracy, never has there been so much greed shown or so much squandering of noble blazons and titles as in our times, even though this is an era of true democracy and of the maximum political equality.[39]

Because of the abuse and the proliferation of titles rife in the second half of the nineteenth century, it is impossible (or at least extremely difficult) to conduct quantitative-statistical analysis of the southern aristocracy. I shall therefore examine more closely the forty-four individuals in the sample, but restrict my analysis to 1881.

A rapid scan of the list reveals the total absence from it of the great families of the most opulent and influential Neapolitan aristocracy. Moreover, closer scrutiny of the names of the aristocratic professionals reveals that almost half of them (twenty, to be precise) had no official authorization to use a noble title. Most of them belonged to families which were mentioned neither in the list of the noble and titled families of Naples and its province nor in Spreti's *Enciclopedia Storico Nobiliare*, nor in similar works. In certain cases, they were individuals who bore the same surnames as families recorded by these sources but who certainly did not belong to them.

As regards the other twenty-four names, one notes those of certain individuals or families of only very recent ennoblement and who had very little in common with the Neapolitan or southern aristocracy in general. For instance, the list includes the name of Guglielmo Capitelli, a well-known member of the circle of anti-Bourbon and liberal professionals in Naples. Capitelli was, in fact, the son of Domenico Capitelli, who was born in the province of Caserta in 1794 and, in the words of Raffaele De Cesare, was 'the greatest luminary of the Neapolitan law-courts'[40] as well as a patriot, and president of the Neapolitan Parliament in the short-lived constitutional period of 1848. Godfather to the Prince of Naples, the future King Vittorio Emanuele III, Guglielmo Capitelli served as mayor of Naples and was created a Count by Vittorio Emanuele II in 1869.

Also conspicuous is the name of Matteo Mazziotti. His father, Francesco Antonio Mazziotti, was a noted patriot from the Cilento: a deputy after the granting of the constitution and then exiled in Genoa, he returned to Naples in 1860 and campaigned for the rapid annexation of the *Mezzogiorno* to the Kingdom of Savoy. He then served as a parliamentary deputy during the legislatures of 1861–65 and 1867–70. Mazziotti's elder brother, Pietro, sat in the Chamber of Deputies from

[39] F. Bonazzi, *Elenco dei titoli di nobiltà concessi o legalmente riconosciuti nelle provincie meridionali d'Italia dal 1806 al 1891*, Naples, 1891, p. 5.
[40] R. De Cesare, *La fine di un regno*, Milan, 1969, p. 355.

1878 until his death in 1886. Matteo Mazziotti himself was a politician and a historian: he too was a deputy and subsequently served as an under-secretary, first at the Ministry of Posts and then at the Ministry of Finance with Zanardelli. He was appointed senator in 1919. The family title of Barons of Celso was bestowed on Francesco Antonio Mazziotti in 1868 by Vittorio Emanuele. A similar case is that of Francesco Saverio de Cillis. The de Cillis family belonged to the Benevento patriciate: Francesco Saverio, a lawyer and later professor of law at the University of Naples, received the title of Count in 1902.

There was also a group of aristocratic professionals who belonged to families of functionaries, officials and administrators in the Kingdom of the Two Sicilies. Notable among these were the lawyers Gennaro Zelo and Nicola Santangelo, of whom the latter was a nephew of another Nicola Santangelo, formerly Minister of the Interior under the Bourbons. The architect Count Cesare di Gaeta was the son of the Bourbon general Emmanuele di Gaeta and was himself, prior to the dissolution of the Kingdom of the Two Sicilies, an artillery officer. The lawyer Gaetano Viti, a nobleman of Altamura, was the son of Francesco Viti, the superintendent of the province of Terra di Lavoro (now the province of Caserta). The engineer Ferdinando Montemayor, a former captain in the navy, was the second son of Emmanuele Montemayor, a general of the engineering corps in the Bourbon army.

The sample also comprises a number of impoverished aristocrats who had drifted into the professions because they could find no other source of income. The most representative of these is Alfredo Morbilli, Duke of S. Angelo a Frosolone. The younger brother of Gustavo − killed in the revolution of 1848 − Alfredo Morbilli was the son of Duke Giuseppe Morbilli. The Morbilli family was already in straitened circumstances in the generation preceding that of Duke Giuseppe, who was obliged to serve as a common soldier in Murat's army throughout the 1814 campaign in Italy. He was then promoted to the rank of quartermaster and billeting officer, in which capacity he served during the 1815 campaign. On his return to Naples, Giuseppe Morbilli eked out a living by giving fencing lessons. He married Rosa Degas, daughter of a banker of French origin with business in Naples, who brought with her a dowry of 20,000 ducats − but of which Giuseppe's father-in-law only disbursed the interest. On his death, the family's last remaining apartments in via Toledo were confiscated and consigned to its creditors.[41] Alfredo Morbilli was an engineer in the civil engineering corps. Of his two brothers, Edmondo married Maria Teresa

---

[41] R. Raimondi, *Degas e la sua famiglia in Napoli 1793–1917*, Naples, 1958, pp. 142–9.

270   GIOVANNI MONTRONI

Degas, sister of the painter, while Adelchi became director of the *Banca Nazionale*. With this family background, Alfredo's only son, Gustavo, heir to the title of Duke of S. Angelo a Frosolone, not surprisingly chose a career in the judiciary.

The sample also comprises the representatives of a Neapolitan patriciate who for many years formed the most influential and prestigious section of the professions. One of these, for example, was Marchese Giuseppe Perez Navarrete della Terza, son of Pietro Navarrete, a civil lawyer of great fame.[42] We then finds other nobles who moved into Naples from outlying towns for reasons of work: among them, the engineer Luigi Amadei, a Roman patrician employed in the provincial technical office at Naples, and the Torinese nobleman and engineer Nicola Melisurgo. The case of the Melisurgo family is of particular interest because it provides an example of a family whose members had all opted for the professions and the civil service. Nicola Melisurgo's brothers, in fact, were Michelangelo, a secretary at the Ministry of Agriculture, Industry and Commerce; Enrico, an employee in the Revenue Office in Rome; Luigi, who worked in the technical service of the railways in northern Italy; Giuseppe, an engineer in the Italian corps of naval constructors; Guglielmo, an engineer.

The largest group, however, belonged to a patriciate or an aristocracy which was richer in sons than it was in economic resources, and which originated in the various urban centres of the *Mezzogiorno*. And also worth noting is the fact that most of these professionals had followed the traditional pattern of migration to Naples from the southern provinces. It is certainly not easy to measure the size of this phenomenon during the period with which we are concerned: the only figures available refer to the 1840s and show that 44.2 per cent of free professionals were provincial migrants into the city.[43]

The general picture that emerges from the lists of professionals compiled in 1915 is substantially similar to that of the 1880s. Rapid inspection of the list of aristocratic professionals reveals that only 29 out of a professional group comprising fully 3,254 individuals were lawyers or attorneys.[44] The marginal role of this noble component is further confirmed by the absence of nobles both from the *consiglio dell'ordine degli avvocati* (council of the order of lawyers) and from the *consiglio di disciplina dei procuratori* (the prosecutors' disciplinary council). Although it is evident from the foregoing discussion that the relationship between

[42] R. De Cesare, *La fine di un regno*, p. 356.
[43] C. Petraccone, *Napoli dal '500 all'800. Problemi fi storia demografica e sociale*, Naples, 1974, p. 240.
[44] *Guida annuario dell'industria, commercio e professionisti, anno 1915*, Naples, undated.

the aristocracy and the professions was certainly closer in the legal field, the group of twenty-nine noble lawyers/attorneys comprises no fewer than twelve who used an aristocratic title which was not officially recognized. A further nine of them bore surnames of families which had indeed been decorated with a title, but they were impossible to trace in the genealogies of these families – which suggests that even in the best of cases they were very distant relations. Only the remaining eight can be readily identified as individuals fully entitled to use a noble title. Of these, the Marchese Serafino de Gennaro and Count Francesco Antonio Pironti belonged to families traditionally employed in the judiciary of the Kingdom of Naples. But whereas the de Gennaro had been ennobled in 1747, the title that the Pironti bore was of Savoy origin. Francesco Antonio Pironti, in fact, was the son of Michele, a magistrate prior to 1848, a patriot, a deputy in the Neapolitan parliament of 1848, and after Unification president of the *Corte di Cassazione* in Naples, deputy, senator of the Kingdom, keeper of the seals in the Menabrea cabinet, and created Count by Vittorio Emanuele II in 1869. Together with Prince Girolamo Ruffo, a member of a minor branch of the Ruffo di Bagnara, we find representatives of families belonging to the local patriciate of towns in the *Mezzogiorno* or at any rate, like the D'Aubert family, extraneous to the Neapolitan aristocratic milieu.

A further interesting finding is that the social area from which the aristocratic lawyers – at least those whom it has been possible to identify with confidence – recruited their wives was certainly not that of the nobility. Exceptions were Prince Girolamo Ruffo, who married Antonia Folgari, Marchesa di Ducenta; and Ferdinando Ferrari, who, as the son of Vincenzo Ferrari, Barone di Silvi e Castiglione, married Princess Emilia Pignatelli di Strongoli and was thus authorized to assume, *maritali nomine*, the title of Principe di Strongoli. His elder brother Bernadino, a judge in the *Corte di Cassazione*, married Giovanna Caracciolo Ginetti of the Princes of Avellino.

Two preliminary conclusions seem incontrovertible. Firstly, it was patently not the great landowning southern aristocracy that forged the relationship between the professions and the nobility; instead, it was a patriciate or an impoverished nobility originating mostly from the provinces of the *Mezzogiorno* that did so. Secondly, in Naples, only very rarely did the nobility enter professional occupations which lay outside the field of the law. Engineers and architects of aristocratic birth almost never undertook independent professional activity; they much preferred to work for the public administration.

In order to understand this extremely low level of social mobility, one must bear in mind certain aspects of the position and the role of the aristocracy in southern society from the Restoration onwards. After the end of the Napoleonic decade – in the course of which a patrimonial hierarchy was established which then proved to be extremely long-lived – the fragmentation of the aristocracy characteristic of the highly conflictual period that preceded it produced two distinct alignments: the nobility who participated in the life of the court on the one hand, and the nobility excluded from it on the other. The court made an obvious attempt to create a new noble tradition, and it indeed achieved tangible results. The demarcation line between these two components of the aristocracy was very evident in marriage alliances during the Bourbon period, but it was even more conspicuous in their economic choices. Whereas the nobility extraneous to the court restricted its economic activity to the agricultural sector, the courtly nobility tended to engage in business and finance. The probable reason for this latter behaviour is the courtly nobility's ability to gain legitimation for its status not so much from its choice of economic activities, which then led to acceptance of rent-earning alone as a 'respectable' occupation, as from its position close to the king. The fact that these activities ceased with Italian Unification is further evidence in support of this assertion. It should also be added that, in the *Mezzogiorno*, the above-discussed international aristocracy sprang from the courtly nobility. National Unification was a further factor which accentuated the isolation of the aristocracy. Now impoverished or entirely deprived of the privileges of rank, it was in defence of its status and in obedience to a rigorous code of membership that the Neapolitan aristocracy found the stimulus to reconstruct its collective identity. Aristocratic investment in landed property increased (although it was already substantial in the 1850s), but there was no apparent change in the system of the dual marriage market, although it now expanded to cover an increasingly broader geographical area. The professions for their part, even as regards the most prestigious ones like the law, henceforth grew, paradoxically, even more distant from the culture and the aspirations of the aristocracy. By now the professions and the aristocracy were two entirely separate worlds. The use of bogus titles and the parading of the noble titles or honours bestowed by the new royal house further widened the rift between them. And when one considers, furthermore, that the group of the professions tended to merge with the new liberal ruling class while the urban aristocracy adhered to positions which were called disparagingly, and not without a certain degree of superficiality, 'Bourbonic', the divide between them is even more evident.

6. I have so far only considered the case of Naples, even though it cannot be plausibly taken to represent the country as a whole: indeed, one may presume that in other parts of Italy the situation was very different. For instance, the city of Milan between the 1880s and the First World War, as described in the writings of Marco Meriggi on associationism,[45] was a setting generally much richer in relations, exchanges and alliances between the aristocracy and the bourgeois groups. The Milanese aristocrats revealed themselves much more willing to embark on professional careers. In contrast to Naples, in Milan we find a number of aristocrats practising as notaries (2 in 1877, 4 in 1888 and in 1903) or physicians (7 in 1877, 6 in 1888 and 7 in 1903).[46] The aristocratic class was well represented among lawyers and attorneys, and also among engineers and architects, with, in 1877, 24.4 nobles per thousand lawyers and attorneys, and 33.1 per thousand engineers and architects; in 1888, the figures were 40.5 per thousand lawyers and attorneys and 26.5 per thousand engineers and architects. In 1903 the numbers diminished to 19.6 and 21.8 per thousand, respectively; a decline, however, which was due mainly to a marked expansion in the professional group which was not matched by a corresponding increase in the share of aristocratic professionals. The figures therefore reveal a much larger number of aristocratic professionals in Milan than in Naples. However, a feature common to both cities is the rarity of marriages between professionals and aristocrats: the proportion of Milanese lawyers who married women of aristocratic birth was, in the matrimonial cohorts between 1840 and 1860, lower than 2 per cent.[47] In 1888 there were 52 aristocratic professionals in Milan practising as lawyers, attorneys, engineers, architects, notaries and doctors. Shedding illuminating light on this group is the fact that, apart from eight Counts, all its other members used the title of mere '*nobile*'.

Examination (if somewhat superficial) of the group of Milanese aristocratic professionals as a whole confirms Siegrist's finding as specifically regards the legal profession:

> Almost none of the Milanese lawyers of noble birth came from the most important Milanese patriciate, and only a few of them from the truly entrenched ancient nobility. Just one lawyer bore the title of Count; all the

---

[45] M. Meriggi, 'Lo "spirito di associazione" nella Milano dell'Ottocento (1815–1914)', *Quaderni Storici*, 26, 77, 1991, pp. 389–417; *idem, Milano borghese. Circoli ed élites nell'Ottocento*, Venice, 1992.

[46] The figures are taken from *Guida industriale e commerciale di Milano per l'anno 1877*, Milan, 1877; G. Savallo, *Guida di Milano del 1888 (anno VII)*, Milan, 1888; *Guida generale amministrativa, commerciale, industriale, professionale di Milano e provincia*, x, 1903–4.

[47] H. Siegrist, 'Gli avvocati nell'Italia del XIX secolo', p. 58.

others were '*nobili*', that is, cadets, the sons of marquises and counts with no rights of inheritance. Most of them were recruited from aristocratic families who had migrated to the city, or from families ennobled during the Napoleonic or Restoration periods.[48]

In this respect, therefore, Milan resembled Naples more closely than one might suppose, and more closely than is usually claimed. Further confirmation is provided by the finding that, in both cities, the proportion of nobles in the legal professions tended progressively to diminish between the mid-nineteenth century and the first decades of the twentieth.[49]

The situation in central Italy was rather different – although here again the reference is specifically to lawyers, who, as we have seen, accounted for the majority of the aristocratic professionals. Siegrist's research shows that in Tuscany, the relationship between the legal profession and the aristocracy during the period prior to national Unification was particularly close (as it was for that matter in most of the country, with the exception of certain major urban centres) and that it remained just as close thereafter. Eleven per cent of the Tuscan lawyers who received their training between 1840 and 1858 – a group which comprised the lawyers active for at least the following thirty years – were noblemen.[50] Here too, however, the aristocrats who entered the legal professions came, according to Siegrist, from the patriciate of the small and medium-sized towns: 'the scions of the most important noble families did not become lawyers'.[51]

7. We may therefore conclude that very different patterns of behaviour were displayed by what we can call, somewhat crudely, the high nobility and the lesser nobility. Until the First World War, the former were much more concerned to maintain rigid endogamy, and they were mostly uninterested in the exercise of a profession. The professions – including the more prestigious and politically advantageous legal occupations – failed to attract a great deal of interest among the aristocracy, with the exception of *de facto* restricted groups with smaller economic resources. Aristocratic families instead found a satisfactory source of income for their cadets – who in the meantime increasingly resorted to marriage for the same purpose – by placing them in the upper echelons of the civil service. The diplomatic corps, the judiciary, the army, the navy, and the other sectors of the state were environments that the

[48] Ibid., p. 162.
[49] Ibid., p. 165.
[50] Ibid., p. 161.
[51] Ibid., p. 163.

aristocracy found more congenial than professional firms. The lesser nobility, for its part, increasingly resorted to matrimonial alliances with partners from the world of the professions. This was a tendency which enabled the minor nobility to narrow the distance between the bourgeoisie and the high aristocracy. It also gave this group a polymorphism which enabled it to assume a leading role in political affairs while simultaneously moving into those professions more easily exploited to gain office in local government or a seat in parliament.

The extremely close relationship between the legal profession and political leadership thus accounts for the interest that the former aroused among the nobility. It was, however, a phenomenon that concerned the specific component of the nobility which did not possess the property and the deep roots in a local milieu that could legitimate its aspiration to a seat in Parliament or – and this has more explicit significance – a seat in the Senate under the provisions of the twenty-first category of eligibility defined by the Constitution.

Particularly significant is the finding that in all areas of the country in the late nineteenth and early twentieth centuries, aristocratic professionals declined in numbers compared with the mid-1800s. And it is a fact which acquires even greater significance if we bear in mind that these few aristocratic professionals belonged to a minor nobility which was almost entirely provincial in origin; and, moreover, that most of these minor nobles were impoverished younger sons excluded from their families' wealth. Again: the numerous professionals who paraded titles which were not rightfully theirs, or at any rate not officially recognized as such, together with the large number who were only distant relatives of the families whose noble name they bore, distort the features of this group even further. And if one then adds that the contiguity between professionals and nobles, which was in any case slight, can only be distinguished at the margins of the aristocracy (where the group's distinctive features begin to fade), social mobility between the Italian aristocracy and the professions may have been even less marked than this chapter has indicated.

CHAPTER 8

THE PROFESSIONS IN PARLIAMENT

FULVIO CAMMARANO

INTRODUCTION[1]

Largely neglected by Italian historiography, the subject of the professions in Parliament is nevertheless an important aspect of the broader issue of political representation in post-Unification Italy.[2] Of course, criticism of the shortcomings of historiography does not apply to the numerous studies in parliamentary sociology or to research into individual professions, since these have frequently also addressed the topic of the political representation of the professions. Such criticism concerns the more complex question of the overall role of free professionism in parliament, and the historical influence exerted by the socio-occupational backgrounds of parliamentary deputies on the relationship between general political representation and the representation of specific interests. This is a problem that resists easy solution and which requires analysis to shift from sociographic factors (such as profession, religion, social class) to the parliamentary behaviour of deputies free from narrow political-party constraints – which was the case of parliamentary deputies in liberal Italy. The aim of this essay is to conduct only preliminary and broad-gauge investigation. It therefore restricts itself to providing data and interpretations which, for the reasons given

[1] I am indebted to Maria Rita Tattini for her help in gathering the materials for this research. I also wish to express my thanks to Carla Venturi for her assistance in compiling the statistical tables.
[2] The outstanding analysis of the political role of self-employed professionals in the liberal parliament is by P. Farneti, *Sistema politico e società civile. Saggi di teoria e ricerca politica*, Turin, 1971. On historiographical neglect and the methodological problems encountered in analysis of the parliamentary class, see F. Andreucci et al., 'I parlamentari in Italia dall'Unità all'oggi. Orientamenti storiografici e problemi di ricerca', *Italia Contemporanea*, 153, 1983, pp. 145–64. Useful interpretative insights are offered by M. Cotta, 'L'analisi della classe parlamentare: problemi e prospettive', *Rivista Italiana di Scienza Politica*, 3, 1975, pp. 473–514.

below, should be taken as purely indicative – although they represent the first 'in-the-field' verification of the few but well-established hypotheses in this area of inquiry. Before we move to the main body of analysis, however, a number of introductory aspects (including methodological ones) require elucidation, and beginning with the institutional setting for the action of the professional categories examined: lawyers, engineers, doctors and notaries.

The Chamber of Deputies was instituted in 1848 by Article 39 of the Statute of Carlo Alberto (the *Statuto Albertino*), and thereafter legislatures followed each other in an uninterrupted sequence. The number of deputies progressively increased as the Kingdom of Savoy annexed more and more territory. Four hundred and forty-three deputies sat in the first Italian parliament, which met in February 1861; the number rose to 493 following the annexation of Venetia in 1866, and then to 508 with the fall of Rome four years later. The electoral system was created by a special law promulgated in March 1848 and which was subsequently extended to the Kingdom of Italy after Unification. This law granted voting rights to those male citizens aged over 25 who possessed a basic level of literacy, and who paid taxes amounting to at least 40 lire annually. The voting system was based on the single-member constituency and on a two-ballot majoritarian system which guaranteed the election of one candidate for every constituency. At the elections held on 27 January 1861 for the first Italian parliament (8th legislature), 1.9% of the population was enrolled on the electoral registers, but of those eligible to vote only 57.2% actually did so. The electoral law was reformed in 1882 when, with the voting age reduced to 21, literacy was given precedence over wealth. The minimum requirement became the effective demonstration of literacy or, failing this, personal wealth equivalent to an annual tax outlay of at least 19.80 lire. The extension of suffrage increased the numbers eligible to vote from 621,896 in 1880 to 2,017,829 in 1882, with an electors/overall population ratio of 6.9%. The party list system was also introduced, without proportional representation, so that between two and five candidates were elected for each constituency on the basis of a simple majoritarian system. The pre-existing 508 single-member constituencies were reorganized into 135 constituencies of varying sizes. The single-member system was reintroduced in 1891, while the law of June 1912 granted voting rights to all male citizens aged over 30 – or over 21 if they met the literacy or wealth requirements, or if they had completed their military service.

The gathering of the data presented below has been hampered by the scarcity and imprecision of the available sources. The main reference text is the three volumes by Alberto Malatesta.[3] Although this work represents the most complete collection of biographical data on members of parliament in the period in question, it lacks reliable criteria for their classification. For this reason, it was necessary to cross-check with other sources[4] whenever possible or, more frequently, to extrapolate. I encountered the greatest difficulty in establishing the actual profession of certain deputies, given that these biographical collections give priority to political and intellectual achievements and omit information on professional matters. It is indicative, for example, that definitions such as 'landowner' or 'property-owner' are never used.

The survey considered the biographical data of all the deputies who, between 1861 and 1913, possessed an educational qualification which entitled them to practise as lawyers, engineers, doctors or notaries. On the basis of this information it was possible to establish the quantitative size of the phenomenon by calculating the distribution of deputies across legislatures (from the 8th to the 24th) by educational qualification, by profession, by electoral constituency and by political affiliation. This last feature proved extremely difficult to specify, because in this period the party-political positions of deputies in the broad political spectrum of Italian liberalism were nebulous and constantly shifting. For this reason the sources restrict themselves to providing, when they do, vague political labels (except for 'socialist' or 'catholic', which unequivocally indicate political position vis-à-vis the liberal alignment). Therefore in a study so broad in scope, simplified indicators of political affiliation had inevitably to be used. Nevertheless we sought to adopt the most homogeneous criterion possible, based on the information provided by our sources and bearing in mind that the categories Right, Centre and Left frequently represent contingent nuances, perhaps not even political ones and in any case always within the liberal area. The term 'Right' covers all deputies defined by the sources as: Destra Storica, Liberali Temperati, Moderati, Costituzionali

---

[3]   A. Malatesta, Ministri, deputati, senatori dal 1848 al 1992, 3 vols, Milan, 1940–41.

[4]   In particular, T. Sarti, Il parlamento subalpino e nazionale. Profili e cenni biografici di tutti i deputati e senatori eletti e creati dal 1848 al 1890, Rome, 1896; V. Porto, Gli onorevoli del Veneto durante la XVII legislatura, Rome, 1892; L. Pallestrini, I nostri deputati: XIX legislatura, Palermo, 1896; F. Bartolotta, Parlamenti e governi d'Italia dal 1848 al 1970, Rome, 1971; I 508 deputati per la XXIII legislatura, Milan, 1910; I 508 deputati al Parlamento per la XXIV legislatura. Biografie e ritratti, Milan, 1914; A. Tortoreto, I parlamentari italiani della XXIII legislatura. Cenni biografici dei deputati e senatori, Rome, 1910; A. De Gubernatis, Dizionari biografici, 2 vols, Rome, 1895; A. Brunialti, Annuario biografico universale, Turin, 1884; Dizionario biografico degli italiani, 39 vols, Rome, 1960–91.

Moderati, Gruppo Agrario (literally, historical right, middle-of-the road, moderate liberals, moderate constitutionalists, agrarian group). The 'Centre' comprises deputies indicated as belonging to the centre-right and centre-left, and those whose political allegiance is not otherwise specified. The term 'Left' refers to the *Sinistra Storica*, the *Liberali Democratici*, and the *Liberali Progressisti* (historical left, the democratic liberals, and the progressive liberals). 'Extreme Left' applies mainly to radicals and the republicans. In assigning these labels, possible shifts and changes in a deputy's political career have been taken into account. It should also be mentioned that the number of deputies was calculated on the basis of the total number of candidates elected for each legislature. That is to say, also included are deputies who entered parliament as a result of by-elections. Consequently, the overall figure for the deputies in each legislature used for percentage comparisons includes deputies who entered parliament in the course of individual legislatures.[5]

The legislatures have been grouped into chronological blocks of relative political homogeneity in order to give a broad and easily consultable overview. Accordingly, the data have been aggregated into three periods: from Unification to the eve of the electoral reform of 1882 (8th–14th legislatures); the twenty years from the birth of transformism to the political and institutional crisis of the end of the century (15th–20th legislatures); and the period of the political ascendancy of Giovanni Giolitti (21st–24th legislatures). A specific interpretative criterion has also been adopted in the geographical classification of the constituencies represented by deputies in parliament. Classified as 'northern' are constituencies in the traditional regions of the North, with the exception of the provinces of Romagna (Forli and Ravenna), which have been assigned to the Centre together with the provinces of Tuscany, Marche, Umbria and Latium. The remaining regions, including Sicily and Sardinia, have been taken to constitute the Italian South.

It is necessary to make a further point as regards the educational qualifications of deputies, since these are qualifications for entry to the professions, not university degrees. The concept of 'profession' obviously has no correlation with the economic and social condition of the deputies concerned, for it is indicative neither of their personal assets nor of their professional success. The alternative occupations given in tables 8.11(a) to (c), have been deduced from biographical descriptions which tend to exclude the exercise of the profession normally associated with the qualification as the only or principal activity.

---

[5] I am indebted to Maria Serena Piretti for my figures on the numbers of deputies entering parliament as a result of by-elections.

This quantitative analysis has been flanked by sample-based analysis of parliamentary behaviour. That is to say, I examined speeches made in the Chamber of Deputies during general debate, and also voting records, in order to assess to what extent the parliamentary behaviour of deputies belonging to the professions corresponded to their corporatist affiliations. I selected parliamentary debates according to their relevance to the professional categories concerned. Analysis of the votes cast by professionals in parliament was also conducted on a sample basis and by professional training, but here I encountered an insurmountable difficulty: most of the voting of potential interest was by secret ballot.[6] However, to the roll-call votes analysed I added, for the purpose of contrast, roll-call votes on motions of confidence. These latter I took to be a proxy for the 'party' or 'conscience' vote and therefore as usable for verification of the existence and incidence of 'professional' votes. Excluded from this latter sub-category – which we may call 'behavioural' – were notaries, given the negligible number of deputies who belonged to that profession.

LAWYERS

The percentage figures on lawyers in parliament show very clearly that this category constituted the backbone of the Italian political class from the earliest days of the Kingdom of Italy. A law degree, indeed, appears to have been an essential prerequisite for a career in politics – as witness the fact that from the 13th legislature onwards (with the advent of the *Sinistra Storica*, and especially after the 15th legislature and the electoral reform of 1882), the number of deputies with a law qualification (see table 8.1) increased substantially, although this increase was not paralleled by a similar rise in the number of lawyers in the Chamber of Deputies (table 8.2). This is an interesting discrepancy, and especially in the light of the figures set out in table 8.11, which show that in the years between the 15th and 20th legislatures there was a sharp rise in deputies with degrees in law but who practised other professions, most notably journalism. Also significant is the homogeneity of geographical provenance: from the 15th legislature onwards, the ratio in the Chamber of Deputies between lawyers from the North and lawyers from the South remained stable (table 8.6). In fact, although until the early 1880s there were distinctly more lawyers from the North than from the South, in subsequent legislatures an equilibrium of sorts was established.

[6]   On voting regulations in the Chamber of Deputies see U. Galeotti, *Il regolamento della Camera dei Deputati*, Rome, 1902, and *Manuale ad uso dei deputati al Parlamento nazionale – XXV legislatura*, Rome, 1919.

Table 8.1 *Distribution of deputies by educational qualification and legislature (rounded percentage values)*

Legislatures*	Educational qualification							
	Law		Medicine		Engineering		Total	
	No. deps	%	No. deps	%	No. deps	%	No. deps	%
VIII	246	36.61	35	5.21	29	4.32	672	100.00
IX	210	41.92	24	4.79	19	3.79	501	100.00
X	250	40.85	24	3.92	26	4.25	612	100.00
XI	268	43.86	21	3.44	34	5.56	611	100.00
XII	247	44.67	30	5.42	25	4.52	553	100.00
XIII	270	46.31	27	4.63	34	5.83	583	100.00
XIV	265	47.58	27	4.85	29	5.21	557	100.00
XV	280	48.53	24	4.16	31	5.37	577	100.00
XVI	277	46.95	26	4.41	35	5.93	590	100.00
XVII	281	51.47	25	4.58	32	5.86	546	100.00
XVIII	290	53.21	27	4.95	32	5.87	545	100.00
XIX	276	51.88	24	4.51	36	6.77	532	100.00
XX	298	53.21	28	5.00	33	5.89	560	100.00
XXI	311	53.71	33	5.70	30	5.18	579	100.00
XXII	321	55.63	41	7.11	32	5.55	577	100.00
XXIII	318	55.11	38	6.59	39	6.76	577	100.00
XXIV	301	57.55	37	7.07	24	4.59	523	100.00

Notes:
* Legislatures 1861–1914: durations and prime ministers

Legislature	Duration	Prime Minister
VIII	1861–65	Cavour, Ricasoli, Rattazzi, Farini, Minghetti, La Marmora
IX	1865–67	La Marmora, Ricasoli
X	1867–70	Ricasoli, Rattazzi, Menabrea, Lanza
XI	1870–74	Lanza, Minghetti
XII	1874–76	Minghetti, Depretis
XIII	1876–80	Depretis, Cairoli, Depretis, Cairoli
XIV	1880–82	Cairoli, Depretis
XV	1882–86	Depretis
XVI	1886–90	Depretis, Crispi
XVII	1890–92	Crispi, Di Rudinì, Giolitti
XVIII	1892–95	Giolitti, Crispi
XIX	1895–97	Crispi, Di Rudinì
XX	1897–1900	Di Rudinì, Pelloux
XXI	1900–4	Pelloux, Saracco, Zanardelli, Giolitti
XXII	1904–09	Giolitti, Tittoni, Fortis, Sonnino, Giolitti
XXIII	1909–13	Giolitti, Sonnino, Luzzatti, Giolitti
XXIV	1913–19	Giolitti, Salandra, Boselli, Orlando, Nitti

Table 8.2 *Distribution of deputies by profession and legislature*
(rounded percentage values)

Legislatures	Profession									
	Lawyers		Doctors		Engineers		Notaries		Total	
	No. deps	%	No. deps	%	No. deps	%	No. deps	%	No. deps	%
VIII	189	28.13	28	4.17	26	3.87	1	0.15	672	100.00
IX	163	32.53	18	3.59	17	3.39	1	0.20	501	100.00
X	187	30.56	20	3.27	23	3.76	3	0.49	612	100.00
XI	199	32.57	19	3.11	29	4.75	1	0.16	611	100.00
XII	179	32.37	26	4.70	20	3.62	2	0.36	553	100.00
XIII	195	33.45	21	3.60	29	4.97	3	0.51	583	100.00
XIV	190	34.11	21	3.77	25	4.49	1	0.18	557	100.00
XV	190	32.93	21	3.64	26	4.51	1	0.17	577	100.00
XVI	190	32.20	22	3.73	29	4.92	3	0.51	590	100.00
XVII	196	35.90	20	3.66	26	4.76	1	0.18	546	100.00
XVIII	191	35.05	23	4.22	27	4.95	1	0.18	545	100.00
XIX	183	34.40	21	3.95	30	5.64	2	0.38	532	100.00
XX	208	37.14	24	4.29	24	4.29	4	0.71	560	100.00
XXI	219	37.82	29	5.01	21	3.63	2	0.35	579	100.00
XXII	228	39.51	36	6.24	25	4.33	2	0.35	577	100.00
XXIII	229	39.69	33	5.72	30	5.20	1	0.17	577	100.00
XXIV	215	41.11	33	6.31	20	3.82	1	0.19	523	100.00

So much, therefore, for absolute numerical values. In terms of 'density' (that is, the ratio between professionals elected to the Chamber and the number of electors per geographical area), the situation was very different, and here the South noticeably predominated.[7] There was a rather sharp percentage increase in the number of lawyer deputies in the years of the *Sinistra*, especially from the 1890s onwards and during the Giolitti period. From a political point of view, however, the situation was extremely diversified. Whereas in the North and Centre, the majority of lawyers with seats in the

---

[7] In 1865 the ratios between lawyer-deputies and electors were approximately as follows: 1 : 1,900 in the North, 1 : 2,480 in the Centre and 1 : 2,850 in the South. These ratios, however, were completely transformed by the 1882 elections: the ratio became 1 : 13,450 in the North, while there were 11,260 electors for every lawyer deputy in the Centre and only 7,960 in the South. This trend was confirmed by the elections of 1895 (15,200 in the North, 13,275 in the Centre and 7,200 in the South) and then by the elections of 1909 (16,550 in the North, 12,997 in the Centre and 8,725 in the South) which increased the gap between the density ratios. Although the elections of 1913, with universal male suffrage, reduced the percentages, considerable differences still persisted (1 : 43,080 in the North, 1 : 47,300 in the Centre and 1 : 35,000 in the South). My calculations are based on data from *Statistica delle elezioni generali politiche 1861–1913*, Florence–Rome, vols 1–13.

Chamber belonged to the centre-right, in the South their colleagues from the 'governmental' left maintained a constant and considerable numerical superiority until the 24th legislature (table 8.10). Generally, the substantial decline in the numbers of rightist lawyer deputies from one block of legislatures to the next was much more marked in northern and central Italy, where, in the period from the 8th to the 14th legislatures, lawyer deputies belonging to the moderate tradition (right and centre) remained in the overwhelming majority (tables 8.8 and 8.9). In the South, by contrast, from 1861 onwards only a small minority of lawyer deputies belonged to the right (table 8.10). Thus, even when centrist tendencies are taken into account, the parliamentary balance of power was tipped decidedly in favour of the left (table 8.10). In central Italy, however, the period between the 15th and 20th legislatures saw a significant change in political allegiance by almost half of the lawyers present in the Chamber who, after spending the first two decades after Unification on the right, transferred to the more tranquil and anodyne pastures of the centre (table 8.9). Nevertheless, and again as regards lawyer deputies from central Italy, it was these that comprised the highest percentage of members of the extreme left in the years between the Unification of Italy and the end of the century. With the Giolitti period, a sizeable number of socialist lawyers (9.42% of all lawyer deputies from the North and 8.78% from the South) began to enter parliament from constituencies in central–northern Italy, although the figure was much lower for the South (2.49%) (tables 8.8, 8.9 and 8.10). Apart from the obvious consideration that the socialist movement was more developed in northern Italy, these figures suggest that, whereas in the Centre–North the choice of the legal profession was a question of 'culture' (and, in the positivist climate of the time, culture leaned towards the left), in the South this choice was still made to gain entry into the traditional ruling class, albeit only in the subordinate role of 'adviser'. As a general political category, lawyers represented the best barometer of political change in the country. Changes in the composition of political representation in Italy after 1882 were epitomized by the collapse of the central–northern right among lawyer deputies; a collapse, moreover, which was not followed by any alternative political alignment. The steady increase in the numbers of lawyers elected to parliament in those years,[8] and their homogeneous political and

---

[8] The figure for the effective presence of members of the professions in the chamber has been calculated on a sample of eighteen votes of confidence in the executive between 1862 and 1912. On average, 61% of the lawyer-deputies were present in parliament during this period.

geographical distribution, provide striking evidence of how closely profession and politics had become fused together.

Indeed, if we move from the numbers of lawyers in parliament to their behaviour, their keen awareness of the political potential of their professional expertise is immediately apparent. As early as 1861, two days before the official proclamation of the Kingdom of Italy, almost all the lawyer-deputies asserted their political role, rejecting that of experts and defending the prerogatives of the Chamber against any mixing of legislature and executive. When minister Cassinis proposed the appointment of a committee to draft the civil code,[9] he provoked the following response from lawyer-deputy Mellana:

> I see no reason for the appointment of a Committee to do the work of the judiciary and of all the other experts called in as consultants to convey their wisdom to the executive. The Chamber should remain extraneous to everything pertaining to government, it should keep its place [...] We sit here as legislators and not as counsellors to anyone; each of us may, as an individual, convey that advice or that knowledge which he sees fit to the Government, but when he comes here he takes his seat as a legislator.

Later in his speech, Mellana declared that 'the government knows how many of us sit here and which of us has most to contribute in terms of knowledge and advice to this great enterprise of civil legislation',[10] but, he added, the government should consult these deputies in private. This line of argument, with its blend of political ethics and defence of professional monopoly from outside interference, was pursued in speeches by other lawyer deputies, even those of opposing political persuasions.[11] It was, in fact, yet another example of that ambiguous overlapping of public and private interests which constituted the distinctive feature of legal professionism in Italy. This was an ambivalence that was most forcefully expressed in the Chamber during debate on the law establishing the first regulatory professional code in Italy (the *legge forense* of 1874). On that occasion the inherent contradiction between the professional and institutional aspects of the Italian lawyer became manifest. The ostensible aim of the government's bill was to create an order of attorneys and prosecutors, but it also served the ulterior purpose of regulating a profession which the new state intended to utilize for more general public ends. The existing distinction under the law between the professions of *avvocato* (roughly equivalent to a prac-

---

[9] *Atti Parlamentari, Camera, Discussioni*, 15-3-1861.
[10] Ibid., *on.* Mellana, 15-3-1861.
[11] Ibid., *on.* D'Ondes and *on.* Giorgini, 15-3-1861.

tising attorney) and *procuratore* (prosecutor) [12] was regarded by many lawyer deputies as signalling a 'bureaucratization' which must perforce be rejected.[13] The Honourable De Portis argued vigorously against the creation of a 'Chamber of attorneys and prosecutors', declaring that he failed to understand

> why it is necessary to create these castes and, as the report states, to revive the corporations. The report wisely notes that, whenever the need arose, these free institutions gradually formed by themselves, without the law being required to intervene [...] Let us therefore leave it to the lawyers, let us leave it to those concerned to create these institutions.[14]

If anything, the defence of the dignity and the value of the profession was to be entrusted to the regulations governing admission to it. Deputy Massei (a lawyer), for example, argued that two years of practice were not enough to exercise the profession of attorney, especially in view of the fact that even undergraduates could join legal chambers as trainees. Massei concluded by dismissing as 'too generous, as well as inappropriate, this ease of entry to the ranks of the attorneys'.[15]

Significant, moreover, was the renewed emphasis with which the speakers – who not coincidentally were all lawyers – sought to glorify the Italian legal tradition. This was a tendency which stemmed from the need to nurture a founding myth that could be used to legitimate a category which, on the eve of the rise to power by the *Sinistra Storica* (that is, at the beginning of a period in which there was a greater requirement for mediation between society and state), was assuming a more complex political and professional dimension. According to Massei,

> The prestige of the Italian jurisconsult [...] reaches back to our forefathers, the Romans; we may with good reason affirm that our

[12] A distinction that the Minister of Justice Vigliani explained as follows: '[...] the profession of public prosecutor, which our law considers as necessary in civil proceedings, concerns itself only with the preliminary proceedings for criminal trials and the application of the rules of civil procedure. The profession of attorney concerns itself with the doctrinal component of law, the application of the Civil Code and of the other laws that pertain to it. This brief explanation suffices to demonstrate the great distance that divides the two professions. The one is entirely scientific; as regards the other, I would not say that it has absolutely no need of science, but the element of doctrine attaching to the functions of a prosecutor is certainly much less than that required to practise as an attorney, that is, to be a jurisconsult [...]': Ibid., *on.* Vigliani, 23-3-1874.

[13] See ibid., *on.* De Portis, 23-3-1874.

[14] Ibid., *on.* De Portis, 23-3-1874.

[15] Ibid., *on.* Massei, 23-3-1874.

law is not inferior to that of any other country, we may hold our heads up high.[16]

Those who opposed the bill similarly resorted to tradition by contrasting the ancient and glorious figure of the 'jurisconsult' with the 'pettifoggers' bred by what they regarded as the reprehensible fusion between the professions of prosecutor and attorney.[17]

According to the political scientist Paolo Farneti, the lawyers' over-representation of their status can be interpreted as an attempt – albeit a weak and confused one – by certain sectors of the middle class to find a functional alternative to the direct political involvement that they had so far failed to achieve, and, especially, as their attempt to build a mass party of their own.[18] If Farneti is right, then it should be possible to use the various Italian 'schools' of legal thought that confronted one another in parliament in those years as a criterion for identifying political alignments, although these obviously did not always coincide. Confirmation is provided by the heated debate of 1879 in which no fewer than fifteen of the eighteen speakers were jurists. At issue was a government bill which stipulated that couples could not be married in church if they had not first gone through a civil marriage. The question was of great importance because it marked a further step in the secularization of the state undertaken by the governments of united Italy. The clash was orchestrated on the basis of a conflict among schools of legal thought, which thus apparently assumed the role of groupings enabling determination of the political, cultural and geographical differentiation among deputies. The proponents of the rigid separation of state and church accused certain deputies – especially those from the southern region of Campania – of still being influenced by *giurisdizionalismo* (the doctrine of the state's right to supervise church affairs) and of creating a 'crime for merely political purposes'.[19] The Minister of Justice rebutted these charges on formal grounds:

[16] Ibid., *on.* Massei, 23-3-1874.
[17] See Ibid., *on.* Farina and *on.* Piroli, 23-3-1874.
[18] See P. Farneti, *Sistema politico*, p. 249. Farneti, however, warns that this was not simply a question of finding a 'functional alternative to an organized middle class party', but rather the representation 'of a composite and heterogeneous "middle class"' (p. 254).
[19] *Atti Parlamentari, Camera, Discussioni, on.* Puccioni, 14-5-1879. Of the same opinion was the extreme left-wing lawyer Arisi: 'I do not accept, gentlemen, that freedom can ever be restricted, with just one exception; namely when a right in jeopardy must be defended. Now I ask you what is the right that is to be defended by the bill on religious matrimony. Perhaps the right of the state?': Ibid., *on.* Arisi, 13-5-1879.

The first article of our criminal code runs as follows: 'Any violation of criminal law is an offence.' This indicates the source of our right to punish and the eminently political nature of the definition of crime.[20]

It was Deputy Varè, a lawyer, and a member of the *Sinistra Storica* like the minister, who pointed out the political importance of the distinctions among the various schools of legal thought:

> Our ministers of justice – and this is an observation which does nothing to detract from my esteem for the authority of our ministers – have almost all come from the same region [Campania: Editor's Note]. And it is quite natural for this to be so, because jurisprudence has always flourished greatly in that region. These outstanding minds come from a rightly celebrated school which in the last century was greatly praised by lay society, but which today I believe has run its course. They have studied canon law carefully and they know it well. No one speaks of *exequatur* and of *placet* with more enthusiasm than they do. And they are eager to discuss theological distinctions. They have a certain tendency to don the cope and mitre and to address the Chamber as if it were an Ecumenical Council [...] But we in Italy, we who wish the two powers to be separate, are too intimately and too conscientiously secular to take theological discussion, discussion of the sacraments, seriously.[21]

Deputy Indelli, a lawyer belonging to the political centre, sprang to the defence of the school and of the minister:

> Gentlemen, I belong to that mitred school of which *onorevole* Varè has spoken. I am not a bishop, but permit a modest sidesman to remind you of certain of that school's principles; the principles on which the bill before you rests. That school, gentlemen, has its precedents. [...] Gentlemen, this bill has a basis which I believe to have been forgotten in this discussion. And this basis consists of those jurisdictionalist traditions described by *onorevole* Varè [that] led to the grand school of the encyclopaedists, who taught us our ideas of freedom and gave us our free institutions. And yet, gentlemen, the French Revolution which reconstituted the State was the first great claim for its rights that civil society brought against the Church.[22]

Also the radicalization of parliamentary conflict during the political crisis at the end of the century stemmed, of course, mainly from political and class-based cleavages. Nevertheless it was often expressed in the languages of antagonistic schools of legal thought. In 1899, the socialist lawyer Ferri, a leading exponent of the positivist school of crim-

[20] Ibid., *on.* Tajani, 15-5-1879.
[21] Ibid., *on.* Varè, 14-5-1879.
[22] Ibid., *on.* Indelli, 14-5-1879.

inal law, argued in favour of government measures to deal with 'habitual delinquents' as follows:

It is only because the criminal code of 1890 is doctrinaire and bears no relation to the realities of Italian life that we are obliged to patch it together and shore it up against the effects that its application has had, or has been unable to avert, on crime in Italy. And one understands why the *onorevole* Lucchini (who belongs instead to the classical school of criminal law and is opposed to this bill), and who was one of the most assiduous manipulators of the criminal code, has made the first move to say that the criminal code alone suffices for the defence of society, and that special laws are not necessary [...][23]

And in a rejoinder to Lucchini's sarcastic interruptions, Ferri declared that 'this law is an acknowledgement, more or less obligatory, of the positive truth of the scientific doctrine that we represent [...]'.[24]

Lucchini countered that positivist doctrine was 'fine for Russia'. The quarrel grew even more rancorous when Ferri denounced the practice of basing university appointments on the candidates' membership of the various schools of legal thought. This discrimination, contended Ferri, had used Mafia-style methods to deny chairs in criminal law

to outstanding young criminalists like Sighele, Florian, Majno, only because they belonged to the positivist school, favouring others who merely parroted your treatises and your codes. Whatever the case may be, I was rejected five times in my applications for a university chair until I was eventually appointed under article 69 of the Casati law. I was as indifferent to my rejections as I now am to my so flattering appointment. I have always expressed my love for science and have sometimes paid for it in first person by conducting meticulous study in hospitals, in prisons and in anatomy rooms, while those who decided and decide the allocation of our university chairs have barred entry to young men who are the glory and the epitome of Italian science only because they have heterodox ideas. These gentlemen do nothing for Italian science and they boast that they have compiled a criminal code which, in my opinion, is truly a legislative disgrace to our country.[25]

This interweaving of politics, legal culture and academic squabbling was vividly apparent in Lucchini's reply to Ferri:

If his speech was aimed at me personally then it missed its mark: because I answer only to my conscience regarding the judgments I make either as magistrate or as a member of the university appointments board. However, I can tell him frankly that I would never offer a chair in criminal law to anyone who proposed to teach the criminal code as he muti-

23 Ibid., *on*. Ferri, 8-3-1899.
24 Ibid., *on*. Ferri, 8-3-1899.
25 Ibid., *on*. Ferri, 8-3-1899.

lated it yesterday before us [...] But the scientific intolerance to which my honourable colleague Ferri alluded is often a slogan used to palm off substandard goods; like the slogan of the political intolerance with which some professors sought to denigrate the good service received from entire university faculties because it did not constitute a school.[26]

In 1914, the fierce conflicts among the various political-ideological components of the category subsided as the urgent necessity arose to reform a judicial system which all members of the profession, albeit from different points of view, regarded as unsatisfactory.[27] The principal component of this reform was a revival of the panel judge system – when only two years previously the law instituting the single judge system had been passed; a measure, most commentators believed, prompted more by a desire to cut costs than to improve the administration of justice. The law had been vociferously opposed by the lawyers: even though the single judge system 'lasted fewer than ten months, [it] began amid the protests and threats of lawyers, who created uproar in the halls of justice and at professional conferences and meetings'.[28]

The successful campaign waged by the lawyers (accompanied, as was usual during debate on major legal reforms, by substantial doses of self-aggrandisement)[29] brought, amongst other things, improved economic conditions for judges and for courtroom personnel. That a law should be changed within the space of a few months, and without its being given time to prove itself, testified to the political power of these professionals – whose particular interests, when they coincided with those of the occupational category as a whole (in this case also the judiciary), closely conditioned a Chamber in which the lawyers were then at the height of their parliamentary influence.

If we pass from speeches in parliament to analysis of the sample of parliamentary roll-call votes, we find confirmation of a substantial identity between political class and lawyers in the Chamber of Deputies – particularly as regards the behaviour of the lawyer-deputies belonging to the traditional liberalist factions. On both technical issues and confidence in the government, the lawyers voted in a way that faithfully reflected the pattern of the country's overall poli-

[26] Ibid., *on.* Lucchini, 9-3-1899.
[27] 'Thirty-nine or forty projects have so far been discussed, proposals of every kind, studies by innumerable committees have been conducted, in order to solve the relatively simple problem of ensuring for Italy a judiciary which is morally, intellectually and economically worthy of its role': Ibid., *on.* Cotugno, 7-12-1914.
[28] Ibid., *on.* Cotugno, 7-12-1914.
[29] See Ibid., *on.* Sichel, 7-12-1914.

tico-parliamentary life.[30] A clearer picture emerges from their parliamentary oratory, which over the years became increasingly technical in character and was often intended to neutralize the polemical thrust of most debate on social order.[31]

ENGINEERS

Only a handful of engineers sat in the parliaments of post-Unification Italy, and their numbers remained practically unchanged (an average of 25 deputies) throughout the fifty-year period considered (table 8.2). To a greater extent than any of the other categories examined by this study, however, the geographical provenance of these engineer deputies reveals a distinctive pattern: over half of them (in some legislatures even three-quarters) came from northern Italy, whilst the engineer deputies from constituencies in the Centre (with a slight but significant increase during the Giolitti period), and in the South, never amounted to more than one-quarter of the total number of engineers in the Chamber of Deputies (tables 8.3 to 8.6). Parliamentary representation therefore reflected the strength of the northern engineering class deriving from the greater industrialization of North Italy. The northern engineers, moreover, made a more prominent contribution to parliamentary debate than did their colleagues from central and southern Italy. In general, together with the closer correlation − compared with lawyers and doctors − between educational qualification and profession (table 8.11), another finding warrants particular mention: namely that a higher

[30] The large numbers of deputies in this occupational category who voted in the Chamber enabled quantitative analysis of more general significance. Considered as 'party voting' were cases in which at least 40 per cent of lawyers belonging to one of the political alignments considered (right or left) voted for or against a motion, and when they amounted to more than twice the number of those voting otherwise. Defined as 'non-party voting' (which in most instances was transformist) were cases in which these minimal criteria were not met. On this basis, analysis of the eighteen sample ballots showed nine cases of party voting: 17-3-1862, 20-6-1863, 26-2-1866, 22-12-1867, 25-7-1870, 30-11-1880, 15-5-1888, 16-12-1892, 12-6-1906; and nine cases of non-party voting: 11-12-1878, 25-6-1884, 11-3-1887, 19-12-1890, 7-12-1891, 3-12-1895, 6-2-1901, 30-6-1905, 24-5-1912. As is evident from the dates, fully six of the nine cases of party voting belong to the years before transformism, and eight cases of non-party voting to the subsequent period. The five ballots on 'technical' issues exhibit the same pattern: party voting took place on 12-3-1869 and 24-6-1871, while non-party voting took place on 13-3-1865, 1-12-1888, 18-5-1894.

[31] A striking example is provided by the speech in which the lawyer Nocito opposed the bill stiffening the penalties for recidivists. Entirely non-political in purpose, Nocito's speech relied solely on technical arguments. See Ibid., on. Nocito, 9-3-1899.

percentage of engineers belonged to the nobility (table 8.11). This is a feature probably accounted for by the closer links in the North (especially in Lombardy) between the aristocracy and the productive fabric of civil society. Politically, too, the engineers were markedly different. Compared with the other professions examined, they comprised the highest number of members of the rightist parties (table 8.7). This was a northern right, in fact, given that after 1882 no southern engineer belonging to a rightist party was elected to parliament (table 8.10): indeed, the engineers from the Centre and South of Italy identified principally with the *Sinistra Storica* (tables 8.9 and 8.10). Another noteworthy feature is that almost none of the engineer deputies were socialists: the only two identified were elected in the North during the Giolitti period (table 8.8). This figure correlates significantly with the higher percentage of catholic engineers (table 8.7) compared with the other professions.

Inspection of the parliamentary behaviour of engineers yields no information on their possible corporatist tendencies. The sample of parliamentary debate examined deals largely with the question of transport, in particular the railways; a topic of major importance throughout the period and which, because of the interweaving interests involved, could have generated pressure groups aligned on the basis of professional ambition. However, the issue that actually predominated – in the few speeches to the Chamber made by the engineer deputies – was defence of the interests of the electoral colleges, which were invariably described as safeguarding the interests of the collectivity. The engineer deputies rarely deployed their expertise to advance political arguments, although they were certainly aware that they possessed knowledge which parliamentary decision makers would find useful. In 1872, in reply to a deputy who had doubted the technical abilities of a parliamentary committee appointed to study the feasibility of a rail link between Udine and Pontebba, an engineer, Deputy Monti, declared:

> ... if *onorevole* Porta has the goodness to consider that it [the committee] contains five engineers, he will realize that the committee has thoroughly discussed the bill [...] in every particular.[32]

The engineers did display, therefore, a certain degree of solidarist spirit – as testified in 1882 by the passionate address to the Chamber by

[32] Ibid., *on.* Monti, 15-6-1872. On another occasion, Monti defended the 'mechanical school' against the claim by the 'military school' that it was more expert on railway engineering; a defence made 'I permit myself to say, with the seriousness of one who can speak as a practitioner': Ibid., *on.* Monti, 4-6-1873.

Table 8.3 Distribution of deputies by profession, legislature and geographical area: North (rounded percentage values)

Legislatures	Lawyers			Doctors			Engineers			Notaries			National total of deputies
	No. deps North	No. deps Nat.	North /Nat. %	No. deps North	No. deps Nat.	North /Nat. %	No. deps North	No. deps Nat.	North /Nat. %	No. deps North	No. deps Nat.	North /Nat. %	
VIII	80	189	42.33	4	28	14.29	14	26	53.85	1	1	100.00	672
IX	82	163	50.31	7	18	38.89	13	17	76.47	1	1	100.00	501
X	94	187	50.27	8	20	40.00	16	23	69.57	2	3	66.67	612
XI	90	199	45.23	10	19	52.63	19	29	65.52	1	1	100.00	611
XII	73	179	40.78	14	26	53.85	12	20	60.00	1	2	50.00	553
XIII	85	195	43.59	12	21	57.14	20	29	68.97	0	3	0.00	583
XIV	78	190	41.05	11	21	52.38	18	25	72.00	1	1	100.00	557
XV	79	190	41.58	11	21	52.38	19	26	73.08	1	1	100.00	577
XVI	70	190	36.84	10	22	45.45	19	29	65.52	2	3	66.67	590
XVII	69	196	35.20	5	20	25.00	17	26	65.38	1	1	100.00	546
XVIII	82	191	42.93	8	23	34.78	19	27	70.37	1	1	100.00	545
XIX	75	183	40.98	7	21	33.33	20	30	66.67	1	2	50.00	532
XX	94	208	45.19	8	24	33.33	18	24	75.00	3	4	75.00	560
XXI	98	219	44.75	9	29	31.03	12	21	57.14	2	2	100.00	579
XXII	98	228	42.98	11	36	30.56	15	25	60.00	2	2	100.00	577
XXIII	97	229	42.36	10	33	30.30	15	30	50.00	1	1	100.00	577
XXIV	89	215	41.40	9	33	27.27	10	20	50.00	1	1	100.00	523

Table 8.4 *Distribution of deputies by profession, legislature and geographical area: Centre (rounded percentage values)*

Legislatures	Profession												National total of deputies
	Lawyers			Doctors			Engineers			Notaries			
	No. deps Centre	No. deps Nat.	Centre /Nat. %	No. deps Centre	No. deps Nat.	Centre /Nat. %	No. deps Centre	No. deps Nat.	Centre /Nat. %	No. deps Centre	No. deps Nat.	Centre /Nat. %	
VIII	28	189	14.81	8	28	28.57	10	26	38.46	0	1	0.00	672
IX	22	163	13.50	5	18	27.78	4	17	23.53	0	1	0.00	501
X	28	187	14.97	4	20	20.00	3	23	13.04	1	3	33.33	612
XI	40	199	20.10	3	19	15.79	3	29	10.34	0	1	0.00	611
XII	31	179	17.32	6	26	23.08	3	20	15.00	0	2	0.00	553
XIII	33	195	16.92	4	21	19.05	4	29	13.79	0	3	0.00	583
XIV	33	190	17.37	2	21	9.52	4	25	16.00	0	1	0.00	557
XV	31	190	16.32	2	21	9.52	3	26	11.54	0	1	0.00	577
XVI	31	190	16.32	2	22	9.09	6	29	20.69	0	3	0.00	590
XVII	35	196	17.86	4	20	20.00	3	26	11.54	0	1	0.00	546
XVIII	31	191	16.23	3	23	13.04	2	27	7.41	0	1	0.00	545
XIX	31	183	16.94	5	21	23.81	3	30	10.00	1	2	50.00	532
XX	35	208	16.83	8	24	33.33	3	24	12.50	1	4	25.00	560
XXI	36	219	16.44	8	29	27.59	5	21	23.81	0	2	0.00	579
XXII	36	228	15.79	10	36	27.78	4	25	16.00	0	2	0.00	577
XXIII	41	229	17.90	7	33	21.21	8	30	26.67	0	1	0.00	577
XXIV	35	215	16.28	5	33	15.15	5	20	25.00	0	1	0.00	523

Table 8.5 Distribution of deputies by profession, legislature and geographical area: South

Legislatures	Profession												National total of deputies
	Lawyers			Doctors			Engineers			Notaries			
	No. deps South	No. deps Nat.	South /Nat. %	No. deps South	No. deps Nat.	South /Nat. %	No. deps South	No. deps Nat.	South /Nat. %	No. deps South	No. deps Nat.	South /Nat. %	
VIII	81	189	42.86	16	28	57.14	2	26	7.69	0	1	0.00	672
IX	59	163	36.20	6	18	33.33	0	17	0.00	0	1	0.00	501
X	65	187	34.76	8	20	40.00	4	23	17.39	0	3	0.00	612
XI	69	199	34.67	6	19	31.58	7	29	24.14	1	1	50.00	611
XII	75	179	41.90	6	26	23.08	5	20	25.00	1	2	33.33	553
XIII	77	195	39.49	5	21	23.81	5	29	17.24	1	3	0.00	583
XIV	79	190	41.58	8	21	38.10	3	25	12.00	0	1	0.00	557
XV	80	190	42.11	8	21	38.10	4	26	15.38	1	1	33.33	577
XVI	89	190	46.84	10	22	45.45	4	29	13.79	3	3	0.00	590
XVII	92	196	46.94	11	20	55.00	6	26	23.98	0	1	0.00	546
XVIII	78	191	40.84	12	23	52.17	6	27	22.22	0	1	0.00	545
XIX	77	183	42.08	9	21	42.86	7	30	23.33	2	2	0.00	532
XX	79	208	37.98	8	24	33.33	3	24	12.50	0	4	0.00	560
XXI	85	219	38.81	12	29	41.38	4	21	19.05	0	2	0.00	579
XXII	94	228	41.23	15	36	41.67	6	25	24.00	0	2	0.00	577
XXIII	91	229	39.74	16	33	48.48	7	30	23.33	0	1	0.00	577
XXIV	91	215	42.33	19	33	57.58	5	20	25.00	0	1	0.00	523

Table 8.6 *Distribution of professional deputies by geographical area and block of legislatures (rounded percentage values)*

Legislatures	LAWYERS North		Centre		South	
	No. deps.	%	No. deps.	%	No. deps.	%
VIII–XIV	582	44.70	215	16.51	505	38.79
XV–XX	469	40.50	194	16.75	495	42.75
XXI–XXIV	382	42.87	148	16.61	361	40.52

Legislatures	DOCTORS North		Centre		South	
	No. deps.	%	No. deps.	%	No. deps.	%
VIII–XIV	66	43.14	32	20.92	55	35.95
XV–XX	49	37.40	24	18.32	58	44.27
XXI–XXIV	39	29.77	30	22.90	62	47.33

Legislatures	ENGINEERS North		Centre		South	
	No. deps.	%	No. deps.	%	No. deps.	%
VIII–XIV	112	66.27	31	18.34	26	15.38
XV–XX	112	69.14	20	12.35	30	18.52
XXI–XXIV	52	54.17	22	22.92	22	22.92

Legislatures	NOTARIES North		Centre		South	
	No. deps.	%	No. deps.	%	No. deps.	%
VIII–XIV	9	75.00	1	8.33	2	16.67
XV–XX	9	75.00	2	16.67	1	8.33
XXI–XXIV	6	100.00	0	0.00	0	0.00

Table 8.7 *Distribution of deputies by profession, block of legislatures, political position (rounded percentage values)*

	LAWYERS					
	Legislatures VIII–XIV		Legislatures XV–XX		Legislatures XXI–XXIV	
	No. deps.	%	No. deps.	%	No. deps.	%
Right	387	29.72	174	15.03	156	17.51
Centre	390	29.95	378	32.64	225	25.25
Left	488	37.48	464	40.07	269	30.19
Extreme Left	37	2.84	137	11.83	165	18.52
Socialist	0	0.00	4	0.35	58	6.51
Catholic	0	0.00	1	0.09	18	2.02
Total	1,302	100	1,158	100	891	100

	DOCTORS					
	Legislatures VIII–XIV		Legislatures XV–XX		Legislatures XXI–XXIV	
	No. deps.	%	No. deps.	%	No. deps.	%
Right	46	30.07	15	11.45	9	6.87
Centre	63	41.18	44	33.59	34	25.95
Left	24	15.69	40	30.53	36	27.48
Extreme Left	20	13.07	26	19.85	32	24.43
Socialist	0	0.00	6	4.58	20	15.27
Catholic	0	0.00	0	0.00	0	0.00
Total	153	100	131	100	131	100

	ENGINEERS					
	Legislatures VIII–XIV		Legislatures XV–XX		Legislatures XXI–XXIV	
	No. deps.	%	No. deps.	%	No. deps.	%
Right	74	43.79	46	28.40	22	22.92
Centre	48	28.40	49	30.25	26	27.08
Left	37	21.89	48	29.63	22	22.92
Extreme Left	10	5.92	19	11.73	17	17.71
Socialist	0	0.00	0	0.00	3	3.13
Catholic	0	0.00	0	0.00	6	6.25
Total	169	100	162	100	96	100

	NOTARIES					
	Legislatures VIII–XIV		Legislatures XV–XX		Legislatures XXI–XXIV	
	No. deps.	%	No. deps.	%	No. deps.	%
Right	3	25.00	1	8.33	0	0.00
Centre	2	16.67	0	0.00	0	0.00
Left	7	58.33	7	58.33	2	33.33
Extreme Left	0	0.00	4	33.33	1	16.67
Socialist	0	0.00	0	0.00	0	0.00
Catholic	0	0.00	0	0.00	3	50.00
Total	12	100	12	100	6	100

Table 8.8 *Distribution of deputies by profession, block of legislatures, political position and geographical area: North (rounded percentage values)*

LAWYERS

	Legislatures VIII–XIV		Legislatures XV–XX		Legislatures XXI–XXIV	
	No. deps.	%	No. deps.	%	No. deps.	%
Right	214	36.77	93	19.83	78	20.42
Centre	178	30.58	147	31.34	105	27.49
Left	178	30.58	161	34.33	77	20.16
Extreme Left	12	2.06	64	13.65	71	18.59
Socialist	0	0.00	3	0.64	36	9.42
Catholic	0	0.00	1	0.21	15	3.93
Total	582	100	469	100	382	100

DOCTORS

	Legislatures VIII–XIV		Legislatures XV–XX		Legislatures XXI–XXIV	
	No. deps.	%	No. deps.	%	No. deps.	%
Right	19	28.79	6	12.24	1	2.56
Centre	30	45.45	7	14.29	7	17.95
Left	12	18.18	11	22.45	7	17.95
Extreme Left	5	7.58	19	38.78	8	20.51
Socialist	0	0.00	6	12.24	16	41.03
Catholic	0	0.00	0	0.00	0	0.00
Total	66	100	49	100	39	100

ENGINEERS

	Legislatures VIII–XIV		Legislatures XV–XX		Legislatures XXI–XXIV	
	No. deps.	%	No. deps.	%	No. deps.	%
Right	49	43.75	42	37.50	20	38.46
Centre	35	31.25	38	33.93	12	23.08
Left	21	18.75	17	15.18	6	11.54
Extreme Left	7	6.25	15	13.39	8	15.38
Socialist	0	0.00	0	0.00	2	3.85
Catholic	0	0.00	0	0.00	4	7.69
Total	112	100	112	100	52	100

NOTARIES

	Legislatures VIII–XIV		Legislatures XV–XX		Legislatures XXI–XXIV	
	No. deps.	%	No. deps.	%	No. deps.	%
Right	2	22.22	1	11.11	0	0.00
Centre	1	11.11	0	0.00	0	0.00
Left	6	66.67	4	44.44	2	33.33
Extreme Left	0	0.00	4	44.44	1	16.67
Socialist	0	0.00	0	0.00	0	0.00
Catholic	0	0.00	0	0.00	3	50.00
Total	9	100	9	100	6	100

Table 8.9 *Distribution of deputies by profession, block of legislatures, political position and geographical area: Centre (rounded percentage values)*

LAWYERS

	Legislatures VIII–XIV		Legislatures XV–XX		Legislatures XXI–XXIV	
	No. deps.	%	No. deps.	%	No. deps.	%
Right	98	45.58	27	13.92	21	14.19
Centre	62	28.84	84	43.30	41	27.70
Left	44	20.47	36	18.56	44	29.73
Extreme Left	11	5.12	46	23.71	27	18.24
Socialist	0	0.00	1	0.52	13	8.78
Catholic	0	0.00	0	0.00	2	1.35
Total	215	100	194	100	148	100

DOCTORS

	Legislatures VIII–XIV		Legislatures XV–XX		Legislatures XXI–XXIV	
	No. deps.	%	No. deps.	%	No. deps.	%
Right	15	46.88	3	12.50	0	0.00
Centre	12	37.50	13	54.17	15	50.00
Left	3	9.38	1	4.17	3	10.00
Extreme Left	2	6.25	7	29.17	9	30.00
Socialist	0	0.00	0	0.00	3	10.00
Catholic	0	0.00	0	0.00	0	0.00
Total	32	100	24	100	30	100

ENGINEERS

	Legislatures VIII–XIV		Legislatures XV–XX		Legislatures XXI–XXIV	
	No. deps.	%	No. deps.	%	No. deps.	%
Right	19	61.29	4	20.00	2	9.09
Centre	5	16.13	0	0.00	4	18.18
Left	6	19.35	12	60.00	11	50.00
Extreme Left	1	3.23	4	20.00	5	22.73
Socialist	0	0.00	0	0.00	0	0.00
Catholic	0	0.00	0	0.00	0	0.00
Total	31	100	20	100	22	100

NOTARIES

	Legislatures VIII–XIV		Legislatures XV–XX		Legislatures XXI–XXIV	
	No. deps.	%	No. deps.	%	No. deps.	%
Right	1	100.00	0	0.00	0	0.00
Centre	0	0.00	0	0.00	0	0.00
Left	0	0.00	2	100.00	0	0.00
Extreme Left	0	0.00	0	0.00	0	0.00
Socialist	0	0.00	0	0.00	0	0.00
Catholic	0	0.00	0	0.00	0	0.00
Total	1	100	2	100	0	100

Table 8.10 *Distribution of deputies by profession, block of legislatures,
political position and geographical area: South (rounded percentage values)*

| | LAWYERS | | | | | |
| | Legislatures VIII–XIV | | Legislatures XV–XX | | Legislatures XXI–XXIV | |
	No. deps.	%	No. deps.	%	No. deps.	%
Right	75	14.85	54	10.91	57	15.79
Centre	150	29.70	147	29.70	79	21.88
Left	266	52.67	267	53.94	148	41.00
Extreme Left	14	2.77	27	5.45	67	18.56
Socialist	0	0.00	0	0.00	9	2.49
Catholic	0	0.00	0	0.00	1	0.28
Total	505	100	495	100	361	100

| | DOCTORS | | | | | |
| | Legislatures VIII–XIV | | Legislatures XV–XX | | Legislatures XXI–XXIV | |
	No. deps.	%	No. deps.	%	No. deps.	%
Right	12	21.82	6	10.34	8	12.90
Centre	21	38.18	24	41.38	12	19.35
Left	9	16.36	28	48.28	26	41.94
Extreme Left	13	23.64	0	0.00	15	24.19
Socialist	0	0.00	0	0.00	1	1.61
Catholic	0	0.00	0	0.00	0	0.00
Total	55	100	58	100	62	100

| | ENGINEERS | | | | | |
| | Legislatures VIII–XIV | | Legislatures XV–XX | | Legislatures XXI–XXIV | |
	No. deps.	%	No. deps.	%	No. deps.	%
Right	6	23.08	0	0.00	0	0.00
Centre	8	30.77	11	36.67	10	45.45
Left	10	38.46	19	63.33	5	22.73
Extreme Left	2	7.69	0	0.00	4	18.18
Socialist	0	0.00	0	0.00	1	4.55
Catholic	0	0.00	0	0.00	2	9.09
Total	26	100	30	100	22	100

| | NOTARIES | | | | | |
| | Legislatures VIII–XIV | | Legislatures XV–XX | | Legislatures XXI–XXIV | |
	No. deps.	%	No. deps.	%	No. deps.	%
Right	0	0.00	0	0.00	0	0.00
Centre	1	50.00	0	0.00	0	0.00
Left	1	50.00	1	100.00	0	0.00
Extreme Left	0	0.00	0	0.00	0	0.00
Socialist	0	0.00	0	0.00	0	0.00
Catholic	0	0.00	0	0.00	0	0.00
Total	2	100	1	100	0	100

Table 8.11 *Deputies qualified to practise a free profession. Distribution of seats in Parliament by occupation.*

(a)

LAW

OCCUPATION

Legislatures	Lawyers	Of which nobles	Notaries	Of which nobles	Journalists	University professors	Businessmen	Property owners
VIII–XIV	1,302	120	12	–	83	54	13	25
XV–XX	1,158	124	12	–	146	53	51	38
XXI–XXIV	891	67	6	–	108	34	43	29

(b)

MEDICINE

OCCUPATION

Legislatures	Doctors	Of which nobles	Journalists	University professors	Businessmen	Property owners
VIII–XIV	153	12	3	2	7	–
XV–XX	131	2	8	2	3	–
XXI–XXIV	131	2	8	3	2	1

(c)

ENGINEERING

OCCUPATION

Legislatures	Doctors	Of which nobles	Journalists	University professors	Businessmen	Property owners
VIII–XIV	169	14	–	8	–	–
XV–XX	162	27	–	2	3	–
XXI–XXIV	96	16	–	4	9	1

engineer Lugli in defence of the technicians engaged in building the St
Gothard tunnel:

> I believe that if there is anything to say about the St Gothard enterprise it
> can only be words of praise. And since I am talking about that under-
> taking [...] whose slowness is criticised by *onorevole* Meardi, allow me to
> send from this place a word of praise for the director of works *onorevole*
> Giambastiani, our ex colleague, and to all the engineers who have been
> working on that railway line, who have made many sacrifices and have
> shown great self-denial and great skill in completing the line without
> extra expense and ahead of schedule [...][33]

This legitimation of the engineers' professional role was again confirmed in parliamentary discussion of financial allocations for the urban
renewal of Naples.[34] This legitimation, however, never induced the
engineers – as a professional group which was heterogeneous from the
point of view of its expertise and still in search of a specific professional
identity – to take cognizance of their public role. Caught between an
uncertain social role and the demands of their constituencies, the engineers in parliament therefore did not act as a mouthpiece for any comprehensive political design. Nor did they distinguish themselves by the
assiduousness of their parliamentary activity, although in percentages
they were the professional category most frequently present in the
Chamber, with an average attendance of 68% (see note 8). Transformist criteria, often tied to specifically pro-government choices, directed their voting on railway affairs[35] and on motions of confidence
in the government[36] throughout the period examined. The roll-call
ballots taken as a sample – with the due caution required by the ran-
domness of the sampling method and the paucity of the statistics –
seem to show a greater homogeneity of voting behaviour among the
engineer deputies (probably because of their greater political compact-
ness) compared with the other professional groups in parliament,

[33] Ibid., *on*. Lugli, 21-6-1882.
[34] The presenter of the bill, Deputy De Zerbi, praised the Naples urban plan, 'made
by public competition', precisely because the adjudicating panel had consisted of
'Cipolla, Alvino, Mendia and other illustrious engineers'. Ibid., *on*. De Zerbi,
20-12-1884.
[35] See the votes on motions relating to railway transport on 16-7-1864, 31-7-1870,
22-12-1884, 6-3-1885, 24-6-1891, 3-6-1903, 17-5-1906. Only those of 27-6-1876
and 7-7-1906 seem to have been party-based.
[36] In no fewer than 13 out of the 18 confidence votes examined between 1862 and
1912, the great majority of engineers in parliament voted in support of the government; 12 of these votes were obviously party-based. See the votes of 17-3-
1862, 20-6-1863, 26-2-1866, 22-12-1867, 25-7-1870, 11-12-1878, 30-11-1880,
25-6-1884, 11-3-1887, 15-5-1888, 19-12-1890, 7-12-1891, 16-12-1892, 3-12-
1895, 6-2-1901, 30-6-1905, 12-6-1906, 24-5-1912.

although no signs of a profession-based stance, even less a corporatist one, can be discerned. The engineers in parliament, therefore, possessed scant political and numerical weight at the turn of the century and during the Giolitti period. Nevertheless, the Chamber of Deputies felt the repercussions of the increasing professionalization of an occupational category whose social prestige increased in direct proportion to the transformation of a society now advancing towards industrialization.[37]

DOCTORS

Like the engineer deputies, there were relatively few doctors with seats in the Chamber in the period from Unification to the end of the century (an average of twenty-four doctors per legislature). However, this minority group, always slightly smaller in size than that of the engineers, grew considerably during the Giolitti period (table 8.2). In the period 1870–90 most of the doctors in the Chamber came from the North of the country (from the 11th to the 15th legislatures, those elected by northern constituencies amounted to more than 50% of all doctor deputies: see table 8.3). But from the 16th legislature onwards the trend was reversed, so that the South became the area of provenance of the majority of the doctors in the Chamber (table 8.5). If we use the 'density' criterion, we find that the 'southernization' of the category had already begun with the elections of 1882, and that it continued thereafter.[38]

Also the doctor deputies – who registered the lowest percentage of members of the nobility (table 8.11) as well as the lowest percentage of presences in the Chamber (an average of 52% of all doctors elected: see note 8) – exhibited a relatively clear-cut political profile. With no Catholics among them and relatively few right-wingers, the political sympathies of the doctors tended to shift towards the radical left with

[37] The engineers were also distinguished by the greater agility of the technical language employed in their speeches to the Chamber. For examples, see Ibid., *on.* Artom, 6-2-1892; Ibid., *on.* Engel, 5-12-1896; Ibid., *on.* Carmine 10-6-1908.

[38] In 1865 there were approximately 22,250 electors for every doctor elected in the North, 10,900 in the Centre and 28,050 in the South. In 1882 in the three geographical areas of the country there were 96,650 electors for every doctor elected in the North, 174,500 in the Centre, and 79,650 in the South. In 1895 and 1909 the change in the ratios continued. 1895: 164,900 in the North, 82,300 in the Centre, and 61,700 in the South; 1909: 160,400 in the North, 76,150 in the Centre, and 49,600 in the South. The trend persisted despite the major expansion of the electorate in 1913: 348,500 electors for every doctor in the North, 331,000 in the Centre, and 167,500 in the South. My calculations on data from *Statistica delle elezioni.*

successive legislatures. Indeed, although the main nucleus of doctors revolved around the centre-left, one notes that from the 1880s onwards they comprised the highest percentage, compared with the other professions, of members of the extreme leftist parties and of socialists (table 8.7). These data, however, require geographic specification. First of all, the socialist 'vocation' of the doctor deputies seems to have been wholly restricted to the regions of northern Italy. In the last two decades of the century, the few professionals who declared themselves socialists were almost all doctors from the northern regions; and even when the socialist component expanded percentage-wise during the Giolitti period, the sixteen socialists elected by northern constituencies (41% of the doctors from the North) were matched by only three from central constituencies (10% of doctors from the Centre) and just one from southern constituencies (1.61% of those from the South). One therefore finds profound differences in political position among doctor deputies from the North, the Centre, with a sizeable group of extreme left-wing deputy professionals, and the South, where the eclipse of the extreme left among the medical deputies during the 15th–20th legislatures was not, however, a prelude to the growth of a socialist tradition during the Giolitti period (tables 8.8, 8.9 and 8.10).

Analysis of the parliamentary behaviour of the doctor-deputies highlights their more pronounced ability to link general interests to those of their occupational category. This was in part due to the greater scientific homogeneity of medicine and its increasing emotional impact, which rendered the doctors better able than the engineers to defend their technical prerogatives and professional status. Analysis, however, is made difficult by the absence of roll-call votes on health issues, while, as in the case of the engineers and the lawyers, voting on confidence motions was uniformly party-based until 1880, and decidedly less so thereafter as a clearly transformist tendency emerged.[39] Richer information, though, can be gained from reading the speeches made in the Chamber by the doctor deputies.

In the first decades after Unification, these speeches were frequently defensive in character. Their aim was to gain acceptance for the idea that the public status of medicine could not be separated from the defence of the autonomy and scientific dignity of a discipline often criticized and often dismissed as simply a branch of the public administration and, as such, subordinate to the authority of the prefects or mayors.

[39] See the parliamentary votes of 17-3-1862, 20-6-1863, 26-2-1866, 23-12-1867, 25-7-1870, 11-12-1878, 30-11-1880, 25-6-1884, 11-3-1887, 15-5-1888, 19-12-1890, 7-12-1891, 16-12-1892, 3-12-1895, 6-2-1901, 30-6-1905, 12-6-1906, 24-5-1912.

Representative of this mentality was the derisive speech delivered by Bixio on the Maritime Health Bill of 1866.

> Whenever maritime health is discussed, the doctors belonging to the various medical schools of thought vie with each other to save humanity. I am not a doctor, but of quarantines I have had some experience [...] yet I must reject all these laws on maritime health care, which in my view is nothing but an absurdity [...] I do not wish to give lessons to the honourable minister of the interior, but let him be certain, and likewise *onorevole* Morelli and the members of the Committee, that medicine has no remedies [...] All doctors, all those who sit on the Health Councils, are nothing but hindrances to commerce.[40]

The bill provoked the indignation of the doctors because it envisaged the assignment of maritime health management to the prefects, and the creation of maritime health offices which would depend on the provincial administrations. The two doctors who addressed the Chamber on the matter (out of a total of ten deputies) opposed the measure because it perpetuated, as Deputy Morelli put it, 'the extraordinary practice in Italy whereby health functions are performed by non-technical officials'.[41] Morelli contended that neither the minister's nor the committee's proposals gave sufficient emphasis to the need for

> the cooperation of the health officials, who represent those technical functions indispensable if public health is to be safeguarded. And believe me, gentlemen, by making this observation I do not intend to perorate in the interest of my profession, but only to make public safety more secure. If the prefect is to have responsibility and authority for the management of administrative matters, I do not understand why there should not be technical officials who share them with him and exercise them under his guidance [...].[42]

The controversy between doctors and the government over the priority of technical expertise in health matters continued to simmer until the end of the century. In 1882 it boiled over in the debate over transferring the university clinics and the institutes of the Naples faculty of medicine. Deputy Buonomo, a doctor from Naples, complained that the bill had not been submitted to the scrutiny of experts but had been 'sent straight to the Budget Committee [...] appointed to examine more the financial part than that part of it of especial merit'.[43] Buonomo's remark provoked

---

[40] *Atti Parlamentari, Camera, Discussioni, on.* Bixio, 25-4-1866.
[41] Ibid., *on.* Morelli, 25-4-1866.
[42] Ibid., *on.* Morelli, 25-4-1866.
[43] Ibid., *on.* Buonomo, 22-6-1882.

uproar. In his sarcastic rejoinder, the spokesman for the committee raised the perennial problem of the relationship between general and particular interests:

> I understand his affection for the work of 'Gesù e Maria' [the hospital that was to be transferred: Editor's Note], since he himself is its superintendent, as well as being the director of the provincial lunatic asylum [...] which is located in the vicinity. One understands therefore that having therein the most conspicuous site of his scientific functions, he should be devoted to an institution for whose promotion and management he is responsible, and that he should feel affection for the places wherein he is accustomed to discharge his functions as a doctor.[44]

Until the 1880s, debate in the Chamber regarded the issue of health care as closely bound up with the more general question of public order. As such, health was viewed as nothing more than a problem of 'education in hygiene'; a problem which the civil authorities could handle without resorting to costly investment in health care programmes – the value of which, moreover, many deputies doubted. It was between 1884 and 1888 – that is, between the parliamentary debate on the measures in favour of Naples and the health-care plan introduced by the Crispi government – that the nation's health became a more explicitly political issue, one closely associated with the culture of a developing industrial society. The cholera epidemic in Naples brought the conflict with the denigrators of the autonomy and importance of medicine to a head, and enabled the doctors to emerge as an compact occupational category whose knowledge served as much political purposes as altruistic ones. By dramatically highlighting the impotence of the traditional political and administrative powers, the epidemic restored the prestige and credibility of the medical profession,[45] attributes which were ratified by the health law of 1888. The aim of the reform was to create a public health system based on medical officers stationed in every part of the country. The socialist doctor Badaloni, although scheduled to speak against the bill, praised its endeavour to give greater prominence to technical aspects. In his reminder to the Chamber of the efforts of *onorevole* Bertani, whose contribution to

---

[44] Ibid., *on.* Branca, 23-6-1882.

[45] 'It has been said that hygiene measures are useless because they cannot prevent the spread of the disease. Now the general discussion is closed, but if it were not, it would be sufficient to utter that bizarre paradox of the uselessness of sanitation in the building industry to see all the illustrious doctors in this Chamber rise as one man [...]': Ibid., *on.* De Zerbi, 20-12-1884.

the preparatory work for the health reform had been crucial, Badaloni declared:

No work of inquiry has been more thorough and conscientious than [that] carried out by Bertani, who began by interviewing municipal doctors [...] rather than mayors and prefects [...] Gentlemen, it is undoubtedly the case that there can be no real and effective health reform unless the state's health administration is based upon real expertise and unless it is removed from an interfering bureaucracy which until recently, in Italy and elsewhere, resisted the entry of doctors into the administration, and was the principal cause of the sterility of the state's management of public hygiene.[46]

It was comparisons with the past, especially, that highlighted the importance of the bill under discussion. Even for a deputy of the political centre, Senise (a doctor),

rather than being the activity of a body naturally suited to the purpose, [the administration of health in Italy] was imposed on an artificial, heterogeneous and therefore impotent organism. What did the administrative bodies and agencies know [...] about public health or medical policy? We may all agree at least on this: that the great merit, the true merit (as *onorevole* Badaloni said) of this bill is that it gives to our country something that it has never had before and always needed: namely a technical body organized to safeguard our health.[47]

Despite strong resistance to the bill,[48] the positions taken up by the doctors in the Chamber remained substantially uniform; a somewhat rare occurrence, apparently, given that one deputy felt it necessary to comment on the existence of this 'agreement in favour of the law [...] even among the opinions of the doctors, who [...] cannot often boast a similar consensus of points of view'.[49]

Not surprisingly therefore, the doctors – especially those most closely involved with the project (the general practitioners or *medici condotti*) – sought to exploit this attempt to bring far-reaching reorganization to the public health system, hoping thereby to secure ratification

[46] Ibid., *on.* Badaloni, 12-12-1888.
[47] Ibid., *on.* Senise, 12-12-1888.
[48] 'It is important not to exaggerate: there are indeed extremely serious questions which can only be resolved scientifically, but there are others which because of their simplicity, and because of the experience and good sense of the committees presently at work, can be resolved straightforwardly, without the need to create numerous Health Councils which overburden the already aggravated conditions of the public administration': Ibid., *on.* Arnaboldi, 12-12-1888.
[49] Ibid., *on.* De Renzi, 13-12-1888.

of their public role with the consequent recognition of their profession and image. [50]

Onorevole Panizza, spokesman for the committee responsible for drafting the bill, admitted that

> the stability that the present bill confers on the meritorious class of general practitioners, with the purpose of raising their scientific and professional status, does not have an immediate bearing on the health reforms now being proposed. It is certainly not a necessary condition for them; [nevertheless] the bill provides [...] a favourable opportunity to grant this benefit to the general practitioners [...] Today medical studies are much longer, more laborious and difficult than they used to be [...] It therefore seems just that the municipal doctor should be rescued from a condition that is humiliating to him. [51]

The Chamber therefore managed to meet two distinct but concomitant political requirements: on the one hand, it ensured the 'public' promotion of an emerging occupational category; on the other, it dispelled the danger of the already well-advanced alliance between democracy and medicine. In other words, the indispensable nature of the doctors – whom the Prime Minister himself had called 'the honest labourers of public health'[52] – was ratified within that process of the institutionalization of the state which Crispi regarded as the precondition for Italy's modernization. As Panizza pointedly observed,

> the general practitioner is the sole representative of science in its most modern form among the numerous inhabitants of the countryside. In consideration of this, the state will become increasingly aware that [the doctor] is an apostle of civilization, and also aware of how much the country can rely on his patriotism. [53]

Debate in the Chamber grew acrimonious as sixteen different speakers intervened, nine of whom were doctors (that is, just under half of all the doctors elected in that legislature).

[50] According to Badaloni, 'Public opinion has already rendered justice to these obscure martyrs who daily struggle for their existence, without any other comfort than the knowledge of duty fulfilled. It is now, therefore, that such justice is also rendered to them by the written law [...] Assured therefore the moral security, and with the pension the future material security of the general practitioners, you may now safely and serenely proceed with health care reforms: because with the general practitioners you have not only skilled professionals but also sagacious interpreters who, with wise application, will enable the law to bear fruit': Ibid., *on.* Badaloni, 12-12-1888. Another doctor deputy recommended that 'for the sake of equity, the benefits already enjoyed by schoolteachers should also be granted to general practitioners': Ibid., *on.* Petronio, 13-12-1888.

[51] Ibid., *on.* Panizza, 13-12-1888.

[52] Ibid., *on.* Crispi, 13-12-1888.

[53] Ibid., *on.* Panizza, 13-12-1888.

The doctors saw the law as enhancing their prestige and therefore their capacity to apply political pressure. This capacity reached its maturity in the Giolitti period, when an intense programme of professional organization outside parliament led in 1905 to the creation in the Chamber of the *Fascio Medico Parlamentare*, to which almost all the doctors present in that legislature belonged. This attempt to organize what was effectively a lobby was frustrated by political and professional conflicts and collapsed after only a year; nevertheless, there was no diminution in the profession's ability to apply pressure – as witness, for example, the discussion in 1907 on making a degree in medicine a compulsory requirement for those wishing to practise as a dentist.[54] The evident improvement in the legal, organizational and economic status of the Italian doctor, however, had little effect on the close relationship between medicine and the *questione sociale*; at least not in relation to the substantial percentage increase, compared with the other professions, in the number of extreme left-wing and socialist doctors elected to the Chamber during the Giolitti period.

CONCLUSIONS

We may conclude this brief discussion of the professions in the Chamber of Deputies of liberal Italy with a number of general remarks on the results of the analysis. First of all, the importance of the inquiry has been confirmed – for obvious quantitative reasons, given that deputies practising a 'liberal' profession invariably comprised between 40% and 50% of the total membership of the Chamber. But also, and especially, it has yielded valuable information on Italy's paramount political institution in the light of a factor – profession – which is of major importance in understanding the relationship between representatives and represented, as well as the character itself of liberal parliamentarianism.

One feature, however, should be given greatest emphasis: the constant recurrence in parliament of the question of the relationship between the deputies' political role and their private interests.[55] In

---

[54] See ibid., *on.* Rampoldi, 11-5-1907.

[55] In *Il regolamento della Camera dei Deputati*, Galeotti wrote: 'All deputies have the right to vote. Not translated into law, in fact, is that part of the proposal submitted on 31 March 1865 by Minister Lanza which required those deputies with some interest in the matter at hand to abstain from voting [...]': quoted in M.S. Piretti, G. Guidi (eds), *L'Emilia Romagna in Parlamento (1861–1919)*, vol. I, Bologna, 1993, p. 16.

1884, the moderate deputy Bonghi repeatedly, but unsuccessfully, sought approval for a bill whereby:

> No deputy may vote on matters in which he has a particular or personal interest, whether as an advocate for private individuals or of companies, whether as their administrator or in some other capacity in connection with them [...] A deputy proven to be in breach of this rule will be deprived of his mandate.[56]

In the years between the 1870s and the end of the century, the proliferation of proposals and initiatives to deal with the problem confirms that it was a constant source of tension between the realm of private and clientary interests on the one hand, and a liberal political culture extremely hostile to the idea of organized and particularist interests on the other. Frequently advanced, for example, was a demand that the names of deputies owning shares in companies affected by bills put to the vote should be made public;[57] a proposal which was bound to aggravate the controversy. This is precisely what happened when, in 1893, the radical Fortis invited the Chamber to examine

> the issue even more carefully. I ask you, why did you not ask for the list of landowners when the proposal was made to reduce the tax on rural landholdings by two-tenths? Why did you not ask for the list of industrialists when laws for the protection of large-scale industry were proposed?[58]

The question of private interest was obviously of close concern to the professionals elected to the Chamber – even when it was disguised as the professional specialism frequently invoked to impose a political point of view. The left-wing deputy Branca, a lawyer, declared:

> I believe that the true incompetents in adjudication of a question are precisely those who are competent in the specific matter under discussion. Nonetheless, it should not be forgotten that the Parliament is the grand jury of the national interests, and those who declare themselves competent in a matter are always those who are most directly concerned by it. And when I say 'interests', I do not refer to those interests that stem from private considerations; there may be interests of science, interests of profession. [...] I say that all the members of the Chamber, whether soldiers,

---

[56] *Atti Parlamentari, Camera, Discussioni*, 19-6-1884.

[57] For the motions and proposals intended to regulate the parliamentary vote in this way, see M.S. Piretti, G. Guidi, *L'Emilia Romagna in Parlamento*, pp. 16–17.

[58] Quoted in M.S. Piretti, G. Guidi, *L'Emilia Romagna in Parlamento*, p. 17. Although such lists were sometimes published, they did not set impediments on voting by deputies, according to Article 1 of the *Regolamento*.

whether engineers, whether doctors, have the right to discuss, but not the right to judge; judgement is the more impartial the more it is passed by men who feel neither professional passions nor jealousies.[59]

The educational qualifications and professions that quantitatively predominated in the Italian parliament, from 1861 onwards, were those that pertained to legal culture.[60] The proportion reached its maximum in the Giolitti period but thereafter went into progressive decline.[61] It is important to bear in mind, however, that the Italian law faculties prepared their students for what was generically known as the 'public dimension' – a milieu which comprised occupations ranging from civil servant to what the rhetoric of the time called 'jurisconsult', the interpreter (manipulator) of the legal system.

Significantly low, by contrast, are the absolute figures for the professions of doctor and engineer; and those relative to notaries (whose few representatives came mostly from the North) are negligible.[62] This numerical paucity is all the more striking when we remember that the overall number of lawyers practising in the country in the period 1871–1911 was slightly higher than that of doctors, just over double that of engineers, and only three times higher than that of notaries.[63] Accordingly, there is no proportion between these figures and the numerical ratios among the professional categories in parliament.

As far as doctors and engineers are concerned, therefore, we may endorse Farneti's finding (which he based on analysis of the shorter period 1891–1913) that, 'given the exiguousness of the number of these professions in the political class' we may exclude even the most timid of 'corporatist' tendencies.[64] What is instead evident is that Parliament was exploited to promote the image of their category – and

[59] *Atti Parlamentari, on.* Branca, 23-6-1882. An opinion expressed in various forms in speeches delivered by deputies anxious to avert accusations of particularist interest. The issue continued to be a lively one, as witness an article in the doctors' journal *Il medico condotto*, which maintained that 'in parliament there must not be and cannot be doctors, teachers, lawyers, owners or workers, but only deputies who have been sent there to study and solve the general problems of the country': quoted in T. Detti, *Medicina, democrazia e socialismo in Italia tra '800 e '900*, 'Movimento operaio e socialista', 1979, p. 37.

[60] For evaluation of this finding, also in comparison with other European parliaments, see P. Farneti, *Sistema politico e società civile*, pp. 242–57.

[61] For figures on this decline after the 1920s see L. Lotti, 'Il Parlamento italiano 1909–1963. Raffronto storico', in *Il Parlamento Italiano 1946–1963*, Naples, 1963, pp. 156–62.

[62] Several notaries, whose profession was not indicated in the records, have been included in the overall calculation of notaries present in the Chamber thanks to information kindly provided by Marco Santoro.

[63] The relative figures are set out in the essay by A.M. Banti in this book.

[64] P. Farneti, *Sistema politico*, p. 247.

also obviously of themselves – by deputies who did not hesitate to stress the self-sacrifice of their colleagues and the civil and patriotic role of their profession. And this, moreover, was also a convenient way to pay political and social homage to, and to maintain contacts with, their profession.

Of course, as we have seen, this is not to imply that doctors and engineers in the Chamber failed to perceive their profession as a source of scientific power, especially in debate on matters which concerned their expertise; only that such power was dissipated within the politico-institutional mechanisms of parliament. Put otherwise: their expertise failed to create the 'alternative' channels of representation able to move scientific and professional interests to the centre of a political design broader in scope than that strictly necessary to ensure the personal political success of the individual deputy. Indicative of this was the failure of the *Fascio Medico Parlamentare*, which, in 1906 and only a few months after its creation, was disbanded because parliamentarians refused to formalize its relationship with the *Associazione Nazionale dei Medici Condotti*.[65] More debatable, though, is Farneti's contention that these two professions 'acceded to politics to the extent that they grew and gained in importance as a social category'.[66] I have been unable, in fact, to establish a close correlation between professional prestige and the parliamentary influence of these categories, given that the evident growth of the former factor between the end of the century and the Giolitti period was not matched by a parallel and equally marked increase in the numbers of these professionals in the Chamber of Deputies.

The problem takes a different form as regards the lawyer deputies, since their numerical and cultural preponderance within the Chamber, as well as the social role and bureaucratization of their professional order outside it, helped to transform them into a political category ready to identify with the institution itself of political representation. Nor should one underestimate the fact that, probably, this preponderance and the relatively uniform distribution of legal practitioners in the country was a major factor in the political nationalization of Italy, and that it also curbed the much more dangerous process of its politicization.[67] It is therefore plausible that the over-representation of lawyers in the parliaments of the liberal era constituted one of the few channels of communication between civil society and the state; a role

[65] See T. Detti, *Medicina*, pp. 36–7.
[66] P. Farneti, *Sistema politico*, p. 211.
[67] See F. Cammarano, 'Nazionalizzazione della politica e politicizzazione della nazione. I dilemmi della classe dirigente liberale 1861–1914', in M. Meriggi, P. Schiera (eds), *Dalla città alla Nazione*, Bologna, 1993, pp. 139–63.

which was ideally suited to a professional figure divided between private practice and public function. It was no coincidence, therefore, that growing demand for political participation, the lack of political parties, and the inflexibility of the institutions – the conditions, that is, of the crisis that marked the end of the century and in some respects the Giolitti period – became factors which enhanced the presence of lawyers in the Chamber. In fact, whereas for the nascent party organizations of those years political representation was inseparable from that of the *notabilato collettivo* or collective notability,[68] then one may argue that, for the category of lawyers (the profession with easiest access to the political arena[69]), the quality of 'being notable' and judicial patronage were directly connected to a function that we may call 'collective political representation'.[70]

[68] See P. Pombeni, *Autorità sociale e potere politico nell'Italia contemporanea*, Venice, 1993, p. 72.

[69] P. Farneti, *Sistema politico*, p. 255.

[70] From this point of view, we can dispute the 'hierarchical' order established by Farneti, and his contention that 'the lawyers grew and maintained their importance as a social category to the extent that they acceded to politics': Ibid., p. 211.

CHAPTER 9

PROFESSIONALS IN POLITICS.
CLIENTELISM AND NETWORKS

LUIGI MUSELLA

I. INTRODUCTION

In recent years the social sciences have had a salutary influence on both political history and the history of the professions. However, a great deal of research has apparently not acquired a conception of historical social science with which one can agree. In particular, the transformation of history into a social science with fixed socio-economic categories is an operation open to criticism.[1] The denial of the individual through the adoption of larger aggregates, in fact, prevents evaluation of the relations between professions and politics that still persisted in Italy in the late nineteenth and early twentieth centuries. Many of these problems obviously stem from a view which opposes the individual and society, so that persons and extra-individual aggregates are perceived as two distinct realities.[2] In what follows I do not describe professions, groups or political parties as free-standing entities, almost as if they were not the outcome of relations among individuals. Convinced as I am that it is the chain of constantly changing relations and interdependencies that shapes different patterns, and therefore different groups and parties, and that it is the interweaving of reciprocal relationships which generates social organizations, I intend to describe the careers of certain individual members of the professions in order to shed light on the political forms that they engendered. The aim of this biographical approach is to reconstruct the political settings and

---

[1] I refer in particular to certain German historiographers who, more than others, have in recent years developed the study of the professions in relation to political history. See G. Iggers (ed.), *The Social History of Politics. Critical Perspectives in West German Historical Writing since 1945*, Leamington Spa, 1985; H. Medick, 'Missionare im Ruderboot? Ethnologische Erkenntnisweisen als Herausforderung an die Sozialgeschichte', *Geschichte und Gesellschaft*, 10, 1984, pp. 295–319.

[2] See N. Elias, *Über den Prozess der Zivilisation. I. Wandlungen des Verhaltens in den Wetlichen Oberschichten des Abendlandes*, Frankfurt, 1969 (2nd edn).

contexts of these professionals, thereby recreating a political era and the groups that typified it. Thus individual history has been chosen as providing access to relations and as yielding a more finely drawn picture than that resulting from an objectifying interpretation.[3]

2. MASTERS, FELLOW STUDENTS, COLLEAGUES BETWEEN THE MID-1800S AND 1880

Reconstruction of the biographies of those Italian professionals-politicians who played a significant part in the *Risorgimento* almost invariably leads us to the same educational institutions, the same salons, and the same meeting places. The personal and professional careers of these men, their friendships and their relationships, appear similar if not identical. We meet them time and again in the same private houses, doctors' surgeries, lawyers' chambers, newspaper offices, party offices, parliament, and municipal and provincial councils. Even such diverse settings as these, therefore, combined to assume a single function in the political and professional ascent of these individuals.

Giuseppe Pisanelli, the author of the new civil code of united Italy, first met Paolo Emilio Imbriani in 1835 at the home of Giuseppe Poerio. 'An indomitable patriot', as Pisanelli called him,[4] Poerio tutored numerous young men in law and politics. 'Imbriani and I', Pisanelli recalled, 'were among them, and with us also Alessandro and Carlo Poerio, Giovanni Manna, Giuseppe Miraglia, Leopoldo Tarantini, Francesco Torelli, Nicola Di Giovanni, Giuseppe Savastano'. After 1825 it was instead the law firm of Marquis Basilio Puoti – located in Palazzo Bagnara on Largo Mercatello (now Piazza Dante) in Naples – that provided southern Italy's most brilliant young lawyers with their intellectual training. Between 1834 and 1837, Pisanelli and De Vincenzi were Puoti's pupils, and before them Paolo Emilio Imbriani and Antonio Ranieri. Diomede Marvasi, also in Naples to pursue his legal studies, made friends in Puoti's chambers with Silvio and Bertrando Spaventa, with De Sanctis, with Settembrini, with the Poerio brothers, and also with Angelo Camillo De Meis, Pironti, Nisco, Massari and Pica.[5] Many of these pupils soon became teachers in their turn. In 1839,

---

[3] On the use of biography and the interpretative problems arising from the use of biographical sources, see G. Levi, 'Les usages de la biographie', *Annales ESC*, 6, 1989, pp. 1325–36; N.K. Denzin, *Interpretative Biography*, London, 1989.

[4] L. Stampacchia, *Giuseppe Pisanelli. La biografia e il suo progetto del codice civile*, Lecce, 1880.

[5] Almost all lawyers and deputies for southern provinces after 1861.

Pasquale Stanislao Mancini[6] began to give lectures in law and criminal and civil procedure. He charged a monthly fee of twelve *carlini* paid in advance 'with no exemptions or exceptions'. Mancini delivered his lectures at his own home, which in 1842 was located at 22 via Cisterna dell'Olio. Again in 1839, chambers were opened at 5 vico Bisi by Roberto Savarese and Giuseppe Pisanelli, who, according to Settembrini, had around four hundred auditors (*uditori*), including Enrico Pessina, Filippo de Blasio, Filippo Capone. Numerous students studied under Giovanni Manna[7] after a decree of 16 May 1840 granted him permission to open an office of civil and administrative law.

In Bologna, a role similar to Giuseppe Poerio's was performed by Gabriello Rossi, tutor to many of the city's professionals and politicians. One of the founders of the *Società Medica* in 1823 and a doctor by profession, Rossi was also a scholar of economics and the social sciences and, in the years prior to Unification, included Luigi Tanari, Marco Minghetti and Luigi Pizzardi among his pupils and friends. In the home of Marquis Gioacchino Pepoli and in the other salons of the Bolognese nobility, numerous young men met leading members of their chosen profession who coached them in the intricacies of political debate. Minghetti in turn taught public economics and constitutional law, and his office and home were centres of learning and intense discussion for the future ruling class. Finally, in 1860 the lecture-halls of the university faculties of law were frequented by numerous students with successful careers ahead of them.

Outstanding among the young Bolognese lawyers were Giuseppe Ceneri and Camillo Casarini. Ceneri is probably the best example of a professional who combined technical expertise with political practice. After graduating in May 1848, by the following year he was already practising as a lawyer. In 1850 he began teaching a private course in pandect and was shortly afterwards appointed to a university chair. An expert on Roman law, Ceneri was regarded by many of his students as a good teacher of law but not as a particularly original thinker. His activities as a scholar, university teacher, and lawyer for the most powerful families of mid-nineteenth-century Bologna gave powerful impetus to his political career first as a municipal councillor and then as a senator of the Kingdom.

After 1861, it was principally their legal work that enabled these lawyers to establish the connections and relationships that they required to build their political careers. 'Not a lawyer by nature and

---

[6] Several times Minister of Justice.
[7] Minister of Agriculture from 8 December 1862 to 27 September 1864.

passion like his father', wrote Benedetto Croce, Carlo Poerio 'used the practice of his profession chiefly in order to gain acquaintance and familiarity with the Neapolitan middle class'.[8] In certain cases, the 'practice of the profession' became a frenetic affair: it was said of *avvocato* Pica in the early 1860s that 'he has not yet come to parliament because, being left almost alone, he is extremely busy with adjusting torts, and having become what for the councillors and the judiciary is Father Christmas for children, every morning he hurries from one ministry to another with long lists of business to attend to'.[9]

The lawyers' clients had rights to enforce against private individuals and public bodies, or they had to defend themselves against the public administration (in matters concerning taxation, bankruptcy, and so on). Suits were therefore pursued at all levels according to the legal and administrative procedures provided by the law. The revenue office, the fiscal prosecutor, and other offices were administered locally, but there were then the tribunals, the judicial courts at various levels, and ultimately the ministries. The lawyer therefore had to navigate through the dense labyrinth of an institutional structure which was still almost as complex as it had been prior to Unification.

A political career became the final and indispensable accomplishment for the successful lawyer, because it enabled him to forge close connections with the inner circles of the state administration. The lawyer's clients – who belonged to the 'middle class' and to the most active sector of the electorate – were transformed into political clients and, as voters, into citizens concerned to ensure the election of their patron.

For the lawyer-deputy, the *raccomandazione* (the person-to-person soliciting of a favour from those in a position to bestow it) became an essential part of his stock in trade. When the protégé applied for promotion in his administrative career or for some benefit pertaining to his position in the hierarchy, the lawyer specified the laws that applied to his particular case. Antonio Ranieri, for example, deputy for a district of Naples, was highly systematic in these matters: he ordered the petitions and the relative 'pleas' of his protégés according to the competences of the various ministries, and according to those of his friends employed in these ministries who could be counted on to accelerate the bureaucratic process. Ranieri attended to the interests of a varied mix of clients: he was advocate for the Prince of Fondi in his application for settlement of a lawsuit concerning the waters of the river

---

8   B. Croce, *Una famiglia di patrioti*, Bari, 1949, p. 35.
9   Biblioteca Nazionale di Napoli, *Carte Ranieri*, busta 86, lettera 310.

Sarno; but he also represented an ex-Bourbon official seeking a better position in the new Italian state apparatus. A police agent applied to Ranieri for a promotion or a 'transmutation', as he put it, while the Duke of Marigliano hired him to press his claim for war damages.[10]

It was, however, the assistance itself that the lawyer gave to his client that consolidated his relationships with civil servants, politicians and influential voters. In the dispute over the assignation of funds to the church of Santa Chiara, involving Monsignor Michele Salzano and the state, Ranieri, as defender of the former, engaged in voluminous correspondence with, apart from his client, Cavalier Francesco Taranto, Superintendent of Naples and already a personage closely 'devoted' to Ranieri, with Guglielmo Semmola, a functionary in the Ministry of Justice, and with the Minister of Justice himself, the lawyer Tommaso Villa. Ranieri exploited friendships already cultivated for professional reasons, but which subsequently, because of the administrative nature of the case, became political as well. He obviously resorted to the relationships established in the everyday practice of his profession, but he also benefited from his political role and from relations which derived from wholly political connections. With various vicissitudes, the dispute dragged on from 1866 to 1881, and it consolidated relationships which constantly shifted from the professional to the politico-personal sphere and back again.[11]

3. THE FAMILY

Many professionals relied on their families as the first network[12] through which to build their careers. They frequently received their early professional training in the offices of relatives or of family friends: an opportunity which was important not only because of the training and experience that it provided, but also because of the numerous clients that the young professional was able to acquire. At the same time, the broad network thus created enabled him to develop social strategies and to advance his career. The sons of the wealthy urban bourgeoisie were often articled in the chambers of well-established criminal and civil lawyers, and behind the professional success of nine-

[10] Ibid., busta 30.
[11] Ibid.
[12] This concept takes account of the literature which uses the term 'network' in a political context. See in particular J. Boissevain, *Friends of Friends. Networks, Manipulators and Coalitions*, Oxford, 1974; J. Clyde Mitchell, 'The Concept and Use of Social Networks', and J.A. Barnes, 'Networks and Political Process', both in J. Clyde Mitchell (ed.), *Social Networks in Urban Situations. Analyses of Personal Relationships in Central African Towns*, Manchester, 1969.

teenth-century advocates stood many a barrister, magistrate or attorney who had managed to introduce a son or a nephew with the appropriate training to the right circles. In many cases it was kinship relations that enabled the offspring of rural landowners to gain positions in the most successful law firms in the chief town of the province.

For many parents, the search for a 'situation' for their sons and the cultivation of the manifold relationships that would help him acquire professional skills and launch him on a successful social and professional career were a major undertaking. A letter of thanks to a leading member of the Avellino bourgeoisie from an aspiring lawyer aptly illustrates how such relationships were deployed to obtain a good position:

> For five days now I have assisted at the chambers of Baron Raffaele Magliani, to whom I was proposed by the attorney general Lanzara. He seems an extremely brilliant person, and as far as I can tell, learned in law. He combines the two branches of criminal and civil law, a most difficult enterprise in Naples, and he has laboured much because of this choice [...] Signor Landolfi, to whom you recommended me, was also party to the choice and assures me that I could have found no better for all my requirements.[13]

Whilst family-run chambers were most common in the provincial towns, most legal firms in the cities employed lawyers who were not necessarily connected by kinship ties. The youngest lawyers frequented the law-courts where they attended to the preparation of legal briefs. The more senior members of the firm analysed the material, suggested strategy and drew up the legal text. Family and personal relations predominated in the firm, but they also enabled relationships to be established between the professional and his clients. A client never hired a member of the professions because of his specific expertise; he did so on the promptings of direct acquaintance, or on the suggestion of a friend, or of a friend of a friend. A network therefore grew up around the professional which, although structured by technical relationships, often developed at other levels as well. The office became a meeting place for friends with the same political allegiance and who, by discussion and analysis of local administrative matters, were spurred to direct action and to organize a consensus often difficult to find in other forms.

In many cases, a member of the professions already belonging to a family of professionals would resort to marriage in order to establish new relations, and to buttress his social position further. In northern Italy and also in Naples marriages frequently took place between

---

[13] Biblioteca Provinciale di Avellino, *Archivio Trevisani*, contenitore 41, fascicolo 2.

members of the liberal professions and women from the propertied class. In Florence, it was usually the son of the property-owner who married the daughter of the professional. Matrimonial strategy was therefore of considerable importance. For example, the Pisan lawyer Olindo Barsanti (1806–1905), first a deputy and then a senator, and for many years president of the council of the Florentine law association, married into a noble family.

Family links were also important for the development of a political clientele. 'Outside the family', Turiello writes of the southern regions of Italy, 'there was practically no other moral bond'.[14] The clientele and the family, according to Turiello, even managed to subvert the 'new orders' – the municipality and the state – and to exploit them for their gain. Personal interests thus usurped the impersonal function of the local and central institutions. But it was above all in mobilizing the vote for elections that the family exerted its influence. 'The nephew of my lady, with her brothers and relatives',[15] a chief elector assured the prefect of Bari in July 1885, intended to vote for the government candidate; but, he added, the mayor of her town and his brothers, one of whom was a canon and another a doctor, worked 'industriously' for the other candidate. The electoral campaign therefore pitted entire families against each other; families who were often already at loggerheads over questions of prestige and local interests. On other occasions, 'a certain number of influential families', 'linked by ties of kinship or of good neighbourliness' and 'lending each other mutual support', were able to conquer an 'invulnerable preponderance'. These were veritable 'clans' which, 'tied by blood and by shared interests and ambitions', dominated 'the administrations of the municipalities' because they were able to exploit the fact 'that various of their members were mayors, two or three were provincial councillors, and one was a parliamentary deputy'.[16]

4. THE UNIVERSITY, THE OFFICE, THE CAFÉ, AT THE TURN OF THE CENTURY

In the last twenty years of the nineteenth century, aspiring lawyer-politicians followed a route to success which differed from that of their precursors of the *Risorgimento*. In earlier years, first attendance at university, then private courses, and finally attachment to legal chambers,

[14] P. Turiello, *Governo e governati in Italia*, edited by Piero Bevilacqua, Turin, 1980, p. 60.
[15] Archivio di Stato di Bari, *Gabinetto di prefettura*, fascio 29.
[16] E. D'Orazio, *Fisiologia del parlamentarismo in Italia*, Turin, 1911, p. 190.

320 LUIGI MUSELLA

introduced the fledgling lawyer into the professional world and brought him the clients with which he would build his future career. This 'sociability conditioned by family structure and more closed both socially and spatially' (homes, private schools) now became 'open sociability enacted in public places'[17] (universities, offices and chambers, cafés). The salon, domestic settings, and to a certain extent all the places tied to an aristocratic and traditional world, were replaced by the bourgeois public domain.

In Naples, Eduardo Ruffa belonged to the school of Marini Serra, Alfonso Vastarini Cresi to the school of Casella, Pasquale Placido to that of Castriota. Francesco Girardi studied under Tarantini, Achille de Nicola under Casella, Pietro Rosano under Nicola Amore and, finally, Giacomo Russo under Casella.[18] These were men all more or less of the same age, who were fellow students at university, and friends. And they subsequently all became close political colleagues in the upper echelons of the administrative and parliamentary system, where they learnt the doctrine, practice and the rules of the game which tied the professions to civil society and politics. Through their offices and the cultivation of leading members of the professions they then began to re-establish and to strengthen relations with their provinces of origin. Although a multitude of links existed between Naples and the provinces of the *Mezzogiorno*, it was the legal profession that exploited them for influential clients who resided in the city but still maintained economic interests in their province of origin. The high southern bourgeoisie continued to reside in the ex-capital and, by entrusting their lawyers with more delicate matters regarding their property, enabled them to operate in two different spheres which subsequently proved decisive for their political-parliamentary careers. The client, in fact, was often also highly influential in the lawyer's constituency and could thus secure his election to parliament. It was, for instance, undoubtedly their common origins in the region of Lucania, the friendship between their families, and their shared experience of migrating to Naples, that brought Emanuele Gianturco and the lawyer-deputy Plastino together; and it was always Gianturco's Lucanian friends who enabled him to build his illustrious career in the profession. But it was the apprenticeship that, like most lawyers, Gianturco had served which enabled him to consolidate his position in the bourgeois society of the city as he followed the well-trodden path of

[17] The expression is taken from M. Malatesta, 'La democrazia al circolo', preface to the Italian edition of M. Agulhon, *Il salotto, il circolo e il caffè. I luoghi della sociabilità nella Francia borghese (1810–1848)*, edited by M. Malatesta, Rome, 1993, p. VIII.
[18] All lawyers and deputies from the south of Italy.

university, private school, legal chambers, and then his own private
school and his own pupils, his own legal firm and his own collaborators
and articled clerks, and finally his own clients. As time passed, the
network grew more closely knit, and it reinforced Gianturco's status as
both a professional and a public figure. The priest Peppino Gianturco,
the elder brother of Emanuele and a friend of Vincenzo Nitti, took
charge of the education of Francesco Saverio Nitti as a boy. But it was
then Emanuele Gianturco who received the young man into his firm
as an articled clerk between 1889 and 1892. Just as it was the Nitti
family, for its part, which acted as electoral agents for the aspiring
deputy Gianturco. Nitti then opened his own firm in 1903, specializing
in administrative and financial matters. In 1917 his most important
clients were Società Meridionale di Elettricità (SME; Southern Electricity Company), Maira, Peirce and Cattori, Lioy and Enrietti, and the
Istituto Marittimo.[19] He became prime minister in 1919.

Gianturco had graduated in 1879 on submission of a thesis entitled
La fiducia nel diritto civile italiano and supervised by Giuseppe Polignani –
a leading authority on Roman and civil law, who had studied with
Roberto Savarese and received his training in Giuseppe Pisanelli's law
firm. Gianturco began to practise his profession in the offices of Nicola
Alianelli, a lecturer in commercial law at the University of Naples.
After brief experience of handling lawsuits in the magistrate's court of
Avigliano, Gianturco, with the support of Giustino Fortunato, secured
a position in the offices of the Plastino brothers: only then did he
begin to practise his profession with profit, and to frequent the best
circles of the Neapolitan legal profession. From the 1880s onwards, in
fact, Gianturco contributed frequently to the journal *Il Filangieri* edited
by Giuseppe Pisanelli, Federico Persico, Enrico Pessina and Polignani.
In December 1882, through the good offices of Plastino – and perhaps
even more so through those of Fortunato, who wrote to the general
secretary of the Minister of Education asking for Plastino to be appointed to the selection board awarding qualifications as *libero docente*
(the entitlement to teach university-level courses, like that of the
Privat-Dozent in German universities) – Gianturco received his *libera
docenza* and opened a private school of civil law. Students flocked to
the Lucanian jurist's lectures (Gianturco himself counted eight
hundred of them in 1890) and many others studied his *Istituzioni di
diritto civile*, a manual on the principles of civil law. Gianturco continued to combine his teaching with the exercise of a profession begun
'without help of any kind, with a sparse and modest clientele'. His pro-

---

[19] See F. Barbagallo, *Francesco S. Nitti*, Turin, 1984, pp. 182–216.

minence in the law courts and in the lecture halls of the university brought him to the attention of a wider public. Because of his achievements as a lawyer and as a lecturer in civil law, his rise to political prominence was by now imminent, but it was once again the Lucanian brotherhood that had constantly helped him in his professional career – Plastino, Fortunato, Michele Torraca – that ensured his success.

In 1889, a seat in parliament fell vacant on the death of the deputy Correale, and the third constituency of Potenza elected Gianturco as its representative. Nitti, now a journalist, had mounted a press campaign to promote Gianturco's candidature; he subsequently joined him as a colleague, first in the Naples law faculty and then in parliament. Of the ten deputies from Basilicata, it was Fortunato, Gianturco and Nitti who had the closest affinities. All three lived in Naples, except when professional or political duties called them to Rome. They cultivated each other's company and met regularly at the Caffè Calzona in the Galleria Umberto I, where they were often joined by Plastino. The Caffè Calzona was a meeting place for many young lawyers – as evidenced by the following extract from a memoir written by Alberto La Pegna about Francesco Perrone, a lawyer and lecturer in commercial law at the University of Naples, and Lucanian deputy in the 24th, 25th and 26th legislatures:

> We thus met, by chance, twenty-five years ago. We frequented, almost at the same hour, in the same room, every day, Caffè Calzona in the Galleria Umberto I; but we belonged to different cliques. In the late hours of the afternoon, after the exhausting *via crucis* of Castelcapuano [the Naples hall of justice], a group of lawyers, with few briefs, many honest ambitions and great fervour of faith, met to converse on literature, politics, art [. . .] Opposite us, around a table near the entrance, sat at the same hour a small group of men. They were almost all professors and students from the fertile region of Basilicata, presided over by the great authority and grandiose personality of Giustino Fortunato. The tone of their conversation was always muted, discreet, subdued; only Fortunato sometimes spoke loudly and excitedly. We boisterous lawyers would immediately fall quiet when the Master on the other side of the room raised his voice.[20]

Unlike Gianturco, whose career had begun on a much more uncertain footing, Tancredi Galimberti's future was decided well before he began his studies as a law student. His father set out his ambitions for him very clearly in a letter written in April 1877, when the Galimberti family had just moved house: '(Y)our mother and family already call

---

20 A. La Pegna, 'Al Caffè Calzona', in G. Fortunato, *Pagine e ricordi parlamentari*, II, Florence: Vallecchi, 1927, pp. 54–5.

the Blue Room the Lawyer's Room. It is detached from the house and has its own entrance'.[21] The Galimberti residence, therefore, had already been prepared to function as an office.

Galimberti attended the University of Rome for a year and then transferred to Turin. In the capital he attached himself to numerous politicians of democratic and pro-republican leanings. In Turin he was instructed in administrative law by Giusto Emanuele Garelli della Morea, in political economy by Salvatore Cognetti de Martiis, and in constitutional law by Attilio Brunialti. Galimberti's flourishing legal practice began in 1904 at the law courts of Cuneo and other judicial seats in northern and central Italy. Frequently involved in political trials, Galimberti defended a number of newspapers against the libel suits brought against them for their denunciations of political and administrative malpractice. In the spring of 1904 he sprang to prominence as one of the lawyers defending Linda and Tullio Murri, the sons of a famous clinician of the time. Galimberti thus acquired fame as a clever and accomplished barrister ready to do battle against the constituted powers.

The exercise of his profession, in effect, enabled Galimberti to build 'a ramified network within the electoral college of Cuneo'. His involvement in various political trials of those years gained him a great deal of sympathy in democratic circles and, in the elections of June 1895, also the official support of the socialists. His contacts with influential members of the judiciary and with his clientele – though this was certainly much more circumscribed for a criminal lawyer than for a civil lawyer – proved crucial in his mobilization of electoral support. After Galimberti had wound up his law partnership, his collaborators not only helped him to edit the local newspaper (which he also owned) but became his electoral agents when he stood as a candidate in the general election.[22]

For Giuseppe Zanardelli, instead, the legal profession afforded an opportunity to organize a network in Brescia which, in many respects, developed into a full-blown patron–client system.[23] Entirely aware that 'the inhabitants of the provinces feel more passionately about matters close to them, even though of minimal importance, than about matters at a distance, even though of maximum importance',[24] Zanardelli

[21] The quotation is taken from E. Mana, *La professione di deputato. Tancredi Galimberti fra Cuneo e Roma (1856–1939)*, Treviso, 1939, p. 20.

[22] Ibid., p. 263.

[23] On clientelism see S.N. Eisenstadt, R. Lemarchand (eds), *Political Clientelism, Patronage and Development*, London, 1981.

[24] E. D'Orazio, *Fisiologia del parlamentarismo in Italia*, Turin, 1911, p. 211

always followed 'local questions' from very close at hand. He never left his constituency of Iseo (in the province of Brescia) for Rome, and he attended to the individual and personal cases that proliferated in it with zeal. Zanardelli organized consensus by exerting iron control over the strategic nodes of the administration. Municipality, provincial administration, mayors and prefects, magistrates and simple employees were the organizations and officials that he manipulated with trade-offs and controls. Favours to influential voters, needs satisfied, bureaucratic procedures accelerated, interests promoted, were the mechanisms with which he tied the periphery and the political centre together. It was thus that the chain 'voters–deputy–government' found its maximum expression in the Brescian deputy. Zanardelli's profession enabled him to build his network horizontally and to extend it to the middle and upper ranks of society.

5. PROFESSIONALS AND THE LOCAL ADMINISTRATIONS

In the first decades of unified Italy, 'the tightening of the interest networks which centred on the economic management of the urban centres'[25] altered the relations between professions and politics. The importance acquired by the local administrations – most notably as regards the financing of public works, education, sanitation and health – as well as increasingly close relationships among administrators, technicians and businessmen, also saw the involvement of numerous politician-professionals. In certain cases, there appeared 'on the scene of municipal political life personnel more competent and culturally better equipped to deal with the problems raised by industrialization and the modernization of services'.[26]

Nicola Amore had been a pupil of Giacomo Savarese in Naples. In 1850 he graduated in law and entered the firm of Giuseppe Marini Serra. In 1860 he left the legal profession to embark on a career in the judiciary, and in 1862 was appointed Chief of Police in Naples. After spending a brief period in parliament, he resumed his legal activities, which he combined with his duties as a city councillor. Between 1868 and 1876 he was returned to parliament as deputy for Campobasso, although he continued to live in Naples. In 1879 he was reappointed to the city council and in May 1884 became mayor.

Amore served as mayor from 1884 to 1887 and from 1888 to 1889; years, these, which marked a true turning-point both in the political

[25] P. Frascani, *Finanza, economia ed intervento pubblico dall'unificazione agli anni Trenta,* Naples, 1988, p. 70.
[26] Ibid.

management of the city – with increasingly massive spending on public works – and in the relationships among civil servants, entrepreneurs and members of the professions. In particular, with the approval of the special law on urban renewal, Amore found himself at the centre of a web of relations which conditioned the life of the city for many years to come, as well as determining political-entrepreneurial behaviour throughout the first three decades of this century.

In Bologna, heightened awareness of the problems of health and sanitation led to a wide-ranging programme of public works. The building and management of the mains water supply, of the municipal slaughterhouse, of the market, and of the judicial and municipal offices forged close links between the political class and the doctors. Bologna's ambitious urban project of the late 1860s and early 1870s was realized through close collaboration among professionals, civil servants and technicians. The city council elected in 1868 numbered among its members an engineer, Alessandro Maccaferri, a teacher, Enrico Panzacchi, a doctor, Augusto Siccardi, and five lawyers (Ferdinando Berti, Casarini, Pompeo Guadagnini, Gustavo Vicini, Gustavo Sangiorgi).

A leading figure in the Bolognese professional class of those years was Antonio Zannoni. After receiving his degree in engineering in 1861, Zannoni entered the public works department of the city council, where he was assigned specific responsibilities for various architectural projects in the city centre. In 1863 he became 'engineer of the first department' and in this capacity 'executed the studies and designs for the municipal water supply while at the same time following the prestige building projects'.[27] Zannoni's professional activities enabled him to gain control over the city's large-scale construction work of the early 1860s and the development schemes, especially in services and infrastructures, undertaken in the years that followed. Zannoni's relations developed at the professional level, and then expanded in the political-administrative sphere as well. He thus managed to establish close relationships with other professionals and politicians of the city and to propagate the exchanges realized through the municipal machinery among the professional class, the political class and the world of business.

Control of the local council also provided the key to political success for the Pisan engineer Ranieri Simonelli, who first attracted public attention when, in 1865, he set up a joint-stock company to build a theatre in Pisa. In 1867 he managed to secure election as a provincial

[27] A. Alaimo, L'organizzazione della città. Amministrazione e politica urbana a Bologna dopo l'Unità (1859–1869), Bologna, 1990, pp. 154ff.

councillor and member of the provincial committee. Simonelli's power
in the administration enabled him to promote a vigorous programme of
public works and to build what was a *de facto* political machine. In the
course of the 1870s he gained increasingly closer control over the construction work carried out by the city council: work which benefited
doctors, lawyers and industrialists alike. Once he had achieved control
over the board of directors of the *Banca del Popolo di Pisa*, Simonelli
mixed its exponents of the old political class with new men from the
world of the professions and business. The consequent use of the bank
for clientelistic purposes cemented the economic and political interests
of the city firmly together. In 1871 Simonelli was elected parliamentary
deputy – as a result of his patient 'building of links in the province' – for
the constituency of Lari (Pisa). From 1876 onwards he was a member of
parliament for no fewer than five legislatures, and he also sat on the provincial council uninterruptedly from 1867 to 1880. Simonelli received
his most solid electoral support from those municipalities in which his
bank had branches, and those with a particular interest in the public
works policy – especially as regards railway construction – implemented
by the provincial administration after Simonelli had joined it in 1867.[28]

After a first phase – especially the years from 1861 to 1874 – in
which numerous politicians were criminal lawyers and law lecturers by
profession, from the mid-1870s onwards their ranks were swelled by
growing numbers of experts in administrative and civil matters. With
increasing frequency, the municipal and provincial councils became
litigants in disputes over bids for tender, contracts and auctions, and
hence the assiduous clients of a large number of lawyers. In many
cases, the lawyers used their political activities in order to buttress their
professional position with the relations and alliances that they had developed in their administrative experience: indeed, the fortunes of
many law firms of those years were built on municipal interests.

In Naples, constant litigation by or against the *Comune* (Municipality) enabled a group of lawyers in the city to specialize in administrative law and to base their careers on lawsuits of this kind. Gianturco,
a parliamentary deputy and twice a minister, handled a number of important lawsuits brought against the Municipality, including the suit
filed by the gas company and one of the many brought by the con-
tractor building the city's sewage system; Pasquale Grippo, parliamentary deputy and former local councillor, defended other building
contractors against the *Comune*; Francesco Spirito, a parliamentary

[28] See A. Polsi, 'Possidenti e nuovi ceti urbani: l'élite politica di Pisa nel ventennio
post-unitario', *Quaderni storici*, 19, 56, 1984, pp. 493–516.

deputy, represented several council engineers against the Municipality; Fusco, a municipal and provincial assessor and parliamentary deputy, defended the *Comune* on several occasions, but on many others represented litigants against the Municipality. And mention should also be made of Alberto Marghieri, who, after starting his career as chief lawyer for the Municipality, became one of the most respected professionals in Naples and a political figure at the centre of the city's most powerful economic and financial relations of the beginning of this century.

A striking example of the extent to which the legal and political profession benefited from litigation between companies and the Municipality is provided by the Apulian deputy Roberto Vollaro de Lieto, who handled the legal affairs of the waterworks company *la Compagnia delle Acque di Serino*. According to contracts signed in 1878 and 1882, the *Compagnia* was appointed by the Naples city council to build 'the water conduit from Serino to Naples, and also to construct three reservoirs and the water mains in the city and villages'.[29] The *Compagnia*, however, did not itself lay the water pipeline system but subcontracted the work to the *Società Veneta per Imprese e Costruzioni Pubbliche*. Litigation broke out between the two companies and was concluded in 1892 by adjudication in favour of the *Società Veneta*. The delay in the construction work and the verdict against the *Società del Serino* substantially inflated the costs of the project, with the consequence that the *Società*'s requests for more funds once again brought the issue before the courts. 'The situation that obtained at the time [1890] and for some years thereafter was constituted by the numerous lawsuits, generated by the conflict of interests between the contracting parties, begun, suspended, and postponed; by the claims of the *Compagnia* for an unpaid sum of six hundred lire; by the Municipality's unsatisfied demands.'[30] The affair dragged on for almost twenty years, from the mid-1880s until the early 1900s. The many lawsuits, the various attempts to reach agreement, constant re-examination of the contracts and the drafting of further amendments, brought steady and profitable employment for Vollaro de Lieto – 'the fortunate advocate of the waterworks Company', as he was called, 'who from near and afar followed developments with the greatest interest, fearing that some unforeseen circumstance might compromise' a contract and a commission 'so beneficial to the Company itself'.[31]

[29] Regia Commissione d'Inchiesta per Napoli, *Relazione sull'amministrazione locale*, II, Rome, 1901, p. 59.

[30] Ibid., p. 66.

[31] Ibid., p. 117.

The personal relations that Vollaro was able to establish during the *Compagnia del Serino* affair were a decisive factor in his political career. The dispute between the company and the city council, in fact, was not restricted to its local setting: the government was often consulted, and the technical offices of the state were, perforce, contacted. Vollaro therefore established close relations with the national leaders of the time and from them gained first-hand political experience. His professional and political activities reinforced each other, with the consequence that, not unexpectedly, between 1892 and 1904 he was elected parliamentary deputy for the constituency of San Nicandro Garganico. Vollaro's direct acquaintance with Crispi, Sonnino and Pelloux undoubtedly helped him in his prosecution of the lawsuit against the Naples city council: the government's constant approval of contracts, which were then ruled invalid on technical grounds, was frequently the fruit of the good relations that the Apulian lawyer had cultivated with the authorities in Rome.

Political and professional activities thus fused and reinforced each other. Many lawyers of those years were at the centre of manifold and disparate interests which gravitated around the local administrations; and in many cases they became the legal and political representatives of those economic groups which built their fortunes on public resources. Their offices became meeting-places for city officials, industrialists, financiers, politicians, and the places where political and social alliances were forged. Stipulating and drawing up contracts and inventories enabled the lawyers to deepen their knowledge of administrative matters, but also to develop the personal relations from which they drew professional advantage. Professional practice therefore led them increasingly further into political terrain; and politics, in its turn, with its burgeoning need for legal expertise in order to modernize the administration, perfected the knowledge these lawyers had acquired through professional practice.

However, a great deal more can be said on the political function of the lawyer and, in general, of the expert on administrative and civil law. As we have seen, from the 1870s onwards the celebrated criminal lawyers of the pre-Unification years, already engaged in the struggle for national liberation, were joined on the political stage by the many civil lawyers who had begun their professional and political careers in litigation for, or against, the local administrations. These new luminaries of the legal profession conducted their politics under the aegis and with the support of the Left. And it was during the predominance of the leftist party that they managed to develop a political and professional clientele that brought them to the summit of the parliamentary deputations and of the politico-administrative systems of many cities, and for many years – almost indeed until the end of the Giolitti period.

6. PROFESSIONALS AND THE SOCIALIST PARTY

Very similar career paths were followed by the first socialists, many of whom belonged to families with long legal traditions. Francesco Saverio Merlino, for instance, was the son of a councillor at the court of appeal and brother to a King's prosecutor. He graduated in law at an extremely early age and – already well known for his lively intelligence and legal expertise – practised as a lawyer for many years and with considerable success. In 1876, after the outcry in condemnation of the attempted insurrection of San Lupo (Benevento) instigated by an Internationalist plot, and with its leaders being pilloried in even the democratic press, Merlino wrote the first articles in their defence. When Cafiero and Malatesta were brought to trial at Benevento, Merlino succeeded in obtaining a verdict of not guilty for both of them.

The clients of the socialist lawyers were frequently subversives or party comrades; for all that, however, they were just as needful of their lawyers' manipulation of relations with the local administrations and the state offices as any ordinary client. Not surprisingly, therefore, almost all the political leaders of the first workers' movement in Naples were lawyers. Many of them first decided to join the socialist party while students in university law faculties and following the courses taught by Bovio, Colajanni and Loria. Many of them, therefore, were initially Mazzinians, Republicans and radicals like their teachers. They then joined the new movement which, because it embraced Bakunin's ideas, was not rigorously Marxist in attitude but embraced a libertarian and sometimes populist ideology. Their bourgeois origins and liberal culture – appearances notwithstanding – were therefore unaffected, and almost all the early socialist leaders propounded liberal political ideas which garnered votes among social ranks with no direct experience of working class life or the factory floor.

Like Francesco Merlino, Luigi Alfani, a magistrate's son, as well as Arnaldo Lucci and Silvano Fasulo, were also practising lawyers. Irredentists first, and Republicans later, were the Neapolitan socialists who congregated at the Caffè de Angelis, a Mazzinian haunt where 'from time to time' even 'the great patriot' Roberto Mirabelli himself made an appearance, and where the students from the provinces met to discuss 'more politics than pandects'. It was at this café that they also found their new leader. General secretary of the Republican party in Naples, Pasquale Guarino exercised a kind of 'moral authority' over the young socialists of the city: aware of 'all the facts' and 'all the families' of these young men, he was the father-figure 'to whom all turned to seek advice'.[32]

The friends of the Caffè de Angelis gradually matured into their new political faith; Pasquale Guarino first of all, and then Arturo Labriola, Ettore Croce and others, followed by Enrico Leone, Ernesto Cesare Longobardi and Giuseppe Caivano. The café thus became a hotbed of discussion on the most varied aspects of Marxist theory. This was a theory that Antonio Labriola too, when spending his summer holidays in Naples, expounded to the young men who gathered around him and every evening accompanied him 'down to the seashore, dawdling and with long pauses' while he spoke of Kautsky and Bernstein.

Almost all the Italian universities were preparing the socialists of the future in those last years of the century. Debate on Marxism, and on sociological and economic problems, was further stimulated by courses taught by lecturers who, although not themselves socialists, were nevertheless political activists. 'More than from motives of intellectual reaction and moral opposition to conservative professors, many students were persuaded to join the Workers' Party (the first socialist party in Italy) by the socialist ideas professed by many other university lecturers.'[33] Giuseppe Emanuele Modigliani[34] also decided to join the socialist party while attending the law faculty of the University of Pisa. In those years, in fact, Pisa contained a large group of scholars who had built their academic careers elsewhere and had then come together in the Tuscan city to create a rich and stimulating intellectual environment. Giuseppe Toniolo, who had received his training at the school of catholic spiritualism, developed many of the sociological ideas that inspired political catholicism. Adolfo Zerboglio was a *libero docente* of law and criminal procedure; Ludovico Mortara, a lecturer in civil procedure and the legal system, was the city's leading proponent of socialist doctrine. And also highly influential was Edoardo Bonardi, who, although he taught in the Faculty of Science, imparted his ideas to the many Pisan students who attended his extra-mural courses and lectures. Extremely active both politically and socially, Bonardi was one of the most dynamic representatives of social medicine and, in the eyes of his

---

[32] On the relationships between socialists and professionals an important reference is still R. Michels, *Il proletariato e la borghesia nel movimento socialista italiano. Saggio di scienza sociografico-politica*, Turin, 1908.

[33] R. Michels, *Storia critica del movimento socialista italiano*, Florence, 1926, p. 185.

[34] On Modigliani see D. Cherubini, *Giuseppe Emanuele Modigliani. Un riformista nell'Italia liberale*, Milan, 1990.

young followers especially, the epitome of the 'heroic and anonymous combatant, constantly struggling against natural suffering, to which he sought a remedy that was often frustrated or hampered by the social miseries of which he was a witness but which he was unable to alleviate'.[35] The Pisan students also associated with their masters outside the university lecture halls; the *Circolo di Studi Sociali* founded in 1892 by Ferri and Mortara, the Caffè Ussero and the Caffè dell'Arno, were places of meeting and discussion where socialist doctrine was examined and political action analysed in the detail that was inevitably lacking from the examination syllabuses.

But certainly the most outstanding professional–university–lecturer–politician to teach the Pisan students (and also the future socialist lawyer Modigliani), was Enrico Ferri. Born in San Benedetto Po (Mantua), Ferri studied under Ardigò, the 'high priest' of positivism, and attended the law faculty at Bologna where he met Turati, Bissolati and Loria, and became the favourite pupil of Ellero. Awarded his degree in 1877 on discussion of a thesis entitled *La teoria dell'imputabilità e la negazione del libero arbitrio*, he specialized in criminal law at Pisa under the tutorship of the celebrated criminalist Carrara. Ferri soon became one of the country's leading experts on criminal law and divided his energies between profession and politics. Between 1884 and 1885 he defended the Mantuan peasants arrested for the 'La boje' riots. The quality of his oratory, as well as his economic and social knowledge of the Mantuan countryside displayed at the trial, attracted widespread attention. His success and popularity swiftly secured him a seat in the Chamber of Deputies at the elections of 1886. With time, Ferri gained increasing authority in his professional field, but he was above all an example of how professional activity and political commitment could be combined. Not by chance, then, at the end of the 1890s Ferri was joined as defence counsel by the young Modigliani – who thereby became a member of that group of lawyers who, in every part of the country, placed their profession at the service of political ideals.

Previous experience in the democratic sphere, sound intellectual training, a professional practice, and origins in the petty bourgeoisie were therefore features shared by many of the leading socialists of the time. As Malagodi wrote, 'From this bourgeoisie, which could not expect its sons to live on the fractions of their inheritance, there emerged young men who were sent to the gymnasiums, the lycées, the universities to pursue the mirage of the profession [...] These,

[35] E. Ciccotti, *Psicologia del movimento socialista*, Bari, 1903, p. 52.

therefore, were studious young men who were soon attracted by the great scientific ideas.'[36]

However, these characteristics also provided the Socialist Party with easy access to the electoral and political-administrative world of the turn of the century. Analysis of the socialist lists for the council elections in the larger cities shows that professionals predominated: mainly lawyers, but also doctors and pharmacists. Of course the proportions varied: in Naples, in the period 1899–1914, professionals accounted for more than 50 per cent of these lists, while members of the working class invariably comprised around 30 per cent. In Florence, between 1902 and 1914, the percentage of professionals increased (from 25% to 43%) while that of factory workers fell (from 41 per cent to 17 per cent) and that of office workers rose steeply (from 8% to 23%). In Turin in 1899, there was a clear predominance of workers over professionals (35% against 29%), but by 1914 the percentages of these two groups and that of civil servants had equalized (25%).[37]

7. PROFESSIONALS AS BROKERS

Italian society at the end of the nineteenth century, it seems, was cemented together by the professions. A multitude of ties connected the rural elites to the urban bourgeoisies; and the doctors, lawyers and engineers found themselves at the centre of extensive networks which rendered centre and periphery mutually dependent. The link between landowners and professionals was solidly established: often related to each other, they frequented the same circles and they lived in close proximity. Many members of landowning families practised as professionals – lawyers principally, but also doctors. The legal profession in particular was closely involved with the administration of land.[38]

The network constituted by the professional's clientele reinforced his mediatory function. Not coincidentally, the handbooks on professional ethics gave specific instructions on how to behave with clients: although they might comprise the 'thoughtless', the 'boring', the 'sly', all of them were to be treated with equal efficiency and helpfulness. In many cases, almost indissoluble bonds were created among lawyers,

[36] The quotation is taken from M. Ridolfi, *Il Psi e la nascita del partito di massa 1892–1922*, Rome–Bari, 1992, p. 127.

[37] For these figures see M. Ridolfi, *Il Psi e la nascita del partito di massa 1892–1922*.

[38] See P. Macry, 'I professionisti. Note su tipologie e funzioni', *Quaderni storici*, 16, 48, 1981, pp. 922–43; P. Frascani, 'Les professions bourgeoises en Italie à l'époque liberale (1860–1920)' and P. Macry, 'Notables, professions libérales, employés: la difficile identité des bourgeoisies italiennes dans la deuxième moitié du XIXe siècle', *Mélanges de l'Ecole Française de Rome*, tome 97, 1985–6, pp. 325–59.

doctors and their respective clients. The professional, it was said, 'is privy to every interest, to every family event; he is an intimate confidant without whom nothing could be accomplished in economic and civil life'[39] And sometimes considerable interests were at stake: 'there are other law firms where not minor profit and not minor advantage derive from the representation of some wealthy client who entrusts the administration of his entire estate to the lawyer'.[40] In this context, the passage from a professional to a political clientele was straightforward. In effect, the professionals became the brokers *par excellence* within civil and political society.[41] In Italy, for most of the period considered, this role was performed principally by the lawyer. It is therefore to this latter category that the following general remarks apply.

Research has yet to provide a comprehensive picture of the role of lawyers in the political system of liberal Italy. Still less has it provided a thoroughgoing account of the relationships between civil society, the legal profession, institutions and politics. None the less one may still offer a number of observations which may help to illuminate the topic.

First of all, it is not a particularly fruitful exercise to interpret the political rise of the lawyer as an effect of modernization and to narrow the focus to those lawyers who achieved conspicuous political success. The selectivity of these two historiographical approaches has led, in the former case, to a teleological description of the history of the lawyer-politicians,[42] in the latter to underestimation of the relations between civil and political society brokered by lawyer-politicians of middle and, sometimes, low professional rank.[43]

Although research is still in its early stages, it has furnished two main findings: (1) the lawyer-politician can be considered a variable in, and simultaneously an indicator of, the slow growth of the unitary state and its adhesion to civil society at both the centre and the periphery; (2) research should be extended to include those politicians and lawyers who were less successful on the national scene but who were nevertheless a constant feature of Italy's political and parliamentary

---

[39] G. Zanardelli, *L'avvocatura*, Florence, 1891, p. 16.

[40] D. Giuriati, *Come si fa l'avvocato*, Livorno, 1897, p. 114.

[41] On the concept of 'broker' see Boissevain, *Friends of Friends*, cited above (note 12) and E.R. Wolf, 'Kinship, Friendship and Patron–Client Relations in Complex Societies', in M. Banton (ed.), *The Social Anthropology of Complex Societies*, London, 1966.

[42] The reference is principally to P. Farneti, *Sistema politico e società civile. Saggi di teoria e ricerca politica*, Turin, 1971.

[43] The reference is principally to the political historiography still common in Italy which maintains that biographical reconstruction is only useful as regards institutionally representative figures.

system. It was in fact through the more unremarkable lawyers and politicians that the channels transmitting political demands from civil to
political society were created and consolidated.

Comparison between the figures on lawyers with seats in
parliament[44] and the figures on the professional composition of a
sample of city councils (see tables 9.1, 9.2 and 9.3), as well as my foregoing analysis, may not lead to solid conclusions; but they at least
suggest a transformation in the relationship between the institutions
and lawyer-politicians at the end of the nineteenth century and the beginning of the twentieth. Italian lawyers, in fact, apparently concentrated principally on parliament until the early 1890s; thereafter their
interest focused also on the local administrations. This slow process
whereby political power was redistributed from centre to periphery
seems confirmed by the behaviour of those who – even before 1861
and then again during the liberal era – were the true protagonists of
Italian politics.

The years from 1861 until the mid-1870s saw the rise of lawyers
with shared experience of the *Risorgimento*, most of whom eventually
moved in to occupy the institutions; after the mid-1870s, lawyers with
professional expertise in civil law, and political experience gained
mainly in the local administrations, came to the fore. The lawyer-
deputy of the early years was usually a man of prestige, and by virtue of
his birth or wealth he enjoyed moral legitimacy among the electorate.
Most of the lawyer-deputies of the 1870s and subsequently were political brokers whose power derived from their ability to control actors
with access to resources and to mediate among them.

This process is evidenced by the city councils. The numerical increase in lawyers was probably caused by the expanding functions of
the local administration in the urban economy, and by the corresponding expansion in the professional and political opportunities
available to those who drew their power from brokering activity.
The constant presence of *proprietaires*-aristocrats confirms the image
of cities still largely dependent on notability-run politics and in
which a compromise was reached between old and new forms of
political representation.

More in general, I do not believe it is possible to identify a specific
point in time which marks the onset of a different form of participation by lawyers in political life. Therefore, a watershed – as an aspect
of the more comprehensive transformation of the political system
('modernization' and 'democratization') and of politicians (the advent

[44] See the essay by F. Cammarano in this book.

Table 9.1 *Members of the city council of Pisa, 1869–85*

Profession	Served on the council for at least 3 years	Served on the council for more than 6 years
Lawyers and doctors of law	19	8
Notaries	2	–
University lecturers	15	5
Engineers	6	3
Doctors	2	–
Veterinary surgeons	1	1
Office workers	9	1
Industrialists	3	2
Tradesmen	5	1
Property-owners	15	7
Unspecified	2	2
Total	79	30

Table 9.2 *Professional composition of the city council of Naples, 1901–10*

	1901	1904	1906	1907	1910
Property-owners/ aristocrats	15	17	16	19	19
Property-owners	8	4	2	–	–
Lawyers	15	13	22	27	30
Engineers	5	5	–	3	1
Doctors	4	4	3	1	1
University lecturers	12	12	12	4	7
Publicists	2	–	–	–	–
Tradesmen	2	6	7	11	12
Craftsmen	2	1	1	–	1
Industrialists	2	2	2	–	–
Factory workers	5	2	1	1	1
Soldiers	2	2	3	–	–
Deputies/senators	2	3	4	12	5

Table 9.3 *Professional composition of the city council of Bologna*

	1868	1889
Property-owners	14	32
Tradesmen, industrialists, bankers	11	11
Lawyers	11	24
Notaries	1	1
Doctors	5	8
Engineers	1	10
Accountants	1	4
University lecturers	4	12
Magistrates	2	1
Other	5	10

of the 'politician by profession') – is impossible to specify. In fact, lawyers occupied an important role[45] in many cities of Italy and Europe throughout the late eighteenth and early nineteenth centuries, apart from any quantitative analysis that one may make. What changed was the socio-political context and the manner in which lawyers participated in it. Even before the building of the unitary state, lawyers operated in various spheres (professional, political, personal) and as the years passed they modulated their relationships not only with these but with all the actors that belonged to them. Their capacity to adapt to the changes that occurred in these various milieux made (or marred) the fortunes of many politicians–lawyers.

[45] See H. Siegrist, 'Gli avvocati e la borghesia. Germania, Svizzera e Italia nel XIX secolo', in J. Kocka (ed.), *Borghesie europee dell'Ottocento*, Venice, 1989; and *idem*, 'Gli avvocati nell'Italia del XIX secolo', *Meridiana*, 14, 1992.

INDEX

337